Early Modern History and the Social Sciences

Habent sua fata libelli

EARLY MODERN HISTORY AND THE SOCIAL SCIENCES

Testing the Limits *of* BRAUDEL'S *Mediterranean*

Edited by
JOHN A. MARINO

Copyright © 2002 by Truman State University Press
100 East Normal Street, Kirksville, Missouri 63501-4221 USA
http://tsup.truman.edu

Library of Congress Cataloging-in-Publication Data

Early modern history and the social sciences : testing the limits of Braudel's
Mediterranean / John A. Marino, ed.
    p.   cm. — (Sixteenth century essays & studies ; v. 61)
   Includes bibliographical references and index.
   ISBN 1-931112-06-1 (casebound : alk. paper) — ISBN 1-931112-07-X (pbk. : alk.
paper)
    1. Mediterranean Region—History—1517–1589—Congresses. 2. Human geog-
raphy—Mediterranean Region—Congresses. 3. Social sciences—Congresses. 4.
Braudel, Fernand—Congresses. 5. Mediterranean Region—Civilization—Con-
gresses. 6. History—Philosophy—Congresses. I. Marino, John A. II. Series

   DE96 .E28 2002
   909'.091822—dc21   2002020630

Cover art: "View of Toledo" by El Greco. The Metropolitan Museum of Art,
H. O. Havemeyer Collection, Bequest of Mrs. H. O. Havemeyer, 1929 (29.100.6).
Photograph © 1992 The Metropolitan Museum of Art.
Cover design by Teresa Wheeler
Printed by Thomson-Shore, Dexter, Michigan
Set in Adobe Garamond and Bauer Text Initials

∞The paper in this publication meets or exceeds the minimum requirements of the American National Standard—Permanence of Paper for Printed Library Materials, ANSI Z39.48
(1984).

CONTENTS

ACKNOWLEDGMENTS

The essays in this volume were first presented at the Rockefeller Foundation Bellagio Study and Conference Center, 23–27 June 1997. Participants are grateful for the generous support and hospitality of Susan E. Garfield, secretary to the Bellagio Committee and manager of the Bellagio Center office; Pasquale Pesce, director of the Conference Center in Bellagio; Nadia Gilardoni, the Conference Center assistant in charge of our accommodations; and the Conference Center's most attentive staff.

Other participants who delivered or sent papers, provided formal comments, and engaged in the lively discussion and exchange are warmly thanked for their contributions to our collective intellectual work: Yves-Marie Bercé, Marco Diani, Nicholas B. Dirks, Cornell Fleischer, Dale Kent, Julius Kirshner, Giovanni Levi, Michael Meeker, Diego Moreno, and Immanuel Wallerstein. Thanks also to Anthony Grafton, Anthony Molho, and Stanley Chodorow for their letters of support for this project. Above all, the conference could not have been planned or held without the enthusiastic encouragement and strong support of Maurice Aymard and Julius Kirshner.

Financial support for travel was provided by the Maison des Sciences de l'Homme, by the University of California San Diego Academic Senate Committee on Research, and by the Rockefeller Foundation.

Raymond A. Mentzer of the Sixteenth Century Essays and Studies, Paula Presley, and Nancy Rediger, have been most supportive and encouraging as the manuscript went through Truman State University Press. Special thanks to the University of California, San Diego, Subvention Fund for Scholarly Publication.

INTRODUCTION

JOHN A. MARINO

To commemorate the fiftieth anniversary of Fernand Braudel's *The Mediterranean and the Mediterranean World of Philip II*, which Peter Burke's *History and Social Theory* calls "a book with a good chance to be regarded as the most important historical work of the century,"[1] the Rockefeller Foundation Study and Conference Center in Bellagio sponsored a conference (23–27 June 1997) on early modern history and the social sciences. The conference was neither a celebration nor a revision of Braudel and his works, but rather used Braudel as a point of departure to further the dialogue between early modern history and the social sciences in light of contemporary social theory and historical practice.[2] Conferees were well aware that Braudel's *Mediterranean* (defended as a thesis in 1947 and published in 1949) should be read together with other exemplary theses of his generation, such as Maximilien Sorre's *Les fondements biologiques de la géographie humaine* and Claude Lévi-Strauss's *The Elementary Structures of Kinship*,[3] as part of an important French postwar "structuralist" contribution to the cross-fertilization of twentieth-century social science.[4]

1. Peter Burke, *History and Social Theory* (Ithaca: Cornell University Press, 1992), 16.
2. For Braudel as a point of departure on Mediterranean history, see the exemplary book of Pergrine Horden and Nicholas Purcell, *The Corrupting Sea: A Study of Mediterranean History* (Oxford: Blackwell, 2000).
3. Maximilien Sorre, *Les fondements biologiques de la géographie humaine*, 3 vols. (Paris: Amand Colin, 1943–52), and Claude Lévi-Strauss, *Les structures élémentaires de la parenté* (Paris: PUF, 1949). For Braudel on Sorre, see Fernand Braudel, *On History*, trans. Sarah Matthews (London: Weidenfeld & Nicholson, 1980), "Is There a Geography of Biological Man?" (written 1944), 105–19; for Braudel on anthropology and Lévi-Strauss, see Girolamo Imbruglia, "Braudel, le *Annales* ed il miraggio dell'antropologia," in *Fernand Braudel: Il mestiere di uno storico*, ed. Bianca Arcangeli and Giovanni Muto (Naples: Edizioni Scientifiche Italiane, 1988), 17–25, and Charles Tilly, "Anthropology, History and the *Annales*," in *Review* 1:3/4 (1978): 207–13.
4. Burke, *History and Social Theory*, 110–14, emphasizes structuralism's debt to linguistic theory.

Braudel's own conversation with the social sciences grew out of his "faithful[ness] to the teachings of Lucien Febvre and Marcel Mauss...always wish[ing] to grasp the whole, the totality of social life."[5] In a 1951 *Annales* article, "Geography Confronts the Human Sciences," Braudel expressed his views on the exchange of ideas among the social sciences in an extended metaphor of a building, one perhaps not unlike Philip II's monastery-palace-mausoleum El Escorial whose concord and harmony among its parts and whose communicating rooms and courtyards have been shown to exemplify an Augustinian aesthetics:[6]

> For me, the human sciences do not exist behind limited confines. Each of them is an open door onto a hallway of the social, which opens to all the rooms and leads to all the floors of the building on the condition that the researcher does not stop in his own steps halted by self-regard in the face of other neighboring specialists, but on the contrary, is ready to use, when it may be necessary, their doors and their stairs. Thus each social science possesses its own specific path, its own perspectives and its own methods. Every separation, every barrier between the social sciences is a regression. There does not exist a history sufficient unto itself, nor a geography, nor a political economy. There does exist a group of researches joined together which need not be separated apart.[7]

And just as the convent church lies at the center unifying Philip II's ideal palace complex of the Escorial in Franz Hogenberg's 1572 engraving in Georg Braun's *Civitats Orbis Terrarum*,[8] so too history takes primacy of place in Braudel's human sciences.

One could faithfully describe Braudel's openness to the social sciences—their interconnections, confluences, and limitlessness—with another metaphor, that of the Mediterranean, not his book, but the sea itself. For Braudel,

---

5.   Braudel, *On History*, "History and Sociology" (written 1958), 76.

6.   George Kubler, *Building the Escorial* (Princeton: Princeton University Press, 1982), 125–34.

7.   Fernand Braudel, "La géographie face aux sciences humaines," *Annales: Economies, Sociétés, Civilisations* 6, no. 4 (1951): 491–92.

8.   Georg Braun and Franz Hogenberg, *Beschreibung und Contrafactur der vornembster Stät der Welt*, 6 vols. (orig. *Civitates Orbis Terrarum* [1572–1618]; facs. ed., Plochingen: Müller & Schindler (1965–70), vol. 6.

the inland sea had "at least two faces": peninsulas ("miniature continents") and seas (or rather "a complex of seas"), which could not be understood without their near neighbors—the vast, boundaryless stretches "from the Atlantic Sahara to the Gobi Desert and up to the gates of Peking" and "northern Europe beyond the olive trees…with its Atlantic horizons."[9] Braudel's study of the Mediterranean Sea (and social science) would be more than a series of sea voyages from one port to another, but would explore the structures of an inexhaustive, expansive, and ever-changing world.

The genesis of the book, for its part, is like its argument, a story about time and space, an artifact layered with the theses and trends of social scientific research across the first two thirds of the twentieth century. How Braudel's *Mediterranean*—a monumental work in breadth, scope, and erudition—evolved far beyond the rather conventional, diplomatic history of the author's 1923 thesis proposal on the Mediterranean policy of Philip II (a reflection of his Parisian education at the Lycée Voltaire [1913–20] and the Sorbonne [1920–23]) into an ambitious portrait of the historical trajectory of the Mediterranean basin at large has been well rehearsed.[10] While teaching lycée in Algeria (1923–32, with a 1925–26 interlude for military service in the Rhineland), the original thesis was conceived and Braudel gathered archival materials on the thesis "between 1927 and 1933, when I lived in the archives without hurrying—not even hurrying to choose my subject—…[and] my decision ripened of its own accord" to shift the emphasis from Philip II to the Mediterranean.[11] Reinforced by the fortuitous encounter with Lucien Febvre on the twenty-day return voyage from Brazil in 1937, which changed his professional career and found him an adopted father, Braudel had worked out his thesis "in its main lines, if not written entirely, by 1939, at the close of the first youthful resplendence of the *Annales* of Marc Bloch and

---

9. Fernand Braudel, *The Mediterranean and the Mediterranean World of Philip II*, trans. Siân Reynolds, 2 vols. (New York: Harper & Row, 1972–73), trans. of *La Méditerranée et le monde Méditerranéen à l'époque de Philippe II*, 2d ed. (Paris: A. Colin, 1966); 1:3–24.

10. Fernand Braudel, "Préface à la seconde édition," in *La Méditerranée*, 2d ed., 11–12; idem, "Personal Testimony," *Journal of Modern History* 44 (1972): 448–54; and idem, "Une vie pour l'histoire, propos recueillis par François Ewald et Jean-Jacques Brochier," in *Magazine Littéraire*, no. 212 (November 1984): 18–24. See also, Giuliana Gemelli, *Fernand Braudel e l'Europa universale* (Venice: Marsilio Editore, 1990); Pierre Daix, *Braudel* (Paris: Flammarion, 1996); William H. McNeill, "Fernand Braudel, Historian," *Journal of Modern History*, 73 (March 2001): 133–46.

11. Braudel, "Personal Testimony," 452.

Lucien Febvre, of which it is the direct fruit."[12] Recalled to military service, Braudel was captured in 1940, and while a prisoner of war until 1945, he wrote out his chapters and mailed them to Febvre. By 1947 the thesis was ready to be defended at the Sorbonne, published in 1949, and completely revised and enlarged in its two-volume second edition in 1966.[13] Braudel's work thus provides readers at the beginning of the new century with a kind of archeological dig to uncover half-forgotten theories, speculative hypotheses, and superseded propositions—all embedded in a grand geohistorical design and enriched with a gold mine of enduring archival value, literary exempla, and personal passion.

To prove its chief claim that historical time moved with different rhythms over long-term geographical structures, middle-term socioeconomic structures, and short-term individual events, Braudel argued that the traditional history of Philip II's Mediterranean policy was explicitly tied to the constraints imposed upon politics by geography, economy, sociology, and human psychology. For Braudel, constraints or limits meant possibilities, not probabilities. He, therefore, emphatically defended human freedom and consciously avoided the dangers of determinism, as he summarized in his 1950 inaugural lecture to the Collège de France:

> The dangers of a social history are clear to us all, and in particular the danger of forgetting, in contemplation of the deep currents in the lives of men, each separate man grappling with his own life and his own destiny; the danger of forgetting, perhaps even of denying, the inimitable essence of each individual. For to challenge the enormous role that has sometimes been assigned to certain outstanding men in the genesis of history is by no means to deny the stature of the individual as individual and the fascination that there is for one man in poring over the fate of another.[14]

---

12. Braudel, "Préface à la seconde édition," 1:11. See also George Huppert, "Storia e scienze sociali: Bloch, Febvre e le prime *Annales*," in *Gli strumenti della ricerca*, pt. 2, *Questioni di metodo,* Il Mondo contemporaneo, vol. 10 (Florence: La Nuova Italia, 1983): 734–50.

13. Samuel Kinser, "Annaliste Paradigm? The Geohistorical Structure of Fernand Braudel," *American Historical Review* 86, no. 1 (1981): 63–105, and Gemelli, *Fernand Braudel e l'Europa,* offer the two best comparisons of changes between the two editions.

14. Braudel, *On History,* "The Situation of History in 1950," 20.

Despite such disclaimers the inextricable structures of time and place define Braudel's historical practice.

The multiplicity of historical rhythms or time spans to be employed for historical analysis were only one of the possible "common languages" that Braudel argued were available for the development of the social sciences. His goal was to foster discussion across disciplinary boundaries and to encourage venturing outside one's own specialty in order "to orient some kind of collective research and make possible the first stages of some sort of coming together."[15] For Braudel, other possible common research programs for the social sciences might include the languages of social mathematics (the languages of necessary facts, of contingent facts, and of conditioned facts); of communications (the languages of the exchange of women, of goods and services, and of messages); and of place, geography, or ecology. What Braudel's prescience saw so clearly at midcentury—history's "formidable but challenging responsibilities" and "a general crisis in the human sciences...all overwhelmed by their own progress"[16]—is as much with us today as it was then, and is the injunction inspiring the present collection.

As the postmodernist crisis in social thought and the linguistic turn in historical studies have increasingly called into question social scientific epistemologies, the relationship between history and the social sciences has strengthened. While still focusing on the problem of social change, such historically focused and self-reflective tendencies have shifted research in both history and the social sciences to include both spatial and temporal as well as comparative dimensions. This collection of essays is not interested in a revision of Braudel's text, in reevaluating and correcting his theses in terms of present methodologies or new knowledge. Individual essays do indeed review various historiographical traditions to arrive at conclusions about their disciplines, but the overall thrust of each contribution is grounded in present practice in the respective social scientific disciplines (geography, economics, sociology, anthropology, political science, psychology, and their relationship to history; that is, the problem of social change) and geared toward influencing prospective trends in their development in the twenty-first century. Here Braudel's insights offer a double inspiration, for he was deeply concerned about the totality of the social and about the exchange of ideas across disciplinary boundaries as they affected the great issues of early modern European history—the rise of

15. Braudel, *On History*, "History and the Social Sciences: The *Longue Durée*," 40–52.

16. Braudel, *On History*, "The Situation of History," 6, and idem, "History and the Social Sciences," 25.

capitalism, the growth of the middle classes in developing urban areas, the emergence of the modern state, and the role of culture, thought, and belief in the transformation to the modern world.

The present essays begin with five divisions that correspond to the Mediterranean world's (1) long-term structures of geography, (2) economic theory and practice, (3) social and cultural understanding and trends, (4) politics, and (5) mentalities as defined by law and religion. Part 6 broadens the perspective beyond the spatial boundaries of Europe and the Mediterranean in order to provide a critical vantage point from China and the Americas to view and review Eurocentric models and preoccupations of the early modern period.

In chapter 1, John Marino reviews the historical roots of Braudel's *géohistoire* from developments in the discipline of geography. The essay looks back to contemporary sixteenth-century ideas and practices in describing and representing space in words and maps through the early-twentieth-century crisis around geographic determinism in order to uncover the assumptions underlying Vidal de la Blache and the French school of geography, the single most powerful influence in the early formation of Braudel's conceptual framework. By following the trajectory of twentieth-century geography through its interaction with economics and statistics up to its postmodern rethinking of space as a reflection of power, geography emerges as a vibrant discipline that has changed its analytical program from cataloguing landscape to explaining land use in order to reassert individual freedom (and constraints) by emphasizing the role of human agency and political action in the control and change of space over time.

In part 2, Bartolomé Yun Casalilla and Jan de Vries show how new theories in economic history help to explain long-term changes in the European economy and thus update and refine one of Braudel's fundamental areas of inquiry.[17] Yun's focus in chapter 2 on Spain, the home base of Philip II's empire, introduces the conceptual tools available to economic historians to study the institutional and cultural inputs that allow us to understand city/countryside relations more fully. The rise and decline of Spain is seen in a more nuanced and sophisticated analysis that links questions about land, labor, and markets to the broader context of early modern political economy. De Vries in chapter 3 similarly reviews the developments in economics—institutional economics (the new organizational and inferential economics),

---

17. See also John Day, *Money and Finance in the Age of Merchant Capitalism* (Oxford: Blackwell, 1999), 110–50.

new growth theory, the concept of "path dependency," and cultural factors drawn from a model of *homo economicus*—that help to explain the interaction or reciprocity between event and context, producer and consumer, countryside and city. The essay aims at showing how early modern urbanization was a precondition for modern industrialization through a process of interrelated household decisions that he has called "the industrious revolution."

Social and cultural considerations played a lesser role in the construction of Braudel's methodology and organization than geography and economics. Both society and culture often appeared as unambiguous givens, the unproblematic background or starting assumptions invoked by a literary example from Bandello or a "timeless" proverb. In chapter 4 Ottavia Niccoli shows how "Images of Society" were themselves a language operating not as metaphors, but literally as the political creations of political thought. This essay outlines the ideas behind representations of society as a political body (from functional or reciprocal relationships of parts to the whole to a shift to hierarchy; in the dichotomy between health and disease or infirmity) and as a ship of state (with replaceable captains or magistrates). Above all, Niccoli demonstrates how such images take on a life of their own in institutions, through political propaganda, and how they affect behavior. Peter Burke's review of the recent anthropological literature on the Mediterranean world in chapter 5 contrasts Braudel's macrosocial concerns with anthropology's microsocial insights in order to privilege concepts, theories, and methods that come out of the study of honor and shame, insults and feuds, the family and its values, saints and pilgrimages/festivals, patronage and friendship, gifts and hospitality, domestic rituals such as weddings and funerals, gender, and beliefs or modes of thought. Problematizing society and culture makes us aware that structural systems are constructs, neither unities nor cultural islands, but arenas of interaction, encounter, and exchange. Thus, the historian's analytical vocabulary is enriched with the concepts of acculturation, syncretism, creolization, and resistance in confronting the complexities of the Mediterranean's symbolic boundaries or the false binary opposition between Ottoman and Habsburg empires, Christian and Muslim, Jew and Arab, inquisition and *convivencia*.

One of the strongest reactions to Braudel's *Mediterranean* comes in part 3 from political, diplomatic, and military history and from the study of comparative revolution by historians, political scientists, and sociologists. Because Braudel reduced the political world to ephemeral events yet kept the last third of his two-volume revised edition focused on them, one must ask what he had in mind. Was he reluctant to jettison his hard-won cache of archival references still tied to an inadequate framework? In chapter 6 M. J. Rodríguez-Salgado takes aim at Braudel's structural focus "on mountains and water" and its analysis of Philip II's Mediterranean policy as untenable or completely misguided, since the complexities of Philip II's world would be better explored by examining both sides (Ottoman and Habsburg) of the political and ideological divide or by a more in-depth study of the political, economic, and ideological worlds of the monarch and his worldwide empire. From Rodríguez-Salgado's perspective on political policy and practice, John Elliott serves as a better example of the new diplomatic history with its avoidance of the overly rational and illusory limits of personality, strategies, and economic trends in favor of a broader understanding of local elites, court society, and ideologies such as religious or confessional commitments, patriotism, and the like to get at the powerful underlying role of individuals and states in political decision making. Sociologist Jack Goldstone in chapter 7, on the other hand, remains inspired by Braudel's commitment to "total history." Goldstone argues for comparative study of larger cycles of recurrent waves of social and political revolts (roughly 1280–1380, 1580–1680, 1770–1870, and 1910–present) in order to discern the process of change. In his review of four macrohistorical explanations of these waves of revolt (climate, technological innovation, shifting political culture, and demography) he finds no convincing single general theory. Instead, he counsels looking for the processes and factors that "interfere with the reproduction of relationship across time and across generations" as part of a feedback loop that sees changes deriving from both material and ideological causes in a constant interaction between "both social and political relationships [on the one hand] and values and *mentalités* [on the other]."

Part 5 addresses the topics of law and religion—both greatly underdeveloped, if not completely absent—in the Braudelian program. António Manuel Hespanha's "Early Modern Law and the Anthropological Imagination of Old European Culture" is closer to Lucien Febvre's project of recovering the "mental tools" that underlay thought and action in the early modern period. Instead of the decontextualized appeals to universal principles of much contemporary legal and institutional history, chapter 8 aims at restoring the unexpected strangeness of medieval and early modern legal imagery by decoupling it from anachronistic contemporary categories and by rejecting its study as anticipations of modern concepts or rules. The blurred distinction between persons and things, the rigid contingency between emotions and external behavior, the irrelevance of free will in the shaping of human interaction, the surprising contiguity between law and love, justice and grace lead us to consider that the cluster of values such as fidelity, friend-ship, liberality, charity, service, and gratitude that constituted the political reality and natural order of things in medieval and early modern legal and institutional culture were far removed from current assumptions about both human nature and common sense as well as law and society. In a similar move to get beyond universal generalizations about religious difference, Henry Kamen's chapter 9 on the uneasy coexistence (*convivencia*) of many diverse ethnic and religious groups, especially the strategies of survival among minority populations, emphasizes community contexts and local cir-cumstances. Below the surface of any formal conflict between Christians, Muslims, and Jews in Spain, Kamen sees local and regional variation, that is, community-based multiculturalism and a community-centered evolution of cultural identities conditioned by geography, jurisdiction, and language. *Mentalité* by definition must return to commonly held mental habits and practices that often remained uncodified and unarticulated, but which nev-ertheless structured the unconscious assumptions in the practice of daily life.

In the comparative finale, part 6 looks at Asia and America in the making of the early modern world. While China specialist Mark Elvin praises Brau-del's poetic power in an artistic evocation of the Mediterranean world in chapter 10, his main focus is Braudel's misunderstanding of China in *Civili-zation and Material Life*. Elvin identifies Braudel's sharp insights and intui-tions on China, as he points out major gaps and misinformation in Braudel's attempt to explain why Chinese economic development did not lead to a breakthrough to capitalism. Here Elvin provides a formidable summary of the problem limiting Chinese economic development and why Braudel was unable to utilize the information available to him at the time to draw a more accurate picture of the Chinese situation. To Braudel's material world, Elvin's China offers a nuanced challenge to rethink the mechanisms of change in early modern economic development. Anthony Pagden's concluding chapter examines the relationship between the idea of America and the concept of Braudel's *longue durée*. He argues that America was not just an extension of Mediterranean Europe, but its "discovery" required a complete remaking and rethinking of the Old World. For Pagden, Braudel's question was badly framed because with America's entry into European time—actually a reorder-ing of historical time—modernity and its meaning took new form and direc-tion. As America burst the formerly understood limits of time and space—those still operative in Braudel's frame—the future no longer had a fixed end, but offered the possibility of a limitless one. "Total history" here takes on a new meaning, and we have come full circle to take critical stock of Braudel's *Mediterranean* in a way that he himself would no doubt have found to be exactly what he had in mind—a heuristic exercise in rethinking the way we do history by linking all aspects of the social together through heightened insights derived from the cooperative efforts of the social sciences.

Braudel's *Mediterranean* fifty years later is clearly a document, not a monument. In comparing the first edition of 1949 and the second edition of 1966 one cannot help but be struck by development of two interrelated topics—the theoretical or methodological arguments and the infusion of new research findings. On this first point, Braudel's *Mediterranean* is an artifact that reflects the growing sophistication of twentieth-century social science and the growing relationship between history and the social sciences. At the same time, as a touchstone of scholarship—the second point—few books can boast such immediate and direct influence in framing and organizing research on not only Philip II, Spain, and the Mediterranean world, but the social and economic history of the early modern world in general. The 1966 edition and the present volume's revisions and reflections on such details are testimony to Braudel's inspiration and impetus.

From today's vantage point, fifty years after the first edition, we see more clearly what Braudel left out. His highlighting of structures—long-term, medium-duration, and short-run events—underplayed mentalities and human agency. The confidence of postwar imperialism failed to understand the reaction against colonial dependence in North Africa, Asia, and the Americas. Subsequent poststructuralist perspectives have broken down preconceived patterns and relationships, and have opened the door to the rediscovery of the "other" as well as the self.

None of our new knowledge and consciousness, however, should detract from what were the truly important contributions of Braudel's work. He taught us the centrality of the interaction between space and time that articulated for the first time two fundamental insights: first, the sixty-day world—what Immanuel Wallerstein calls the "economic world"—which united the far-flung continents and societies of the early modern period into one self-contained system;[18] and second, the idea of social times, which identified the varying rhythms of change from the slow processes of the long term to medium conjunctures and short-term events. Above all, Braudel's insistent quest for the holy grail of "total history" is what brought all the disciplines of

18. Immanuel Wallerstein, *The Modern World-System* (New York: Academic Press, 1974–).

the social sciences in play together to interrogate the multifaceted complexities of the routines of daily life and the imperceptible movements and discontinuities that were constantly changing it. For Braudel, this quest was itself in constant flux: "all the social sciences find their tasks shifting all the time, both because of their own developments and because of the active developments of them all as a body." This perpetual motion machine is what makes history itself so polyvalent: "For me, history is the total of all possible histories—an assemblage of professions and points of view, from yesterday, today, and tomorrow. The only error, in my view, would be to choose one of these histories to the exclusion of all others."[19] If one were to appropriate this one of Braudel's numerous insights and injunctions to answer questions about the overall conclusions of these essays, one could best describe their message to history and the social scientific disciplines as the importance of continuing to test the limits of the possible.

19. Braudel, *On History*, "History and the Social Sciences," 34.

PART 1

Reconstructing
and Representing
the Original Landscape

Chapter 1

ON THE SHORES OF BOHEMIA

Recovering Geography

JOHN A. MARINO

"Le maniere de' terreni sono tre, di campo, di collina, di monte." This simple
sentence dividing the earth into the three qualities of soil to be found in the
plains, hills, and mountains, is not taken from the 1952 Italian translation of
the first edition of Braudel's *Mediterranean*.[1] This short quotation comes
instead from the 791-page text of Ferrante Imperato's *Dell'historia naturale*,
which was published in Spanish Naples in 1599, the year after Philip II's
death.[2] Because natural history played such an important role in the emergence of geography as a scientific discipline,[3] Imperato's late-sixteenth-century
encyclopedic natural history provides an excellent point of departure for an
examination of the relationship between geography and history.

Imperato and his pre-Cartesian naturalist circle help to problematize a
number of concepts or categories about geography and history which have
held hard-and-fast paradigmatic value for almost four centuries up through
Braudel's reliance on geography as the cornerstone of his *Mediterranean*;
namely, environment (the interaction between nature and society), place (the

---

1. Fernand Braudel, *La Méditerranée et le monde Méditerranéen à l'époque de Philippe
II,* 1st ed. (Paris: Armand Colin, 1949), 2d ed., 2 vols. (Paris: Armand Colin, 1966); Italian
trans., *Civiltà e imperi del Mediterraneo nell'età di Filippo II*, trans. Carlo Pischedda (Turin:
Einaudi, 1953).

2. Ferrante Imperato, *Dell'historia naturale. Libri XXVIII* (Naples: Stigliola, 1599), 5.

3. David Stoddart, *On Geography and Its History* (Oxford: Blackwell, 1986); on the
discipline of natural history, see Michel Foucault, *The Order of Things: An Archaeology of the
Human Sciences* (1966; repr. New York: Vintage Books, 1994), 125–65; N. Jardine, A. Secord
and C. Spary, eds., *Cultures of Natural History* (Cambridge: Cambridge University Press,
1996); Ann Blair, *The Theater of Nature: Jean Bodin and Renaissance Science* (Princeton:
Princeton University Press, 1997); Lorraine Daston and Katharine Park, *Wonders and the
Order of Nature, 1150–1750* (New York: Zone Books, 1998).

interconnection between regions and culture), and space (the intersection of ideas about space and time). Thus, returning to the original sixteenth-century time frame of Braudel's study of Philip II's Mediterranean world aids in uncovering the roots of Western geographic consciousness and its modern mapping mentality as they developed from the Renaissance recoveries of ancient books and artistic monuments and from the Renaissance discoveries in geography and science. From its origins in the European Renaissance, Reconnaissance, and Scientific Revolution, geography has constantly struggled between a number of contending dualities in the relationship between nature and culture: a methodology caught between scientism and humanism, the applied action of social criticism or political cooperation, the objectivity of critical distance versus the subjectivity of Eurocentrism, and a debate over the role of free will or determinism.

Reconstructing that original mental landscape *before* the *episteme* of modernity's project had been established will prepare us for the present examination of the current state of geographic epistemologies and practices.[4] For the last quarter of the twentieth century, the theoretical foundation of geography has been in flux as the unresolved tensions embedded in geography's program and practice—problems shared across the social sciences and humanities—have been called into question. In order to authorize the postmodern geographical discourse on the construction and production of space, the postmodern geographical critique has rejected two formative moments in the discipline's development: first, its "positivist" roots and manifestations in turn-of-the-century environmental determinism—what Braudel's 1949 first edition "possibilism" via Lucien Febvre was correcting and modifying; second, its scientism in post–Second World War spatial and economic science—what Braudel's 1966 second edition was trying to incorporate.[5] What the promises of postmodern geography will deliver and how its insights are being integrated into the discipline at large remain an open question—a question, however, that shows how central geography continues to be to the modern social sciences and humanities.

---

4.   Stephen Toulmin, *Cosmopolis: The Hidden Agenda of Modernity* (Chicago: University of Chicago Press, 1992).

5.   David Harvey, *The Condition of Postmodernity: An Enquiry into the Origins of Cultural Change* (Cambridge, Mass.: Blackwell, 1989); Edward W. Soja, *Postmodern Geographies: The Reassertion of Space in Critical Social Theory* (London: Verso, 1989); and Derek Gregory, *Geographical Imaginations* (Cambridge, Mass: Blackwell, 1994).

GEOGRAPHICAL TRADITIONS AND INTERACTIONS IN EARLY MODERN EUROPE

In the same way that the study of nature is foundational for the emergence of the natural sciences as modern disciplines in early modern Europe, the social sciences employ geography as the key discipline linking the study of the physical and biological with the social and cultural world. In addition to geography's initial focus on human-environment relationships, geography also emphasizes two other long-standing traditions.[6] Regional analysis, a second area of study, examines the differentiation of place, such as the connections and conflicts between town and country or the particularities and power of various landscapes. A third research agenda, the study of space itself and the processes which structure it, reflects the importance of systems and organizational principles. Another way of articulating the three distinctive perspectives of geography would be to emphasize their respective approaches: (1) in the synthesis of human action and physical environment, that is, the linking of environment to social dynamics, environmental dynamics to physical systems, and human-social dynamics to economic, social, and political systems; (2) in the observation of place, space, and scale to establish integration and interdependencies; and (3) in the representation of spatial relationships visually, verbally, mathematically, digitally, and cognitively.[7]

Understanding the relationship between human society and the natural world both as a shift in modern mentality and in scientific paradigm is, however, only a partial approximation of what geography does vis-à-vis the social sciences.[8] Because geographers claim to have special expertise about the physical world, they not only attempt to control, channel, and change it, but in turn they also use their knowledge to reform and condition political and

---

6. Richard L. Morril, "A Theoretical Imperative," *Annals of the Association of American Geographers* 77 (1987): 535–41. For a classic account, William Patterson, "The Four Traditions of Geography," *Journal of Geography* 63 (1964): 211–16, identifies (1) regional or area studies; (2) physical geography or earth science; (3) ecological or man-land relationships; and (4) location theory or spatial studies, with cartography and behavioral geography closely allied to it.

7. National Research Council, *Rediscovering Geography: New Relevance for Science and Society* (Washington, D.C.: National Academy Press, 1997), 28–29.

8. Keith Thomas, *Man and the Natural World: A History of the Modern Sensibility* (New York: Pantheon Books, 1983); David Arnold, *The Problem of Nature: Environment, Culture and European Expansion* (Oxford: Blackwell, 1996); and Lorraine Daston, "The Nature of Nature in Early Modern Europe," *Configurations* 6 (spring 1998): 149–72.

social policy. Thus, whether the applications of contemporary geography affect the Malthusian dilemma between population and resources, the economic imperatives over the transformation of the earth, the destruction of the Amazon rain forest, or the sustainability of the biosphere, the environmental tradition of geography has long had practical and ethical implications.[9]

Our natural historian, Ferrante Imperato, here too has more to teach us because in addition to being a representative voice in the developing discipline of natural history, he also participated in a highly visible naturalist circle that had unusual influence in the development of politics and culture in Philip II's late-sixteenth-century Naples.[10] After the 1585 *popolo* bread riot, murder, and ritual cannibalism of the commoners' city council representative, the political implications of the naturalist circle's freethinking found expression in direct political action. Ferrante Imperato himself was involved at the center of the *popolo* party as captain of the *popolo* quarter Piazza di Nido (one of the twenty-nine *ottine* or commoner districts that comprised Naples' *piazza del popolo*), in charge of defense of the city gates around 1585, and elected as *popolo* representative to the Annunziata's board of governors overseeing poor relief in 1587 and again in 1594.[11] His studies and activism nurtured a deep commitment to the commoners' cause in his son Francesco, who published under Stigliola's press the year before his father's magisterial *Natural History*, a 1598 discourse on the organization of the twenty-nine *ottine* and the office of captain, with documents substantiating its antiquity, dignity, and prerogatives.[12]

Ferrante Imperato's monumental collection of information on the four elements (earth, water, air, and fire) and on things animal, vegetable, and mineral in his *Natural History* was not an isolated book that catalogued the natural order. From the mid-sixteenth century, the first museums of natural history, which were dedicated to the marvels of nature, had appeared in Italy.[13] Paula Findlen has demonstrated that, in its mania for collecting, the

9. Robert W. Kates, "The Human Environment: The Road Not Taken, the Road Still Beckoning," *Annals of the Association of American Geographers* 77 (1987): 525–34.

10. William Eamon, *Science and the Secrets of Nature: Books of Secrets in Medieval and Early Modern Culture* (Princeton: Princeton University Press, 1994), 194–233.

11. Rosario Villari, *The Revolt of Naples*, trans. James Newell with the assistance of John A. Marino (1967; repr. Cambridge: Polity Press, 1993), 29, 65–66, 220 n. 3.

12. Francesco Imperato, *Reformatione di nuovo fatta per lo regimento de le piazze populari de la città de Napoli con un breve discorso intorno all'officio di Capitanio d'Ottine* (Naples: Stigliola, 1598).

discipline of natural history blurred the boundaries between the ancients and moderns, because the desire to recover the knowledge of the ancients and to develop new textual and experimental study merged. At the same time, this widely diffused passion for "possessing nature" among nonuniversity scholars in scientific societies, religious orders, and princely courts mediated old and new forms of knowledge through its examination of facts and evidence with the result that it challenged the dominant Aristotelian ideas about nature and proved a formative influence on the burgeoning scientific revolution.[14]

Whereas Imperato cited classical sources of medicine and agronomy—Agricola, Galen, Pliny, and Columella—near the beginning of his treatise as points of departure, another member of the Neapolitan naturalist circle, Fabio Colonna, invoked the authorities of antiquity—Theophrastus, Dioscorides, Pliny, and Galen—in the subtitle of his 1592 book on plants and fish in order to engage the ancients in disputation.[15] While the Neopolitan naturalist circle's debt to the ancients never strayed far from view, their 1590s output could not have existed without its dependence on Bernardino Telesio (1509–88) and Giambattista della Porta (1535–1615), two local innovative and revisionist natural philosophers, masters of the arts and sciences.[16]

In the intellectual world of Spanish Naples, the whole reign of Philip II lay under the double spell of Telesio and della Porta. Telesio, a Benedictine monk from Cosenza, had published the first two books of his *De natura juxta propria principia* in 1565, and his teaching in Naples inspired a generation of students striving to rethink the authority of Aristotle by relying upon sensory evidence drawn from the natural world. With the appearance in 1586 of the complete edition of the *Rerum natura*,[17] Sertorio Quattromani's short and accessible Italian translation of Telesio's ideas, available only three

13. Paula Findlen, *Possessing Nature: Museums, Collecting, and Scientific Culture in Early Modern Italy* (Berkeley: University of California Press, 1994).

14. Lorraine Daston, "Marvelous Facts and Miraculous Evidence in Early Modern Europe," *Critical Inquiry* 18, no.1 (1991): 93–124.

15. Imperato, *Dell'historia naturale*, 5; Fabio Colonna, *Phytobasanos [Φυτοβαεανος] sive Plantarum aliquot historia* (Naples: Carlino & Pace, 1592), frontispiece: "in qua describuntur diversi generis plantae veriores, ac magis facie, ombusque reispadentes antiquorum Theophresti, Dioscoridis, Pliny, Galeni, aliorumque delineationibus, ab alijs huisque non animadversae."

16. Amedeo Quondam, *La parola nel labirinto* (Bari: Laterza, 1975), 107–11.

17. Bernardino Telesio, *De rerum natura iuxta propria principia, libri IX* (Naples: Horatius Salvianus, 1586). See Luigi De Franco, *Introduzione a Bernardino Telesio* (Soveria Mannelli [Catanzaro]: Rubbettino, 1995).

years later in 1589,[18] and Tommaso Campanella's five-hundred-page defense of Telesio, *Philosophia sensibus demonstrata*, published in 1591,[19] Telesio's teachings on the existence of two elements (heaven and earth) instead of four, and their parallel hot and cold forces at war, became local Neapolitan orthodoxy as much as the new sensory-based, empirical method.[20] Della Porta's 1558 four-book first edition of his *Magia naturalis*, dedicated to Philip II only two years after his accession, proposed to show how magic worked as one of the instruments to understand the causes of natural phenomena. Its 1589 second edition expanded the argument to diverse phenomena in twenty books and had its *nihil obstat* and imprimatur dated from the seat of the university in Naples, the Dominican monastery, S. Domenico Maggiore, where the young Tommaso Campanella first studied upon his arrival in Naples that same year.[21] Della Porta's scientific investigations extended to a wide range of topics related to natural magic, astrology, and alchemy, which included major works on human physiognomy (1586), agronomy (1592), optics and refraction (1592), astrology (1601), pneumatics and geometry (1601 and 1610), and meteorology (1610), with minor works on cryptology (1563), the art of memory (1566), the distillation of spirits (1608), and military architecture (1608). Parallel to this scientific career, della Porta crowned his literary success with seventeen dramas (fourteen comedies and three tragedies) published between 1589 and 1614.[22] On the eve of the "scientific revolution," philosophy, literature, history, and science formed an indissoluble body of knowledge in the Italian heart of Philip II's empire.

The great Neapolitan publisher of much of the naturalist circle's work, Nicolà Antonio Stigliola, was himself a scientist. His 1597 *Degli elementi mechanici* provided not only an exposition of the elements and laws of mechanics, but also pointed to the not-so-veiled connection between science

18. *La philosophia di Berardino Telesio restretta in brevita et scritta in lingua Toscana del Montano Academico cosentino alla eccellenza del Sig. Duca di Nocera* (Naples: Cacchi, 1589; modern edition, ed. Erminio Troilo (Bari: Società Tipografica Editrice Barese, 1914).

19. Tommaso Campanella, *Philosophia sensibus demonstrata* (Naples: Horatius Salvianus, 1591; modern edition, ed. Luigi de Franco (Naples: Vivarium, 1992).

20. *Bernardino Telesio e la cultura napoletana* (Naples: Guida, 1992).

21. Giovanni Battista della Porta, *Magiae naturalis, libri XX* (Naples: Horatius Salvianus, 1589); English translation, *Natural Magick*, trans. anon. (London, 1658; facsim. New York: Basic Books, 1957).

22. *Dizionario Biografico degli Italiani*, s.v. "Della Porta, Giovambattista"; Louise George Clubb, *Giambattista Della Porta, Dramatist* (Princeton: Princeton University Press, 1965).

and society. The first proposition explained how smaller and slower bodies could use leverage to move larger bodies—"let us discover how a smaller potential energy can overcome a greater force; and a slower potential energy overcome a faster movement"—from which one might readily infer the possibility that the smaller subject kingdom of Naples could displace the larger Spanish empire.[23] Such "naturalism" and freethinking precipitated the scrutiny of the Inquisition, and Stigliola, like della Porta and Campanella before him, was subject to an inquisitorial trial (Telesio's work was only placed on the Index posthumously, "pending correction").[24]

Stigliola's involvement in practical politics was limited to the "public sphere" of his press and to private conversations and counsel to his friends, although as mathematician/geometrician he did collaborate between 1590 and 1594 with Mario Cartaro, the official cartographer of the Spanish viceroyalty of Naples since 1583.[25] Stigliola's mathematics helped Cartaro generate maps of the kingdom's twelve provinces, modeled on two earlier 1560s exemplars of Giacomo Gastaldi.[26] The Cartaro-Stigliola maps identified provincial town locations; by 1613, town hearth figures had been penned onto eight of the twelve maps as part of the state bureaucracy's practice of visualizing the space that it administered, here the Camera della Sommaria's fiscal responsibility over the hearth tax, the kingdom's largest source of income.[27]

This kind of administrative use of cartography had become commonplace in Italy by Philip II's reign in the third quarter of the sixteenth century.[28] The lag time of almost 150 years between the introduction of

23. Nicolà Anonio Stigliola, *Degli elementi mechanici* (Naples: Stigliola, 1597), 1: "Cerchiamo come possa la potenza minore vincer di forza la maggiore: e la potenza più tarda, vincer di movimento la più veloce."

24. Luigi Amabile, *Il Santo officio della inquisizione in Napoli* (1892; repr. 2 vols. in 1: Soveria Mannelli: Rubbettino, 1987), and John M. Headley, *Tommaso Campanella and the Transformation of the World* (Princeton: Princeton University Press, 1997), 26–32.

25. Viceroy Cardinal Granvelle licensed state offices requiring cartographic or mathematical skills as early as the 1570s, when the land surveyors (*agrimensori* or *compassatori*) in the provincial customshouse of Foggia were ordered to verify their competence and ensure impartiality, quoted in John A. Marino, "Administrative Mapping in the Italian States," in *Monarchs, Ministers, and Maps: The Emergence of Cartography as a Tool of Government in Early Modern Europe*, ed. David Buisseret (Chicago: University of Chicago Press, 1992), 19.

26. Vladimiro Valerio, "The Neapolitan Saxton and His Survey of the Kingdom of Naples," *The Map Collector* 18 (March 1982): 14–17; and idem, *Società uomini e istituzioni cartografiche nel Mezzogiorno d'Italia* (Florence: Istituto Geografico Militare, 1993), 50–59.

27. Marino, "Administrative Mapping," 13–15.

28. Marino, "Administrative Mapping," 5–25.

Ptolemy's *Geography* to Italy and the use of cartography as a tool of state administration in the Italian states, should give us pause in our historical investigation into the roots of geographical representation and the emergence of mapping as a conscious mental habit. The links between geometry and cartography, we might say even the reception of geography as a science, was one of the earliest fruits of the transmission of Greek learning to the Italian Renaissance.[29] Manuel Chrysoloras, who began teaching Greek in Florence in 1398, brought a copy of Ptolemy's text from Constantinople and between 1406 and 1409 Jacopo Angeli di Scarperia completed Chrysoloras's translation. Ptolemy provides an introduction to his methods and two projections of the οἰκουμένη [the inhabited world] in book 1; the longitude and latitude of about eight thousand locations are in books 2 through 7, while he concludes with instructions for a perspective representation of a globe of the inhabited world on a grid, and twenty-six regional maps with their principal places to be represented in hours and fractions of hours in book 8. Ptolemy gives instructions for making maps, but no evidence exists that maps ever circulated with the text save for one Arabic manuscript of 1295. Renaissance Italy's newly translated Latin Ptolemy, however, soon had maps associated with it from 1427, and forty such Latin manuscripts with maps survive albeit in an unwieldy format of about 61 x 45.7 cm (which when opened to facing pages are 61 x 91.4 cm) or slightly smaller at 45.7 x 30.5 cm.[30]

Samuel Edgerton has argued that this infusion of geometric cartographic knowledge into early-fifteenth-century Florence led directly to the Florentine development of linear perspective as a representational style in the

29. N. M. Swerdlow, "The Recovery of the Exact Sciences of Antiquity: Mathematics, Astronomy, Geography," in *Rome Reborn: The Vatican Library and Renaissance Culture*, ed. Anthony Grafton (Washington, D.C.: Library of Congress, 1993), 125–67; esp. 158–64.

30. Larger-format Ptolemys are: Biblioteca Apostolica Vaticana, Urb. Lat. 277 (Florence, 1472), 59.8 x 43.8 cm; Vat. Lat. 5698 (Florence, 15th c.), 57.0 x 42.0 cm; and Vat. Lat. 5699 (Florence, 15th c.), 59.7 x 43.8 cm; smaller formats are Urb. Lat. 273 (Florence, 1482), 45.8 x 31.2 cm; Urb. Lat. 274 (Florence, 15th c.), 44.4 x 29.9 cm; Urb. Lat. 275 (Florence, 15th c.), 42.1 x 28.4 cm; Vat. Lat. 3810 (Florence, 15th c.), 42.5 x 28.0 cm; Vat. Lat. 3811 (Florence, 15th c.), 43.0 x 31.5 cm; and Vat. Lat. 7289 (Florence, 1480), 45.7 x 30.5 cm. For the maps, Urb. Lat. 277 can be studied in facsimile, *Die Cosmographia des Claudius Ptolemäus codex Urbinas Latinus 277: Einführungsband zur Faksimileausgabe*, ed. Arthur Dürst (Zurich: Belser, 1983), and contains one world map of the οἰκουμένη; ten regional maps of Europe, four of Africa, and twelve of Asia; seven "new" maps of new countries; and ten city maps (Milan, Venice, Florence, Rome, and Volterra in Italy; Constantinople, Damascus, Jerusalem, Alexandria, and Cairo in the East).

1420s.[31] If the confluence of science and art in visual representation under the tutelage of Alberti and Brunelleschi did indeed lead to the rediscovery of linear perspective, coming as Edgerton claims from geographic geometry, one might ask why it wasn't also more immediately applied to cartography and why such maps didn't become everyday tools in popular thought and administrative practice.[32] Instead, the ptolemaic manuscript maps were reproduced as luxury display pieces, and maps as domestic decorations or collector's items became highly valued commodities that spawned the geographic imagination and gradually whet consumer demand—but were not then readily available or affordable objects of use.[33]

Further evidence for the delay in perspectival and state-sponsored map making taking root in fifteenth-century Italy comes from the paucity of extant administrative maps. P. D. A. Harvey finds three distinct subjects among the precocious works of cartographers of the northern Italian plains: district maps, maps and plans of particular localities and plots of land, and plans or bird's-eye views of towns.[34] These maps derived from two different traditions and served two different purposes. Some, such as district maps from the areas around Brescia, Verona, Padova, and Parma and general views of Lombardy, emphasized military and strategic details; others, such as the mural maps in the Palazzo Comunale at Siena in 1413–14 and in the Doge's palace in Venice in 1474, focused on the city walls and pictures of outstanding monuments. Military maps differed from decorative maps as much as both differed from

31. Samuel Y. Edgerton, Jr., *The Renaissance Rediscovery of Linear Perspective* (New York: Basic Books, 1975).

32. Vladimiro Valerio, "Astronomia e cartografia nella Napoli Aragonese," *Rivista Geografica Italiana* 100, no. 1 (1993): 291–303, gives evidence of the close connection between art, economics, mathematics, and astronomy with humanist cartography; Samuel Y. Edgerton, Jr., "From Mental Matrix to *Mappamundi* to Christian Empire: The Heritage of Ptolemaic Cartography in the Renaissance," in *Art and Cartography: Six Historical Essays*, ed. David Woodward (Chicago: University of Chicago Press, 1987), 10–50, argues that the new cartographic knowledge affected the making of world maps and the Spanish imperial vision of Charles V and Philip II.

33. Chandra Mukerji, *From Graven Images: Patterns of Modern Materialism* (New York: Columbia University Press, 1983), argues that maps as objects of display are evidence of the role of consumer demand in fostering capitalism.

34. P. D. A. Harvey, *The History of Topographical Maps: Symbols, Pictures, and Surveys* (London: Thames & Hudson, 1980), 58–83; and J. B. Harley and David Woodward, *The History of Cartography*, vol. 1: *Cartography in Prehistoric, Ancient, and Medieval Europe and the Mediterranean* (Chicago: University of Chicago Press, 1987), 476–98. This applies equally well to the new discoveries for Argonese Naples; see Valerio, "Astronomia e cartografia."

portolan charts, and while the strategic and seafaring purposes of two of these examples are self-evident, it remains unclear why decorative maps were made and how they were used.

Jurgen Schulz concludes his magisterial article on the "moralized geography" of Jacopo de' Barbari's 1500 *View of Venice* with a clear explanation of the *meaning* of it and other engraved city views, as opposed to their *purpose*.[35] By interpreting textual inscriptions and iconographic figures with the town views, he argues that "medieval and Early Renaissance artists…used city views in emblem of abstract ideas." For Barbari's Venice, then, with Mercury, the patron of commerce, shining above the city and Neptune, lord of the seas, propping it up from below, the subject is not the physical city per se, but the commonwealth of Venice, "premier trading and maritime power of Europe." Similarly, Schulz interprets a number of other city views in this same vein of an "integrated cosmography" of spiritual and geographic knowledge. Francesco Roselli's Rome of circa 1490 asks "where are" the grandeurs of the past ancient empire? An anonymous 1515 view of Antwerp "illustrates the city as a fount of prosperity"; Jörg Seld's 1521 bird's-eye view of Augsburg carries a double meaning of dedication to its patrons and of fulfilling viewers' longing for it; and Anton Woensam's 1531 Cologne presents the city as the embodiment of its entire corporate, historical, and spiritual being. Fathoming the purpose of the works for Schulz is problematic. The humanist concept of fame helps explain something of the purpose, but "the particular circumstances or considerations that prompted [these artists] to celebrate the city in this way remains obscure." In a concluding counterargument, Schulz finds that prints "published for no reason other than to represent a faithful likeness of the subject city do not appear before the 1540s." In other words, city representations of purely aesthetic interest began to be produced at about the same time that the expertise of surveyors and cartographers joined together to replace artist mapmakers.[36]

The lag in the spread of perspectively inspired views a full century after the development of linear perspective in painting and drawing must be accounted for. How did map-visualization as a mental habit and map use as

35. Jurgen Schulz, "Jacopo de' Barbari's *View of Venice*: Map Making, City Views, and Moralized Geography before the Year 1500," *Art Bulletin* 60 (September 1978): 425–74, esp. 467–72.

36. John Hale, *The Civilization of Europe in the Renaissance* (New York: Macmillan, 1994), 15–27, argues that maps became "part of the mental furniture of educated men: indeed of their actual furniture" as a result of the new mathematical interest in cartographic projections.

a common practice come into being?[37] The map boom that established mapping in European consciousness by the 1560s was unleashed by the six-teenth-century economic recovery, the Indian summer of the Italian econ-omy after the end of more than a half century of the Habsburg-Valois wars. Increased population and wealth fueled the pent-up demand for map prod-ucts that had been available only to an elite few. And with the widening dis-tribution of maps and the decline in their price, maps became the everyday administrative tool of state government and the everyday mental tool for representing spatial relationships.

The components of the rise of mapping mentality in the Renaissance—where French as opposed to anglophone histories of geography begin[38]—made up the spatial play between the rebirth of ancient knowledge and encounters with the heretofore unknown New World so that geography became the means to understand and explain difference, whether of limits or frontiers, dominant powers or colonial resistance.[39] The geographical imagination in the Renaissance was essentially a moral one in its assertion of property, priority, and privilege in space, just as history was also moral philosophy teaching by examples; similarly, in the eighteenth century, eco-nomics distinguished itself from moral philosophy as moral economy.[40]

37. David Woodward, *Maps as Prints in the Italian Renaissance: Makers, Distributors and Consumers,* 1995 Panizzi Lectures (London: British Library, 1996), 76, 101, 119 n 6, takes strong exception to my formulation of the problem by quibbling with my use of the word "normal" (by which I meant common) and dismissing the argument altogether because we cannot say that earlier administrative mapping was "abnormal" based on the absence of sur-viving maps since "an important map trade...particularly in Florence" was already established at the turn of the century. We both agree, however, that the fifteenth-century roots of modern cartography reached fruition in the explosion of the map trade by the mid-1560s and cer-tainly by the end of the third quarter of the sixteenth century. The point is that the ability to map did not create a map market, and that mapping did not become a common mental habit to visualize space before the midcentury economic recovery.

38. Numa Broc, *La géographie de la Renaissance (1420–1620)* (Paris: Bibliothèque Nationale, 1980); idem, *Regards sur la géographie française de la Renaissance à nos jours,* 2 vols. (Perpignon: Presses Universitaires de Perpignon, 1994–95); and disseminated in introductory textbooks such as Paul Claval, "Histoire de la géographie," in *Les concepts de la géographie humaine,* ed. Antoine S. Bailly et al., 3d ed. (Paris: Masson, 1995), 33–42.

39. Frank Lestringant, *Mapping the Renaissance: The Geographical Imagination in the Age of Discovery,* trans. David Fausett (Berkeley: University of California Press, 1994), and Chris-tian Jacob, *L'Empire des cartes: Apprendre théorétique de la cartographie à travers l'histoire* (Paris: Albin Michel, 1992).

40. Albert O. Hirschmann, *The Passions and the Interests: Political Arguments for Capital-ism before Its Triumph* (Princeton: Princeton University Press, 1977).

Renaissance geography was the construction of a Eurocentric world with the mapmaker's home—whether in Italy or Germany—at the visual center of his chart. Such representation was like Thomas More's *Utopia*, an imaginary world inhabited by "natural" men in "natural" landscapes.[41] But just as linear perspective was a constructed ideal space to allow artists to project a three-dimensional world on a two-dimensional surface and to create a sense of proportion and order through the embedding of perfect geometric shapes (circles, squares, and equilateral triangles), so too the space of Utopia was consciously manipulated into a perfect "natural" harbor whose arms reached around a tranquil sea in order to create a "natural" island paradise where no settlement was too far from the sea.[42]

With the recording of greater and greater differences in the accumulation of its "natural" history, then, Renaissance science created its imaginary world at home and abroad, in the Old World and the New, out of its own self-referential perceptions, not those of the people Europeans encountered.[43] Thus, Renaissance observers attempted to construct typologies and universal laws that underlay all things. Jean Bodin's encyclopedic *Method for the Easy Comprehension of History* is an influential example of the kinds of conclusions that natural law theory would teach and ingrain in European consciousness.[44] The *Methodus*, in its thirteen Latin editions between 1566 and 1650, cut to the quick of historical causality in its attempt to identify how a people's character was formed. Bodin's seminaturalist theory of history finds nature and training as the two factors that affect the character of a people. And the determinant factor influencing human nature is geography—hot climes produce hot bodies; cold climes, cold; thus, the humoral

41. Louis Marin, *Utopics: Spatial Play*, trans. Robert A. Vollrath (1973; repr. Atlantic Highlands, N.J.: Humanities Press, 1984), "The City: Space of Text and Space in Text" (113–42), and "The City's Portrait in Its Utopics" (201–32).

42. Woodcut representations of the island of Utopia appeared in the earliest editions of More's *Utopia*: Louvain, 1516; Paris, 1517; and Basel, 1518; see *Utopia*, ed. E. Surtz, S.J., and J. H. Hexter, vol. 4 in *The Complete Works of St. Thomas More* (New Haven: Yale University Press, 1964). See also, Alphonse Dupont, "Espace et humanisme," *Bibliothèque d'Humanisme et Renaissance* 8 (1946): 7–104.

43. Walter D. Mignolo, *The Darker Side of the Renaissance: Literacy, Territoriality, and Colonization* (Ann Arbor: University of Michigan Press, 1995); Antonello Gerbi, *Nature in the New World from Christopher Columbus to Gonzalo Fernandez de Oviedo*, trans. Jeremy Moyk (Pittsburgh: University of Pittsburgh Press, 1985), dissects the sources behind the references and metaphors in accounts of first contact with the New World.

44. Jean Bodin, *Method for the Easy Comprehension of History* (1566), trans. Beatrice Reynolds (New York: W. W. Norton, 1969), esp. 86–145.

theory of medicine fitted in lock step with a geographical determinism. Giovanni Botero, the ex-Jesuit tutor of the Savoyard monarchy's progeny, popularized the pseudoscience of geographic determinism in his *Relationi universali*, with information drawn from the Peruvian missionary account in José de Acosta's 1590 *Natural and Moral History of the Indies*.[45] The dilemma of Renaissance discovery was a permutation on the central problem of Renaissance moral philosophy, what a human being could or could not do on one's own, *fortuna* versus *virtù*, free will or predestination.

The Bodin, Acosta, or Botero brand of wide-ranging generalization gave sixteenth-century speculation a "rather curious air" ("cet assez curieux passage"), in the words of Fernand Braudel's first edition of *The Mediterranean*, in the conclusion to part 1 on the *longue durée*, and later deleted in the second edition. Braudel cites Botero's 1592 part 2 of the *Relazioni universali* on Spain and Italy. For Spain, Braudel quotes Botero directly:

> [T]he inhabitants of the plains, it is said, by reason of the commodities which they possess, by reason of their ease of commerce and of mercantile traffic, have the habit of being prudent and wise; whereas on the contrary, those who inhabit the high elevations, by the fact of the barrenness of the sites which they cultivate, of the crudeness of their customs...are also high in courage and hardiness. Such they are in Spain— the Biscayans, the Aragonese and the other peoples of the more barren and more mountainous regions of the Peninsula. Despite the fact that they have a king, it is true, their multiple privileges are great, and they live in liberty under a republic. On the contrary, the Castilians and the Andalusians in their even lower and more fertile lands, are willingly pliant to the pleasure of the Prince.

For Italy, Braudel paraphrases:

> [I]f Naples is unquiet, is it not because of the diversity of its landscape, of the mixture that results from a people "frustrated and almost savage," and from men "pacific and controlled," the latter inhabitants of the grassy plains and the former children of

---

45. For the first complete edition, Giovanni Botero, *Relationi universali devise in quattro parte* (Bergamo, 1596). José de Acosta, *Historia natural y moral de las Indias* (1590), ed. J. Alcina Franch (Madrid: Historia 16, 1987).

the mountains? In Naples, by reason of nature, there is an incessant melange of those violent and contradictory human types. Botero affirms that Milan, for sake of comparison although it is composed of diverse locales, has a less agitated history than Tuscany "divided into mountains and villages." Wisdom on the plains, in sum, and semi-madness in the wild mountains.

A rhetorical question ends this long citation of Renaissance geographical determinism: "Is this image even discussable?"[46]

BRAUDEL'S *GÉOHISTOIRE*

Natural history as a Renaissance science, the first wave of European expansion, and their descriptive rationalization in Botero have led us to Braudel's excursus on what he thought his work should be called, "the barbaric sounding" *géohistoire* instead of *géopolitique*.[47] Here in Braudel's first edition we are

---

46. Braudel, *La Méditerranée*, 1st ed., 303–4: "nous terminerons: 'les habitants des plaines, proclame-t-il, par les commodités dont ils disposent, par la facilité des commerces et du trafic, ont l'habitude d'être prudents et sages: au contraire ceux qui habitent les hautes régions, du fait de l'âpreté des sites qui les abritent, de la rudesse de leurs moeurs…ont assez de courage et de hardiesse. Tels sont en Espagne, les Biscayens, les Aragonais et les autres peuples des régions les plus âpres et les plus montueuses de la Péninsule: au-dessus d'eux un Roi, mais, au vrai, si grands sont leurs multiples privilèges, qu'ils vivent en liberté et en république. Au contraire les Castillans et les Andalous, dans leurs pays aplanis et plus doux se plient volontiers à ce qui plaît au Prince….' Et d'ajouter encore: si Naples est inquiète, n'est-ce pas à cause de la diversité de ses étages, du mélange qui en résulte de gens 'frustres et quasi sauvages', et d'hommes 'pacifiques et policés', ceux-ci habitants des grasses plaines, ceux-là enfants de la montagne? A Naples, du fait de la nature, il y a un mélange incessant d'eaux humaines violentes et contradictoires. Botero affirme que Milan, à ce compte-là, compte des diversités locales, a une histoire moins agitée que la Toscane 'distinta in monti e in valli.' Sagesse des plaines, en somme, et demi-folie des montagnes sauvages. L'image est-elle tellement discutable?"

47. Braudel, *La Méditerranée*, 1st ed., 295: "*Géohistoire*: notre essai mériterait-il de porter ce nom si nous réussissions jamais à acclimater, en français, ce vocable à consonances barbares? Il évoque celui de *géopolitique*, beaucoup plus acceptable d'ailleurs pour nos oreilles. Mais si nous sentons le besoin de forger un mot différent de ce mot allemand adopté par quelques Français, c'est qu'en parlant de *géohistoire*, nous entendons désigner autre chose que ce qu'implique la *géopolitique*, autre chose de plus historique à la fois et de plus large, qui ne soit pas seulement l'application à la situation présente et future des états, d'une histoire spatiale schématisée et, le plus souvent, infléchie à l'avance dans un certain sens." See Samuel Kinser, "Annaliste Paradigm? The Geohistorical Structure of Fernand Braudel," *American Historical Review* 86 (1981): 63–105.

in the middle of an important debate long resolved, but important in the formation of Braudel's mind and for the fortunes of the Annales School. What was Braudel's intent and why did he suppress his "invented" name for the genre of his project?

Obviously, Botero's type of late-Renaissance determinism is clearly absurd, if not outright racist. Neither topography (mountains or plains), nor climate (hot or cold, wet or dry), nor region (north or south, east or west) produces a characteristic civilization. Certainly Braudel himself did not believe in a facile geographic determinism either. Instead, his was a complex and contradictory, almost literary and poetic, idea of geographic "possibilism" derived from the 1922 Lucien Febvre revision of geographic determinism, *La Terre et l'évolution humaine*.[48] Braudel, through Febvre, would have rejected Benedetto Croce's 1925 taunting criticism of any kind of geographic determinism—"If the natural condition of the earth were to determine political history, that history would be written by agronomists, and not by politicians; which is too hard for me to concede"[49]—at the same time that he embraced the agronomists as a committed follower of Paul Vidal de la Blache (1845–1918) and the French school of *géographie humaine*.

Vincent Berdoulay has carefully traced the formative period of French academic geography in the crisis between the wars of 1870 and 1914, as the Third Republic grappled with the underlying ideological and social problems of modernization.[50] France, from its German defeat and borrowing of German sociopolitical forms, through the construction of its colonial empire and reorganization of its educational system at home, was committed to establishing a new social order. Different traditions of geographic research, for example an old style historical geography, a descriptive physical geography, and a statistical population geography, vied for ascendancy in this dynamic period of

48. *La Terre et l'évolution humaine,* ed. Lucien Febvre (Paris: Albin Michel, 1922); English trans. E.G. Mountford and J. H. Paxton, *A Geographical Introduction into History* (New York: Knopf, 1925).

49. Benedetto Croce, *Storia del regno di Napoli* (Bari: Laterza, 1925; 1972), 40: "Ma poi da queste osservazioni si vuol trarre la conseguenza che il Regno non potesse avere storia se non miserabile; ed é illazione arbitraria, perché in terre povere si è svolta vigorosa storia politica quando i loro abitatori hanno dispiegato animo grande, e terre fertilissime sono state asservite e sfruttate da stranieri. Se la condizione naturale delle terre determinasse la storia politica, questa dovrebbe essere scritta dagli agronomi, e non dai politici: il che par duro a concedere."

50. Vincent Berdoulay, *La Formation de l'école française de géographie,* 2d ed. (Paris: Comité des Travaux Historiques et Scientifiques, 1995), and Paul Claval, *Essai sur l'évolution de la géographie humaine* (Paris: Les Belles Lettres, 1976).

reorientation; Vidal's human geography group—energized by his position at the Ecole Normale from 1877 to 1898, his acquisition of a chair at the Sorbonne to direct theses, and the foundation of his influential journal, *Annales de géographie,* in 1891—won out. Not by chance, geography found a favorable moment in other Western university systems: Friedrich Ratzel (1844–1904), whose project was to make a role for history in the study of "Naturvoelker" in opposition to the ahistorical ethnologists, died in Germany in 1904, the same year that twenty-six American scholars organized the Association of American Geographers and one year after the founding of the first United States graduate department of geography at the University of Chicago.[51]

Vidal himself, for founding the modern discipline of geography in France, should be placed in the same company as his slightly younger colleague Emile Durkheim (1858–1917), for sociology. Despite their differences in defining the domains and boundaries of their respective disciplines,[52] they shared a fundamental understanding of both the breadth of their inquiries (for Vidal, the whole surface of the earth) and the uniformity of forms they encountered (for Vidal, the idea of terrestrial unity and correspondence). Vidal's geography, like Durkheim's sociology, attempted to define social facts and to establish methodological rules.[53] Vidal's underlying theoretical framework was a neo-Kantian science founded on observation, classification, and relativist rather than positivist laws. Its epistemology carried with it the air of the debate, especially the quarrel over human origins that links Vidal to Lamarck, Darwin, and natural history.[54] At the same

51. *Annals of the Association of American Geographers* 69 (1979), commemorates seventy-five years of American geography with thirty articles "of personal observation by those who were participants in the history leading up to the present" (3).

52. Vincent Berdoulay, "The Vidal-Durkheim Debate," in *Humanistic Geography: Prospects and Problems,* ed. D. Ley and M. Samuels (Chicago: Maaroufa Press, 1978): 77–90.

53. Paul Vidal de la Blache's major theoretical articles are: "Le principe de la géographie générale," *Annales de géographie* 5 (1986): 129–42; "Les conditions géographiques des faits sociaux," *Annales de géographie* 11 (1902): 13–23; "La conception actuelle de l'enseignement de la géographie," *Annales de géographie* 14 (1905): 193–212; "Les genres de vie dans la géographie humaine," *Annales de géographie* 20 (1911): 193–212, 289–304; "Des caractères distinctifs de la géographie," *Annales de géographie* 22 (1913): 289–99.

54. Vincent Berdoulay and O. Soubeyran, "Lamarck, Darwin et Vidal: Aux fondements naturalistes de la géographie humaine," *Annales de géographie* 100 (1991): 617–34; M.-C. Robic, "L'invention de la géographie humaine au tournant des années 1900: Les vidaliens et l'écologie," in *Autour de Vidal de la Blache,* ed. Claval, 137–44, and idem, "Géographie et écologie végétale: Le tournant de la Belle Epoque," in *Du milieu à l'environnement,* ed. M.-C. Robic (Paris: Economica, 1992), 125–65.

time, Vidal's antigeographic determinism was committed to notions of intentionality, human initiative, and free will; that is, his explanations were based on the contingency of the laws of nature.[55] Vidal avoided monocausality in favor of the interaction of all elements relative to the man-nature relationship. Vidal's geography led logically to his 1911 idea of *genre de vie*, the relationship between environment and human social, economic, and cultural forms, an idea that contradicted political economy's idea of evolutionary epochs and livelihood hierarchies in favor of balanced interactions between the natural world and human work. This perspective derives from the fundamental Vidalian principle of emergence, that is, an approach to place which recognizes that new forms of landscape and their corresponding social arrangements appear, develop, and over time reach a finite sort of equilibrium or stability.[56] In Vidalian *géographie humaine* the problematic of time and space are intrinsically linked.

French geography had come a long way from its positivist, scientist definition in the Enlightenment. The author of the 1757 *Encyclopédie* entry on "Geography," Robert de Vaugondy, who was the Royal Geographer, began his definition in classic scientific terms as "the description of the earth."[57] The Enlightenment understood modern geography to exist midway between two liberal arts in the quadrivium, namely, astronomy and geometry. Geography, thus, was a quasi-liberal art which possessed a distinct language or way of knowing between geometry and astronomy's spatial organization of earth and sky. As a science, Enlightenment geography could be subdivided into six constituent parts according to subject matter:

1. Natural geography studied the natural divisions on the surface of the earth
2. Historical geography described the changing circumstances in a country or town over time
3. Civil or political geography drew the political map of governments and states

55. Vincent Berdoulay, "French Possibilism as a Form of Neo-Kantian Philosophy," *Proceedings of the Association of American Geographers* 8 (1976): 176–79; and idem, *La formation*, 214–26.

56. Vincent Berdoulay, "Place, Meaning, and Discourse in French Language Geography," in *The Power of Place: Bringing Together Geographical and Sociological Imaginations*, ed. John A. Agnew and James S. Duncan (Boston: Unwin Hyman, 1989), 126–27.

57. "Géographie," in *L'Encyclopédie, ou Dictionnaire raisonné des sciences, des arts et des métiers*, ed. D. Diderot and J. d'Alembert (1751–65), vol. 7 (1757): 608–613.

4. Sacred geography treated church history in various lands
5. Ecclesiastical geography traced ecclesiastical divisions and jurisdictions (patriarchates, dioceses, and archdioceses)
6. Physical geography (which also merited its own distinct entry) considered what we would today call geology.

The definitive breakthrough to modern geography came in France in the period 1760 to 1830, immediately following Vaugondy's summary statements on geography's goal to create a unified, true, and complete picture of the earth. The key figure was Alexander von Humboldt (1769–1859), who resided in Paris from 1804 to 1827, where contact with the leading scientific community of the day aided in the analysis and publication of the data gathered during his previous five-year South American expedition. His works established a modern geography grounded in two principles: first, "that landscapes and natural regions [are] worthy objects and scales of analyses"; second, "that comparison of like phenomenon across space can reveal much about the past and present nature of Earth."[58] Vidal's geography studied such landscapes and natural regions in comparative focus with a new humanistic framework that emphasized man-land interaction rather than positivist certainties. Thus, the regional monograph was a means to this end of understanding man-nature relationships from the point of view of closely described local studies.

When Lucien Febvre took up his pen in support of the two Vidalian themes of environmental possibilism and regional studies in historical perspective in *La Terre et l'évolution humaine*, he had already worked in the same vein in his 1911 thesis on the Franche-Comté at the time of Philip II.[59] Begun before the Great War and only published in 1922, the Annales School cofounder championed geographic possibilism as part of the worldwide dismantling of the exaggerated claims of a radical geographic determinism mounted against such works as Friedrich Ratzel's 1912 *Anthropogeographie* and Ellsworth Huntington's 1915 *Civilization and Climate*.[60] Since geographical determinism was disapproved rather than disproved, Febvre was

58. Anne Marie Claire Godlewska, *Geography Unbound: French Geographic Science from Cassini to Humboldt* (Chicago: University of Chicago Press, 1999).

59. Lucien Febvre, *Philippe II et la Franche-Comté: Étude d'histoire politique, religieuse et sociale* (1912; repr. Paris: Flammarion, 1970).

60. Ellen Semple, *Influences of Geographic Environment, on the Basis of Ratzel's System of Anthropo-geography* (New York: Holt, 1911), and Ellsworth Huntington, *Civilization and Climate,* 3d rev. ed. (New Haven: Yale University Press, 1924).

able to salvage the French human geography tradition for its possibilist strengths and regional details by making them an objective and empirical set of observations introductory to regional historical studies. The marginalization of geography by historians of the Annales School to a scholastic subordination not only relegated geography to an ancillary discipline but paved the way for the next wave of economic empiricism, led by Ernest Labrousse.

Not only in France, but also in the Anglophone world, geographic revolutions reshaped the discipline after both world wars. Whereas post-First World War scholarship turned against geographic determinism, post-Second World War scholarship turned toward a quantitative approach.[61] The clinical objectivity and empirical optimism of the Cold War 1950s in the West fostered a geography dedicated to the application of statistical methods, simple optimization techniques, systems analysis, and operations research to geographic problems. For most geographers, geography became a subset, no longer of history, but of economics.

Braudel's *Mediterranean* as a *géohistoire* fits in the middle of these two revolutions. The structure of part 1, "La Part du milieu," follows the outline of Vidal de la Blache's 1922 posthumous *Principes de géographie humaine* quite literally.[62] Vidal's chapter 5 on Mediterranean regions is divided into six parts—transhumance, arboreal cultivation, plains, hills, mountains, and the arable. Further, Vidal's book is divided into three parts: "Human distribution on earth" (corresponding to Braudel's interest in physical features as slowly changing variables like climate and as they affect *genre de vie*), "Forms of civilization" (corresponding to Braudel's speculations on towns), and "Circulation" (corresponding to Braudel's emphasis on routes and distances as measured by time, not light-years but letter-delivery days). Since we know from his own testimony that the young Braudel was researching a rather traditional diplomatic history until his fortuitous meeting with and adoption by Lucien Febvre in 1937, *géographie humaine* enters and reorganizes his work under Lucien Febvre's influence, but with Vidal's imprint and ideas.[63]

More important even than Vidal's tripartite spatial divisions into mountains, plateaus, and plains or even than Braudel's tripartite temporal division into long-, medium-, and short-term—in my opinion—is Braudel's appropriation of

61. Peter Gould, "Geography 1957–1977: The Augean Period," *Annals of the Association of American Geographers* 69 (1979): 139–51.

62. Paul Vidal de la Blache, *Principes de géographie humaine* (Paris: Colin, 1922).

63. On Braudel's meeting and friendship with Lucien Febvre, see Fernand Braudel, "Personal Testimony," *Journal of Modern History* 44 (1972): 448–67.

Vidal's unified culture area.[64] With the Mediterranean as a whole, he could tell a metanational story beyond Philip II's empire in the west and the Ottoman empire in the east. With the idea of circulation, he could cross the Alps as easily as he traversed the Sahara, or sail through the straits of Gibraltar as often as he landed on the shores of the Black Sea and entered the Eurasian steppe.[65]

Different in scale from the microscopic regional studies of geographers and historians of the time and sparkling with the erudition of a dozen years of archival work, Braudel's 1949 *La Méditerranée* found few imitators. Some forty years later, two studies of non-Western areas employed Braudel's culture area method to organize books on China around the Yellow River and on Southeast Asia around the Indian Ocean. Both Lyman Van Slyke's self-conscious "little book," *Nature, History and the River,* and Anthony Reid's two-volume *Southeast Asia in the Age of Commerce 1450–1680* aim at Braudel's ambitious "total history" with the conception of their subject as not just a body of water, but as the center of exchanges with the coherence of a "common arena toward which all were oriented."[66] And only in 2000, fifty years after Braudel, did the first comprehensive study that systematically rethinks the Mediterranean as a distinct unity across time and space from prehistory to the present appear, in Peregrine Horden and Nicholas Purcell's extraordinarily rich and provocative *The Corrupting Sea.*[67]

The real reason for the failure of culture area imitation—as opposed to the legion of monographic studies on specific socioeconomic topics inspired by Braudel's *Mediterranean*—was already well known by Braudel as early as 1951.[68] In an *Annales* article commending the "courageous" 1949 essay of Maurice Le Lannou on *géographie humaine* at an opportune moment in the

---

64. Marvin Mikesell, "Geographic Perspectives in Anthropology," *Annals of the Association of American Geographers* 57 (1967): 617–34, details how anthropologists adapted the idea of "cultural area" just about the time that the geographers had rejected it. Such cross-fertilization among the social sciences is typical of the borrowing of hypotheses (both heuristic and controversial) that may go in and out of fashion.

65. Despite Braudel's insistence on the more expansive idea of "géohistoire," there is no doubt that a much older "géopolitique" informs his *Mediterranean*. See Leopold von Ranke, *The Ottoman and the Spanish Empires in the Sixteenth and Seventeenth Centuries*, trans. Walter K. Kelly (1843; repr. New York: AMS Press, 1975); translation of vols. 1 and 2 of *Fürsten und Volker von Sud-Europa*.

66. Lyman Van Slyke, *Nature, History and the River* (Reading, Mass.: Addison-Wesley, 1988), 1, and Anthony Reid, *Southeast Asia in the Age of Commerce 1450–1680*, 2 vols. (New Haven: Yale University Press, 1988–93).

67. Peregrine Horden and Nicholas Purcell, *The Corrupting Sea* (Oxford: Blackwell, 2000).

great contemporary geographical debate, Braudel hypothesized on the reasons for the then current grave crisis of the so-called human in geography. According to Braudel, postwar geography was changing all over, not only in France, because the new generation of geographers were less well rounded than Vidal's students, because the older methods and perspectives had come under recent attack, because of the spread of increased knowledge, and because an expanded physical geography made claims of scientific progress. Further, geography has always been extremely receptive to new ideas in exchange with both the natural and human sciences, but has been relatively weak in retaining its own identity as the other sciences sack, assimilate, and annex it.

When Braudel's *La Méditerranée* appeared in 1949, he tells us that it was almost ten years after it had been worked out. Thus, in many areas—most notably the debate about determinism—Braudel rehashed a summary of old disputes that had long since played themselves out. For the 1966 second edition fifteen years later, Braudel recognized that some questions and debates had fallen out of fashion as "our polemics of yesterday follow into the shadows."[69] The second edition takes the occasion, therefore, to update the text in a number of ways: to add graphics not originally available; to correct, revise, and even add new problematics; to synthesize a generation of outstanding new social-economic research; to add new archival references; but finally, most important to the argument advanced here concerning the postwar crisis in geography, to change his perspective. Since "l'auteur lui-même a changé," Braudel tells the reader that he gives greater emphasis to economics, political science, a revised conception of civilization, and demography.[70] Despite his lament for geography and never, of course, losing his personal

68. Fernand Braudel, "La Géographie face aux sciences humaines," *Annales E.S.C.* 6, no. 4 (1951): 485–92.

69. Braudel, *La Méditerranée*, 2d ed., preface, 1:11, explains that it was first published in 1949 from the defense of his 1947 Sorbonne thesis as "le fruit direct" of the *Annales* of Marc Bloch and Lucien Febvre and "était fixée dans ses grandes lignes, sinon écrite entièrement, dès 1939.... Aussi bien le lecteur ne se trompera-t-il pas à tels arguments de la préface de la première édition: ils se dressent contre des positions anciennes, aujourd'hui oubliées dans le monde de la recherche, sinon dans celui de l'enseignement. Notre polémique d'hier poursuit des ombres."

70. Braudel, *La Méditerranée*, 2d ed., preface, 1:12: "Toutes ces gerbes, il a fallu les engranger. Alors se sont reposées les insidieuses questions de méthode. Elles interviennent aussitôt à l'échelle d'un livre qui met en scène l'espace méditerranéen, pris dans ses plus vastes

artistic flair for the human, he too had become converted to the new "positivism" and scientific optimism of postwar reconstruction.[71]

POSTMODERNISM AND GEOGRAPHY

No doubt up to this point, the outline of geography—as a discipline shaped in the late nineteenth century in reaction against positivism, that then survived the post-First World War crisis of environmental determinism and evolutionism by embracing environmental "possibilism," in order to join the ranks of the other social sciences after the Second World War in its fascination with statistical scientific methodology—is an old story. Soon after Braudel published his revised and updated second edition in 1966, the political and intellectual displacements of 1968 found a home in a challenging new geography that continues to develop with epistemological innovations. Three important perspectives have shaped post-1968 geography: Marxism and political consciousness; feminism, aware of both a patriarchal establishment and a skewed research agenda that missed one half of the world's population; and the philosophical rethinking of space that is the centerpiece of postmodernism.[72] In addition, geographers like other social scientists have

---

limites et dans toute l'épaisseur de sa vie multiple. Grossir l'information, c'est, forcément, déplacer, rompre les anciens problèmes, puis en rencontrer de nouveaux, aux solutions difficiles et incertaines. D'autre part pendant les quinze années qui séparent cette nouvelle édition de la rédaction initiale, l'auteur lui–même a changé. Toucher à ce livre était impossible sans que se déplacent d'eux–mêmes aussi certains équilibres du raisonnement, et même la problématique qui en est l'articulation majeure, cette dialectique espace-temps (histoire-géographie) qui en justifiait la mise en place initiale. Cette fois, j'ai dégagé et accentué des perspectives à peine esquissées dans le premier texte. L'économie, la science politique, une certaine conception des civilisations, une démographie plus attentive m'ont sollicité. J'ai multiplié des éclairages qui, si je ne m'abuse, portent des lumières neuves jusqu'au coeur de mon entreprise."

71. Giuliana Gemelli, *Fernand Braudel e l'Europa universale* (Venice: Marsilio, 1990). Two geographic examples of this paradigm in English are J. M. Houston, *The Western Mediterranean World: An Introduction to Its Regional Landscapes* (London: Longmans, 1964), and Catherine Delano Smith, *Western Mediterranean Europe: A Historical Geography of Italy, Spain and Southern France since the Neolithic* (London: Academic Press, 1979).

72. Two new geography journals, which began publishing in response to the post-1968 crisis, are exemplary: *Antipode: A Journal of Radical Geography* (August 1969–) and *Hérodote* (1976–).

come to question their "objectivity" and have become keenly aware of their own value-laden agendas in a postcolonial, postindustrial world.[73]

David Harvey is one of the leaders of the postmodern movement—not only in geography, but as a philosophical perspective. His 1989 book, *The Condition of Postmodernity: An Essay into the Origins of Cultural Change,* may be his most well known work, but only one of a number that derive their argument from a Marxian political commitment and analysis of the "political-economic transformation in late-twentieth-century capitalism."[74] For Harvey, postmodernism grows out of geography because he focuses on the "new dominant ways in which we experience space and time."

In simplest terms, Harvey argues that "the rise of postmodernist cultural forms (in architecture and the arts, for example) are only shifts in surface appearance that reflect the emergence of more flexible modes of capitalist accumulation." Harvey defines the post-Second World War boom between 1945 and 1973 as a Fordist-Keynesian *regime of accumulation* and its associated mode of *social and political regulation,*" transformed after the early 1970s to "a 'flexible' regime of accumulation." What Harvey focuses on is the "time-space compression," in other words, how the communication and transportation revolutions have shrunk the time horizon of both private and public decision making. Harvey does not see postmodernism as a question of perspective or interpretation, but as a fundamental shift in the way the material world is organized—anyone remembering Braudel's sixty-day world of space defined by time/distance knows what Harvey's geography is all about. Further for Harvey, money, time, and space form a substantial nexus of social power. In his recent 1996 book, *Justice, Nature and the Geography of Distance,* Harvey goes even further in trying to "construct a general theory of dialectical and historical geographical materialism," here emphasizing how the present dialectical way works (grounded in process, flux, and flow) versus the past idea of fundamental certainties and permanencies.[75]

Much of the theoretical underpinning for Harvey comes from the French: Michel Foucault's understanding of space as defined/measured/limited by the human body; Michel de Certeau's use of the human scale of a walker as establishing the practices of everyday life; and also Pierre Bourdieu's emphasis on

73. Gregory, *Geographical Imaginations,* 36–37.

74. Harvey, *Condition of Postmodernity,* "The Argument" (vii), pt. 2, on the transformation (119–97), and pt. 3, on the time-space experience (199–323).

75. David Harvey, *Justice, Nature and the Geography of Difference* (Oxford: Blackwell, 1996), 6–10.

the household as the unit of spatial measurement.[76] But above all, it is Henri Lefebvre's 1974 book, *La Production de l'espace*, that develops a historical and philosophical rationale to differentiate space in three modes: as experienced, perceived, and imagined.[77] Lefebvre's book revels in triads: space exists also in the physical (that is, in nature and the cosmos), the mental (as logical and formal abstractions), and the social (as a product of capitalists' power relations). Marx is the point of departure, and a historical materialism divides traditional Western Civilization periods into triads: the Greco-Roman Christian world used private property to demarcate its space in villas, villages, and towns that gave way to a medieval spatial organization of town, country, and power relationships; in the Renaissance city, architectural, urbanistic, and political codes operated; in nineteenth-century industrialization, land, labor, and capital created a fetishized, fragmented, and hierarchical space; and currently, spatial production can be geometrical (a la Euclid), optical or visual, and phallic in the erection of a contemporary architecture embodying the police, the army, and bureaucracy.

French geographers themselves participated in this philosophical debate either to challenge or preserve the structural orientation of classical geography. Antoine Bailly could write in a 1984 article, "Probabilités subjectives et géographie humaine," that what was once thought of as a science of space is now seen to be subjective, relative, and mediated by culture.[78] Semiotics was employed to explore the meaning of arrangements in space; in their words, the organization of geographical space by society constitutes its means of reproduction and development. Paul Claval even tried to develop a "grammar

76. Michel Foucault, *Discipline and Punish: The Birth of the Prison* (London: Allen Lane, 1975), and idem, "Questions on Geography," in *Power/Knowledge: Selected Interviews and Other Writings* (Brighton: Harvester Press, 1980), 63–77; Michel de Certeau, *The Practice of Everyday Life*, trans. Steven Rendall (Berkeley: University of California Press, 1984), pt. 3, "Spatial Practices" (91–130), esp. chap. 7, "Walking in the City"; Pierre Bourdieu, "The Kabyle House, or the World Reversed," in *Algeria 1960* (Cambridge: Cambridge University Press, 1979), 133–53, and idem, *Outlines of a Theory of Practice* (Cambridge: Polity Press, 1977).

77. Henri Lefebvre, *La Production de l'espace* (Paris: Anthropos, 1974); *The Production of Space*, trans. Donald Nicholson-Smith (Oxford: Blackwell, 1991), afterword by David Harvey.

78. Antoine S. Bailly, "Probabilités subjectives et géographie humaine," in *Géographes aujourd'hui: Mélanges offerts en hommage au doyen F. Gay* (Nice, 1984); idem, "Distances et espaces: Vingt ans de géographie des représentations," *L'Espace géographique* 3 (1985): 197–205; and Antoine S. Bailly and Bernard Debarbieux, "Géographie et répresentations spatiales," in *Les concepts*, 157–64.

of social relationships grounded in the interaction between space and types of power in order to explain the structure and emergence of place configuration," that is, how spatial structure or form constrains social structures and how the social for its part determines spatial structures. French geographers were not only interested in grammar, but also semantics, the meaning of place—both in its cognitive as well as emotive response to lived space. And so, "the urban place for example is no longer the center city, but rather it takes the form of a network of various locations (friends, restaurants, theaters, offices)." Finally, completing the linguistic model of geography as a grammar and a semantic system, geography also has a rhetorical dimension as discourse, embodying a strong narrative component and a distinctive method of argument and criteria for evidence in order to persuade.[79]

Edward Soja is another important geographer in the understanding and use of power in defining space. As early as 1971, he wrote an American Association of Geographers pamphlet on *The Political Organization of Space,* and in 1989, the same year as Harvey's *Postmodern Condition,* Soja published *Postmodern Geographies: The Reassertion of Space in Critical Social Theory.*[80] Soja's own research has often focused on the contemporary city, with Los Angeles as the quintessential postmodern place for his source of examples.

Both Harvey and Soja are dissected in Derek Gregory's 1994 *Geographical Imaginations,* where contingency and complexity, difference and indeterminacy are bywords to help explain (especially in the city) how urban places are produced and how we represent our understanding of them.[81] Harvey especially receives strong criticism for his neglect of the feminist critique; Soja in terms of his interest in environment and planning.

The explosion of creativity within geography over the last twenty-five years is legion: failures like that of the chorologists who tried to identify choremes as elementary structures in the organization of geographical space; great successes like Geographical Information Systems (GIS), which store, retrieve, and map large volumes of overlapping data sets using satellite photography and computer correlations; or even the historical/artistic contribution that comes into the critique of Western ethnocentric concepts of space

79. Berdoulay, "Place, Meaning, and Discourse," cites: Paul Claval and Gilles Ritchot (129–30), G. Burgel (130–31), his own articles and J. Schlanger (134–36), and Claval and Roger Brunet (328–29).

80. Edward W. Soja, *The Political Organization of Space,* Commission on College Geography, no. 8 (Washington, D.C.: Association of American Geographers, 1971).

81. Gregory, *Geographical Imaginations,* 317–416, on Harvey, and idem, 256–313, on Soja.

from Guaman Póma, the Peruvian chronicler/illustrator whose late-six-teenth-century American Indian perspective turns our visual assumptions upside down.[82] What all this innovation and experimentation in the discipline has in common, the primary point that postmodern geographers teach us, is, above all, that space is constructed and, therefore, representing it visually in maps or reconstructing it historically in our writing is like playing a Platonic shadow game of reflected and ephemeral images darting across the wall of a cave. We are always constructing and reconstructing space since there is no such thing as an "original" landscape.

GEOGRAPHY'S PRESENT STATE AND FUTURE PROMISE

As in the earlier paradigm shifts within geography, the current contentious environment has breathed new life into the discipline by making space matter, not only for geography but for all the human sciences. A genuine confluence of diverse perspectives from the other social sciences and from different national geographic traditions has created a convergence of thought bristling with new research questions. The extreme breadth of geographic interests and practices, however, makes it seem that geographers may be talking past one another. In 1980, Chauncy Harris's third edition of his authoritative *Annotated World List of Selected Current Geographical Serials* counted 443 geographical periodicals from seventy-two countries, while the professional societies and subspecialties of study groups proliferate with eight in Canada, eighteen in Britain, and forty-one in the United States.[83]

Two recent American publications attest to geography's optimistic future. In 1992, the Association of American Geographers initiative to summarize the current state of the field resulted in a collaborative volume of sixteen essays, which emphasized that the various geographic schools and divergent tendencies had more in common than disciplinary disputes suggested and that instead of a crisis of confidence, the current debate had become a source of renewal.[84] About that same time, in 1993, the National

82. Roger Brunet (1969, 1972, and 1980), cited in Berdoulay, "Place, Meaning, and Discourse," 128–29; Rolena Adorno, *Guaman Póma: Writing and Resistance in Colonial Peru* (Austin: University of Texas Press, 1985).

83. Chauncy D. Harris, *443 Current Geographical Serials from 72 Countries* (Chicago: University of Chicago Department of Geography, 1980).

84. R. F. Abler, M. G. Marcus, and J. M. Olson, eds., *Geography's Inner Worlds: Pervasive Themes in Contemporary American Geography* (New Brunswick, N.J.: Rutgers University Press, 1992).

Research Council (the principal opinion agency of the National Academy of Sciences) established the Rediscovering Geography Committee "to identify ways to make the discipline more relevant to science, education, and decision making."[85] The committee's conclusions, published early in 1997, have four aims: (1) on research—to improve geographic understanding; (2) on education—to improve geographic literacy; (3) on organization—to strengthen geographic institutions; and (4) on cooperation among the various related institutions—to implement the report's recommendations.

For the National Research Council, geography provides untapped potential for fundamental contributions to the President's National Science and Technology Council's recently identified eight strategic fields of research, education, and information transfer. Since our focus is more concerned with epistemological questions than policy issues, I should emphasize that the committee's report also recognizes "the more basic questions that underlie" policy issues as fundamental research problems in which geography participates, such as "relationships between macroscale and microscale phenomena and processes, understanding complex systems, developing integrative approaches to understanding complexity, and understanding relationships between form and function."[86]

How geographers and historians confront similar questions in different ways can be seen in some work using this new scientific approach. In ecological or environmental history, the work of two scholars comes to mind: Alfred Crosby's *Columbian Exchange* and *Ecological Imperialism*, and J. R. McNeill's *The Mountains and the Mediterranean* (which compares five depopulated and eroded regions in Turkey, Greece, Italy, Spain, and Morocco).[87] In reviewing McNeill's book, Karl Butzer emphasizes how different would be the geomorphologist or polymologist's attempt to exploit a

---

85. Abler et al., *Rediscovering Geography*, ix–x.

86. See Abler et al., *Rediscovering Geography*, 13–14: "Five are fields in which geography should be a central contributor: global change research; environmental research; high-performance computing and communications (e.g., geographic information systems and visualization); civil (public) infrastructure systems; and science, mathematics, engineering, and technology education consonant with the Educate America Act. Geography is also relevant in more subtle ways to the other three fields—biotechnology, advanced materials and processes, and advanced manufacturing technology—through its focus on environmental and social issues, resource use, locational decisions, and technology transfer."

87. Alfred W. Crosby, *The Columbian Exchange: Biological and Cultural Consequences of 1492* (Westport, Conn.: Greenwood Press, 1972), and idem, *Ecological Imperialism: The Biological Expansion of Europe, 900–1900* (Cambridge: Cambridge University Press, 1986); J. R.

wider source base, to develop more detailed land-use studies, and to theorize with a more nuanced understanding of causality and contingency.[88] Similarly, on the vexed question of original Amerindian population, a topic pioneered by the Berkeley school—Sherburne Cook, Lesley Byrd Simpson, and Woodrow Borah (1948; 1963; 1968), with roots back to Carl Ortwin Sauer[89]—no consensus estimate has emerged despite the ingenuity of research methods, including geographer Thomas Whitmore's human ecological situation model that accounted for demographic changes in age structure, mortality, fertility, and migration in terms of variables of disease, food shortage, homicide, climate, and labor withdrawal.[90]

For the United States' educational policy, geography's future success seems to be in turning itself once again into a "science" at the same time that the cutting-edge postmodernists among the geographers have convinced the discipline that they have been studying constructed phenomena. Unlike the other social sciences in the United States' academic labor market, geography's main problem is unmet demand rather than oversupply. While geography's inverse demographic profile may reflect how low the discipline had fallen by the early 1980s, its recovery has been quite extraordinary. From the time of

---

McNeill, *The Mountains of the Mediterranean World* (Cambridge: Cambridge University Press, 1992); Salvatore Ciriacono, *Acque e agricoltura: Venezia, l'Olanda e la bonifica europea in età moderna* (Milan: Franco Angeli, 1994); Richard C. Hoffman, "Economic Development and Aquatic Ecosystems in Medieval Europe," *American Historical Review* 101 (1996): 631–69; and Mauro Ambrosoli, *The Wild and the Sown: Botony and Agriculture in Western Europe, 1350–1850*, trans. Mary McCann Salvatorelli (New York: Cambridge University Press, 1997).

88. Karl W. Butzer, book review of McNeill, *Mountains of the Mediterranean World* in *Annals of the Association of American Geographers* 86 (1996): 780–82.

89. Carl Ortwin Sauer, chair of the University of California–Berkeley department of geography (1923–57), defined the "Berkeley school": see *Encyclopedia of the Social Sciences* (1931), s.v. "Cultural Geography;" idem, "Forward to Historical Geography (1941)," in *Land and Life: A Selection from the Writings of Carl Ortwin Sauer*, ed. John Leighly (Berkeley: University of California Press, 1963), 351–79; idem, *The Early Spanish Main* (Berkeley: University of California Press, 1966); and idem, *Sixteenth Century North America* (Berkeley: University of California Press, 1971). See also Sherburne Cook and Lesley Byrd Simpson, *The Population of Central Mexico in the Sixteenth Century* (Berkeley: University of California Press, 1948); Sherburne Cook and Woodrow Borah, *The Aboriginal Population of Central Mexico on the Eve of the Spanish Conquest* (Berkeley: University of California Press, 1963); and idem, *The Population of the Mixteca Alta, 1520–1960* (Berkeley: University of California Press, 1968).

90. Abler et al., *Rediscovering Geography*, 72, cites T. M. Whitmore, *Disease and Death in Early Colonial Mexico: Simulating Amerindian Depopulation* (Boulder: Westview Press, 1992).

the well-publicized 1986 survey of adults in nine countries, which ranked United States' young adults' geographic knowledge last in any age group, efforts to improve the discipline have borne fruit both in the schools and in government support. In university education, for example, in the eight academic years between 1986–87 and 1993–94, undergraduate geography majors increased 47 percent (60 percent in Ph.D.-granting departments), and graduate student enrollment in the seven years between 1985 and 1991 grew by 33.4 percent in comparison to a 15.3 percent increase for the social sciences and 5.4 decrease for the environmental sciences.[91] Geographical knowledge and expertise does indeed seem to be recovering, both its intellectual underpinning and its institutional infrastructure.

If "recovering geography" as a medical metaphor for a patient etherized upon a table is not to dissolve into another less attractive metaphor for the stuffed armchair of some avant-garde reupholsterer, geography must keep its eye on its history and be ready to recover—with the meaning of "to reclaim"—something of its tradition.[92] What was lost that must now be refound or rediscovered? Geography as a discipline occupying the space between the liberal arts of geometry and astronomy, that is, as a recovered science with its unique way of knowing, should *not* be geography's goal. Vermeer's 1669 *The Geographer*, which is often associated with his similar painting of *The Astronomer*, provides a visual image of the unacceptability of a neoclassical or Enlightenment geography.[93] Both Vermeer's "scientific" geographer of the earth and his "scientific" astronomer of the heavens are represented in the same way, as an early modern doctor doing a dissection or as scientists at experiment. The chiaroscuro emphasis on the scientist/principal investigator at the center of the action, the object of study (patient's body or map), and the tools of the trade (scalpel or compass) focuses our attention on the act of creation taking place in the highlighted, concentrated light streaming in from some window to the world. The closed study functions as a camera obscura to produce "scientifically objective" representations of the outside world. But rather, geography's recovery of the contingency of space,

91. Abler et al., *Rediscovering Geography*, 8.

92. Postmodern geography is fond of such puns; see David Harvey, "From Models to Marx: Notes on the Project to 'Remodel' Geography," in *Remodelling Geography*, ed. Bill Macmillan (Oxford: Blackwell, 1989), 211–16.

93. Gregory, *Geographical Imaginations*, 34–35, cites Jonathan Crary, "The Camera Obscura and Its Subject," *Techniques of the Observer: On Vision and Modernity in the Nineteenth Century* (Cambridge: MIT Press, 1990), 25–66.

like history's rediscovery of the contingency of time, should place the discipline within the tradition of the studia humanitatis, that is, as a rhetorical practice of representation leading to ethical decision making and moral conduct. Thus, geography operates like history—which constructs meaning out of a chronicle of events—by constructing and reconstructing meaning from its presentation and representation of space/time (as a single, unbreakable unit). The end result is not an explanation of change over time, but a more nuanced understanding of change over time *and* space, in order to inform individual action and state policy.

My thanks to Andrew Zimmerman for his comments and suggestions.

PART 2

Economic Theory and Practice in Early Modern History

Chapter 2

CITY AND COUNTRYSIDE IN SPAIN

Changing Structures, Changing Relationships, 1450–1850

BARTOLOMÉ YUN CASALILLA

The task assigned me presents some concerns. As I understand it, each author—from the perspective of his or her own specialization—is to offer a series of reflections on what the various social sciences (sociology, anthropology, economics, and others) can provide to help us improve our understanding of history. We must do this not only theoretically and generally, but also through an assessment of the changes that have taken place since the publication of Fernand Braudel's *La Méditerranée* and by examining a specific problem, in my case, the relationship between the countryside and the city in Spain. This was a topic of great concern to Braudel while he was writing his masterpiece, and it continued to preoccupy him for the rest of his life.[1] It is not that economic history is so much more difficult than other disciplines, but it seems that in the particular case of urban-rural relations in Spain, the problems multiply. These difficulties exist—partly as a result of Braudel's legacy—because economic history has long been at the center of our conceptualization of the past and our explanations of the present. To further complicate the situation, the field of economic history is undergoing a kind of crisis related to its connection with the field of economics.[2] This brings to mind the words of E. P. Thompson (so politically incorrect that I should not even repeat them here—but those were other times!). When referring to the one-sided relationship

---

1. Fernand Braudel, *The Mediterranean and the Mediterranean World in the Age of Philip II,* 2d ed., 2 vols., trans. Siân Reynolds (London: Collins, 1973), 1:275–352. It is widely recognized that this theme appears repeatedly in Braudel's writings and played a fundamental role in his second great work, *Civilization and Capitalism, 15th to the 18th Century,* 3 vols., trans. Siân Reynolds (New York: Harper & Row, 1981).

2. See "What Is Economic History?" *History Today* (February 1985), for a report on the responses to a questionnaire administered to a group of distinguished economic historians.

often created by a coupling of the social sciences and history, Thompson complained of the image of a frigid and passive history succumbing to the potency of sociology, anthropology, and—I would add—economics.[3]

LA MÉDITERRANÉE, CITY AND COUNTRYSIDE, AND BRAUDELIAN ECONOMIC HISTORY

Economic history was the undisputed star for more than forty years, from the time Fernand Braudel wrote his masterpiece until the 1980s. Nor is there any question that the relationship between economics and history is complex. It is enough to look carefully at his chapters that deal specifically with economics, that is, part 2 "Collective Destinies and General Trends," which analyze long-term trends that, Braudel reminds us, constitute the appropriate time span for the economic historian in contrast to the economist.[4] In these chapters, the long cycles appear to be marked by short-term events and activities. An occurrence such as the relocation of the Besançon fairs constitutes "the event of the century from the point of view of the history of capitalism."[5] These chapters present advances in navigation techniques as being critical to northern Europe's superiority over southern Europe. Moreover, as the reader follows the narrative's sinuous but steady course, it is apparent that the economy cannot be explained in isolation. The power of cities, institutions, and politics appears to be decisive in the economy's expansion and contraction; the spaces of exchange or of production and information are not uniform, as postulates of neoclassical economics predict, but instead are irregular, made up of complicated networks, fragmented by superimposed administrative districts and by a complex jungle with areas of varying monetary circulation. And this is proven—why shouldn't it be?—when one examines cities. Salamanca or Venice are not market centers but jurisdictional entities that control their territories by force. When it comes to the development and, above all,

---

3. E. P. Thompson, "Anthropology and the Discipline of Historical Context" (review of Keith Thomas, *Religion and the Decline of Magic* [1971], and Alan MacFarlane, *The Family Life of Ralph Josselin, A Seventeenth-Century Clergyman* [1970]) in *Midland History* 1, no. 3 (1972): 41–55. Thompson speaks of an anthropology and a sociology that inseminate a frigid Clio, but the metaphor could be applied to economics as well.

4. Braudel summarized his thoughts on the subject in one of his few theoretical essays; see "Pour une économie historique," *La Revue économique* 1 (May 1950): 37–44; English trans. in Fernand Braudel, *On History*, trans. Sarah Matthews (London: Weidenfeld & Nicholson, 1980), 89–130.

5. Braudel, *The Mediterranean*, 2d ed., 1:379.

the decline of the Mediterranean cities, these up-and-down trends are presented not just as the result of economic vicissitudes but page after page affirms that the "modern state" is to blame for asphyxiating the political potential and, ultimately, the economic vigor of the urban centers.[6]

However, things look very different when we get out from under the luxuriant oak of Braudelian erudition and face the bare branches of his conclusions. The economy, the long term, the cycles having little or nothing to do with politics, these are presented as the passkeys to the historical explanation of acts and events, all at the expense of the short term. Because they depend on its resources, the economy explains the vicissitudes of states and empires, and this, in turn, explains the cycle of growth that began in the fifteenth century and its decline starting at the end of the sixteenth century. This is true to such a degree that it is this fact that unites "the giant political combinations built up by the Ottoman and the Habsburg."[7] In this view, says Braudel refuting Joseph A. Schumpeter, chance scarcely plays a role.[8] The "secular trend" is, above all, an economic trend, and the economy governs circumstances, even as these are made up of "economic" and "noneconomic" fluctuations. This is precisely why the fundamental question of Braudel's second edition focuses on the length of the cycle. Did expansion end in 1620, as claimed in the first edition? Or should the "'long' sixteenth century" be said to last until 1650?[9] The answer is telling: "alongside such problems" (Braudel is referring to cycles and long-term economic rhythms), "the role of the individual and the event necessarily dwindles." These events ("essentially ephemeral") form the "brilliant surface," important to the historian but, in the end, nothing more than "footnotes" written within the "pentagram of history." The individual is seen as being "imprisoned within a destiny in which he himself has little hand, fixed in a landscape in which the infinitive perspectives of the long term stretch into the distance both behind him and before." The "long run always wins in the end," "annihilating innumerable events"; it is understood, of course, that the "long run" is not just economic but also the economic time frame of the historian, as Braudel explained.[10]

---

6. See Braudel, *The Mediterranean*, 2d ed., 1:615–41, "The brilliant victory in the seventeenth century of English and Dutch … was the result of a series of technological improvements in the design and handling of ships" (636). See also ibid., 1:325, 326, 340, 352, 355–94.

7. Braudel, *The Mediterranean*, 2d ed., 2:678.

8. Braudel, *The Mediterranean*, 2d ed., 2:678–81.

9. Braudel, *The Mediterranean*, 2d ed., 2:893–94.

10. Braudel, *The Mediterranean*, 2d ed., 2:1240–44.

In Braudel, we find some of the principal threads of historical analysis that would dominate the field until the 1980s. Like Braudel, the Annales School and various Marxist lines of thought also used the study of economic fluctuations as the backbone upon which to base their general interpretations. The cycles of production, population, and prices, or the expansion and contraction of income or property rents, have often been taken to be the forces governing history. The culmination of the cycle in the Mediterranean—aggravated by the "betrayal of the bourgeoisie" and "refeudalization" (a term liked by few, including Braudel)—resulted from cyclic change. The seventeenth century was analyzed in economic or, more precisely, fiscal terms, even in regard to its political conflicts. Examples abound, even for the case of Castile and Spain generally, but this is not the best place to enumerate them.[11] In any case, the prevalence of these assumptions makes perfectly understandable many of the criticisms or concerns about Braudel and the Annales School that have been voiced by historians who study institutions and politics, such as Felix Gilbert, J. H. Hexter, or Lawrence Stone; by those, like Jonathan Israel, who defend an economic history more deeply rooted in its political context and the influence of the short term on the economy;[12] and by a Marxist historiography, concerned as it is with class relations, which finds that the Malthusian prism fails to explain cycles.[13] And it makes it possible to appreciate the accusations of determinism hurled against "such borrowings from the social sciences," to which Stone refers.[14]

---

11. The ideas are summarized in Bartolomé Yun Casalilla, "Cambiamento e continuità: La Castiglia nell'Impero durante il secolo d'Oro," *Studi Storici,* no. 1 (1995): 9–103.

12. Felix Gilbert, "Intellectual History: Its Aim and Methods," *Daedalus* (winter 1971); J. H. Hexter, "Fernand Braudel and the *Monde Braudelian*," *Journal of Modern History* 44 (1972), 480–539; Lawrence Stone, "A Demurral," *The New Republic* (October 1, 1984): 31–34; J. Israel, *Dutch Primacy in World Trade, 1585–1740* (Oxford: Clarendon, 1989), 4–11, and "The Phases of the Dutch *Straatvart,* 1590–1713: A Chapter in the Economic History of the Mediterranean," in *Empires and Entrepôts: The Dutch, the Spanish Monarchy and the Jews, 1585–1713* (London: Hambledon, 1990), 133–62.

13. For a critique of the theory, see J. Fontana, "Ascenso y decadencia de la escuela de los 'Annales,'" in *Hacia una nueva Historia,* ed. E. Balibar, M. Barceló, et al. (Madrid: Editorial Akal, 1976), 109–27. On the other hand, everyone recognizes the existence of this comparison in the so-called Brenner Debate. T. H. Aston and C. H. E. Philpin, eds., *The Brenner Debate: Agrarian Class Structure and Economic Development in Pre-industrial Europe* (Cambridge: Cambridge University Press, 1985).

14. Lawrence Stone, "History and the Social Sciences in the Twentieth Century," in *The Past and the Present Revisited* (London: Routledge & Kegan Paul, 1987), 19–20.

Nevertheless, neither Braudel's economic conceptualization nor the one we economic historians have long applied has succeeded as much as might have been hoped when one considers economic history's indisputable reign. The French scholar's use of terms such as "marginal crisis" to refer to the Malthusian crisis at the end of the sixteenth century indicates a certain theoretical (or, at least, terminological) vagueness at the same time that the application of categories from national budgetary accounts (such as GDP, GNP, etc.) raises questions, as even the author himself acknowledges.[15] In *La Méditerranée*, the application of the theory of diminishing marginal returns is only one part of the Ricardian formulation which, instead of a working hypothesis, is applied as a metaphor for the process that it supposedly produced. Braudel's recognition of the fragmentation of economic space or the irregularity of markets never led him to consider the theories that Ronald Coase formed in the late 1930s nor to analyze the phenomenon in light of transaction costs that fragmentation and market characteristics imply for economic agents. Such a contemplation might well have rounded out or improved Braudel's arguments in later editions of his masterpiece. Malthusian visions have often been put forward in simplistic models limited to comparing population and production curves without considering the internal logic of economic processes in their historical context. When we have used concepts like market, demand, consumption, investment, and so forth, we have frequently had recourse to the most abstract and simplistic definitions of these terms. Clearly, we are lacking an analysis that would explain, not the cycles, but the economic decision-making process in its specific social, institutional, and ideological context or one that would seek out, within the ample field of modern economic theory, the most appropriate model to apply to each case. It is not surprising that one economist has insinuated that even today, "the fundamentals of economics remain inaccessible to historians." Nor is it surprising that this deficiency is attributed not only to a lack of knowledge on the part of historians but above all to the development of economics along abstract lines that failed to consider achievements of historians or the findings that they could have provided through an analysis of the real world.[16] This view echoes E. P. Thompson's accusation of asymmetry in the partnership between history and the social sciences.

15. Braudel, *The Mediterranean*, 2d ed., 1:585, 1:418–61.
16. Thomas G. Rawski, "Economics and the Historian," in Thomas G. Rawski et al., *Economics and the Historian* (Berkeley: University of California Press, 1996), 2–4.

Our notion of the relationship between the countryside and the city, in the case of Castile specifically and of Spain generally, could not be more coherent with that position. From the point of view of Braudel and his followers, Castilian cities witnessed the rise of territorial states, yet the belief continues that they are governed by the economy, or more precisely, by economic cycles. Both the economy and the cycles (fundamentally agrarian cycles) are taken in their simplest sense as the explanatory key to urban development, surpassing the influence of political history, which is important but always overly detailed and never decisive.[17] Cities are nodal points in a network of commercial circuits and information exchange. They are centers of consumption, which the surrounding countryside supplies only with difficulty. They grow until the decade of 1580–90 while the countryside allows such expansion, but it would be the very same agrarian blockages that limited their development. Thus, the urban decline of Castile is, at root, economic, Malthusian, and provoked by problems of supply[18] or by the exhaustion of a cycle that pumped agrarian rents toward the cities and urban consumers;[19] although it is also recognized that the towns' loss of political power had severely restricted their capacity for response. Cities (the agents of civilization, as Braudel expounded elsewhere) met their downfall as fundamentally commercial centers squashed by a low ceiling of agricultural productivity.

The next phase of the cycle, the Castilian cities' recessive phase, Braudel does not explain, neither in *La Méditerranée* nor in later works, where it is even more noticeably lacking. This phase has, nevertheless, preoccupied many of his successors, and it lends itself to a continued application of the conceptual scheme. The seventeenth century would be a century of Malthusian, or at least Smithian, readjustments. Declining populations had adapted to diminishing resources, generating a new urban model. The result is clear: the expansion of the eighteenth century is the least that could be expected, but it was built on structures identical to those that caused the crisis at the end of the sixteenth century. This assumption has been present,

17. For a lucid consideration of this issue, see Paul M. Hohenberg and Lynn Hollen Lees, "Urban Decline and Regional Economies: Brabant, Castile, and Lombardy, 1550–1750," *Comparative Studies in Society and History* 31 (1989): 439–61. Even though Spanish historians have scarcely noticed, the work of Hohenberg and Lees takes for granted a more sophisticated Ricardian model for the development of Castilian cities in the early modern period.

18. Braudel, *The Mediterranean*, 2d ed., 1:570–76.

19. Hohenberg and Lees, "Urban Decline and Regional Economies," 449–55.

even in later works.[20] The new cycle of agrarian expansion had increased the surplus available to sell to the cities. Only renewed Malthusian asphyxiation, such as occurred at the end of the eighteenth century, would again stop urban growth.

CITY AND COUNTRYSIDE IN EARLY MODERN SPAIN: RECENT FINDINGS AND NEW PROPOSALS

The agrarian limits to urban development are still recognized today, but a belief has emerged that difficulties in many cities began well before rural expansion ground to a halt.[21] A simplistic Malthusian tension between production and population cannot explain this. Instead, in conformity with what might be characterized as a typically Ricardian scheme (but one that is unlike the model mechanically applied until quite recently and based on agricultural output), it is recognized that agrarian expansion led to an increase in land rents. This severely stifled the rural economy's ability to expand, in turn worsening the conditions for growth in urban economies.[22] Along with the sale of common lands (*tierras baldías y concejiles*)—a phenomenon certainly separate from the agrarian cycle itself—rising rents contributed to indebtedness and rural breakdown in a context in which agrarian capitalism, as a potential substitute, simply did not fit the institutional framework of the time.[23]

20. Even in sophisticated studies, such as Hohenberg and Lees, "Urban Decline and Regional Economies," there are no substantial differences between explanations for sixteenth-century urban cycles and later ones.

21. See, for example, the concerns expressed by J. E. Gelabert, "Urbanisation and Deurbanisation in Castile, 1500–1800," in *The Castilian Crisis of the Seventeenth Century: New Perspectives on the Economic and Social History of Seventeenth-Century Spain,* ed. I. A. A. Thompson and Bartolomé Yun Casalilla (Cambridge: Cambridge University Press, 1994), 182–205.

22. Bartolomé Yun Casalilla, *Sobre la transición al capitalismo en Castilla: Economía y sociedad en Tierra de Campos, 1500–1814* (Salamanca: Consejería de Educación & Cultura, 1987), 269–85. In my opinion, Hohenberg and Lees, "Urban Decline and Regional Economies," 450–55, offer the most interesting theoretical assessment of the subject.

23. Concerning the sale of common lands, see the pioneering studies of J. Gómez Mendoza, "La venta de baldíos y comunales en el siglo XVI: Estudio de un proceso en Guadalajara," *Estudios Geográficos,* no. 109 (1967): 499–559, and David Vassberg, *La venta de tierras baldías: El comunitarismo agrario y la Corona de Castilla durante el siglo XVI* (Madrid: Servicio de Publicaciones Agrarias, 1983). David Vassberg, *Land and Society in Golden Age Castile* (Cambridge: Cambridge University Press, 1994), esp. chaps. 6 and 7, summarizes the problems facing peasant economies.

The urban crisis, as has been shown in cases such as Córdoba, also had internal components, both industrial and commercial. These were not unrelated to rigidities in industrial organization (which was, in turn, linked to a system of tax collection that established inflexible units of production), as well as to the type of tax system in force and the contraction of demand in the countryside.[24] The emphasis on Madrid's pernicious effects[25]—so unlike the attraction that other European capitals, such as London,[26] exercised over their surrounding regions—requires an explanatory shift away from the theories of Adam Smith and toward explanations that pay closer attention to the character of capital cities. One must consider Madrid's economic life, as well as Spain's overall economic, social, and institutional structures within which the capital was evolving.[27] At the same time, and despite the vision of absolutism as the annihilator of local power, research in political and institutional history has demonstrated the fiscal and administrative strength of the cities.[28] It has also revealed significant inequalities between the center and the periphery in levels of urban development after

24. José Ignacio Fortea Pérez, *Córdoba en el siglo XVI: Las bases demográficas y económicas de una expansión urbana* (Córdoba: Monte de Piedad y Caja de Ahorros de Córdoba, 1981), 413–75.

25. David Ringrose, *Madrid and the Spanish Economy* (Berkeley: University of California Press, 1983). Notably, the judgment that Madrid negatively influenced the Castilian economy, although not for the same reasons, has been confirmed even by those who had at one time strongly disagreed with Ringrose's explanation. See J. M. López García and S. Madrazo, "A Capital City in the Feudal Order: Madrid from the Sixteenth to the Eighteenth Century," in *Capital Cities and Their Hinterlands in Early Modern Europe,* ed. Peter Clark and Bernard Lepetit (Aldershot: Ashgate, 1996), 119–42.

26. One of the most conclusive works is the pioneering study of Edward Anthony Wrigley, *People, Cities and Wealth: The Transformation of Traditional Society* (Oxford: Blackwell, 1987), chap. 6.

27. See the interesting discussion between S. Madrazo, "La lógica 'smitheana' en la historia económica y social de Madrid: A propósito de una traducción reciente," *Revista de Historia Económica* (1986): 609–18, and David Ringrose, "Poder y beneficio: Urbanización y cambio en la historia," *Revista de Historia Económica,* no. 2 (1988): 375–96. In a book published while I was working on this essay, José Miguel López García, ed., *El impacto de la Corte en Castilla: Madrid y su territorio en la época moderna* (Madrid: Siglo Vientiun de España, 1998), expounded on this particular point.

28. A nearly endless list of works emphasize the high degree of resistance by the urban powers against the crown. For a summary, see P. Fernández Albaladejo, "Cities and the State in Spain" in *Cities and the Rise of States in Europe, A.D. 1000 to 1800,* Charles Tilly and Willem Pieter Blockmans, eds. (Boulder: Westview, 1994), 168–83.

the seventeenth century,[29] which, not occurring elsewhere in Europe, frees us from the responsibility to find consistent explanations.

These new insights invalidate much of the common wisdom about Spain's urban history in existence when Braudel wrote the second edition of *La Méditerranée*. This recognition calls for the construction of a new version of that history, one that would utilize economic categories that fit recent findings better and provide more fruitful answers. The new explanation must be based in the fields of political and institutional history, the disciplines responsible for many of these recent achievements, and it also must incorporate those concepts from the field of economics that are capable of illuminating how political and institutional changes influence economic development. In writing this chapter, I have accepted these requirements while acknowledging the impossibility of addressing all of them. Consequently, I have limited myself to a series of reflections that are offered more as a research agenda than as definitive formulations.

To begin, the influence of strictly economic factors consistent with Braudel's notion of "long-term" changes are visible in the formation and expansion of Castilian and Spanish urban networks. The growing commercialization of the economy, and of agrarian output generally, as well as the location of the Iberian peninsula in trade routes, are essential to understanding the process, as the French historian so strongly emphasized.

The growth of large cities from the fifteenth century—beginning first in the Meseta Norte and later becoming especially vibrant in the south (in Andalucia and Valencia, to be precise, which displaced Barcelona from its position in the trade circuit with Italy)—reflects the increasing importance of the Atlantic economy and its Mediterranean connections, as well as the growing economic articulation of the country's distinct regions. The commercial expansion of the sixteenth century, with the consolidation of international linkages through Burgos and Seville, the flowering of the fairs in Medina del Campo and Medina de Rioseco, and the growth of industry (in cities such as Segovia, Toledo, and Cuenca, or Seville and Córdoba) reinforced urban development, at the same time that interior trade routes were consolidating,

---

29. José Ignacio Fortea Pérez, "Las ciudades de la Corona de Castilla en el Antiguo Régimen: Una revisión historiográfica," in *Boletín de la Asociación de Demografía Histórica*, no. 3 (1995): 21–59. Also V. Pérez Moreda and D. S. Reher, "La población urbana española entre los siglos XVI y XVIII: Una perspectiva demográfica," in *Imágenes de la diversidad: El mundo urbano en la Corona de Castilla (s. XVI–XVIII)*, ed. José Ignacio Fortea Pérez (Santander: Universidad de Cantabria, 1997), 129–63.

both locally and interregionally.[30] Commercial expansion increasingly spilled over political boundaries. This is evident in the relationship between Barcelona and the Castilian fairs, where Catalan products destined for Seville were forwarded under the pretense of originating in Castile. It is also seen in the increasing trade of Valencia's silk textiles for Castilian wheat. The spread of commerce in the interior was accompanied by a growing economic interconnection of the countryside and city, based on commodities marketing, the spread of crops specifically grown to meet urban demand, the extension of urban credit to rural areas, and the development of the putting-out system.[31] These changes favored many small and medium-sized producers.

Not surprisingly, between 1530 and 1590, urbanization rates rose (see table 2.1). This is true whether we measure growth in towns with 5,000 inhabitants or those with more than 10,000. While there were areas that did not experience growth, such as Old Castile, these were located primarily in zones where urbanization, having begun in the fifteenth century, had reached its zenith by 1530.[32] In other regions, urbanization was also conspicuous. Thus, even though in many areas of Extremadura, Andalucia, Murcia-Alcaraz, and New Castile the towns were not strictly commercial or industrial in nature but also supported important agricultural activities, these places exhibit a significant growth rate, surpassing that of the overall Spanish population, and their rates of urbanization also trend steadily

30. Increasing interconnections are seen in the destination for silver minted in Seville during the 1570s, much of which was sent to the Valle del Duero and the region of the fairs, and in the extent of Córdoba's commercial control at this time. For more on the first topic, see José Gentil Da Silva, *Desarrollo económico, subsistencia y decadencia en España* (Madrid: Ciencia Nueva, 1987), 65–83. On Córdoba, see Fortea, *Córdoba*, 349–411. Similar conclusions can be drawn from the case of Burgos's commercial networks; see H. Casado, "Crecimiento económico y redes de comercio interior en la Castilla septentrional (siglos XV y XVI)," in *Imágenes de la diversidad*, ed. Fortea, 283–315.

31. The overwhelming bibliography on this topic, too extensive to cite here, is based on a multitude of local studies. A summary can be found—among others cited in these pages that are perhaps less accessible—in Gelabert, "Urbanisation and Deurbanisation in Castile," 182–205. On the impact of urban credit on rural expansion, see Bartolomé Bennassar, "Ventes de rentes en Vieille Castille dans la première moitié du XVI siècle," *Annales E.S.C.* (November-December 1960): 1115–26. On the textile industry and the formation of networks around the putting-out system, the best known case is undoubtedly that of Córdoba; see Fortea, *Córdoba*, 268–89.

32. In these places, industrial and commercial expansion was more important than size per se, given that upwards of 50 percent of the population was economically active, even in centers as small as those having only 2,000 inhabitants. On the division of economic roles made

TABLE 2.1. RATES OF URBANIZATION IN CASTILE BY REGION
(based on populations of more than 5,000 and 10,000 inhabitants)[a]

Region	1530[b]		1591		1787	
	>5,000	>10,000	>5,000	>10,000	>5,000	>10,000
Extremadura	5%	0%	16%	2%	13%	3%
Andalucía	42%	19%	59%	34%	53%	34%
Murcia-Alacaraz	26%	13%	30%	10%	54%	32%
Castilla la Nueva	7%	4%	25%	13%	26%	17%
Castilla la Vieja	9%	6%	9%	6%	8%	5%
Cornisa Cantábrica	0%	0%	1%	0%	5%	4%
Total	13%	8%	21%	12%	23%	15%

a. Author's own elaboration from J. I. Fortea, "Las ciudades de la Corona de Castilla en el Antiguo Régimen: Una revisión historiográfica," *Boletín de la Asociación de Demografía Histórica* 3 (1995): 21–59; see appendix, 52–53.

b. Excludes population of Granada.

upward.[33] Finally, it is notable that the transfer of the royal court from Valladolid to Madrid increased the population growth rate in New Castile (from 7 percent to 25 percent for towns larger than 5,000 inhabitants and from 4 percent to 13 percent for those over 10,000).

In Castile, the growth in the percentage of the population living in towns with more than 5,000 inhabitants was as great as in England and Holland in the same period (table 2.2). For example, between 1500 and 1600, this figure

---

among the cities of the Meseta Norte, see B. Bennassar, *Valladolid au siècle d'or: Une ville et ses campagnes au XVIe siècle* (Paris: Mouton, 1967), chap. 3. Also, F. J. Vela, "El sistema urbano del Norte de Castilla en la segunda mitad del siglo XVI," in Luis Antonio Ribot García and Luigi De Rosa, *Ciudad y mundo urbano en la Epoca Moderna* (Madrid: Actas, 1998), 15–43. An outstanding study that reveals possibilities for applying sophisticated theories to the study of economics in the *ancien régime* is that of Christaller's theory of central places, revised by Lösch and Berry.

33. F. J. Vela, "Sobre el carácter de la formación social bética en la segunda mitad del siglo XVI," in *Actas II Coloquios de Historia de Andalucía: Andalucía Moderna* (Córdoba: Monte de Piedad y Caja de Ahorros de Córdoba, 1983), 1:377–411.

TABLE 2.2. URBAN POPULATION IN
ENGLAND, FRANCE, CASTILE, AND HOLLAND
(population in towns of more than 5,000 inhabitants)[a]

	France		Castile		England		Holland	
	%	Index	%	Index	%	Index	%	Index
1500	9.1	104.60	13.00	62.00	5.25	65.63		
1550							20.80	71.72
1600	8.7	100.00	21.00	100.00	8.00	100.00	29.00	100.00
1650							37.00	127.59
1700	10.9	125.29			17.00	212.50	39.00	134.48
1750	10.3	118.39			21.00	262.50	35.00	120.69
1800	11.1	127.59	23.00	109.00	27.50	343.75	33.00	113.79

a. Author's own elaboration from E. A. Wrigley, *People, Cities and Wealth: The Transformation of Traditional Society* (1987), and J. I. Fortea, "Las ciudades de la Corona de Castilla en el Antiguo Régimen: Una revisión historiográfica," *Boletín de la Asociación de Demografía Histórica* 3 (1995): 21–59.

rose from 13 percent to 21 percent. In England, in comparison, the figure rose from 5.25 percent to 8 percent, comparable in relative terms; a similar claim can be made about Holland.[34]

Nevertheless, it would be a mistake to view urban growth, especially that of Castile, as a simple consequence of economic forces acting, from an institutional point of view, on a uniform and abstract field. On the contrary, throughout the peninsula and especially in Castile, cities were seignorial seats and centers of bureaucratic organization, and, therefore, also the country's economic centers. During the Reconquest, the crown had granted these places considerable power. A commercially very powerful city, such as Burgos, owed its progress to the imposition of its authority and control over surrounding areas and trade routes and to its capacity to intervene in the life and

34. It appears that the best way to make these comparisons is to take as a reference point the sectoral composition of the economically active population. In any case, it is worth mentioning that the figure for Castile for 1500 corresponds to 1530, which indicates a certain underestimation of the rhythm of the growth rates of Spanish cities in comparison to those in England.

economic activities of its many vassals.[35] Segovia, a textile city, encompassed a large jurisdictional hinterland (*alfoz*) extending to the far side of Spain's central mountain range, the Cordillera Central, and the city's needs mediated the use of these lands and control of the area's natural resources.[36] All the important cities and even some of the second-tier towns benefited from their capacity to regulate supply and the demand for basic goods; to impose—both within and outside their walls—forced purchases of produce when harvests failed; to control the labor market in their *alfoz* and district; and to mediate disputes in their villages. Unquestionably, municipal officials also extended their coercive powers in order to regulate the guilds, the industrial goods markets, and other economic activities.[37] The vigor of medium-sized population centers (precisely those places having between 5,000 and 10,000 inhabitants, which table 2.1 shows as being so dynamic)—Medina de Rioseco, Cuellar, Sepulveda, Calatayud, Siguenza, and even some to the south, such as Trujillo or Carmona—is probably linked to their status as *villas*, around which jurisdictions extended relatively well controlled from a commercial and production-based point of view. This was the basis for their growth and expansion up to and during the sixteenth century, since rather than curtail the power of the *villas* and cities, the crown actually reinforced it. Thus, in 1538, the authority of the urban oligarchies in Castile was strengthened with the establishment of the sales tax, which transferred fiscal powers to them. Cities continued to be highly autonomous links in a chain of feudal authority, and in addition to economic and mercantile interrelationships, the power, jurisdiction, and coercion of these centers extended over the territories under their control. All of these things, inseparable from economics, contributed to growth.

35. Juan Antonio Bonachía, *El señorío de Burgos durante la Baja Edad Media (1255–1508)* (Valladolid: Universidad de Valladolid, 1988).

36. María Asenjo, *Segovia: La ciudad y su tierra a fines del Medievo* (Segovia: n.p., 1986).

37. There are good case studies on Valladolid (Bennassar, *Valladolid au siècle d'or*) and Toledo (Juan Montemayor, *Tolède entre fortune et déclin (1530–1640)* [Panazol: Pulim, 1996]). Some of these questions, particularly those referring to the forced purchase of grains, are also examined in Bartolomé Yun Casalilla, *Crisis de subsistencias y conflictividad social en Córdoba a principios del siglo XVI* (Córdoba: Excma, 1980). For a general perspective on the increase in the powers of the cities over the industries operating within their walls, see Paulino Iradiel Murugarres, *Evolución de la industria textil castellana en los siglos XIII–XVI* (Salamanca: Universidad de Salamanca, 1974). An interesting example of the process for issuing decrees that regulated industry, and on the control by municipal officials, can be found in Montemayor, *Tolèdentre*, 207–14.

To some degree, the differing weight of economic forces and of political and institutional structures can explain the rhythms of urbanization. In the kingdoms of Aragon and Navarre, weaker urbanization and other differences when compared to Castile were due not only to their secondary role in Spain's commercial networks but also to institutional factors. In these regions, a distinct political system determined the relationship of the smaller cities to the monarchy, resulting in two tiers, separate and only weakly connected, which favored certain territorial capitals, such as Zaragoza, Barcelona, and Valencia. Consequently, while the urban network was weaker overall, it was more centralized in regard to these large population centers. Compared to the density of the Castilian network, Zaragoza, Barcelona, Valencia, and to a lesser degree, Pamplona, although urbanized, were located in underdeveloped regions, given the relative unimportance of the towns that lay between these cities.

Urbanization was a multipolar phenomenon, determined by a diversity of factors, many local in character, particularly those of an administrative nature in which endogenous components were paramount. The significance of these features is scarcely compatible with the usual characterization of an export economy and the notion of a semiperiphery, which have often been attributed to Habsburg Spain.

If we take the growth of cities to be a consequence of political and institutional developments, then a similar approach must be used in evaluating the urban decline that began in 1580. Clearly, this process cannot be explained solely in terms of Malthusian maladjustments or the annihilation of local power. Many regions, including the dynamic Meseta Norte, confronted Malthusian blockages beginning, perhaps, as early as 1560. This is indicated by the appearance around that time of a drop in cereal production and a slowing of urbanization. Rising land rents also definitively constricted the maneuver room for agricultural producers, leading to a rural crisis paralleling that of the cities. Nevertheless, these circumstances only have meaning when taken in a wider context. The problem of provisioning the cities of the Meseta Norte are related to commerce in the interior of the peninsula and the flow of products from areas still undergoing expansion, such as La Mancha or Andalucia and Murcia. Moreover, by 1580, not only is agrarian expansion reaching its limit but so is the model of institutional development of the cities. The administrative importance of cities to local growth poles impeded commercial and urban networks from making the leap to a higher level of peninsular or interregional integration. Said another way, the administrative and seignorial character of the cities had nourished urban development but, having reached a certain point, it now acted as a brake on achieving greater integration. Centers of regional networks were ever more outward looking, with weaker links toward the peninsula's interior. This was also true of Murcia, an intensely active zone,[38] of Malaga, and even of Seville, where the growing presence of foreign traders and products destined for the Americas reflects, like nothing else, the centrifugal nature that was still characteristic of urban expansion.

The political process itself contributed to the urban collapse, although not exactly as Braudel explained it. The military effort, the revenues required to convert Castile into the backbone of the empire, which had been behind its tax–collecting autonomy, was also leading to the sale of districts and jurisdictions to many less important towns. Rather than result in the disappearance of local districts—a potential impetus for economic interregionalism—there occurred a pulverization into even more, and smaller, districts. Consequently, large cities lost some of their operational capacity, and bureaucratic organization and economic relations fragmented further. This was particularly true in Castile, where the sale of prerogatives over the second-tier towns was even more intense than in Aragon.[39] This was happening just as the fiscal outlook was turning sour, not because of the size of taxes, which in macroeconomic terms, was not excessive,[40] but because taxation burdened small urban workshops by raising the cost of supporting apprentices and officials, resulting in lower profit margins for producers.[41] This was not a reflection of the crown's attempt to crush the local power structure, but a corollary to changes in the economic foundation of the local oligarchies, and in the pact that expressed the relationship between them and the monarchy. On the one

---

38. María Pérez Picazo and Guy Lemeunier, *El proceso de modernización de la región murciana (siglos XVI–XX)* (Murcia: Editora Regional de Murcia, 1984), 77–88.

39. Helen Nader, *Liberty in Absolutist Spain: The Habsburg Sale of Towns, 1516–1700* (Baltimore: Johns Hopkins University Press, 1990). A provisional but telling comparison among the different kingdoms appears in J. E. Gelabert, "Cities, Towns and Small Towns in Castile, 1500–1800," in *Small Towns in Early Modern Europe,* ed. Peter Clark (Cambridge: Cambridge University Press, 1995), 271–94.

40. I. A. A. Thompson, "Taxation, Military Spending and the Domestic Economy in Castile in the Later Sixteenth Century," in *War and Society in Habsburg Spain* (Aldershot: Variorum, 1992), ii, 1–21.

41. Bartolomé Yun Casalilla, "Estado, y estructuras sociales en Castilla durante el siglo XVI," in *Revista de Historia Económica* 8 (1990): 549–74, and also "Introducción" in Joseph Ruíz de Zelada, *Estado de la Bolsa de Valladolid: Examen de sus tributos, cargas y medios de su extinción, de su gobierno y reforma* (Valladolid, 1777; repr. Valladolid: Secretario de Publicaciones, 1990), 7–41.

hand, this pact made it possible to climb the social ladder by means of a political career as well as by purchasing titles and administrative positions, and through their control of local power and propensity to be rentiers instead of entrepreneurs. This, however, does not quite fit with the phrase "treason of the bourgeoisie," since it was something that had already been going on for some time and may have been a structural problem.[42] On the other hand, urban self-government was a key to diverting the tax burden onto the artisan class and working people generally.

Political developments were also changing the environment in which the economy and urban-rural relations operated. In Castile above all, the military effort and the needs of the crown, as well as the cohesion of a society that saw itself as the defender of orthodoxy in Europe, was leading to a complex melding of the aristocracy and the church into an absolutist system. Although this did not relieve the economic difficulties of the former, it preserved cohesion and promoted the extension of entailment of property and the mortgaging of lands under the control of the church.[43] The concentration of property in the hands of the aristocracy, and above all, the church, meant that in many places the forces of urban demand, already in decline, were felt not so much by direct producers as by rentiers and the holders of seignorial rights.

Thus, the social structure and forms of property ownership interfered with and distorted the supposedly positive effects of the urban market on rural areas, creating a situation very different from that predicted by the abstract reasoning of classical economics and notions of easily transferable resources. Moreover, we are dealing with groups—the middle and high aristocracy and the clergy—whose drive to obtain political rents or whose managerial abilities in regard to assets did not impede capital investment in productive improvements, as has often been claimed, but did divert a significant part of their funds to the social or political promotion of family members, doing little to revitalize the economy. This was a natural consequence of the immense possibilities for social enrichment and political ascent that, as a supranational entity, the Spanish empire could bestow. The accelerated

42. Burgos may best exemplify this long-term—one might even say, structural—phenomenon. Hilano Casado, *Señores, mercaderes y campesino:. La comarca de Burgos a fines de la Edad Media* (Valladolid: Junta Castilla y León, 1987).

43. This summarizes what is explained in detail in Bartolomé Yun Casalilla, "Cambiamento e continuità: La Castiglia nell'Impero durante il sécolo d'Oro," *Studi Storici* 1 (1995): 51–101.

mortgaging and entailment of land immobilized a productive factor, so that it could not circulate in response to fluctuations in the commodities markets nor contribute to output in order to keep pace with the growing needs of the population.

In the context of population-resource imbalances, rising land rents, and blockages in industrial and commercial development (which were especially intense in the Valle del Duero, a primary motor of expansion), political and institutional transformations were decisive and explain the problems that began around 1580. Nevertheless, the medieval model of urbanization did not break down smoothly and evenly.

First, a shadow began to spread across the interior of Spain as early as 1560, particularly in the Valle del Duero. There, interrelated rural and urban problems would ultimately unleash de-urbanization and even a ruralization of the cities during the seventeenth century.[44] Segovia and Toledo, among other places, resisted the trend and may even have benefited from Madrid's demand for goods and the collapse of the other industrial centers. Nevertheless, the installation of the royal court in Madrid and that city's extremely rapid demographic growth (from 10,000 inhabitants in 1560 to 90,000 in 1590, and, after the collapse of 1601 to 1606—when the court returned to Valladolid—130,000 in 1630) disrupted the model of urbanization, which had already been weakened by Madrid's ability to attract migratory flows that until then had fed the growth of other cities.[45] Although still grave, the urban decline was somewhat less severe in the southern part of Spain. Thus, Córdoba began its decline in 1580, but thanks to the second Atlantic cycle, Seville held on, as did Murcia, which resisted until 1630. Urban expansion seems to have also prolonged itself in Catalonia, where, when compared to the Meseta, the cities resisted throughout the seventeenth century.

Second, in accord with our explanation of the mechanisms causing the crisis—particularly the sale of districts dependent on large towns—towns

44. Yun Casalilla, "Estado, y estructuras sociales en Castilla," 549–74.

45. As mentioned, this idea is widely accepted today. A recent review of the problem— using London as a model and Shalins and Wrigley's ideas on urban growth—establishes a correlation between the boom in Madrid and the collapse of the urban network in the interior; see Pérez Moreda and Reher, "La población urbana española," in *Imágenes,* ed. Fortea, 129–63. Fig. 2.1 reflects the perspective of Pérez Moreda and Reher. As can be proven, the revival of Madrid's population, once the royal court had returned there from Valladolid, parallels the definitive collapse of the urban network in the Meseta Norte. Although this does not mean we should assume that these factors are linked in a fatal cause-and-effect relationship, it shows the mechanisms that affected the stagnation in Castilian population growth.

with more than 10,000 inhabitants were profoundly affected, while smaller places resisted better. The urban recession, moreover, must have been long, above all in the cities of the interior (as fig. 2.1, while based on a limited

FIGURE 2.1. BAPTISMS IN MADRID AND SELECTED CITIES OF THE MESETA NORTE[a]

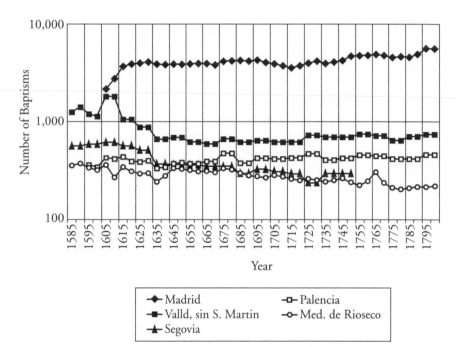

a. Author's own elaboration from B. Bennassar, *Valladolid au siècle d'or: Une ville et ses campagnes au XVIe siècle* (1969); A. Gutiérrez, *Estudio sobre la decadencia...* (1989); M. Serrano, *Geografía urbana de Valladolid en el siglo XVIII*, Memoria de licenciatura leida en Valladolid (1964); A. García Sanz, "Población e industria textil en una ciudad de Castilla: Segovia 1530–1750," in *Evolución demográfica bajo los Austrias*, vol. 3, Valencia (1992); G. Herrero, "La población palentina en los siglos XVI y XVII,"en *Publicaciones de la Institución Tello Téllez de Meneses,"* no. 21 (1958), Appendix 1; A. Marcos Martín, *Economia sociedad, pobreza en Castilla...* (1985), 1:28; B. Yun Casalilla, *Sobre la transición...* (1987), 156–58; M. F. Carbajo, *La población de la villa de Madrid desde finales del siglo XVI hasta mediados del siglo XIX*, Madrid (1987), 45.

FIGURE 2.2. ESTIMATED TRENDS
OF URBAN AND RURAL POPULATION GROWTH IN OLD CASTILE
(Indices, 1630–35 = 100)[a]

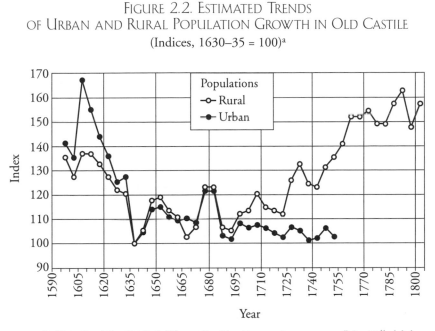

a. B. Yun Casalilla, "Valladolid en Castilla: Economía y consumo" in *Valladolid Historia de una ciudad* (1999).

sample, clearly illustrates). Larger cities, such as Valladolid and Segovia, suffered an intensely sharp decline until the 1630s, and one that was much more serious than what occurred in Palencia or Medina de Rioseco.[46] Although the explanation for the urban decline in Spain's interior cannot be extrapolated to the entire country, it is notable that in these towns the population levels did not show signs of recovery until well into the eighteenth century. This is even more significant since it contrasts with the remarkable expansion of the rural populations in these regions, which was growing steadily before the end of the seventeenth century (fig. 2.2). The prolonged

46. The data on Segovia (apparently a second-tier city) do not include all its parishes, so it seems to be a town similar to Palencia or Medina de Rioseco. What is important for our discussion, nevertheless, is the trajectory of development in these towns, which is undoubtedly similar to what appears in fig. 2.1. Segovia's evolution is similar to that of other industrial centers, such as Cuenca. David Sven Reher, *Town and Country in Pre-industrial Spain: Cuenca, 1550–1870* (Cambridge: Cambridge University Press, 1990), 18–33.

urban decline also explains one of the most important and revealing features of urban history of Castile in comparison to other European countries. Even at the end of the eighteenth century, the rate of urbanization was not much greater than it had been in 1600 (table 2.2). The slowness of economic recovery explains the depth, duration, and complexity of the urban crisis, which again forces us to consider the economy of the time as a system of rigidities vis-à-vis the transfer of factors.

In contrast to other capitals, the influence of Madrid was, at first, decidedly negative and, later, scarcely stimulating. Like other European courts, Madrid amassed industrial and commercial activities along with a big bureaucracy, all nourished by substantial rents collected from the vast empire under the capital's control. However, unlike London, Madrid was far from being a nodal point in a preexisting urban network from whose expansion the capital would benefit. Instead, Madrid superimposed itself artificially, subjecting its network to an overwhelming, violent strain at an already difficult time, and—once economic and demographic growth halted—forcing the system to remake itself traumatically and completely. Madrid's mercantile relations with surrounding areas also differed greatly from those of London. While the capital on the Thames became increasingly involved in an ever more dynamic agricultural and industrial economy, Madrid continued to operate within a rigidly "feudalistic" framework. Instead of revitalizing production, its demand for agrarian products was met largely through the collection of seignorial rents (principally *diezmos* [tithes]), or demand affected sectors that were unprofitable from an investment standpoint.[47] By 1630, the court had become a demand pole too distant for most Castilian growers to stock. Supplying the capital now required the intervention of middlemen and systems of imposed commercial contracts. Thus, its ability to revive the agrarian economy and raise productivity in order to reap the benefits of trade was extremely limited.[48] Despite its expanding role in international trade, Madrid did not control as solid or widespread a market as London, and what trade it did undertake was based on exports of primary materials and, as a consequence of the breakdown of domestic industry, the importation of luxury items.

47. This does not mean that Madrid's growing demand did not result in agrarian improvements, including on estates, as is demonstrated by the permits for loans for improvement of farms owned by the nobility, located in the Archivo General de Simancas.

48. On the obligatory systems for provisioning the capital, which operated during the seventeenth century, see Ringrose, *Madrid and the Spanish Economy*, esp. pt. 2.

Indeed, a large part of Spain's international trade was concentrated in Seville-Cadiz and Barcelona, especially after 1650. This disassociation between the royal court, as the political capital of the empire, and the country's commercial and financial centers also negatively affected Spain's economy. This is especially true if one considers the distance between these three capitals and the declining importance of Seville (controlled by foreign merchants and goods) as a center capable of revitalizing the economy, and above all, domestic industry. It would have been very difficult for the vigor of these three centers, the most dynamic of Spain's cities, to converge and form a new, consolidated network of interregional compass.[49]

The institutional process itself ran counter to any possible strengthening of mercantile circuits within the peninsula's interior. During the seventeenth century, jurisdictional prerogatives spread, further fragmenting the economic map. Since the fourteenth century, cities and district seats regulated supply through a system of *obligados*, which meant they held a quasi monopoly in the sale of, among other products, wine, meat, and oil (which, in turn, determined the availability of hides and industrial-quality oil). This significantly limited the participation of merchants from outside the local network. Numerous things disrupted the free workings of the market: the sale of districts, often bought by individuals or the towns themselves; the sale of offices, including the office of *escribano de millones* (responsible for recording the collection of the royal tax on real and personal property assessed to raise one million ducats in 1590), a phenomenon largely ignored by historians; the sale of brokerages for a variety of commodities; the purchase or exchange of some sort of tax relief on commercial transactions by a given agent, often a nobleman, or by the towns themselves, and many similar stratagems common during the seventeenth century. This was in addition to the continuing tax collection autonomy of municipalities.[50] The tax system, based on the *millones* under the control of the local authorities, was also disruptive, since it not only reinforced the involvement of municipal clientage networks in tax collection—leading to fraud and arbitrariness—but also created a complex fiscal

49. The effect on the Mediterranean of Seville's commerce is traced in Ildefonso Pulido Bueno, *Almojarifazgos y comercio exterior en Andalucía durante la época mercantilista, 1526–1740* (Huelva: n.p., 1993). On Barcelona, see J. Fontana, "Sobre el comercio exterior de Barcelona en la segunda mitad del siglo XVII," in *Estudios de Historia Moderna* (1957): 197–218.

50. Such a claim is based primarily on a study still in progress that uses documents in the Archivo General de Simancas, which clearly shows this, but whose more detailed citation I will spare the reader here.

geography, in which tax structures differed significantly between neighboring localities. On top of everything, crises in the community treasuries led to an enormous diversity in municipal-level taxes, whose levies varied widely from place to place.[51]

Scholars who study the effect of taxation only from the point of view of magnitude have overlooked the true consequence of these practices: a veritable tangle of local variation, which generated high transaction costs and heightened uncertainty among merchants. This situation impeded the formation of flexible and widespread commercial networks. At the same time, currency manipulation, especially intense between 1620 and 1680, made markets less and less predictable. These manipulations could even unleash contractions in supply, bringing on agricultural crises that were caused not only by poor harvests and the lack of transportation but by the combined effect of all these things.[52]

Political and governmental institutions were not alone in impeding economic recovery. Peasant families, the base in many agricultural areas, did not follow the dictates of productivity maximization. Adjustments were indeed taking place, redistributing crop agriculture as dictated by the new circumstances and allowing farmers to accumulate some surplus. Additionally, as Malthusians have noted, the demographic depression had increased the amount of land available per person. Nevertheless, things were more complicated than this. With the decline of the cities, commercialization of goods and its supposed stimulation of production slowed in many places. The Castilian inheritance system, which tends to distribute equally among all heirs, was fragmenting landholdings, particularly in regions well suited to cultivation, such as the Tierra de Campos. Such property division delayed improvements in productivity and profitability, despite family strategies aimed at overcoming the practice. In addition, strategies for preserving family wealth appear to have been behind the establishment of religious foundations (*obras pías, capellanías*) and other practices that required the donation of property, none having productivity maximization as a goal.[53] Clearly, all these factors limited the positive effects of the readjustments.

Urban systems, intrinsically based in commercial networks and trade flows, were also difficult to rebuild. This explains why readjustment came

51. The best description of the variations in local assessments and the tangle of municipal taxes levied on certain products can be found in Ruíz de Zelada, *Estado de la Bolsa de Valladolid*.

52. An excellent work on this topic is Antonio Domínguez Ortíz, *Alteraciones andaluzas* (Madrid: Nárcea, 1973), 32–39.

slowly, and why the agrarian recovery, especially visible after 1650, was not accompanied by an increase in urban population in localities that had been important in the past, including Madrid (fig. 2.1). Only between 1700 and 1750 did a new model of urbanization emerge that, with advantages and disadvantages, would come to provide the foundation for Spain's nineteenth-century industrialization.

The new model's primary feature was the consolidation of overall population growth, particularly urban growth on the coast and in the periphery, the country's most economically and demographically dynamic areas.[54] This development fits Jan de Vries's description for Europe, and specifically, for the appearance in the eighteenth century of a new type of network based on international commerce. In a peninsular country like Spain, this had major consequences for the littoral region and for the expansion of the second-tier towns that had been marginal during the sixteenth century. Notably, the expansion in the periphery, which was also based on the development of short-distance maritime trade that was unaffected by the obstacles that existed in Spain's interior, had at its foundation a more flexible and commercial orientation than the agrarian structures in the hinterlands of cities under discussion.[55] As coastal commercial networks formed, their tentacles extended

53. Without doubt, one of the best works on this subject is that of Francis Brumont, *Paysans de la Vieille-Castille au XVIe siècle* (Madrid: Velázquez, 1993), see esp. 289–301, 343–53. On the Castilian inheritance system, see Maximo García Fernández, *Herencia y patrimonio familiar en la Castilla del Antiguo Régimen (1650–1834)* (Valladolid: Universidad de Valladolid, 1994). Some of the impediments to productive readjustment are outlined in Bartolomé Yun Casalilla, "Poder y economía: Algunas propuestas para el estudio de la historia agraria de Castilla y León durante la Edad Moderna," in *Relaciones de poder, de producción y parentesco en la edad media y moderna,* ed. Reyna Pastor de Togneri (Madrid: CSIC, 1990), 375–409.

54. Pérez Moreda and Reher, "La población urbana española," in *Imágenes,* ed. Fortea, 129–44; David Ringrose, *Spain, Europe and the "Spanish Miracle," 1700–1900* (Cambridge: Cambridge University Press, 1996), part 3.

55. This occurred, for example, in Catalonia, where the involvement of many small-holders in cultivation of *aguardiente* (and its marketing, aimed more and more toward America) was critical to the economy; see Pierre Vilar, *La Catalogne dans l'Espagne Moderne: Recherche sur les fondements économiques des structures nationales* (Paris: S.E.V.P E.N., 1962), 2:242–330. It also occurred in Valencia, a region today recognized as having had a seignorial system that permitted commercial agricultural development, based on profitable peasant farms and increased productivity; see Manuel Ardit, *Els Homes i la Terra del País Valencià (segles XVI–XVIII),* 2 vols. (Barcelona: Curial, 1993). Something similar can be said about Murcia; see M. T. Pérez Picazo, "Crecimiento agrícola y relaciones de mercado en el reino de Murcia durante el siglo XVIII," en *Estructuras agrarias y reformismo ilustrado en la España*

into Spain's interior.[56] Especially in Catalonia, strong connections were forged with its hinterlands, based on the exchange of goods and services and the sustained growth of second-tier towns, where industrial and transport activities were blossoming.[57]

This recuperation contrasts with the slow and delayed changes in the interior of the peninsula: Madrid's population did not grow again until 1740, and other centers such as Valladolid and Medina de Rioseco, for example, barely recovered (which, statistically, served to lower the overall rate of urbanization for the country at century's end).[58] Growth was particularly concentrated in rural areas that had been of only minor importance in the seventeenth century (which explains the lag between urban and rural population growth shown in fig. 2.2). These localities were developing agriculture and, in some cases, transport and protoindustrial activities,[59] very probably displaced from those cutting-edge centers of the sixteenth century, over which they had important advantages in regard to their tax base.[60] Such growth was also the fruit of the concession of exemptions to markets and fairs, so common during the eighteenth century, which helped maintain a "ruralized" exchange that nurtured trade in agrarian products and certain

---

del siglo XVIII (Madrid: Ministerio de Agricultura, 1989), 47–78. Even the agrarian systems in the Cantabrian Mountains became more flexible, based on the introduction of new crops like corn, intensive cultivation on small farms that also raised cattle, and even in the growing peasant commerce that combined with a development of protoindustrial activities; see Rafael Domínguez Martín, *El campesinado adaptativo: Campesinos y mercado en el Norte de España, 1750–1880* (Santander: Universidad de Cantabria, 1996).

56. Ringrose, *Spain, Europe and the "Spanish Miracle,"* part 3.

57. For an interpretative synthesis, see J. Fontana, "Les ciutats en la historia de Catalunya," in *Indústria i ciutat: Sabadell, 1800–1980* (Barcelona: Fundación Bosch i Cardellach, 1994), 9–24.

58. After 1630, the population of Madrid stagnated and did not show signs of growing again until the decade of 1740–50; even after, its expansion is much slower than that of other important European courts, such as Paris or London. By 1800, compared to the 190,000 inhabitants in the Spanish capital, Paris and London had about one million inhabitants respectively. María F. Carbajo Isla, *La población de la villa de Madrid* (Madrid: Siglo Vientiuno, 1987), 227.

59. This is true in cases where towns specialized in transportation and industry that supported agriculture, for example, Villaramiel in the plains of the Duero River (Yun Casalilla, *Sobre la transición al capitalismo en Castilla,* 524–600), La Bañeza and neighboring areas in León; see Laureano M. Rubio Pérez, *La Bañeza y su tierra, 1650–1850* (León: Universidad de León, 1987), and many other places scattered throughout the country, particularly in the valleys connecting the naturally divided geographic regions.

nonessential goods that both urban and rural populations were now consuming with greater frequency.[61]

A new model of urbanization was developing. Its basic component was the slow, tentative domestic market formation within the Spanish interior, which had its roots in separate locales, but which was beginning to converge. These changes were helped along by the erosion of customs regulations between the different territories, the increasing state control in the collection of local taxes, and the decreasing importance of these local taxes, as the tax burden was displaced onto tariffs on foreign trade items and traditional taxes on staples and consumer goods declined. The involvement of thousands of peasants and mule drivers in transporting goods and produce also shaped the new model, as did the "merchant diasporas," which helped to reduce transaction costs through information exchange among its members.[62]

Nevertheless, the slowness of the process and the inertia present in this growth model are evident. Even in the middle of the century, variation in local tax arrangements was still immense,[63] causing the high transaction costs and high risk to continue. For the 1780s, the economist Vicente Alcalá Galiano underlined this when declaring:

> The tax that each individual must pay to the state should be
> established and set in advance, not arbitrarily. The timing and

---

60. The movement of industries to the countryside has been suggested by Gelabert, "Cities, Towns and Small Towns in Castile," 287–93, but in many cases, this may have been a reflection of new industries appearing in response to demand from the agrarian sector and the rural population. Around 1775, Colón de Larreátegui, an essayist from Valladolid, warned how, since the seventeenth century, "wages increase in proportion to growing taxes, and being able to work more easily in neighboring towns, people go there to stock up, and, in short, that poor city [Valladolid] is left unpopulated, without industry, art, nor commerce," in *Informe sobre los Gremios de Valladolid* (Valladolid, 1782), Biblioteca Universitaria de Santa Cruz, Mss. 41, f. 417v.

61. Yun Casalilla, *Sobre la transición al capitalismo en Castilla*, 524–76. As is known, this was true throughout Europe. See, for example, J. Thomas, *Le temps des foires* (Toulouse: Presses Universitaires du Mirail, 1993) and Margaret Spufford, *The Great Reclothing of Rural England: Petty Chapmen and Their Wares in the Seventeenth Century* (London: Hambledon, 1984).

62. The best known example, but certainly not the only one, are the Catalonians, who traveled throughout the peninsula trading their products, primarily woven cloth, for produce and raw materials. Assumpta Muset i Pons, *Catalunya i el mercat espanyol al segle XVIII: Els traginers i els negociants de Calaf i Copons* (Barcelona, Ajuntament d'Igualada, 1997).

63. This subject deserves its own study. The interested reader can get an idea of the diversity of taxes by locality from the work of Carmen García García, *La crisis de las haciendas locales: De la reforma administrativa a la reforma fiscal (1743–1845)* (Valladolid: Universidad Autónoma, 1996), 68–78.

method of payment should also be set, and the taxpayer should know the terms of both. Without such knowledge, a taxpayer can suffer at the hands of a tax collector who, according to his interests and caprices, can either increase or ease the tax burden.... Uncertainty increases the insolence and corruption of those working for the royal treasury, which guarantees that the extreme inequality in tax bills will not cause nor could not cause as much damage to the people as does uncertainty.[64]

A peasant aristocracy was forming (in Andalucia it is even possible to speak of an "agrarian bourgeoisie") that consisted of farmers who had surplus to sell to the cities. Notwithstanding, in Castile even into the middle of the eighteenth century, ecclesiastical institutions controlled 35 percent of all agrarian output, and about 65 percent of commercialized surplus.[65] The nobility relied more and more on the direct management of their lands, and were more motivated by the urban market when introducing improvements in productivity. Even so, many obstacles remained. The practices of mortgaging or entailing of property had been overextended, and especially in Castile, the real estate market responded slowly to changes in the commodities market. Industrial growth was tentative in the interior of the peninsula, and although dynamic urban industries capable of altering the guild system existed, strict controls stifled the operations of most enterprises, while the putting-out system was allowed to operate only in certain localities. The expansion of entailed properties and the clergy's control over credit, especially mortgages, meant that currency markets fell far short of creating the kind of circuit between the countryside and city (merchants and farmers) that was being established in other areas of Europe. The findings of David Reher and other scholars who have studied "ruralized" cities, such as Cuenca in the hinterlands of Castile, are not surprising. Examined from a demographic point of view and in regard to migratory flows from the surrounding countryside, the Braudelian axiom that the city was the instigator of change

64. Vicente Alcalá Galiano, *Sobre la economía política y los impuestos (Segovia 1781–1788)*, ed. and prelim. study by José Manuel Valles Garrido (Segovia: Academia de Artillería, 1992), 321.

65. Grupo 75, *La Renta Nacional de la Corona de Castilla* (Madrid: Universidad Autónoma, 1975). The predominance of ecclesiastical vendors and rentier noblemen among those selling grain to Madrid, as well as the peasants' inability to sell directly after poor harvests, are also indicative of this. Ringrose, *Madrid and the Spanish Economy,* chap. 8.

in the countryside is simply not borne out despite marked differences between the two worlds.[66]

In light of all this, it is understandable that the actual effects of processes emphasized in current historiography are undergoing some qualification. These include such ideas as the "consumer revolution," with its Braudelian connotations that privilege the country-city relationship by making the city the instigator of alterations in rural consumption patterns.[67] Thus, even though changes occurred in consumption patterns overall (and in particular, in cities), their effects seem to have been limited and delayed, above all in the countryside. There rising land rents, *diezmos*, and seignorial prerogatives, as well as inequalities in income distribution, restricted peasant demand.[68] This was unfavorable for a process similar to that which de Vries has baptized "the industrious revolution."[69] Spanish farmers, like their counterparts in the Low Countries, were encouraged to produce commercialized surplus as new consumption norms spread, expanding the demand for durable and semi-durable goods. But, above all in the Castilian hinterlands, the rural economy and the market were only tenuously connected when compared to northern Europe, and the possibility for developing these linkages was limited. The institutional obstacles that controlled access to productive factors made a process of similar dimensions impossible in Spain.

66. Reher, *Town and Country in Pre-industrial Spain*, is an essential text on this topic, which makes special reference to Braudel's views.

67. As is widely known, Braudel was particularly concerned with this issue in his *Civilisation matérielle*, but later scholarship has placed special emphasis on this question. And it is worth noting the importance various authors give to the dynamic effects that the change in urban consumption patterns had on the countryside. In this regard, see the claims made by Neil McKendrick, "Commercialization and the Economy," in McKendrick et al., *The Birth of a Consumer Society: The Commercialization of Eighteenth-Century England* (Bloomington: University of Indiana Press, 1982). Also Peter Borsay, *The English Urban Renaissance: Culture and Society in the Provincial Town, 1660–1770* (Oxford: Clarendon, 1989), 315–19. From a French perspective, Daniel Roche, *La culture des apparences:Une histoire du vêtement, XVIIe–XVIIIe siècle* (Paris: Fayard, 1989).

68. M. García and Bartolomé Yun Casalilla, "Pautas de consumo, estilos de vida y cambio político en las ciudades castellanas a fines del Antiguo Régimen," in *Imágenes,* ed. Fortea, 245–82. For case studies on places as diverse as Catalonia and the Valle del Duero, see Jaime Torres Elías and Bartolomé Yun Casalilla, eds., *Consumo, condiciones de vida y comercialización: Cataluña y Castilla, siglos XVII–XIX* (Valladolid: Junta de Castilla y León, 1999).

69. Jan de Vries, "Between Purchasing Power and the World of Goods: Understanding the Household Economy in Early Modern Europe," in *Consumption and the World of Goods*, ed. John Brewer and Roy Porter (London: Routledge, 1993), 85–133.

Today, for obvious reasons, we emphasize the significance of eighteenth-century economic expansion.[70] However, it is apparent that all the brakes on economic renovation were at work as well. Moreover, the phase of domestic market formation faced a hindrance that cannot be overlooked: the weakness of Spain's interior urban network. A simple visual comparison with France (fig. 2.3) shows the degree to which Spain's urban development posed problems from the seventeenth century onward. By 1787, the two countries look very different. Both French and Spanish port cities involved in international trade had flourished, but France, in addition, had a dense network that articulated its interior markets and transmitted the indirect effects of commerce to the productive structures of its hinterlands. Spain, in contrast, had geographic obstacles, like the Cantabrian Mountains; these lay between the northern ports and the Meseta, and made it nearly impossible to create trade networks in the country's center. This was true despite the notable dynamism of places such as Gijon and Santander, which by 1787 had yet to reach 10,000 inhabitants.

As elsewhere throughout Europe, in Castile between 1500 and 1800, the transformation of urban networks was directly related to flexibility in the interconnections among its cities. And as elsewhere in Europe, this was also behind the rearrangements during the "long" (extremely long in some places!) seventeenth century. Nevertheless, the institutional rigidities that explain the slowness of these transformations and readjustments that accompanied them are frequently overlooked. A better understanding of urban history, and the relationships between the city and countryside as a fundamental component of that history, requires analytical criteria that are more complex and rich than those that were utilized in *La Méditerranée*. The agrarian and demographic cycles of the *longue durée* cannot explain everything. Moreover, institutional changes do not fit with suppositions that Braudel and subsequent historians have accepted about the erosion of local authority. To the contrary, the key to the process is in the complex milieu that developed between the local elites and the crown, and in the conditions that this relationship imposed on the development of cities. The effects of the urban market on the countryside, and on economic development generally, also depend on the institutional context in force, as well as on the social relations and property rights in which the market must operate. Seen this way, it appears that—contrary to what at times has been deduced from the Braudelian *longue durée* and *histoire immobile*—recent history has presided

70. For an analysis in this regard, see Ringrose, *Spain, Europe and the "Spanish Miracle."*

FIGURE 2.3. DISTRIBUTION OF POPULATION CENTERS
IN FRANCE AND SPAIN AT THE END OF THE EIGHTEENTH CENTURY
(populations greater than 10,000 inhabitants)[a]

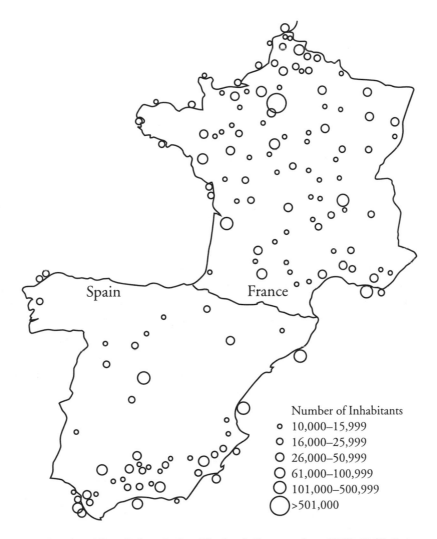

Spain   France

Number of Inhabitants
- ○ 10,000–15,999
- ○ 16,000–25,999
- ○ 26,000–50,999
- ○ 61,000–100,999
- ○ 101,000–500,999
- ○ >501,000

a. Developed from B. Lepetit, *Les villes dans la France moderne (1740–1840)*, Paris:
   Albin Michel, 1988, App. 2, and *Censo de 1787 "Floridablanca,"* Madrid: Instituto Nacional de Estadística, 1986–1991.

over deep structural changes, significant geographic shifts and alterations in the relationships between regions, and changes in the relationships between the city and the countryside and among urban networks. Spain's seventeenth century, so similar to and yet so different from the experience elsewhere in Europe, is, without doubt, the turning point (beyond the explanatory reach of *La Méditerranée*, certainly) for these transformations and other anomalies that appear when comparing Spain to the rest of Europe. These things can still be seen in the nineteenth century, at the moment when modern industrialization takes off, and Spain is forced to confront the Industrial Revolution with a comparatively disarticulated and deficient urban system. Not unrelated to this turning point are the *événements* and the political and social structures and evolution of a society that, in addition to being a product of its economy, also decisively shapes it.

ECONOMIC HISTORY: SOME FINAL REFLECTIONS FROM ECONOMICS AND THE SOCIAL SCIENCES

No one would deny that we should continue to use economic theory in historical analyses. Recent developments have helped to bring the two sciences closer together. Historians are discovering greater complexity in past economies and the decision-making processes that shaped them, at the same time that trajectories, such as the new institutional economics or the more flexible and less theoretical application of Marxist categories, are adding to our analytical tools.

This chapter has applied the concept of transaction costs and a recognition of the market's lack of social and institutional homogeneity. Braudel was aware of these concepts, but he did not actually apply them as conditions influencing an economy's dynamics. Market fragmentation, the scope of local interests (often oligarchic or clientelistic in character), currency manipulation, and entry barriers faced by economic actors were critical to the processes described here. By moving us away from the analysis of abstract economic and productive variables toward the more detailed study of decision-making processes shaping economies, a new field of study, as yet unexplored by historians, opens up. On this point, a few thoughts merit consideration.

First, it is obvious that this analysis should lead to a reaffirmation—increasingly common today—of political economy, understood as economics from an institutional and social perspective. For example, we can study formal institutions (the state, local governments), informal institutions (the family, clientelistic networks, networks of local solidarity), or institutions based in groups and social relations. These approaches are used to understand the functioning of an economy, and even to select from the field of economics the hypotheses to be verified.[71] This chapter, for example, has emphasized the deficiency in investments made by the oligarchy and other privileged groups, which otherwise might have brought about technical and productive improvements. Organization theory, as explained by Herbert Simon and other economists, including Richard Cyert and James March, accounts for this deficiency with the supposition that economic organizations do not always act to maximize profit. Instead, they are subject to internal tensions, which must be offset by transfers destined for something other than productive improvements, and they operate in an environment of uncertainty and hidden variables, conditions very different from what is supposed when we attempt to explain their behavior.[72]

A more historical treatment of the objects under study is also needed. Concepts such as market, demand, consumption, and other things will always require an implicit or explicit understanding of their specific, historical context in order to clarify their operation, and their respective influence on an economy's general trajectory. The case of Spain is indicative of how, for example, social structure, distribution and forms of property holdings,

71. Those who claim that we can always find an economic concept applicable to the problems of the past are correct, but it is also true that in such application, care is needed in the selection of the category and in its adaptation to the real-life situation under study. S. B. Carter and S. Cullenberg, "Labor Economics and the Historian," in *Economics and the Historian*, ed. Rawski et al., 85–121.

72. The body of literature on this topic is too extensive to cover. A basic approach to the field is found in Herbert A. Simon, *Models of Bounded Rationality*, 2 vols. (Cambridge, Mass.: MIT Press, 1982). See also Richard M. Cyert and James G. March, *A Behavioural Theory of the Firm* (Englewood Cliffs, N.J.: Prentice-Hall, 1963). Application of such concepts to lineages and clientele networks among the nobility must be undertaken cautiously and with the recognition that we are often facing a metaphor to describe behavior rather than a truly explanatory key. Even so, the use of such categories can be helpful both to establish an improved common vocabulary between historians and economists and to create working hypotheses of great utility. In fact, this may be what we are looking at when considering that families and aristocratic lineages constitute complex groups where cohesion can be achieved only through "side payments," which among other things, are dispensed in the form of gifts to finance the political career of *segundones* [second sons]. These payments have great strategic value and satisfy the needs of some members of the group, as has been amply demonstrated; see, for example, H. J. Habakkuk, *Marriage, Debt and the Estates System. English Land Ownerships 1650–1950* (Oxford: Oxford University Press, 1954).

and other factors have strongly conditioned the effects of the commodities market on income and economic development. Furthermore, we know that supply and demand for products and factors respond to innumerable disturbances that could be rooted in family relations, reciprocity or negotiations between buyer and seller, or even situations of bilateral monopoly that often resulted from bargaining strategies or from noneconomic circumstances.[73] It is also widely recognized that, in spite of the fact that old regime family economies were not entirely closed units, the market, especially in the countryside, is not the sole determinant of a household's use of resources but rather one element among many.

Consequently, caution is needed when applying a framework based on classical economics, whose body of theoretical literature begins with the assumption that the role of the market and supply and demand for factors and products is the basis for distributing resources and making adjustments in factor inputs. Similarly, the application of the concept of perfect equilibrium, or the idea that disequilibria mitigate toward flexible readjustment in the combination of factors of production (land, work, and capital), may also be inappropriate or insufficient, as demonstrated in this chapter's example of the sluggish recomposition of Spain's urban networks.

Similar observations can be made about demand and consumption, variables strongly influenced by social mechanisms, largely psychological in nature. In fact, such variables are marked by fragmentation and compartmentalization by groups or social sectors, and are very sensitive to apparently irrational stimuli, whose functioning cannot easily be predicted by means of cost-benefit calculations, understood in the strictest economic sense.[74] The need for caution arises exactly at the point of applying models and theories of a universal nature, such as the notions of a "consumer revolution" or the "industrious revolution," discussed earlier.

It is not only when applying classical or neoclassical economic theory that the danger of misuse may arise. It remains astonishing, for example, that Douglass North and Keith Thomas chose property-rights theory to explain

---

73. One of the most impressive studies on this subject is Giovanni Levi's work on real estate markets, *l'Eredità immateriale: Carriera di un esorcista del Piemonte del Seicento* (Turin: Einaudi, 1985), 83–121.

74. Thanks to the debate generated by the notion of a "consumer revolution," this topic has become so popular recently that the literature on it is enormous. A theoretical and historical reevaluation can be found in the anthology, *Acknowledging Consumption: A Review of New Studies,* ed. Daniel Miller (London: Routledge, 1995).

Spain's economic backwardness. According to them, the Mesta (the Castilian organization of transhumant sheep owners) actually impeded agrarian development by generating tremendous uncertainty over the use of the open range and the possibility for peaceful cultivation of lands that their livestock regularly crossed. This interpretation, however, simply does not fit the facts. The Mesta limited itself to those lands that were adjacent to the tracks along which they drove their flocks. Moreover, as an institution, it was compelled to pay remunerations for property infringements. The most damaging aspect of this theory—or of its erroneous application, which assumes an automatic correlation between freely held, capitalist property and economic development—is that the authors overlook the positive impact of communal property rights on agrarian development in sixteenth-century Castile. Had they taken this into consideration, it would have significantly enriched their explanation of economic development.[75]

Thus, vis-à-vis the elaboration and selection of analytical models available in economics, the field of economic history requires more than just an understanding of institutions, society, or even religiosity. We also need to draw closer to anthropology, sociology, and other disciplines (many of which have been unfairly displaced by our use of statistical methodologies). To continue with our examples, while using organization theory to explain patrimony management practices among the aristocracy, we should not forget anthropology's important contribution to the understanding of lineages and family units.[76] It continues to be puzzling—and indicative of the problems and errors we continue to commit—that the specialists in the economic history of

75. The views of Douglass C. North are found in *Structure and Change in Economic History* (New York: W. W. Norton, 1981), 150. Worst of all, like many other claims tossed about in Spanish historiography, these ideas have permeated our thinking on the subject. An example is the even more simplistic observation on the topic presented by Charles Kindleberger, *World Economic Primacy 1500–1990* (New York: Oxford University Press, 1996), 73. Fortunately, the general understanding on the subject is changing thanks to studies such as that of Carla Rahn Phillips and William D. Phillips, *Spain's Golden Fleece: Production and the Wool Trade from the Middle Ages to the Nineteenth Century* (Baltimore: Johns Hopkins University Press, 1997).

76. The solidarities, conflicts, or need for internal coherence, which I referred to before, are issues with which anthropologists are perfectly familiar and which have an internal logic much richer than an exclusively economic one. While there are too many studies on the topic to cite them all, one example of the fruitful combination of anthropology and economics, as auxiliary sciences to economic history, can be found in Levi, *l'Eredità immateriale*. Of course, such a proposal must begin with a rereading from an economic perspective of those anthropologists (and others) who have been most influential in this area, including Malinowski, Geertz, and Polanyi, but who have often been ignored in economic history's official forums.

the firm, who so strongly emphasize the character of family enterprise in many modern companies, entirely forget the weight that family relationships have on the management of those enterprises, and to the contrary and with a reductionism worthy of a more carefully considered critique, they take such relationships to be the consequence solely of cost-benefit analyses, without stopping to consider the inverse relationship.[77] For another example, no anthropologist overlooks the fact that many traits of preindustrial European markets, and more precisely, the bilateral monopolies that often appeared in certain transactions and for certain merchandise match some of the characteristic of a "bazaar economy" that Clifford Geertz described.[78]

As long as we, as economic historians, continue to rely heavily on numbers and statistics, we must also remain aware of the limits of these methods and acknowledge the guesswork they often involve. This is especially important when measuring economic growth, as it affects how we come to terms with the past and the rupture with the notion of an *histoire immobile*, and consequently, with our assessments of modern economic growth.[79] The way

77. While overall a complete and excellent work, *La empresa en la historia de España,* ed. Francisco Comín and Pablo Martín Aceña (Madrid: Esposa Calpe, 1996), contains some odd studies that succumbed to this view. It is not surprising that this perspective of the history of the family, as a means for understanding the conditions under which a firm operates, appears in the work of medievalists as well as in those areas where kinship structures continue to have a significant impact on economic activity. An example of the latter is S. Chaudhury, "Familial and Cultural Networks of Entrepreneurs in India during the Middle Years of the Eighteenth Century" in *Entrepreneurial Networks and Business Culture,* ed. Michael Moss and A. Slaven (Madrid: 12th International Economic History Congress, 1998).

78. Among other studies by the same author, it is necessary to mention Clifford Geertz, *Peddlers and Princes: Social Change and Economic Modernization in Two Indonesian Towns* (Chicago: University of Chicago Press, 1963).

79. Without getting into a discussion of these theories, there comes to mind the revisionism by experts like E L. Jones, *The European Miracle: Environments, Economies and Geopolitics in the History of Europe and Asia,* 2d ed. (Cambridge: Cambridge University, 1981), and idem, *Growth Recurring: Economic Change in World History* (Oxford: Clarendon, 1988), and above all, the attempt to quantify some variables of the past leading to similar conclusions by G. D. Snooks (see especially his anthology, *Was the Industrial Revolution Necessary?* [London: Routledge, 1994]). In any case, it is symptomatic of the need to analyze economic history in light of the social dimensions of the past that an important work which has broken with the myth of *histoire immobile* in ancien régime France emphasizes the need to study the agrarian economy of the period by taking into account "all the details of local life—many of them forever lost—details that impassion social and cultural institutions"; Philip T. Hoffman, *Growth in a Traditional Society: The French Countryside, 1450–1815* (Princeton: Princeton University Press, 1996), 199.

in which data is manipulated affects the results, as de Vries has recently shown for a specific case.[80] While necessary, the calculation of macroeconomic statistics, such as national income, is also problematic in economies where prices vary widely from region to region, do not correspond to an integrated domestic market, and constitute magnitudes of a different nature and type than those of capitalist economies.[81] In the same vein, Thomas Rawski has noted that measurements of growth over the long term—the span of time in which specialists studying the *ancien régime* are accustomed to work—start with an incorrect supposition that time is "in some sense, 'homogeneous,' to use Kuznets' term."[82] This contrasts with the conviction that if the "long term" and the very definition of "growth" itself can be characterized by anything, it is by being accompanied by structural change that affects even the deflators we use, and thus the results of our research.[83] This should not keep us from using economic and statistical categories, but we must remain aware of the reified character of our conclusions, and the need to situate our studies more carefully in order to corroborate or reject hypotheses, even when we are using estimates that are in no way exact.[84]

Today, the relationship between history and economics appears more complex and compels the historian to struggle more than was required when Braudel was writing. This complicates the relationship, but it does not make

80. See his comments on the application of the indexes of Laspeyre and Paasche: de Vries, "Between Purchasing Power," 97–98.

81. In an attempt to calculate rates of gross domestic product (GDP) in Castile during the sixteenth to eighteenth centuries, deviations between regions of as much as 70 percent were found in the price index of certain basic products, including wheat. Although this does not imply different tendencies among these areas, it poses a huge problem when applying deflators to the scarce, and at times chronologically concentrated, available data, and it makes it exceedingly difficult to apply these categories (which were devised in order to analyze integrated economies) to the economies of the past. Bartolomé Yun Casalilla, "Proposals to Quantify Long-Term Performance in the Kingdom of Castile, 1550–1800," in *Economic Growth and Structural Change: Comparative Approaches over the Long Run on the Basis of Reconstructed National Account,* ed. H. Van der Wee and A. Maddison, 11th International Economic History Congress (Milan: Bocconi University, 1994), 97–110.

82. Rawski et al., *Economics and the Historian,* 28.

83. This problem is present in many works such as those of G. D. Snooks, "New Perspectives on Industrial Revolution," in *Was the Industrial Revolution Necessary?* ed. G. D. Snooks, 1–26. This author uses the price of wheat in order to adjust GDP series in England, even though it is amply clear that this commodity did not have the same importance for the English in 1950 as it did in 1300, and when it is also clear that its significance to the diet, and thus to the consumer price index, varied greatly over the last seven centuries.

84. The ideas of Rawski, *Economics and he Historian,* 31–32, seem particularly apt.

it impossible, especially if we consider the enormous advances in material resources (such as access to statistical databases and the progress in cataloging archives) now at our disposal. One key for the future is perhaps to follow the advice of Charles Kindleberger, who said, "we must change from one tool to another as each serves the particular task in hand, and forgo any universal solvent or sovereign explanation."[85] Speaking another way and taking his words to an extreme, the enemy of economic history is the isolation that results from scientific territorialization, meant in the narrowest sense, and from methodological and conceptual self-sufficiency. Therein lie the excellence and the weaknesses of *La Méditerranée* and of the history it—to say nothing of other trends—has influenced us to practice. Because, as has been said too often, history's division into levels and academic specialization (economic, societal, cultural) and time periods (the *longue durée*, in the field of economics; short-term *événements*, in political science), while necessary and fruitful, may have carried a high price. The importance given to economic history may have led us to unilateral interpretations. The study and description of cycles (especially agrarian and demographic cycles) through the superimposition of serial data over the long term not only has left us with an *histoire immobile*, which now must be revised, but in order to give priority to the laws of immobile history, also may have made us conceal the ins and outs of decision-making processes, which rarely operate according to economic criteria, in the strict sense of the word. Certainly, a revision of our discipline along the lines shown in this chapter does not imply the negation of the patterns and laws existing in economic systems, but it does recognize that these laws have a probabilistic and nomothetic nature. Similarly, while conceiving of man as "enclosed in a space that extends before and behind him in an infinite perspective that we have called the 'long term,'" that does not preclude our acknowledgment that events alone are not the brilliant surface of history, that history does not avoid collision with chance, nor does man find himself "the prisoner of a destiny over which he scarcely casts a shadow."

Chapter translated by Patricia Rosas

85. Charles P. Kindleberger, *Economic Laws and Economic History* (Cambridge: Cambridge University Press, 1989), 92.

Chapter 3

GREAT EXPECTATIONS

Early Modern History and the Social Sciences

JAN DE VRIES

This chapter explores the relationship between history and the social sciences with particular reference to the long-term interaction of the urban and rural sectors in European societies. Its starting point is a reflection on the fate of Fernand Braudel's historical project, now that his great work on the Mediterranean is fifty years old. It proceeds to identify new developments in early modern European economic history and then to elaborate on one of the key historical problems of this period, the interrelationships between urban and agrarian economies.

HISTORY AND THE SOCIAL SCIENCES: AN APPRAISAL OF RECENT DEVELOPMENTS

Fernand Braudel is the most celebrated historian of the twentieth century. It is often remarked that if a Nobel Prize had been established for history, he would have been its first recipient. Yet, Braudel's fame far exceeds his intellectual influence on the practice of history. Could it be that the closing paragraph of *La Méditerranée* also applies to him and his work? "So when I think of the individual, I am always inclined to see him imprisoned within a destiny in which he himself has little hand, fixed in a landscape in which the infinite perspectives of the long term stretch into the distance both behind him and before."[1]

---

1. Fernand Braudel, *La Méditerranée et le monde Méditerranéen à l'époque de Philippe II*, 1st ed. (Paris: Armand Colin, 1949), 2d ed., 2 vols. (Paris: Armand Colin, 1966). All citations are from the English translation of the 2d ed.: *The Mediterranean and the Mediterranean World of Philip II*, 2 vols., trans. Siân Reynolds, 2 vols. (New York: Harper & Row, 1972); here, see 2:1244.

What, after fifty years, remains of the intellectual enterprise he championed so effectively both as a prolific writer and formidable academic administrator? Were his actions no more than "une agitation de surface"? I do not propose to address this large question in all its dimensions; indeed, there already exists a substantial literature on Braudel's legacy and on the Annales School.[2] Rather, I will focus on one aspect of Braudel's project: the establishment of history as the central, unifying discipline to the social sciences. It is this extravagant ambition together with the deep pessimism that suffuses his work that initially attracted me to Braudel's writings, and that cemented my allegiance to his vision even as I found myself disagreeing with so many of his subordinate arguments and claims. That he could stake these positions in the age of high modernism and at the same time insist that freedom is to remain within the boundaries of the historically possible astonished me—then as now.

The renovation of history as a discipline, the stated objective of the original *Annalistes*, took on a new, more spacious aspect with Braudel's demonstration of the possibilities of a "total history" in his *La Méditerranée*. His 1958 essay, "History and the Social Sciences," made his agenda explicit. To become the unifying center of all the social sciences, the historical profession had to overcome its continued allegiance to a "pernicious humanism" (what he later describes as a "militant anthropocentrism").[3] Furnished with a "clear awareness of the plurality of social time," and capable of incorporating the dialectics of both time and space, history—and history alone—could reconstitute the global nature of human phenomena. "It alone had access to what [Braudel] called the 'ensemble of the ensembles.'"[4]

Braudel's double critique—of a history too fond of the mere event (those "crests of foam that the tides of history carry on their strong backs"[5]) and of

2. See, among other works, François Dosse, *L'Histoire en miettes: Des "Annales" à la "nouvelle histoire"* (Paris: Éditions La Découverte, 1987); the entire issue of *Journal of Modern History* 44 (1972); Samuel Kinser, "Annales Paradigm? The Geohistorical Structure of Fernand Braudel," *American Historical Review* 89 (1981): 63–105; Trian Stoianovich, *French Historical Method: The Annales Paradigm* (Ithaca: Cornell University Press, 1976); Peter Burke, *The French Historical Revolution: The Annales School, 1929–1989* (Stanford: Stanford University Press, 1990).

3. Fernand Braudel, "Histoire et sciences sociales: La longue durée," *Annales E.S.C.* 13 (1958): 725–53. Quotations are from the English translation: "History and the Social Sciences," in *Economy and Society in Early Modern Europe,* ed. Peter Burke (New York: Harper & Row, 1972).

4. Dosse, *L'Histoire en miettes,* 89.

"imperialistic" social sciences, fragmented and lacking in depth[6]—sought to open a dialogue between the social sciences and history. The intention was not so much to refashion history after the social sciences as to make social science historical. This is an important distinction. History was to become a modern discipline not simply by incorporating existing ahistorical social theory, but by deploying a new concept of duration and periodization, and a radically broadened (less anthropocentric) field of vision with respect to context and agency.

Braudel's formulations of this challenge are unmistakably his own, but the larger agenda of renovating history and entering into a closer dialogue with the social sciences was embraced by a substantial number of other historians, and in several countries. There were, of course, the other members of the Annales School, the economic historians united in the international price history project, the agrarian historians, and the demographic historians. By, say, 1960 they constituted an active body of researchers who were beginning to fashion effective international links (especially the quadrennial International Economic History Congresses) and who shared a more-or-less critical stance toward "traditional" history.

Around this time the "New Economic History" burst onto the historical scene in the United States.[7] This too, was not an isolated movement. There was a sharp increase in interest within the American historical profession as a whole in the theories and methodologies of the social sciences. This new interest was motivated primarily by a desire for a more objective historical scholarship, one with rigorous standards to withstand ideological manipulation. "Nowhere was this search for rigor pushed further in the 1960s than in the field of economic history. There a small group of economists launched a veritable revolution, seizing control of the discipline's organizations and using them to build a coherent and uniquely American body of scholarship based on the application of economic theory and econometric techniques to the study of the past."[8]

---

5. Braudel, *The Mediterranean*, 2d ed., 1:21.

6. See Braudel's 1950 inaugural address to the College de France, in *Écrits de l'histoire* (Paris: Flammarion, 1969).

7. The first major work to which this label was attached appeared in 1958: Alfred Conrad and John Meyer, "The Economics of Slavery in the Antebellum South," *Journal of Political Economy* 66 (1958): 95–130; but the "movement" took its first institutional form in the Purdue University conferences, held annually beginning in 1960.

8. Naomi R. Lamoreaux, "Economic History and the Cliometric Revolution" (unpublished paper, UCLA, 1996), 2.

The New Economic History (which, as it aged, took to calling itself "cliometrics") confronted traditional history with a direct challenge to its practices and norms. The articulation of clear, testable hypotheses needed to be made central to scholarly inquiry in history, as it was already in economics.[9] The practical consequence of this new demand for hypothetico-deductive reasoning in historical analysis was "to upset the long-standing division of labor between economics and economic history—a division of labor that relegated marginalist (neoclassical) economics to the study of short-term phenomena"[10] while economic historians had been free to range more widely in their efforts to understand the long-term processes beyond the reach and ken of neoclassical theory. Now, cliometricians deploying neoclassical theory would emphasize the same market phenomena, the same necessarily short-term processes that preoccupied their economist colleagues.

It will be evident how this "Anglo-Saxon"[11] engagement of history with social science differed from the French School's agenda: the cliometricians (and not they alone)[12] championed a social scientific history while Braudel, as we have seen, advocated a historical social science. As a consequence, while Braudel warned against the explosive event, which "blinds the eyes of contemporaries with clouds of smoke, but [which] does not endure," the cliometricians rushed to embrace an ahistorical theory whose impressive power is precisely in the study of short-term market phenomena.

And yet, there was a brief shining moment—it barely outlasted the tenure of Gerald Ford as president of the United States—when it appeared, from an American perspective, at any rate, that a New History would move from the periphery to the core, and would engage the social sciences in a serious way. The translation of Braudel's *Mediterranean* into English in 1972 and of other *Annales* works in the same period, brought the new ideas to the

9. Major statements of the new agenda include: Robert W. Fogel, "The Specification Problem in Economic History," *Journal of Economic History* 37 (1967): 283–308; Douglass C. North, "Economic History: Its Contribution to Economic Education, Research, and Policy," *American Economic Review* 55 (1965): 86–98; Donald N. McCloskey, "Does the Past Have Useful Economics?" *Journal of Economic Literature* 14 (1976): 434–61.

10. Lamoreux, "Economic History and the Cliometric Revolution," 25.

11. Cliometrics today has established significant beachheads on continental Europe. In July 1997, the Third World Congress of Cliometrics met in Munich, and the recently formed European Historical Economics Society has launched a new *European Journal of Economic History.*

12. The brashness of the New Economic Historians may hide from view the breadth of the movement to incorporate social science theory and method into history. The founding of the Social Science History Association in 1972 helps reveal the scope of the movement.

attention of the (nonfrancophone) historical profession at large. In 1973 and 1974 a leading New Economic Historian, Douglass North, decried the limitations of work within the neoclassical framework and urged a refocusing of attention on long-term economic change. A renewed interest in institutional change emerged from this.[13] 1974 also saw the publication of the first volume of Immanual Wallerstein's *Modern World-System*, a work that attracted broad notice and directed multidisciplinary attention to the place of history in the study of social change and the production of social theory. Shortly thereafter, Robert Brenner's broadsides against the "Smithian and Malthusian interpreters" announced the reintroduction of a rigorous Marxian analysis of long-term change.

In the mid-1970s a broad range of scholars, spanning the ideological spectrum and representing nearly all social science disciplines, were actively engaged in New Historical research and debate. Needless to say, they disagreed with each other on nearly everything. If there was a single point of agreement, it was this: the rejection of narrative history. It led Peter Burke to introduce the final volume of the New Cambridge Modern History, which appeared in 1979, with the following claim: "In the twentieth century we have seen a break with traditional narrative history, which, like the break with the traditional novel or with representational art or with classical music, is one of the important cultural discontinuities of our time."[14] Obviously, no single influence can claim full credit for this historiographical discontinuity, but the most profound factor must be the spread of an uncomfortable feeling that the narrative form greatly restricts the types of possible historical questions and feasible modes of explanation. Narrative history has attached to it like a ball and chain the discrete, short-term historical event—*l'histoire événementielle*.

In the opinion of Bob Dylan, "You don't need a weatherman to know which way the wind blows." But history did have a weatherman, and in the very year that Peter Burke associated the New History with modernity and the future, the weatherman spoke. Lawrence Stone sensed that the vast majority of historians, certainly in Britain and the United States, had no heart for the new scholarship. Moreover, the political sentiments that had

13. Douglass C. North and Robert Paul Thomas, *The Rise of the Western World* (Cambridge: Cambridge University Press, 1973), is the best known of several works. See also, North's presidential address to the Economic History Association, "Beyond the New Economic History," *Journal of Economic History* 34 (1974): 1–7.

14. Peter Burke, "Introduction: Concepts of Continuity and Change in History," in *New Cambridge Modern History* (Cambridge: Cambridge University Press, 1979), 13:1.

nonetheless caused many to pay lip service to material and collective historical analysis were withdrawing that support. Culture, a foundation more trustworthy because less subject to challenge by facts, would take the place of an increasingly uncongenial materialism.

In "The Revival of Narrative: Reflections on a New Old History," Stone foresaw historians' focusing their research increasingly on individual agency and eschewing analytical for descriptive modes of explanation. "If I am right," he concluded, "the movement to narrative... marks the end of an era: the end of the attempt to produce a coherent and scientific explanation of change in the past."[15]

It had been a very brief era. Nor was Stone's prescience limited to "Anglo-Saxon" scholarship, for the shift toward microhistory and a narrowing of the venerable *Annaliste* concept of *mentalité* was underway in France at the same time—indeed, had begun earlier. Braudel's retirement in 1972 from his chief position of influence brought an immediate shift toward cultural and anthropological themes.[16] By the time of the "linguistic turn" of the 1980s the project to integrate history and the social sciences around broadly Braudelian themes seemed bizarre to the great majority of historians, who could only utter the word "science" with an ironic tone of voice.[17]

Which is not to say that postmodern scholarship offered no new possibilities for integrative history, nor that the socioeconomic themes pioneered in earlier decades were not advanced in this period. I will claim, however, that the practical effect of the historical involution of the period since circa 1980 has been to increase the fragmentation of history as a discipline. The postmodern crisis called into question the social scientific epistemologies with which the New History had hoped to enter into dialogue. This, by

15. Lawrence Stone, "The Revival of Narrative: Reflections on a New Old History," *Past and Present* 85 (1979): 3–24; reprinted in idem, *The Past and the Present* (Boston: Routledge & Kegan Paul, 1981), 74–96.

16. The multistranded flight from Braudelian determinism is chronicled in Burke, *French Historical Revolution*, chap. 4, pp. 65–93. Burke judges the Annales School today to be so fragmented and diverse as to no longer exist as a "movement"; ibid., 106–7.

17. The English word "science" has taken on a much more restricted meaning than, say, the German *Wissenschaft*. "Science" is effectively restricted to the nomothetic disciplines, based on deduction and aspiring to lawmaking. The following statement of Braudel, made at the end of the third volume of *Civilization and Capitalism: The Perspective of the World* (New York: Harper & Row, 1982), is today met with incredulity: "Is it not the secret aim and underlying motive of history to seek to explain the present? And today, now that it is in touch with the various social sciences, is history not also becoming a science of a kind, imperfect and approximate as they are..." (619–20).

itself, could have advanced the agenda of those aiming for an historical social science. But another feature of postmodernism raised up a formidable barrier to the advance of this agenda while it powerfully advanced historical fragmentation. There is no empirical refinement in postmodern scholarship. This weakened the always fragile belief that historical knowledge is cumulative and corrective. A discipline without such a sense offers its practitioners no strong reason to pay attention to each other, let alone to the existing stock of empirical findings.

At best, small communities of discourse survive in this process of intellectual involution, and the resulting fragmentation is now a universal lamentation of the historian. Economic historians are acutely aware of their isolation from "general history," and search for ways to restore contact.[18] The same is true of social historians. Adrian Wilson introduced his *Rethinking Social History* with the complaint that "social history lacks a clear sense of direction or unifying perspective," and "is closed off, isolated from the historical disciplines more generally."[19] But, in truth, to invoke Gertrude Stein, "there is no there there." The economic historians, social historians, and so forth are not isolated from anything. They and the other historians are all simply alone.

History is as far as ever from becoming "the queen of the social sciences." But this does not mean that the aspirations voiced by Braudel a generation ago have been abandoned. There are within the social sciences themselves serious movements to develop theories in which duration and space—history and geography—are central dimensions. The general climate of thought, which has scattered historical research to the four winds, has set social scientists to explore nonlinear dynamics and the so-called sciences of complexity. Economists, in particular, are now exploring the implications of bounded and myopic rationality, increasing returns to scale, and "spillover effects"—all of which accord new significance to the details of historical sequence and/or spatial relationships.

In economics, these new developments challenge from within the neoclassical tendency to abstract from time and space. Consequently, institutional economics (including the new organizational and informational economics),[20]

---

18. This is the objective of Lamoreaux, "Economic History and the Cliometric Revolution."

19. Adrian Wilson, "Introduction," in *Rethinking Social History* (Manchester: Manchester University Press, 1993), 23.

20. The "old" institutionalism takes us back to the German Historical School. For a study that blows the dust off this literature, and strips away the hoary myths that allow us so

the new growth theory,[21] the concept of "path dependence,"[22] and models of *homo œconomicus* capable not only of greed, but also of fear and love, not to mention shortsightedness and fairness,[23] all act to convince the economist that "history matters." The new, embryonic historical economics is arguably non-Braudelian in its emphasis on the importance of "adventitious, seemingly transient [events]." Indeed, the concept of path dependence sets as its task the explanation of how some such "mere" events can "become so magnified as to exercise a controlling (and sometimes pernicious) influence over matters of far greater economic and social significance."[24] The emphasis here is on the interaction, or reciprocity, of event and context; not the domination of event by context—but, of course, Braudel argued both ways.

easily to dismiss it, see Heath Pearson, *The Economists' New Science of Law* (Cambridge: Cambridge University Press, 1997). Douglass C. North's approach is represented in *Institutions, Institutional Change, and Economic Performance* (Cambridge: Cambridge University Press, 1990); idem, "Economic Performance through Time," *American Economic Review* 84 (1993): 359–68; and Douglass C. North and Barry Weingast, "Constitutions and Commitment: Evolution of Institutions Governing Public Choice in Seventeenth Century England," *Journal of Economic History* 49 (1989): 803–32.

21. The new growth theory breaks with the neoclassical model by positing pervasive increasing returns to scale and by stressing the importance of (necessarily localized) spillover effects of investment in new technologies. For an overview of what is now a large literature, see Paul M. Romer et al., "Symposium on New Growth Theory," *Journal of Economic Perspectives* 8 (1994): 3–72; Paul M. Romer, "Increasing Returns and Long-Run Growth," *Journal of Political Economy* 94 (1986): 1002–37. The spatial dimension is emphasized in Paul Krugman, *Geography and Trade* (Cambridge, Mass.: MIT Press, 1991); Paul Krugman, "Increasing Returns and Economic Geography," *Journal of Political Economy* 99 (1991): 483–99.

22. The concept of path dependence breaks with the neoclassical assumption that in the long run, all "accidental" forces are shaken off in the process of achieving a unique equilibrium value. Rather, path dependence affirms the existence of positive feedback effects and the consequent possibility of multiple equilibria, including suboptimal "pools of local attraction." See Paul A. David, "Historical Economics in the Longrun: Some Implications of Path-Dependence," in *Historical Analysis in Economics,* ed. G. D. Snooks (London: Routledge, 1993), 29–40; Paul A. David, "Clio and the Economics of QWERTY," *American Economic Review* 75 (1985): 332–37; Brian Arthur, "Positive Feedback in Economics," *Scientific American* (September 1990): 92–99.

23. For a brief discussion of the new strategizing, gambling, and guessing capabilities of "economic man" being developed by economic theorists, see: Richard Sutch, "The Third Task of Economic History," *Economic History Review* 51 (1991): 277–78. See also, Thomas G. Rawski, ed., *Economics and the Historian* (Berkeley: University of California Press, 1996).

24. David, "Historical Economics in the Longrun," 29.

At present, there are some faint signs of a renewed interest among historians in macrohistorical questions and of a disenchantment with the consequences of the "return to narrative." But as so often, historians ride in the caboose; the leaders in the construction of a historical social science are now to be found within the social sciences themselves.

EARLY MODERN HISTORY AND THE SOCIAL SCIENCES: SOME NEW DEVELOPMENTS

At the highest level of generalization about history as a discipline, skepticism, if not pessimism, seems unavoidable. Yet one would go much too far to claim that there have been no important developments in which social science and history engaged fruitfully with each other. In economic history the most consequential development is the reassessment of the Industrial Revolution as the point of origin of modern economic life.[25] I describe this as "most consequential" because the current revisionist literature, while it is often focused on arcane questions of measurement of British industrial performance during the reign of George III, opens the door to a fundamental reperiodization of Western history, one that reduces the size of the barrier standing between "early modern" and "late modern" history, or as many social scientists are still inclined to say, between traditional and modern society.

Such a reinterpretation did not emerge out of nowhere, of course. The revisions of British industrial growth rate estimates could trigger a reconsideration of basic periodization because of the existence of a multistranded critique of a "conventional wisdom" in early modern and *ancien régime* historiography. Some of this critical scholarship, what I have elsewhere called "The Revolt of the Early Modernists,"[26] found its inspiration in Annales School concepts, but much of it is in fact critical of characteristic *Annales* assumptions. For the Annales School, both before and during Braudel's leadership, was as content as any traditional historian to honor the claims to radical historical discontinuity of the twin revolutions of the eighteenth century, the French and the Industrial.

---

25. Representative of the new work on the Industrial Revolution is: N. F. R. Crafts and C. K. Harley, "Output Growth and the British Industrial Revolution: A Restatement of the Crafts-Harley View," *Economic History Review* 45 (1992): 703–30.

26. Jan de Vries, "The Industrial Revolution and the Industrious Revolution," *Journal of Economic History* 54 (1994): 251–53.

Two areas in which early modern economic historians have been particularly active in challenging conventional views are in the classic themes of agrarian and urban history—in city and countryside, and the relations between the two.

RURAL HISTORY

It must be said that Braudel contributed little to the field of agrarian history. For all his sentimentality about the lost village world of his own youth, he was content to leave agriculture as an unexamined black box, submerged in the routine, repetitive realm of material culture. Its structural, barely changing character was implicitly enforced by the rules of Thomas Malthus, a claim made explicit by Emmanuel Le Roy Ladurie, who examined rural society closely, and who went on to provoke historians with his claim that France before the eighteenth century had experienced an *histoire immobile* in which "twelve to thirteen generations of peasants…were busy reproducing themselves within limits of finite possibilities whose constraints proved inexorable."[27] In fact, most of the founding fathers of modern agrarian history— Wilhelm Abel, B. H. Slicher van Bath, even Joan Thirsk—accepted the appropriateness of Malthusian models for European agriculture. And this Malthusianism was powerfully reinforced by the influence of anthropological thinking about the nature of "peasantry" as a category of human civilization. Preindustrial agriculture was a world of culturally different people subject to different economic rules.

The new agrarian history rejects this celebration of the otherness of European cultivators; it explores systematically the possibilities of market-based explanations of rural phenomena and peasant behavior. This literature long had its largest influence in early modern English and Dutch rural history,[28] but more recently has been extended backward to the Middle Ages,[29] and spatially to what had seemed the native habitat of peasant *mentalité*, France.[30]

27. Emmanuel Le Roy Ladurie, "L'Histoire immobile," *Annales E.S.C.* 29 (1974): 673–82. Quotation from the English translation, "Motionless History," *Social Science History* 1 (1977): 122.

28. The early work of E. L. Jones and Donald McCloskey emphasized markets in early modern England, as did, for the Netherlands, Jan de Vries, *Dutch Rural Economy in the Golden Age, 1500–1700* (New Haven: Yale University Press, 1974). See also, E. L. Jones and William N. Parker, eds., *European Peasants and Their Markets* (Princeton: Princeton University Press, 1975).

URBAN HISTORY

The character of early modern urbanism was a special interest of Braudel; he wrote about it at length, and not always consistently. While he did not neglect the ways towns were implicated in structured urban networks and in complex ties of interdependence with the countryside, he took special relish, so it seems, in emphasizing the imperialism and the pretensions of cities. The division of labor between town and country fashioned the cities into worlds of their own, and in these autonomous jurisdictions—the larger ones at least—capitalism nestled: "Capitalism and towns were basically the same thing in the West."[31] Cities were the breeding ground of capitalism, but they were also prone to parasitic relations with their hinterlands, and finally, were increasingly subordinated to the rising national states of the early modern era. In short, Braudel's agenda for the early modern city was a full one. As "transformers" cities set the world of inert material culture and routine market economy in motion; yet the early modern cities, the great cities above all, had lost their way: "It has been shown that these enormous urban formations are more linked to the past, to accomplished evolutions, faults, and weaknesses of the societies and economies of the *ancien régime* than to preparations for the future."[32] The great cities "would be present at the forthcoming industrial revolution as spectators."

29. Here, the work of Bruce M. S. Campbell is fundamental. See Bruce M. S. Campbell and Mark Overton, eds., *Land, Labour and Livestock: Historical Studies in European Agricultural Productivity* (Manchester: Manchester University Press, 1991); Campbell and Overton, "Production et productivité dans l'agriculture anglaise, 1086–1871," *Histoire & Measure* 11 (1996): 255–97.

30. Philip T. Hoffman, *Growth in a Traditional Society. The French Countryside, 1450–1815* (Princeton: Princeton University Press, 1996). Hoffman is admirably clear about his purposes: "[T]he new economic history (now well into middle age) has been pounding at the door of continental Europe with great insistence in recent years. It finally threatens to renew French history in the way that it has already refashioned the past in England, Ireland, and the Netherlands. My book is part of the process of renewal" (5). See also Jean-Marc Moriceau and Gilles Postel-Vinay, *Ferme, entrepise, famille: Grande exploitation et changements agricoles, XIIe–XVIIIe siècle* (Paris: Éditions de l'EHESS, 1992); George Grantham, "Long-Run Agricultural Supply during the Industrial Revolution: French Evidence and European Implications," *Journal of Economic History* 49 (1989): 43–72.

31. Fernand Braudel, *Capitalism and Civilization*, vol. 2, *The Wheels of Commerce*, trans. Siân Reynolds (New York: Harper & Row, 1982), 514.

32. Braudel, *Capitalism and Material Life* (New York: Harper & Row, 1967), 440. The quotation is from the 1st edition. In the 2d English edition of 1979 (*Structures of Everyday Life*), Braudel brings his chapter on cities to a different conclusion. The "backward looking city" concept is toned down, and the emphasis ultimately comes to be placed on the notion of

Braudel, his many insightful and nuanced observations notwithstanding, reinforced an already well established tradition of positing a basic discontinuity between the dynamic urbanism of the Middle Ages (established by the work of Henri Pirenne and Max Weber) and the dynamic urbanism of the industrial age. This left the city of the early modern era in limbo. The stage of urban history in this era was filled with curious facts, but lacked historical depth—a strangely un-Braudelian situation.

Dissatisfaction with this state of affairs surfaced in two works, which appeared in rapid succession in 1984 and 1985. Paul Hohenberg and Lynn Hollen Lees, in *The Making of Urban Europe*, wrote: "We refuse to accept an approach that views half a millennium of urban evolution through the lenses of two models [those of the medieval city and the industrial city], one obsolete the other pre-mature."[33]

In my *European Urbanization, 1500–1800*, I expressed the same dissatisfaction: "In writings about European cities the urbanism of these centuries [the early modern] often seems lost between two well-mapped urban landscapes—those of the medieval city and the industrial city." Yet, "the post-medieval pre-industrial city" was "a term too awkward to endure."[34]

Both books, and others of the past decade,[35] sought to develop concepts drawn from economics, geography, demography, and sociology to establish a framework for urban history—or the history of urbanization—that stresses the networks formed by early modern cities and their relations with their hinterlands. The result, in a nutshell, has been to present early modern urbanization as a precondition for modern industrialization, challenging the view that it was industrialization that called modern urbanization into being.

CITY AND COUNTRY IN EARLY MODERN EUROPE

In this essay's final section, we shall explore the city-country relationship in greater detail. The interaction of the urban and rural economies remains, in

---

transition: "The changing appearance of cities like London and Paris was reflected in the transition from one way of life and art of living to another" (557).

33. Paul Hohenberg and Lynn Hollen Lees, *The Making of Urban Europe, 1000–1950* (Cambridge, Mass.: Harvard University Press, 1985), 104.

34. Jan de Vries, *European Urbanization, 1500–1800* (London: Methuen, 1984), 3–4.

35. Bernard LePetit, *Les Villes dans la France moderne (1740–1840)* (Paris: Éditions Albin Michel, 1988); Ad van der Woude, Jan de Vries, and Akira Hayami, eds., *Urbanization in History: A Process of Dynamic Interaction* (Oxford: Oxford University Press, 1990).

many ways, the site of the most difficult conceptual issues in economic history. They are certainly the most ideologically contested issues. To keep matters as simple as possible, I will focus here on three concepts: the peasant, the market, and the city. Specifically, our concern is the role of the market as the link between the peasant household, as both producer and consumer, and the urban economy, what Adam Smith called "the great commerce of every civilized society."[36] We can think of these markets physically, as thousands of sites forming a thin layer of exchange, "stretching," as Braudel put it, "between the vast world of the producer and the equally enormous world of the consumer."[37]

The market, thus envisioned, was ubiquitous, but it was also ambiguous. Was it a site of mutually beneficial exchange, or an agent of exploitation? Was its role transparent, inert, and routinized, or did it energize the entire economy, setting in motion the very process of economic growth itself?

There is very little in the available tool kit of concepts about peasantry that can encourage the view that a peasant economy could itself foster market relations. Braudel described preindustrial society as waist-deep in the routine of material life, a world of autarkic, autonomous villages. And a distinguished chain of scholars, led by anthropologists, have insisted that this state of affairs was not only a fact, but an ideal. In peasant society "the market is held at arm's length,"[38] for "the major aim of the peasant is subsistence and social status gained within a narrow range of social relationships."[39] Seeking first of all to ensure continuity upon the land, the peasant sees "unlimited involvement in the market [as a threat to] his hold on his source of livelihood."[40] The resulting risk-averse behavior involves the peasant in a cautious, community-oriented strategy that willingly sacrifices profit maximization for the avoidance of disaster and the securing of a "target income, set at a conventional level by a combination of social and economic criteria—the critical or approving behavior of friends, neighbors, and kin, and

36. Adam Smith, *The Wealth of Nations*, ed. Edwin Cannan (1887; repr. New York: Modern Library, 1994), book 1, 401.

37. Fernand Braudel, *Afterthoughts on Material Civilization and Capitalism* (Baltimore: Johns Hopkins University Press, 1977), 16.

38. Robert Redfield, *Peasant Society and Culture* (Chicago: University of Chicago Press, 1956), 45–46.

39. Eric R. Wolf, *Peasant Wars of the Twentieth Century* (New York: Harper & Row, 1969), xiv.

40. Wolf, *Peasant Wars*, xiv.

the amount of reciprocity which they are prepared to give according to what they themselves have received."[41]

The "moral economy" view of peasant behavior, with its emphasis on risk aversion, target income, and community solidarity, is rooted in the assumption that markets are profoundly unnatural, that, as Karl Polanyi claimed, "the alleged propensity of man to barter, truck, and exchange is almost entirely apocryphal."[42] Yet, this literature also acknowledges that the peasant could not be entirely self-sufficient. Besides physical needs that could not be satisfied at home, the peasant had to contend with social and political superiors who required support. Key to the anthropologists' definition of peasantry is the notion that peasants form a "part society," and are linked to power holders outside their own social stratum by asymmetrical, that is, extraeconomic, relations.[43]

If these asymmetrical relations pushed peasants from an ideal of self-sufficiency, incipient market relations could, to some extent, pull them: high prices could encourage the marketing of surplus production, the monetization of which gave the household access to commodities of strategic (for example, salt) or symbolic (for example, silver) value.

The peasant household described here is pushed and pulled from self-sufficiency toward market contact. Its surpluses flow via a mixture of regulated and market mechanisms to support nonagricultural elites and a limited range of producers and traders who cater to the circumscribed markets of the peasants and the elites.

In the northern European context this so-called classic peasant society assumed characteristic forms in the course of the great medieval expansion of the eleventh through thirteenth centuries. Then the basic elements of preindustrial agricultural technology (involving rotation systems, the use of livestock,

41. Robert Firth, "Social Structure and Peasant Economy: The Influence of Social Structure upon Peasant Economies," in *Subsistence Agriculture and Economic Development*, C. R. Wharton, ed. (Chicago: Aldine Press, 1969), 36.

42. Karl Polanyi, *The Great Transformation* (New York: Beacon Press, 1957), 44. On the concept of "moral economy" see also James C. Scott, *The Moral Economy of the Peasant* (New Haven: Yale University Press, 1976); Eric Hobsbawm, *Primitive Rebels* (Manchester: Manchester University Press, 1965).

43. Eric R. Wolf, *Peasants* (Englewood Cliffs, N.J.: Prentice Hall, 1966), 3–4, 11. The preceding paragraphs draw on what is now a venerable literature. It continues to enjoy broad assent. It is in no way challenged in the recent textbook on peasant economics, Frank Ellis, *Peasant Economic: Farm Households and Agrarian Development* (Cambridge: Cambridge University Press, 1992).

the use of plows) became sufficiently common (although by no means universal) to lift grain harvests above the yield ratios (ratios of grain harvested to seed planted) of 2.5 to 3, documented in Carolingian polyptyques. Such meager yields, under the most optimistic assumptions, could support only a tiny nonagricultural population. In a meticulous hypothetical reconstruction of surplus grain output under medieval farming practice, George Grantham has shown that a yield of 5 hectoliters per hectare (roughly equivalent to a yield ratio of 2.5) where 10 percent of the total land area is sown to bread grains requires a provisioning radius of 10 kilometers to supply a nonfarm population of two hundred persons. "It is no wonder then," Grantham observes, "that the Frankish kings and ecclesiastical officers literally ate their way from manor to manor."[44]

But Grantham's calculations also reveal that with yields of 8 to 10 hectoliters per hectare—regularly attainable by the thirteenth century—the same 10 kilometer radius provisioning zone could support from 2,000 to 5,000 nongrain producers.[45] What might seem to have been a modest improvement in yields—from yield ratios of 2.5 to 3 to ratios of 4 to 5—had a huge impact on the formation of towns. Before A.D. 1000 they could be sustained only under special conditions, and with great seignorial effort; by the early fourteenth century most of Europe was covered with a dense network of thousands of market towns and hundreds of cities. The vast majority of all the cities of Europe would have existed by then, and the five hundred or so cities of at least 5,000 inhabitants housed some 8 to 10 percent of Europe's total population.[46]

I have delved into the related issues of agricultural productivity and urban market development in the Middle Ages in order to establish what could be achieved with the small surpluses of millions of peasants: the rapid construction of a vast but thin layer of market economy. Vast, because it embraced thousands of trading sites that left virtually no one untouched;

44. George Grantham, "Espaces privilégiés: Productivité agraire et zones d'approvisionnement des villes dans l'Europe préindustrielle," *Annales: Histoire, Sciences Sociales* 61:3 (1997): 695–725.
45. Kathleen Biddick, "Medieval English Peasants and Market Involvement," *Journal of Economic History* 45 (1985): 823–32.
46. R. H. Britnell, "The Proliferation of Markets in England, 1200–1349," *Economic History Review*, 2d ser., vol. 34 (1981): 209–21. On the urban percentage circa 1300, see: Paul Bairoch, *Cities and Economic Development* (Chicago: University of Chicago Press, 1988), 137; de Vries, *European Urbanization*, 41–43, 69–74.

thin, because it touched most people but lightly.[47] Most output did not leave the farm gate, or the village, and most marketed output did not leave the local provisioning zone.

But there were exceptions. Natural advantages, political privileges, or strategic economic functions could cause the market layer to thicken. In response, what the Germans call *intensitätinseln* could emerge, supplying especially large cities with garden crops, industrial raw materials, and dairy products. These "islands of intensity" extended but a short distance from the gates of the cities and depended on the cities for both markets and capital. Remarkable as they were, they hardly affected the larger structure of local peasant self-sufficiency.

By the sixteenth century Europe began to raise up cities of a size surpassing anything supported by medieval agriculture, requiring provisioning zones that extended far beyond the distances where peasants could directly market their surpluses. Economic historians are fascinated by the spectacle of a Naples or Madrid, a Paris or London straining against institutions and technologies to secure for themselves the wherewithal to live and grow. Braudel thought that "the 'stomach' of London and the 'stomach' of Paris were revolutionary" in the innovations they forced upon the traders, policy makers, and presumably, the producers themselves.[48]

The agricultural productivity of fertile regions in the sixteenth through eighteenth centuries was such that substantial cities could be supplied with grain from provisioning zones defined by the 40- to 50-kilometer radius that ordinarily delimited the distance producers could travel in one or two days.[49] Thus, direct supply from such a zone could suffice, in normal times, to maintain a city of up to 100,000 when grain yields reached 8 hectoliters per hectare and rotation systems were in use allowing one-fifth of the total land area to be under cereal cultivation.[50] Of course, such cities could not leave provisionment to chance; typically, they forced producers in their supply

47. Braudel, *Afterthoughts*, 40: "Until the nineteenth century [the market economy] was merely a layer—more or less thick and resilient, but at times very thin—between the ocean of daily life that lay stretched out beneath it and the capitalistic mechanism that more than once manipulated it from above."

48. Braudel, *Afterthoughts*, 28. For more on comparative metropolitan-hinterland interactions, see Peter Clark and Bernard Lepetit, eds., *Capital Cities and Their Hinterlands in Early Modern Europe* (Aldershot: Scolar Press, 1996).

49. Grantham, "Espaces privilégiés," 708–9; Jean Meuvret, *Le problème des subsistances à l'époque de Louis XIV* (Paris: Mouton, 1977), 3:60–61.

50. Grantham, "Espaces privilégiés," 707, table 2.

zones to market their surpluses directly in the city and forbade them from dealing with middlemen. Paris placed these restrictions on all farmers within 10 leagues of the city (1 league = 4.4 kilometers).[51] Madrid "possessed medieval *señorial* privileges that obliged the towns in its jurisdiction to provide bread to the city at regulated prices." By the early eighteenth century this *pan de obligación* "extended to towns 40–50 miles away."[52] In Portugal, every town council exercised the right to require direct deliveries and forbid middlemen in their supply jurisdictions. In the case of Lisbon, that jurisdiction had a radius of 50 kilometers around the city.[53]

In all of these cities and in others that grew to 200,000, even 400,000 population in the preindustrial era, these marketing zones, however closely controlled, proved insufficient. New mechanisms had to be developed to organize the supply of the emerging urban giants of Europe. But, what innovations could suffice if rural suppliers were as resistant to market orientation as is implied by the characterizations of peasant behavior reviewed above?

Both "push" and "pull" mechanisms—requisitioning and marketing—were employed to secure urban food supplies, but the mix varied among the great cities of Europe. In Madrid "the early seventeenth century saw administered production (the *pan de obligación*) supplemented by regulation of the price and transfer of both bread and grain. The area of control varied with the quality of the harvest, but it tended to grow with the city. In the 1580s bread and wheat embargoes occasionally extended as far as 45 miles; but after 1598, distances of 60 to 70 miles were common—in 1608 and 1631, the distances reached 80 and even 120 miles."[54] Supplementing these measures were edicts fixing rural bread prices below those of the city and the issuance of *tratte*, licenses regulating grain exports from Sicily.

Paris, which continued to regulate closely its primary supply zone, where middlemen were forbidden, unleashed these merchants on communities beyond its provisioning zone as the city grew and when harvests failed. The extended supply areas could not be organized in the traditional manner because of the great distances from the Parisian market. It required investments

51. A. P. Usher, *A History of the Grain Trade in France, 1400–1700* (Cambridge, Mass.: Harvard University Press, 1913).

52. David Ringrose, *Madrid and the Spanish Economy, 1560–1850* (Berkeley: University of California Press, 1983), 144–45.

53. Alvaro Ferreira da Silva, "Lisbon and Its Hinterland in the Eighteenth Century: Some Reflections on a Case-Study" (unpublished paper, New University, Lisbon), 2.

54. Ringrose, *Madrid*, 145.

in transportation, wholesale markets, granaries, and banking services, and of course, arrangements with the many smaller urban centers whose supply zones were being invaded by the expanding Parisian market. Discouraging such investment was the resistance of the local marketing interests plus the extreme instability of the necessary supply zone.

> In poor harvest years provisioning regions were distended beyond the normal range of mercantile networks. Merchants excited and emboldened by high urban prices penetrated virgin territory.... Until late in the eighteenth century, the incapacity of wholesale markets to organize these sporadic thrusts of metropolitan demand into new regions and balance them against local demand resulted in excess exports of grain from the marginal regions of supply.[55]

This is what Jean Meuvret called the market failure of seventeenth-century France.[56]

The fastest growing large city in this era, London, was also the one that came to rely most on market relations as opposed to supply regulation. As its population ballooned, from 200,000 in 1600 to 675,000 by 1750, its supply zone extended beyond the "home counties," and East Anglia until, by 1724, Daniel Defoe could write of the "general dependence of the whole country upon the city of London...for the consumption of its produce."[57] In the early seventeenth century governments persisted in the enforcement of a characteristic medieval provision policy, privileging the London market in times of dearth with export prohibitions and marketing requirements, prohibiting forestalling and regrating, and requiring the livery companies (guilds) to purchase reserve stores of grain for distribution to the poor.[58] By the end of the seventeenth century nearly all regulatory legislation had either been swept away or had fallen into desuetude. The size and relative accessibility of the London market generated price signals that provoked a massive geographical reorganization of agriculture, one cleverly revealed by Ann Kussmaul in her analysis of the changing patterns of seventeenth-century

55. Grantham, "Espaces privilégiés," 715–17; see also, Usher, *Grain Trade.*
56. Meuvret, *Le problème des subsistances.*
57. Quoted in F. J. Fisher, "The Development of the London Food Market, 1540–1650," *Economic History Review* 5 (1935): 51.
58. R. B. Outhwaite, "Dearth and Government Intervention in English Grain Markets, 1590–1700," *Economic History Review,* 2d ser., vol. 34 (1981): 389–406.

marriage seasonality.[59] By 1700 the government's concern was not how to keep a volatile urban population fed, but how to clear the national market of a growing oversupply of grain.

This story of comparative urban food supply, recited here in desperate brevity, is by now a familiar one. In England, urban growth stimulated the creation of a national market, regional specialization, and the reduction of transactions costs. London functions as an "engine of growth." The stomach of Paris may have been "revolutionary," as Braudel avers, but it was a revolution that brought disruption, instability, and constant tension. Meanwhile the claims placed on rural society by a Madrid or a Naples seemed unsustainable except by fiat. In Ringrose's account Madrid's rise enforced the decline of other Castilian towns, the diversion of productive resources for the provision of costly transportation services to a landlocked capital, and the discouragement of agricultural improvement by an oppressive requisitioning system.

How could broadly similar phenomena, the growth of very large urban markets, have had such divergent outcomes? Is the answer to this question to be sought in the character of these cities themselves, and in the behavior of their economic institutions and agents? One is tempted to answer affirmatively, drawing support from the well-entrenched concepts of generative and parasitic cities.[60] In my view there would be little to gain by focusing on the sources of income that sustained urban demand, whether they emanated from London merchants, Paris rentiers, or Madrid landowners. These cities certainly differed from one another, but these differences are easy to exaggerate: eighteenth-century London was, in fact, filled with landowners and officeholders. Braudel's observation that the great cities participated in the Industrial Revolution as spectators applies to London with only slightly less force than it applies to Paris or many other metropolitan centers.[61]

The "market building" activities emanating from the cities at the pinnacles of European urban networks are of greater significance than the scope of urban demand per se. I have already called attention to the varying mix of "push" and "pull," of requisitioning, and of market incentive that

59. Ann Kussmaul, *A General View of the Rural Economy of England, 1538–1840* (Cambridge: Cambridge University Press, 1990).

60. Bert F. Hoselitz, "Generative and Parasitic Cities," *Economic Development and Cultural Change* 3 (1954): 278–94. For an antidote to this way of thinking see E. A. Wrigley, "Parasite or Stimulus: The Town in a Pre-industrial Economy," in *Towns in Society*, ed. E. A. Wrigley and Philip Abrams (Cambridge: Cambridge University Press, 1978), 295–309.

61. Braudel, *Structures of Everyday Life*, 557.

characterized the great cities. The extent of investment in transportation improvements and policies that enabled commercial institutions to keep pace with new needs undoubtedly made a great deal of difference. Indeed, to classical economists such measures were the key to the achievement of economic growth. To them the opportunities for growth were located in the interconnections between market size, transport provision, commercial sophistication, and specialization of function. This "Smithian growth" is encapsulated in the famous dictum "the division of labor is limited by the extent of the market," with its promise that market growth sets the stage for every manner of economizing on transactions cost, which, in turn, encourages the specialization in production that can bring about lower costs.[62]

Differential success in securing Smithian growth can be inferred from these urban food supply situations, described above, and it would be foolish to deny the significance of such commercial advances. But the classical economist is duty bound to add that the achievements of Smithian growth reach their limits: market-driven specialization and the efficiency achieved via trade creation ultimately must yield to the inexorable force of Ricardo's doctrine of declining marginal returns in agriculture. Land is the one factor of production irrevocably fixed in supply: ever larger inputs of capital and labor would be needed to secure future unit increases of food output, and this could lead to nothing other than the stationary state. To the classical economists this was primarily theoretical, having to do with the *ultimate* consequences of certain "laws of economics." But many historians claimed to have found evidence of active constraints on market-driven growth in the preindustrial society. Until rescued by the technological breakthroughs of the Industrial Revolution (according to some), or by the peasantry-destroying institutional revolution of a capitalist bourgeoisie (according to others), preindustrial (feudal) society was confined to strict limits by the feeble power of agricultural productivity. Localized market dynamism, whether in the service of London's stomach, Amsterdam's money, or the Sun King's armies, hardly damages this account, for each of these exceptional situations exploited unique, nongeneralizable situations. Ultimately, the fact that urban Europe grew only from 10 percent of the total population in 1300, and again in 1500, to 13 percent in 1800 is decisive. "The proportion of city residents among the total population is determined by the relative size of the food surplus that country people, voluntarily or not, are able to allocate them." Thus

---

62. E. A. Wrigley, *Continuity, Chance and Change. The Character of the Industrial Revolution in England* (Cambridge: Cambridge University Press, 1988), 17–18.

writes Paul Bairoch in his wide-ranging *Cities and Economic Development from the Dawn of History to the Present*. By his calculations "the most advanced agricultural technology of traditional societies still needed, for the production of food and agricultural raw materials alone, the use of 70 to 75 percent of the entire work force,"[63] and they needed this in 1700 as much as in 1500.

In what has been presented thus far, the role of markets in economic development, while not stripped of all importance, is strictly limited and, in an ultimate sense, impotent. Its role is circumscribed by the suspicions of the "market-insensitive, immutable, unpersuadable peasant" and by declining marginal returns in agriculture. Markets can heighten the efficiency of such an economic regime, but they cannot change the regime itself. The preindustrial economy approaches a dead end, and the stage is set for a history of industrialization that emphasizes discontinuity, dualism, and the importance of exogenous forces, whether technological or political.[64]

What is wrong with this story? It is led astray, I believe, by a too-ready acceptance of the urban and rural sectors as separate worlds. Our attention should not be focused so much on the "stomach" of the growing cities as on the services they render: on their roles as centers of industrial and luxury production, as incubators of commercial techniques, and as agents of investment in transport and communications facilities, linking subordinate market towns in extended commercial networks. Instead of a history of two worlds, urban and rural, confronting each other at market stalls and weigh houses, we need a history of the construction of regional economies, where the urban sector is less remarkable for its aggregate size than for the manner in which it encourages a functional articulation of space. The critical achievement of this process of urban growth and regional development was a market structure in which peasants took the fateful step beyond market *contact* to market *orientation*.[65]

Market *contact* was the common posture of peasants in medieval and early modern Europe. Here, the household is routinely involved in market

---

63. Bairoch, *Cities and Economic Development*, 497; other exponents of agricultural stagnation are: Emmanuel Le Roy Ladurie and J. Goy, *Tithe and Agrarian History from the Fourteenth to the Nineteenth Century* (Cambridge: Cambridge University Press, 1982).

64. This is the message of E. A. Wrigley's classically inspired *Continuity, Chance and Change*.

65. The distinction made here is explored more fully by Jan de Vries, "Peasant Demand Patterns and Economic Development, 1550–1750," in *European Peasants and Their Market*, ed. E. Jones and W. N. Parker (Princeton: Princeton University Press, 1975), 205–66.

transactions—to pay taxes and/or to pay monetized rents, to purchase small amounts of goods not available locally—but this market activity involves "surpluses" in the sense of produce in excess of domestic consumption needs. The household's production system is not much changed from a hypothetical initial posture of self-sufficiency since it continues to be dedicated primarily to supplying directly the household's consumption package. The irregular trickle of marketed surplus flowing from such households, when gathered from thousands of producers, could support substantial concentrations of urban population, as we have seen. But we have also noted the inelasticity and undependability of these strategic supplies. The achievement of an economy characterized by widespread market contact is common enough, and could be brought about through command as readily as through free market mechanisms.

Altogether more consequential was the shift from market *contact* to market *orientation*, for this ordinarily entails a complete reallocation of the productive resources of the household, as well as a complete alteration in its patterns of consumer demand. Goods that had been produced at home are now purchased; services provided for one's self are provided by specialists; consumption habits change since the market offers new goods, old goods with new attributes, and new relative prices to replace those implicit in home consumption. Elsewhere, I have sought to call attention to the importance of this complex of interrelated household decisions by labeling the process whereby this transition could be made an "industrious revolution," driven by essentially Smithian, or commercial, incentives that preceded and prepared the way for the Industrial Revolution, which was driven by technological and organizational change.[66]

How did this industrious revolution manifest itself in preindustrial Europe? The earliest steps occurred in those peasant households that could follow the course of specialization by concentrating household labor in marketed food production. Increased allocational efficiency and the static and dynamic gains from internal trade creation accrued to such households as they reduced the amount of labor devoted to a wide variety of home handicrafts and services and replaced these activities with market-supplied substitutes.[67]

66. I develop the concept of an "industrious revolution" more fully in Jan de Vries, "Between Purchasing Power and the World of Goods: Understanding the Household Economy in Early Modern Europe," in *Consumption and the World of Goods*, ed. John Brewer and Roy Porter (London: Routledge, 1993), 85–132. See also, De Vries, "The Industrial Revolution and the Industrious Revolution," *Journal of Economic History* 54 (1994): 249–70.

A second dimension of the industrious revolution is revealed most clearly by protoindustrial and proletarian households as their underemployed labor on cotter holdings, the voluntary idleness of labor exhibiting a high leisure preference, and the low intensity of effort characteristic of most labor, gave way to longer and harder work. Truly regular, continuous, supervised labor was with few exceptions a product of the factory system, and was rare before the nineteenth century. A vast and evocative literature chronicles the painful adjustments laborers had to make to satisfy the imperious demands of the factory system.[68] However, it would be a grave error to conclude from this literature that the pace and regularity of employment before the factory reflected an unchanging traditionalism. In fact, a major intensification of labor, measurable in labor force participation rates, days worked per year, and effort per unit of labor, occurred in many areas in the course of the early modern era.[69]

A third element in this process of specialization of function and intensification of effort was the increasing efficiency with which the characteristically intermittent demand for agriculture labor was met by rural nonagricultural households, seasonal migrants, and even urban residents.[70] Agricultural labor always features seasonal peaks, and the intensification of agriculture to supply marketed foodstuffs, particularly bread grains, sharpened the demand for harvest labor. This great constraint was not relaxed until harvest mechanization began in the latter half of the nineteenth century.[71]

---

67. De Vries, *Dutch Rural Economy*, 4–17 and appendix C.

68. See Sidney Pollard, *The Genesis of Modern Management* (Harmondsworth: Penguin, 1965), and E. P. Thompson, "Time, Work Discipline and Industrial Capitalism," *Past and Present* 38 (1967): 56–97.

69. See, among others: Gregory Clark, Michael Huberman, and Peter Lindert, "A British Food Puzzle, 1770–1850," *Economic History Review* 48 (1995): 215–37; Gregory Clark, "Productivity Growth without Technical Change in European Agriculture before 1850," *Journal of Economic History* 47 (1987): 419–32; Hans-Joachim Voth, "How Long Was the Working Day in London in the 1750s: Evidence from the Courtroom" (Oxford: Nuffield College Working Paper, 1996); Jan de Vries, "An Employer's Guide to Wages and Working Conditions in the Netherlands, 1450–1850," in *Hours of Work and Means of Payment: The Evolution of Conventions in Pre-industrial Europe,* ed. Carol Leonard and Boris Mironov (Milan: 11th International Economic History Congress, 1994): 47–63.

70. J. Bompard, T. Magnac, and G. Postel-Vinay, "Emploi, mobilité et chomage en France au XIXe siècle: Migrations saisonnières entre industrie et agriculture," *Annales E.S.C.* 45:1 (1990): 55–76.

71. E. J. T. Collins, "Labour Supply and Demand in European Agriculture, 1800–1880," in *Agrarian Change and Economic Development,* ed. E. L. Jones and S. J. Woolf (London:

The production achievements of the industrious revolution were to (1) increase agricultural productivity through market-oriented specialization, (2) increase the flexibility of labor allocation, to provide the seasonal labor required by agricultural technology without enforcing extended underemployment, and (3) increase substantially the output of manufactures by making possible its decentralized location in rural areas.

The European population remained overwhelmingly rural until the nineteenth century, but it did not remain overwhelmingly agricultural, at least not if employment is defined by the actual allocation of days of labor rather than by the persistence of a minimal attachment to the land. In the cases of England and France several scholars have sought to measure an improvement in agricultural productivity in the 1500–1800 period. The efforts vary in method but invariably reveal substantial gains: E. A. Wrigley suggests a doubling of labor productivity between 1520 and 1800;[72] N. F. R. Crafts estimated that total factor productivity in English agriculture grew at a 0.6 percent annual rate early in the eighteenth century, but only 0.2 percent per annum toward its end;[73] Robert Allen, in his work on the English midlands, estimated annual rates of productivity growth of 0.2 to 0.3 percent over the seventeenth and eighteenth centuries.[74] In his recent book, Philip Hoffman, exploiting the evidence of land rents in the Paris basin, estimates the growth of total factor productivity in agriculture at 0.13 percent per annum over the long period 1500 to 1789, with growth concentrated in the sixteenth and eighteenth centuries.[75] The growth in the productivity of inputs speaks to the increased efficiency (via technological and/or organizational change) with which they are deployed. The growth of total output is something else, and this appears to have grown somewhere between 0.2 and 0.36 percent per

---

Methuen, 1969), 61–94; and "The 'Machinery Question' in English Agriculture in the Nineteenth Century," in *Agrarian Organization in the Century of Industrialization: Europe, Russia, and North America,* ed. George Grantham and Carol S. Leonard, Research in Economic History, Supplement 5 (Greenwich, Conn.: JAI Press, 1989), 203–18.

72. E. A. Wrigley, "Urban Growth and Agricultural Change: England and the Continent in the Early Modern Period," *Journal of Interdisciplinary History* 15 (1985): table 4, col. 8.

73. N. F. R. Crafts, *British Economic Growth During the Industrial Revolution* (Oxford: Oxford University Press, 1985), 83–85.

74. Robert Allen, "The Growth of Labor Productivity in Early Modern English Agriculture," *Explorations in Economic History* 25 (1988): 117–46; and idem, *Enclosures and the Yeoman* (Oxford: Oxford University Press, 1992).

75. Hoffman, *Growth in a Traditional Society,* 127–31.

annum over the period 1450–1789. Other regions of France performed differently—generally less well. But, the uniformly somber picture of an immobile French agriculture beloved of *Annaliste* historiography seems no longer tenable. This is a claim that George Grantham had already made effectively for the century after 1750.[76]

In general terms, between 1500 and 1800 broad areas of northern Europe succeeded in reducing the man-days of labor needed per hectoliter of grain produced from between six and eight to four or five, while the yields in hectoliters per hectare rose from between eight and ten up to twelve and fifteen. By Grantham's calculations, the proportion of the total population required to supply total grain needs (not total agricultural output) fell from about 50 percent to about 30 percent.[77] Moreover—and this is the important point of this review of agricultural productivity trends—the technical basis for achieving these high productivity levels existed by the early fourteenth century.[78] Even in 1800 this "medieval potential" was not exploited everywhere, but it had diffused broadly, and as Grantham observes, "it is the history of markets rather than the history of technology which explains the growth of agricultural labour productivity in [what Wrigley calls] the 'late organic economy.'"[79]

In this "history of markets" the growth of large consuming centers played a role, to be sure, but more as organizers of regional economies than as magnets for surpluses. Necessary as they were, by themselves they could transform very little beyond an immediate hinterland, an *intensitätinsel*. The required accompaniment to this initiative "from above" was a response "from below"—the industrious revolution of households using new market possibilities to exploit fully the potential of their available resources using the available technologies.

---

76. George Grantham, "The Growth of Labour Productivity in the Production of Wheat in the 'Cinq Grosses Fermes' of France, 1750–1929," in *Land, Labour and Livestock*, ed. Campbell and Overton, 340–63; George Grantham, "Agricultural Supply during the Industrial Revolution: French Evidence and European Implications," *Journal of Economic History* 49 (1989): 43–72.

77. George Grantham, "Division of Labour: Agricultural Productivity and Occupational Specialization in Pre-industrial France," *Economic History Review* 46 (1993): table 4.

78. Hugues, Neveux, *Vie et déclin d'une structure économique: Les grains du Cambrésis* (Paris: Mouton, 1980).

79. Grantham, "Division of Labour," 2–3.

On the surface the change appears minimal: urban populations, in towns of at least 5,000 inhabitants, rose from 10 to 13 percent between 1500 and 1800. The rural population remained overwhelmingly dominant, but, organized in more effective market networks, it became a much more complicated entity (see fig. 3.1): the 75 percent of the population devoted to agriculture in the early sixteenth century (50 percent growing grain) fell to approximately 50 percent (30 percent growing grain), while a population of craftsmen, industrial workers, transporters, and so forth, grew and emerged to fill, as it were, the interstices of economic life, exploiting opportunities signaled by a maturing market system, and establishing the basis for the Industrial Revolution, an event that continued rather than initiated the growth process.

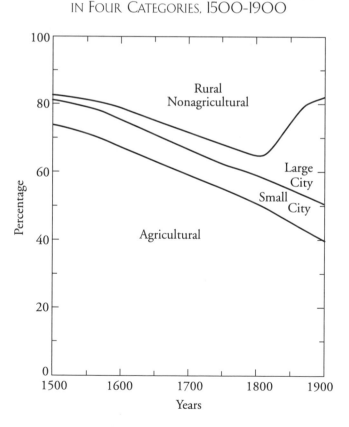

FIGURE 3.1. SHARES OF EUROPEAN POPULATION
IN FOUR CATEGORIES, 1500-1900

This approach to the relationship between urban markets and rural production rejects two common assumptions: that agricultural productivity was held in check by a technological ceiling, and that the inability to enlarge the agricultural surplus acted as a limiting factor to urban growth. While this may have been true generally of the early Middle Ages (and remained relevant to specific cases in later periods), agriculture ceased to act as the *universal* limiting factor thereafter. To put it in the simplest terms, in the early modern period the supply zone needed to support a city with foodstuffs was smaller than that necessary to sustain it demographically (given the excess mortality of large cities).[80] Moreover, large cities had energy needs (for heating, cooking, and industry) that placed claims on land in competition with the needs of agriculture.[81] Figure 3.2 offers a sketch of the various factors that might have placed limits on urban growth over time. One can see that the envelope of active limiting factors shifts, over time, from agriculture, to demography, to energy supplies. But, note also that, in Europe as a whole, the *actual* level of urbanization remained far below the *theoretically possible* level. Preindustrial Europe was "under-urbanized." That is, only a portion of the nonagricultural population actually resided in cities.[82] The explosive urbanization of the nineteenth century was, thus, not so much the result of a technological revolution lifting a ceiling that had long kept the lid on urban growth as it was the result of an organizational change that acted to make a new use of a potential that had long existed. This brings me to the second implication of this approach, which is that agricultural productivity growth before the nineteenth century did not generally face hard technological barriers. The diffusion of "best practice" depended more on markets than on technical knowledge. However, the relevant markets were not only those for the output of peasant enterprise, but also for the goods and services that could spur the household to an "industrious revolution." Without a reorientation toward the market at the household level, a great city's "stomach"

80. See De Vries, *European Urbanization*, 179–97, 231–33.

81. Ad van der Woude, Jan de Vries, and Akira Hayami, "Introduction: The Hierarchies, Provisioning, and Demographic Patterns of Cities," in *Urbanization in History*, 8–14. The significance of energy supplies is also emphasized in Paolo Malanima, *Energia e crescita nell'Europa pre-industriale* (Rome: NIS, 1996).

82. For an effort to measure the size of the nonagricultural population, divided into its urban and rural components, see E. A. Wrigley, "Urban Growth and Agricultural Change," *Journal of Interdisciplinary History* 15 (1985): 683–728.

could grow and grow, the only enduring result being the ill health of the regional economy.

FIGURE 3.2. SKETCH OF THE URBANIZATION CONSTRAINT
IN EUROPEAN DEVELOPMENT

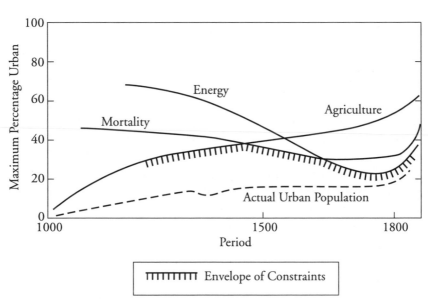

Chapter reprinted with permission from Review 22, no. 2 (1999): 121–49.

PART 3

Social and Cultural Matrices of Collective Destinies

Chapter 4

IMAGES OF SOCIETY

OTTAVIA NICCOLI

SIMPLICIUS AND THE TREE OF SOCIAL ORDERS

In the *Adventurous Simplicius Simplicissimus* by Jacob von Grimmelshausen, one of the most extraordinary works of seventeenth-century European literature, the main character has a peculiar dream. The trees around him were metamorphosing: on top of each tree a knight was sitting, and on the highest branches men, armed with every kind of war instrument—pikes, muskets, guns, drums—were crouched. "The roots, moreover, were made up of folk of little worth: artisans, laborers, mostly peasants, and the like; who, nevertheless, gave the tree its strength, and they renewed this strength when it was lost; they replaced the fallen leaves with their own people, with even greater damage to themselves; and meanwhile they complained of those who were in the tree, and not wrongfully, because the whole weight of the tree lay heavy on them and pressed them down." Other men sat on the intermediate branches, trying to snatch something from those who were higher: they were *landsknechts*, halberdiers, commissioners, unfortunate beings who for many years had grabbed lower branches, and then they had pushed their way up towards the top; so much so that they caused "a perpetual climbing and swarming up the tree, because everybody wanted to sit on the highest and happiest places above them." But suddenly the trees started to push one another and the men fell down heavily in heaps, stone dead, "and while I was watching," concludes Simplicius, "it seemed as if all those trees I was seeing were one single tree on top of which was Mars, the god of war, covering all Europe with its branches."[1]

1. Hans Jacob Christoph von Grimmelshausen, *The Adventurous Simplicissimus*, trans. A. T. S. Goodrick (Lincoln: University of Nebraska Press, 1962), 32–39.

The tree is therefore a representation of the social structure of seventeenth-century Germany and Europe, overwhelmed by the weight of war, which oppressed it with its shade and deprived it of every human and natural resource. The most direct source of Simplicius's dream can be identified in the *Visiones* of Philander von Sittwald, as can be seen in identifiable textual similarities, which, in turn, were based on *Dreams* by Francisco de Quevedo. In other words, this image referred to the late Renaissance extensions of a typically medieval genre. But the fact that Simplicius describes the society of the Germany of his time with the image of its different components climbing the branches of a tree, digging its own roots, and drawing their strength from the weak should not surprise us. It is an image that is not unusual in Counter-Reformation Europe, so much so that we already find a very similar one in a sixteenth-century German xylography, probably carved around 1519/20 by the so-called Petrarca Meister to illustrate a German version of the *De Remediis Utriusque Fortuna* by Petrarch (fig. 4-1). The engraving represents in fact a tree on whose branches sit, from the bottom to the top, artisans and merchants; then princes, nobles, and bishops; finally three kings, the pope, and the emperor. Almost buried amidst the roots, oppressed by the frightful weight of the tree of Christian society and of its components, lie two peasants who hold a pitchfork and a jointed stick. But on top of the tree, almost as a partial retribution for their oppressed comrades, are two peasants playing bagpipes, apparently making fun of all those—pope, emperor, kings—who in spite of everything are below them.

The engraving seems to have a connection with a passage of the text that emphasizes the fundamental equality among human beings:

Blut ist einander gleich	[The blood of the peasant
Des Baurn und Edelmanns....	And nobleman is the same....
Ein Vater mag seinen Son wol lieb haben	A father can love his son
Den Adel aber mag er nicht mit ihm teilen.	But he cannot share nobility with him.]

Because a peasant's blood is equal to that of a noble, a father can love his son deeply, but he cannot transfer nobility onto him; that is, only actions can make one noble, not blood.[2]

2. G. Weydt, "Der Standebaum: Zur Geschichte eines Symbols von Petrarca bis Grimmelshausen," *Simpliciana* 4, no. 5 (1983): 12.

FIGURE 4.1. PETRARCA MEISTER. *VON ADELIGEM URSPRUNG.*
THE PEASANT FOUNDATION OF MEDIEVAL SOCIETY.
(Walther Scheidig, *Die Holzschnitte des Petrarca-Meisters zu Petrarcas Werk von der Artzney bay-
der Glueck, des guten und widerwaertigen* [Augsburg, 1532; 1955]: 60. Reprinted by permission of the Arts Library, Belt Library of Vinciana, of California, Los Angeles.)

The engraving's image was figuratively indebted first of all to similar images present in contemporary manuscripts, in which the various social orders of society, disposed in an orderly way on the branches of a leafy tree, are struck with bow and arrows and caused to fall by Death, who pursues everybody with implacable equity (in the same way the soldiers and the civilians fell from the tree of war dreamed by Simplicius). In this case the metaphor, considering the sympodial ramification of the tree (for example, the nut tree or the chestnut tree), seems to have an agrarian origin. When you beat the branches of a nut tree, a chestnut tree, or an olive tree, the fruit falls randomly, without the possibility of a choice by the farmer; in the same way Death pursues humans randomly, without considering their social role.

But if we shift our attention to the engraving by the Petrarca Meister, which depicts a type of fir or larch with a monopodial ramification, that is, successive and parallel branches that depart from a single trunk, we can understand in a more precise way the meaning of the social stratification (the branches are rigorously one atop the other, not one next to the other). At the same time, it is clear that this representation depends on the iconographic tradition of Jesse's tree, which bears on its branches the successive generations from which the Virgin was born, and on the images derived from it, such as the familiar tree of a religious order, which bears on its branches its own saints and plunges its roots in its founder. Furthermore, if we observe the peasants in whose bodies the tree plunges its roots and therefore those from whom society draws its nutrition, we realize that it is one of the many images of the peasant who supports the weight of society, which in turn were inspired by the image of Atlas, who supports the world on his shoulders.

These are images that will go down to the French Revolution, which has an extensive imagery that shows the Third Estate—represented precisely as that of the peasant—crushed under the weight of France itself, of the monarchy, or of the other two estates.[3] These images have some sharply defined messages. Social stratification, for which the horizontal branches of the tree in the engraving by the Petrarca Meister are a metaphor, is an established fact in which the weakest strata, especially the peasants, support an overwhelming weight, because with their work they support the entire society. Yet, in spite of this, human beings are equal, especially in the face of death.

3. Ottavia Niccoli, *I sacerdoti, i guerrieri, i contadini: Storia di un'immagine della società* (Turin: Einaudi, 1979), figs. 10, 17, 28, 30–33, 35, 38.

METAPHOR AS POLITICAL CREATION THROUGH LANGUAGE

I have lingered on this example in order to introduce more convincingly the first point of my argument. Between the late Middle Ages and the French Revolution, a mass of mental and visual images crowded Europe to describe symbolically and effectively the structure of society, the government of the state, the relations of power between different groups and categories. The images present a literary and metaphorical valence; but they are deeply rooted in the culture that generated them, uniting creativity and long permanence. Our effort to understand the meaning of these images, therefore, should not be merely an examination of the metaphors with the purpose of reaching their true content, while ignoring the images as accessory or ornamental. To do so might be compared to scraping the varnish of a painting in a brutal restoration, or to eliminating all the signs of the times in the restoration of an ancient building. The metaphor and the image must certainly be explained, but always with the knowledge that they are an integral part of the reality that they are used to illustrate.

Researchers in social history and political thought have learned how to value metaphors as a supporting element, not only of language, but of reality itself. An entire science, metaphorology, is in fact born almost as a germination of semiotics and has been concerned, especially in the 1970s and 1980s, with offering us the rules of these rhetorical figures,[4] with classifying them systematically, and with following their progressive shifts of meaning over time. I will not expand on this, referring you to the surveys by Francesca Rigotti;[5] it is sufficient to say that it is a science whose linguistic foundations show a surprising versatility and offer undoubtedly fruitful results for several disciplines. Sociologists, for example, verifying the impact "that metaphors and cognitive paradigms have on our way of understanding reality"[6] and even of constructing it, have used metaphorical structure to read social organizations. Understanding the importance of a society's images owes a lot to

---

4. Harold Weinrich, *Metafora e menzogna: La serenità dell'arte* (Bologna: Il Mulino, 1976), 85–103.

5. Francesca Rigotti, *Metafore della politica* (Bologna: Il Mulino, 1989); idem, "Rassegna introduttiva sulle metafore storico-politiche," in *Il potere delle immagini: La metafora politica in prospettiva storica,* ed. Walter Euchner et al. (Bologna: Il Mulino, 1993), 7–30; in German as *Die Macht der Vörstellung: Die politische Metapher in historischer Perspektive* (Berlin: Duncker & Humblot, 1993).

6. Gareth Morgan, *Images: Le metafore dell'organizzazione* (Milan: Angeli, 1989), 415–16.

---

the recent reflections of social scientists on the role of language in the order-ing of reality. Whereas Bernard Barber in 1957 could consider it "a paradox" that one needed to "create certain abstractions" in order to understand social reality,[7] today the stress is on the priorities of what Barber called abstrac-tions. The fact that language, especially symbolic language, "is the key cre-ator of the social worlds that people experience, not a tool for describing an objective reality"[8] and that it can be ordered and modeled to simplify a sce-nario, such as the ambiguous and complex realities of politics, is certainly a newly acquired understanding. As Michael Walzer has noted, metaphors through their simplicity unify, and therefore, it can be added, they persuade, and are useful government tools.[9]

If this simplifying and remodeling work of political and social experi-ence through language is a relevant aspect of today's world, so much more was it at the beginning of the modern era. Some scholars in Italy and in Ger-many who have studied political metaphors and metaphors of power in a historical perspective have acknowledged, in the best cases, the capacity for social creation by these rhetorical figures. The results of these studies are apparent in the writings of Rigotti,[10] and in the proceedings of the two con-ferences held in Trent, published and edited together by Rigotti, Walter Euchner, and Pierangelo Schiera, as *Il potere delle immagini* and *Die Macht der Vorstellung*.[11] The studies in this collection analyze a fascinating series of specific metaphors actively used in the books of emblems and in political treatises between the sixteenth and nineteenth centuries: the king as a tree in whose shade people rest safely; the card game as a model of political rules; the language of horseback riding used to explain the role of the prince, skill-ful at disciplining horses, capable of inspiring devotion and respect, and ready to use reins and even spurs and at the same time to pet the animal. It is a line of research concerned with the theoretical implications of political dis-course, but perhaps in some cases, less interested in the changing context in which these metaphors are inserted and, therefore, in the variation of their function, in other words, in their historicity. The risk of this kind of research

7. Bernard Barber, *Social Stratification: A Comparative Analysis of Structure and Process* (New York: Harcourt Brace, 1957), 335.

8. Murray Edelman, *Constructing the Political Spectacle* (Chicago: University of Chi-cago Press, 1988), 103.

9. Quoted in Rigotti, "Rassegna introduttiva," 18.

10. Francesca Rigotti, *Metafore della politica*, and idem, *Il potere e le sue metafore* (Milan: Feltrinelli, 1992).

11. See n. 5 above.

appears to be the desire to obtain completeness and most of all its penchant for systematization. The effort to follow each variant of the metaphor can lead to simplistic cataloguing by drawing together similar uses of the image in periods of time chronologically very different one from the other, with little concern about the variables and especially about the diversified use of the images within changing historical contexts.

One example of this risk is found in a ponderous volume by Dietmar Peil,[12] which certainly provides a valuable inventory of these images, but which, by meticulously analyzing every fold or angle of each metaphorical field in all its possibilities and in every time period, makes it difficult to penetrate the specific functions that these images had in any given historical time and the precise motivations of their origin, their transformations, their disappearance or possible permanence (which is exactly what would interest the historian). Thus, here are the shepherd and the flock, the good shepherd and the bad shepherd, the faithful and the unfaithful sheepdog, and the animals of the flock; the hive, the bee, and their queen; the state as a body, and therefore also, as a sick body that requires medical or surgical care; the state as a machine, as a pendulum, as a clock (whence the idea of a functional hierarchy of the parts and the importance of the role of the watchmaker and of the mechanic); the state as a building, in which foundations, walls, doors, windows, and roof can have a meaning; and finally the state as a ship, with each part of the ship and every navigational circumstance given a paragraph, but without a proper treatment of the complete possible evolution of the image. The importance of metaphorical language in the political context and, more generally, in the self-understanding of society is undeniable, but the cataloguing proposed by Peil leads to the transformation of a metaphor from a concrete image to pure rhetorical paraphernalia. In comparison, recent articles with more limited ambitions are much more useful, because they are more specific and more concise, so that they indeed help us to understand a given ecclesiastic or political context, such as, for example, those by Gabriella Zarri on the ship of Saint Ursula, which I will mention later, and those by Robert Descimon on the political metaphor of the king's marrying the republic.[13]

12. Dietmar Peil, *Untersuchungen zur Staats- und Herrschaftsmetaphorik in literarischen Zeugnissen von der Antike bis zum Gegenwart* (Munich: Fink, 1983).

13. Gabriella Zarri, "La nave di Sant'Orsola," *Annali dell'Istituto Storico Italo-Germanico in Trento* 19 (1993): 277–303; Robert Descimon, "Les fonctions de la métaphore du mariage

From the Political Body to the Ship of State

The more interesting metaphors, because they are more concrete and less exposed to the risk of rhetorical dilution, are those, as it has properly been said, that are inseparably connected to the political thesis that they support.[14] An example is the organic image of society, which compares society to a body in which the head and the parts of the body have different roles and functions, but all equally necessary. This image imparts the idea of the social body as a living whole, whose categories are parts each having its own function, and the image cannot be suppressed without the disappearance of the theory to which the metaphor is connected. One of the most interesting aspects of the image of society as a body is that, as one follows the evolution of the image, it is possible to understand the shift in the importance attributed to individual parts and organs of the human body as well as to different parts of the social body. The origin of this image, as it is well known, is in the famous story of the stomach and the feet, which the West had learned essentially in two ways. First, there is the so-called apologue of Menenius Agrippa, which was narrated by Livy in its fullest version, but which is also present in different form in Dionysius of Halicarnassus, in Plutarch, and in numerous other classical authors.[15] The story goes back to the last third of the fifth century and belonged to a large propaganda campaign that aimed at asserting the necessity of *omonoia*, that is, of harmony, in the Greek polis. One ancient version of the story appears in the collection attributed to Aesop, in which stomach and feet contrast strongly: "The feet kept saying that they were superior in strength, that the stomach itself was carried around by them. 'My darlings,' replied the stomach, 'if I did not feed you, you would not be able to carry me.'"

The story had a large success in European literatures, and Peil, in a little volume entitled *Der Streit der Glieder mit dem Magen*, followed its different developments with particular attention to the fifteenth-century tradition.[16] The story continues to emphasize the necessity of harmony in every area of

---

politique du Roi et de la République: France, XVe–XVIIIe siècles," *Annales E.S.C.* 47 (1992): 1127–47.

14. Rigotti, *Il potere e le sue metafore*, 17.

15. Wilhelm Nestle, "Die Fabel des Menenius Agrippa," *Klio* 21 (1926/7): 350–60.

16. Dietmar Peil, *Der Streit der Glieder mit dem Magen: Studien zur Überlieferungs- und Deutungsgeschichte der Fabel des Menenius Agrippa von der Antike bis ins 20. Jahrhundert* (Frankfurt am Main: Peter Lang, 1985).

social life. For example, an Italian sonnet that comments on Aesop's story, which can be dated perhaps around 1462, compares the limbs to foreign merchants far from their homelands and the stomach to the warehouse which they frequent, as a necessary condition for the prospering of their mercantile activity thanks to the solidarity among fellow countrymen:[17]

[Il ventre si simiglia al fontichare	The stomach resembles the frequenting of the warehouse
e si le membra agli altri merchadantix	And the limbs resemble the other merchants.
Finch'al fonticho dura e sta constanti,	As long as the situation is stable at the warehouse,
niun di loro può pericholare;	None of them is in danger;
come il fonticho vien a 'bandonare	As soon as the warehouse is abandoned
e che nel mercandar sono distanti,	And the merchants are far away,
de signori diventa tristi fanti,	The rich men become sad knaves,
nè 'l fonticho non gli può più aiutare.]	And the warehouse cannot help them anymore.

However, the apologue passed to the genre of political treatises primarily through another path. It was well known in Stoic circles, and it is probably there that Paul of Tarsus learned it, drawing from it the famous doctrine set out in the first letter to the Corinthians: "in fact the body, even though it is one, has many parts, and all the parts, even though they are many, are a single body...the eye cannot say to the hand 'I do not need you,' nor the head to the feet 'I do not need you'" (1 Cor. 12:12, 21). This passage, as is known from the work of Ernst Kantorowicz[18] among others, inspired John of Salisbury's *Polycraticus*, which again was the origin of the *Corpus Reipublicae Mysticum*'s image: in the same way as Christ is the head of the church's body, whose members are the faithful, so too the prince is the head of the state's body.

In this form, the image had an immense success, on which I will not dwell, because Peil and others before him have already studied this. I would only like to stress that the apologue in its original form underlines the necessity of harmony between the parts of the body and their reciprocal relations.

17. Peil, *Der Streit der Glieder*, 39.

18. Ernst H. Kantorowicz, *The King's Two Bodies: A Study in Medieval Political Theology* (Princeton: Princeton University Press, 1957), 194–232.

It is, therefore, an image of a functional and not of a hierarchical society, according to the typology laid out by the Polish sociologist Stanislaw Ossowski.[19] The later evolution of the doctrine insists more and more on a hierarchy among the different parts of the body. This is very evident in late Renaissance French and English treatises, which stress the themes of nobility and the honor that is due to it. As the Parisian theologian Jean Michel observed in his *Anatome corporis politici*, published in 1564, the feet should be identified with the farmers, who are low and adhere to the land (a common identification), and the head, "in quo est velut intellectus voluntatis et memoriae domicilium, toti corpori supereminet: sic in corpore politico."[20] Even more defined is, a few years later, the position of François de L'Alouëte, who strongly emphasized the different levels of dignity of different social conditions:

> Les uns avec plus d'honneur et dignité, les autres avec plus basse et vile condition, à l'exemple du cors humain, auquel toutes les partes ne sont pas semblables ni de pareille estime, encores qu'elles soient toutes bien necessaires. Car celles qui sont destinées pour servir au chef, tiennent le premier lieu, et les autres après jusques aus piés, qui tiennent le dernier et le plus vil de tous, encores qu'il soutiennent tout le cors.[21]

The farmers therefore live buried in the earth, and even though they are the lowliest, they sustain the state body; if we imagine it as the trunk of a tree, we return to the *Standenbaum* of the Petrarca Meister. But let us follow instead the fate of the prince, the head of the social body, assuming the same role as Christ in the church (although it is important to specify that in some contemporary treatises the prince is the heart of the state, following Galen's theory according to which the heart is the seat of the vital spirit). One of the most common extensions of the state/body metaphor was the pathological-therapeutic one: if society is like a body, it can be infected by diseases, and it might be necessary to cure it with medicaments, purges, bleedings. We know that Jean Bodin said that revolutions represent the evacuation of the sinful humors of the state body;[22] but common also was the idea of the possible

19. Stanislaw Ossowski, *Class Structure in the Social Consciousness*, trans. Sheila Patterson (New York: Free Press, 1963), 66.

20. Peil, *Untersuchungen zur Staats- und Herrschaftsmetaphorik*, 331.

21. François de L'Alouëte, *Traité de nobles et des vertus dont ils sont formés* (Paris, 1577), 20.

22. Jean Bodin, *Les six livres de la République* (Paris, 1583), 634.

amputation of those members of society who, with their corruption, threatened to infect the entire body. It was understood, James I remarked, that such an operation was feasible for any member of society except the head: "What state the body can be in, if the head, for any infirmity that can befall it, be cut off, I leave to the readers' judgement."[23]

The English monarch could not imagine that in a few years the metaphor he used would become reality in his own country, and that a head would be separated from the body, in the double sense of the physical decapitation of Charles I and of the clear division between the monarch—the head of the state—and the body of English society. It is interesting that Michael Walzer revisited the English Revolution following exactly the history of the organic metaphor of the state. This metaphor appeared more and more unsatisfactory to the Puritan preachers, who felt that it could not render the idea of the radical reformation of society that they upheld. Thus, considering themselves new pilgrims on voyage towards new skies and a new land, they steadily replaced this image in their sermons with that of the ship of state, a ship whose captain, if insane and incapable, could and had to be replaced. This was the argument used in 1649 during the trial of Charles I:

> When the pilot or master of a ship at sea, be either so far over-come and distempered with drink, or otherwise disabled…so that he is incapable of acting the exigencies of his place, for the preservation of the ship, being now in present danger…any one or more of the inferior mariners, having skill, may, in order to the saving of the ship and of the lives of all that are in it, very lawfully assume, and act according to the interests of a pilot.[24]

The image of the ship also had a long history, having originated, like that of the body, in the New Testament. Peter's barque which plied the waves of the Sea of Galilee in Matt. 8:23–26 was the symbol, since Tertullian, of the church which is saved by the presence of Christ.[25] A large iconography, from Giotto's mosaic in the portico of Saint Peter's in the Vatican to a multitude of widely marketed prints and engravings, had spread it to every social level during the Middle Ages and the Renaissance. Among others, a Modenese

---

23. Peil, *Untersuchungen zur Staats- und Herrschaftsmetaphorik*, 459.

24. John Goodwin, 1649, quoted in Michael Walzer, *The Revolution of the Saints: A Study in the Origins of Radical Politics* (Cambridge, Mass.: Harvard University Press, 1965), 181.

25. Rigotti, *Metafore della politica*, 42–46.

engraving, presumably from the early sixteenth century, shows a crowned king who, from his fragile boat, passes into a powerful ship that carries the Virgin pointing to Jesus crucified on the mast. The caption "The Ship of Salvation" is self-explanatory.[26] This type of image had many variants, whose meaning was, however, always to be connected to the idea of salvation offered by the church thanks to the permeating presence of Christ. A peculiar conflation of this representation with that of the voyage of St. Ursula showed Ursula and her companions collaborating with the pope and the bishops in piloting the boat, an iconography that was widespread between 1450 and 1550 as it was used on prints that propagandized St. Ursula's German confraternities. (In fact, the confraternities themselves were called *Ursula-Schiffleine*, Ursula's little boats, because they were meant to be places of refuge for the faithful).[27]

The transfer of the ship and the navigation metaphor from the religious to the political sphere is well detailed by Peil. I will not dwell on it. Rather, I would like to point out an unusual example regarding the iconographic context, even though we only have extant verbal descriptions of it. It is one of those twenty-four paintings, today lost, executed by Nicoló dell'Abate in 1571, the year following the peace of Saint-Germain, for the solemn entry into Paris of King Charles IX and his wife, Elizabeth of Austria. In it the Master of Fontainebleau represented the marriage of Cadmus and Harmony, based on a project that the poet Jean Dorat drew from the Dionysiacs of Nonno of Panopolis, published two years before. Cadmus and Harmony, "qui est la paix," ruled on a big ship, symbol of Paris and France, which finally, after the edict of Saint-Germain, seemed to have found good hopes for calmer seas. The whole ceremony was based on this symbolism. On the bridge of Notre Dame, the royal couple had been offered a large silver ship with the Dioscuri, which on the basis of an emblem by Andrea Alciati, *Spes Proxima*, indicated "certain presage de temps calme…, veu les orages et tempestes qui ont esté depuis dix ans an la France," as the contemporary description of the royal entrance mentions.[28] Even the banquet table was decorated with sugar ships, so that the king would not forget his duty as supreme pilot.[29]

---

26. *I legni incisi della Galleria Estense: Quattro secoli di stampa nell'Italia Settentrionale*, ed. La Soprintendenza per i Beni Artistici e Storici per le province di Modena e Reggio Emilia (Modena: Mucchi, 1986), 87–88 and fig.29.

27. Zarri, "La nave di Sant'Orsola."

28. Simon Bouquet, *Bref et sommaire recueil…de l'ordre tenu à la joyeuse et triomphante entrée de Charles IX…en sa bonne ville et cité de Paris* (Paris, 1572), cc. 3v–34v.

The hopes for a religious peace were to be frustrated the following year with the Saint Bartholomew's Day Massacre. But the maritime theme and the piloting of the ship expressed very well the hopes of the Pléiade poets, who had organized the royal entrance in a moment when the king seemed capable of guiding France out of the tempest of religious wars.

IMAGES OF SOCIETY: FIGURES AND PROPAGANDA

This essay has been more about images than metaphors, an easy transition. There is a very beautiful essay by Fritz Saxl, "Continuity and Variation in the Meaning of Images," which, though published more than a half century ago (originally a lecture given at Reading University in 1947), is most apt to explain this point. Saxl illustrates with a series of examples the variable meaning of the word "image," starting with a simple metaphor that was used in the jurisprudence of the thirteenth century ("my house is my castle"), then recalling the different uses of solar symbolism as an allusion to royalty, finally considering images that are more specifically visual, as for example the representation of Christ as a fish. Metaphors and figures therefore show their reciprocal influences and their strong presence in the history of culture.[30]

As mentioned, Murray Edelman asserted that language does not reflect an objective reality but, rather, creates it. This is even more the case when the image or the metaphor, is figurative, a visual metaphor. Because of this, visual images do not run the risk of literary metaphors, that is, of weakening until they become idioms. A metaphor's universality, when it is visible, appears enormously increased, as does its persuasive power. When an image passes from the imagination to a painting, sculpture, or drawing, it acquires a concreteness, a physicality, a capacity of impact that it would be difficult for a written text to achieve. The Italian word *immagine*, like the English *image*, has in effect a semantic ambiguity (as we have seen, we always need to come to terms with linguistic problems), which allows us to shift quickly from the written word to the visual figure and vice versa, from literature to iconography (metaphor, on the other hand, is only literary), and therefore it allows us to gather a series of words and images, and to read their evolution according to the change in historical context. The place in which figure and

29. Frances A. Yates, "Introduction," in *La joyeuse Entrée de Charles IX Roy de France en Paris, 1572* (Amsterdam, 1572; New York: Johnson Reprints, 1973).
30. Fritz Saxl, *Lectures*, 2 vols. (London: University of London, 1957),1: 1–12.

word meet is the mind, "the high imagination" in which, according to Dante (*Purgatory*, 17.25), images rain down from the sky.

On mental images, on their allowing us to shift from the visual to the written field, and on their importance for the writer, Italo Calvino gave us some enlightening pages in one of his *Lezioni Americane*, the one dedicated to visibility. This might seem a digression from our research, but it is not completely so. Calvino, beginning with the line by Dante cited above, explained that his writing often started with an image that had fallen like rain into his imagination, "an image that for some reason appeared to him dense with meaning,"[31] and which he tried to develop, to correlate to others, and to translate into words. It is surprising that precisely the same procedure was used by Jacob Burckhardt, according to his own explanation, in his *Civilization of the Renaissance in Italy.*

> When I cannot start with an intuition, I am not productive. By intuition I mean also the spiritual perception, for example, the historical impression that is produced by the sources. What I reconstruct historically is not the result of criticism or speculation, but of the imagination, which aims at filling the gaps left by intuition.[32]

It is true that these images were born in the imagination of the Swiss historian because of the sources that he was studying and not spontaneously, but they represented for him a necessary passage in the elaboration of his historical writing, whose object was to render "visible" the reality of the past. Therefore, the mental image is an important passage for the elaboration of and reflection on history and political thought, both today and in the past.

Mental images can become historically relevant metaphors or, to express this better, what we try to investigate is the concrete use of metaphors within the images of society considered as mental configurations and as visual images. As is clear, as explained above, visual images are diffused in strata larger than those that generate the political metaphor, because the diffusion of certain iconographic material is undoubtedly larger than the diffusion of a political metaphor inside a historical treatise could be, and most of all it is addressed to larger social categories. Hundreds of prints were circulated in

---

31. Italo Calvino, *Lezioni americane: Sei proposte per il prossimo millennio* (Milan: Mondadori, 1993), 99.

32. Jacob Burckhardt, *Lettere (1838–1896)* (Palermo, 1993), letter to Willibald Beyschlag, 14 June 1842.

Paris and then in the rest of France in 1789, which illustrate the oppression under which the Third Estate lived with the image of a farmer crushed under the weight of a noble and a priest, and his liberation from the chains around him in the assault of the Bastille. These were certainly more diffused and had a much larger impact than the contemporary pamphlets. It was said that the prints that represented the assault of the Bastille, which were circulated in Paris a few days after 14 July under the title *Le réveil du Tiers État*, were common in bedrooms, in the same way as the fashionable pastoral painting by Fragonard and Boucher had been a few years earlier. They contributed therefore to diffuse the image of an oppression that had been definitively eliminated. Two components of society oppressed the one component that up to that moment had been the weakest, but now, by grabbing a gun, had demonstrated that it was able to use force.[33]

The use, in this as in many other prints, of the image of the three estates showed the persistence in France of the threefold image of society, according to which there exist three social functions and only three, and therefore three estates willed by God, engaged respectively in prayer, war, and working the land. This image, already noticed by Georges Dumézil in the Indo-European sphere, which had surfaced in fourteenth-century England and then had passed through France, has been read by Georges Duby as the most vivid expression of the feudal imagination.[34] In the beginning of the fourteenth century, it had materialized in a specific institution of the French monarchical state, the assembly of the Estates General, which had met a few times during the Middle Ages, then during the religious wars, again in 1614, and finally had been summoned in 1789, and maintained in its immutability the memory of the feudal institutions that it had somehow symbolized. Now, its use in popular prints helped to diffuse the awareness of the iniquity of the clergy and nobility, and of their present weak position, which in turn contributed to the destruction of the privileges that were implied. On the other hand, the representation of the Third Estate as a farmer or as a bourgeois dressed in black and associated with symbols of land cultivation such as a spade or plow, stressed a politically important reality, namely, that delegates of the Third Estate, even if members of the city bourgeoisie, represented a block of composite forces, to which belonged also the general body of farmers that in those same weeks, moved by the *grand peur*, were assaulting the

33. Niccoli, *I sacerdoti, i guerrieri, i contadini*, fig. 27.
34. Georges Duby, *The Three Orders: Feudal Society Imagined*, trans. Arthur Goldhammer (Chicago: University of Chicago Press, 1980).

castles and setting the feudal archives afire. It was probably the awareness that these images expressed, and undoubtedly helped to diffuse, that permitted the antifeudal decrees of 5 and 11 August 1789. This is how an image of society generated an institution, and on the other hand, became an instrument of political propaganda against itself, facilitated in this by its extraordinary simplicity and versatility. It did this even though it could no longer, at least after the thirteenth century, adequately describe social reality. During a conference held in Manchester in 1988, various voices, among those of Peter Burke and William Doyle, rose to express perplexity in the use of the terminology of the social orders, which was appropriately considered incapable of describing a society exhaustively;[35] but there remains the fact that a twisted social awareness can equally have an important political function.

ESTATES, ORDERS, CLASSES

Sociological research about contemporary Europe also stresses the fact that the images of social stratification can influence the preconditions of actions, so much so that we have to refer to them if we want to produce reliable interpretations of a certain behavior.[36] Therefore, we need to study the images of society, in order to understand how humans in every historical time saw and perceived themselves, and acted accordingly. A recent article by Bernard Lepetit in *Annales* proposes a new reading of the "social question" theme, based on a book by sociologist Robert Castel. Lepetit observes that, between the late Middle Ages and the beginning of the modern age, an image of society that represents social relations and functions in a specific order, hierarchical or not, cannot be but alien to a certain number of marginal or supernumerary elements that do not have a precise place in the social structure. Now, the social structure also has a cohesive spatial value: as Georg Simmel wrote, "in the majority of the relations among individuals and groups, the concept of limit becomes somehow important."[37] Therefore, the label that society attributes to those "extras" is that of "vagabonds," people who are devoid of a fixed territorial space, who do not have "a place and a fire," as they used to

35. M. L. Bush, ed., *Social Orders and Social Classes in Europe since 1500: Studies in Social Stratification* (London: Longman, 1992).

36. Carlo Mongardini, "L'immagine della stratificazione sociale," in *Modelli e rappresentazioni della stratificazione sociale,* ed. C. Mongardini and M. L. Maniscalco (Milan: Angeli, 1987).

37. Georg Simmel, *Sociologia* (Milan: Edizioni di Communità, 1989), 531.

say. This happens even though this category includes all sorts of people, from lunatics to unemployed workers to deserters.[38] In this case, society is simply viewed as a closed space: the closed space of the walled city, which protects and sustains the residents, besides the fact that it shuts up the more unstable individuals in hospitals, orphanages, poorhouses or workhouses. We can remark that the "extra" or marginal individuals who are content with their situations will be considered seriously sinful, because they are indirectly harmful to the image of society, and will be appropriately punished, as was a young boy of whom the Modenese ecclesiastic Gian Battista Scanaroli relates that, already poor, but having inherited a large patrimony, he dissipated it all, and was happy (*laetus cantillabat*) about his recovered freedom from riches, going back to his poverty almost greedily. "Non secus ac canis ad vomitum, aut sus ad volutabrum. Dignus sane qui gravissima poena punitus fuisset," concluded the indignant Scanaroli.[39]

In 1957 Stanislaw Ossowski observed that the different ways of conceiving a social structure are themselves elements of the social situation and allow us to understand the founding elements of society for the people that belong to that group. On the basis of these elements, people act on society itself. Its representations, even though they do not correspond to social reality, do in fact influence its programs, its projects, and its institutions.[40] It is precisely on the basis of these considerations that recent research has stressed how the many institutions that blossomed in Italy at the beginning of the early modern period for the support of the so-called shameful poor—those who were ashamed of asking for assistance explicitly, because they had fallen from an honorable condition—are inseparably linked to a specific image of society.[41] That image was of medieval origin, made up of presupposed social positions of divine origin, in which mobility is unacceptable, and even degrading or unthinkable, so much so that, in order to express a similar concept, interpretative categories and even appropriate linguistic instruments are missing. The society between the late Middle Ages and the beginning of the early modern period avoided the obstacle by using, in order to understand and describe those situations, the instruments that it had, in this case the

---

38. Bernard Lepetit, "Le travail de l'histoire (note critique)," *Annales E.S.C.* 61 (1996): 525–38.

39. Giovanni Battista Scanaroli, *De visitatione carceratorum libri tres* (Rome, 1655), 238.

40. Ossowski, *Class Structure in the Social Consciousness*, 9–10.

41. Giovanni Ricci, *Povertà, vergogna, superbia. I declassati fra Medioevo ed Età moderna* (Bologna: Il Mulino, 1996).

symbolic language of a feeling that was widespread and was strongly perceived at that time, in other words, shame.

The impoverished noble is ashamed because he is in a position of emptiness: because society, in the view of the time, was shaped, as it has repeatedly been said, by divine will with fixed social orders, each of which has a specific function in the universal economy of society. Thus, to be excluded from one of them meant somehow annihilating oneself and at the same time contradicting the divine will. Therefore, it becomes necessary, not only for the impoverished noble, but for the whole of society in which he lives, to erase this anomalous situation and reestablish the harmed social order, secretly offering to him the means to reenter, at least apparently, into the order in which he had originally been placed. Alms were to be given not for his survival, but for the dignity that was thought necessary to his condition. "Nobili sane est relinquendum ut possit vivere habita ratione suae nobilitatis," writes André Tiraqueau in the middle of the sixteenth century, "ut proinde non cogatur pauperum cibi vesci."[42] Proper institutions provided for this, not only saving the noble from poverty, but also preserving the *ratio suae nobilitatis*, the principle of the order to which he belongs. This research itinerary demonstrates once again the importance of the links between the so-called history of mentalities and the history of institutions. These two fields of historiography cannot but help each other with reciprocal connections, even though the researcher has to be constantly aware of the distinction between the two plans. In fact, the methodological problem that Ricci had to face is that of a mingling of reality on one hand and of an image of society on the other. This problem can be solved as he did in his book, accepting the creative force of images and of the words that articulate them, and verifying their concrete effects on the institutions.

Linguists and sociologists can therefore give each other a hand, and historians can resort to them for support in their research and in the analysis of the representations of society. In fact, renouncing such assistance in this historical field can create notable setbacks. In 1966, an international conference organized by Roland Mousnier proposed to clarify the historical use of the terminology of social stratification, specifically the terms *castes, orders, classes.*[43] The result of the work was bewildering, showing the difficulties in the reciprocal understanding of the participants, due first of all to the attempt by

42. André Tiraqueau, *De nobilitate et iure primigeniorum* (Lyon, 1559), 168.
43. Rodney Needham, ed., *Problèmes de stratification sociale: Actes du colloque international (1966)* (Paris: PUF, 1968).

some of them—which today frankly appears naive—to overlap and mingle modern terminology and social reality with the terminology of the time, which obviously cannot be reciprocally interchanged; but they can be used alternatively, if the differences are kept in mind. In addition, the participants were insufficiently aware of the history and evolution of the terms discussed, and ignorant of the sociological debate, especially American, on social stratification, as Lawrence Stone noted in reviewing the proceedings. In fact, those scholars would have found useful a 1958 article written by linguist Tullio De Mauro, "Storia e analisi semantica di 'classe,'" which shows the Linnaean origin of the term *class* and the tumultuous evolution during the eighteenth century of the study of botany and of the representation of society.[44] They would also have found useful a few pages on the same topic written by Ossowski in 1957, which, with respect to the larger picture that De Mauro offers, supply some other data, for example, underlining the importance of the revolution in France from the passing of the term *état*, used in the *Encyclopédie* and by Abbé Sieyès, to the term *class* that we find in Babeuf and Saint-Simon.

Equally, those scholars in 1966 could have found useful material in those American sociological essays, which, from Talcott Parson to Kingsley Davis, from Bernard Barber to Melvin Tumin, between the 1940s and the 1960s, had researched the problem of social stratification and of the terminology in which it could be expressed (even though their perspective is today in great part dated). An essay written by Kingsley Davis in 1942 is worth mentioning, because it explains, under a sociological point of view, the terms *class, caste, état;* also useful can be a chapter of the manual *Social Stratification* that Bernard Barber dedicates to the same themes with a slightly different angle. Mousnier, in fact, largely referred to this work earlier in 1965, especially in *Hiérarchies sociales*, even though he simplified terms and only mentioned the work in the final bibliography, as Armand Arriaza pointed out in a quite ironic article in 1980.[45]

---

44. Tullio De Mauro, "Storia e semantica di 'classe,'" *Rassegna di Filosofia* 7 (1958): 309–21.

45. Kingsley Davis, "A Conceptual Analysis of Stratification," *American Sociological Review* 7 (1942): 309–21; Barber, *Social Stratification*; Roland Mousnier, Jean-Pierre Labatut, and Yves Durand, eds., *Problèmes de stratification sociale: Deux cahiers de la noblesse pour les Etats Généraux de 1649–51* (Paris: PUF, 1965); Roland Mousnier, *Social Hierarchies, 1450 to the Present*, trans. Peter Evans (New York: Schocken, 1973); and Armand Arriaza, "Mousnier and Barber: The Theoretical Underpinning of the 'Society of Orders' in Early Modern Europe," *Past and Present* 89 (1980): 39–57.

The debate, which continued until a recent conference, "Social Orders and Social Classes in Europe since 1500,"[46] should not let us forget—with reference to images of society—that those who lived in the Europe of the *ancien régime* undoubtedly saw themselves in terms of orders and not of classes. I do not consider acceptable, at least not completely, Peter Burke's comment (1992) about the fact that these constructions reflected only the interest of nonworking people, and therefore of the well-to-do.[47] The image, even though produced at the high levels of society, had certainly been absorbed by the lower levels too, through channels of communication that were widely diffused, like fabliaux, pictures, or church sermons. This, of course, does not mean that the historian should not consider from a different perspective certain phenomena that the people of the time were not able to see, and describe them with the terminology of today. As Hans-Ulrich Wehler wrote, certain categories used in the social research of the present "can demonstrate their analytical and explicative power as functional concepts (like role, status, reference group, social structure) as well as for previous stages of society."[48]

On a Ladder, in a Town Square

I conclude by touching upon the problem of the articulation of society in spatial terms. "It is virtually impossible to do without spatial metaphors when talking about society," said Peter Burke.[49] In fact, in common language, we speak about a social *ladder* or *stratification*, of superiors and inferiors, of social climbers, and so forth. It is equally evident that these metaphors are rarely neutral, because space is characterized by polarities (up, down, right, left) to which we assign positive and negative values, as it has been shown by a large range of sociological, anthropological, and historical studies.[50] In the images of society, hierarchy is expressed by one of these polarities, and sometimes in combination. We saw that the image of society as body attributed the lowest value to the feet, personified by the farmers; also that the *Standenbaum* attributed to the roots and the branches an increasing value as one moves upward;

46. *Social Orders and Social Classes in Europe since 1500,* ed. Bush.

47. Peter Burke, *History and Social Theory* (Ithaca: Cornell University Press, 1992).

48. Hans-Ulrich Wehler and Jürgen Kocha, *Sulla scienza della storia: Storiografia e scienze sociali* (Bari: De Donato, 1983), 53.

49. Peter Burke, "The Language of Orders in Early Modern Europe," in *Social Orders and Social Classes in Europe since 1500,* 1–12.

and that the characters in Simplicius's dream were also climbing toward the top. But the spatial models of the society of the *ancien régime* are many. *The World Machine: Everyone Tries to Be above Their Friend*, by the engraver Giuseppe Maria Mitelli of Bologna from the late seventeenth century, for example, has ten people form the shape of a pyramid; or *The Ladder of Social Orders*, a German engraving contemporary to that of Mitelli, reproduces another iconographic theme that had an immense success, that of the ladder of the ages; or, to go back to the threefold image of society, we find images in which a farmer carries on his shoulder the priest and the aristocrat, or the table at which they eat, or an egg in which they dip their bread. In 1911 a *Pyramid of the Capitalist System* was printed in Cleveland, in which workers and farmers (who bore labels such as "we feed all" and "we work for all") carried a kind of cake with many layers on which were, in order, lazy bourgeois ("we eat for you"), armed soldiers ("we shoot at you"), priests of different religions ("we fool you"), kings and state leaders ("we rule you"), and finally a big bag of dollars ("capitalism"). All these images evidently referred to a hierarchy, albeit a clearly unjust one.

In a peculiar encyclopedic compilation of the late sixteenth century, we can find a different reading of society as a town square of approximately circular form, in which the spatial values seem to decrease gradually from the center toward a negatively valued periphery. *La piazza universale di tutte le professioni del mondo* [The universal town square of all the professions in the world] by the Lateran canon Tomaso Garzoni was published in 1585 in Venice, dedicated to Alfonso II, duke of Ferrara, and consists of 155 discourses, each of which describes one or more jobs, trades, or positions, for a total of about 400 activities, sometimes mentioned in different parts with a total of 544 different denominations. The work offers us what we could call an all-encompassing vision of the society of the time of Garzoni, rich with interesting and peculiar details, even though a large part of the text comes from other authors or, more often, from sometimes ancient repertoires. But we should still appreciate the extremely detailed descriptions of some craftsman

---

50. Carlo Ginzburg, "High and Low: The Theme of Forbidden Knowledge in the Sixteenth and Seventeenth Centuries," *Past and Present* 73 (1976): 28–41; Robert Hertz, *La preminenza della destra ed altri saggi* (Turin: Einaudi, 1994); J. A. Laponce, "Hirschman's Voice and Exit Model as Spatial Archetype," *Social Science Information* 13 (1974): 67–81; J. A. Laponce, *Left and Right: The Topography of Political Perceptions* (Toronto: University of Toronto Press, 1981); and Rodney Needham, ed., *Right and Left: Essays on Dual Symbolic Classification* (Chicago: University of Chicago Press, 1973).

activities and some long lists of objects or instruments connected with them. On the other hand, what interests us here is that the functional picture of the social articulations that had been expressed by the Middle Ages has completely disappeared in *La piazza universale*. Society appears like a system of atoms that can be infinitely multiplied. It does not look like a tree anymore, or like a pyramid, or the human body, but like a circular town square in which some characters are in the center, some will have to be confined at the margins, and some will even be in the "pissing corners, far away from where the nobility walks, in order not to soil the doctors' gowns or the soldiers' swords."[51] The list of professions, activities, and life situations contained in the work does not appear to have an order, even though the beginning, falsified by later insertions, seems to conserve the traditional scheme of the late medieval list of social orders (emperor, governor, prelates, jurists, surgeons, notaries, attorney). The only clearly defined division is that between "honorable" and "dishonorable" professions or trades, classified independently from the social utility of the job itself, but according to "the nature of the material worked or the material with which one is in contact," or to the "hygienic and clean conditions of the workplace," referring therefore, for example, to the dirtiness of chimney sweepers, tinkers, blacksmiths, dyers, linen drapers, hemp workers, and so forth,[52] considered ignoble, whereas wool workers, for example, would not be considered so, "because the most sumptuous, honorable clothes that can be created for a gentleman are made of the finest woollen draperies."[53]

Today studies on social mobility purposely avoid any term that could make us think in visual terms of a ladder with higher and lower steps, or of an allocation of spatial values, and prefer to speak of passages, paths, mobility, or fluidity.[54] It is difficult to translate these words in a visual image. Is giving up images perhaps the necessary condition for today's research on the structure of society?

Chapter translated by Cristina Farronato

51. Tomaso Garzoni, *La piazza universale di tutte le professioni del mondo*, ed. Paolo Cherchi and Beatrice Collina (Turin: Einaudi, 1996), 1360.

52. Ugo Tucci, "I mestieri nella *Piazza universale* del Garzoni," in *Studi in memoria di Luigi Dal Pane* (Bologna: CLUEB, 1982), 310–31.

53. Garzoni, *La piazza universale di tutte le professioni del mondo*, 1172.

54. Marzio Barbagli, Vittorio Capecchi, and Antonio Cobalti, eds., *La mobilità sociale in Emilia Romagna* (Bologna: Mulino, 1988).

Chapter 5

CIVILIZATIONS AND FRONTIERS

Anthropology of the Early Modern Mediterranean

PETER BURKE

Fernand Braudel demonstrated rather less interest in anthropology than in other social sciences or "sciences humaines," notably geography, sociology, and economics. All the same, the first section of this paper will be devoted to him, in acknowledgment of the debt to his work incurred by subsequent historians of parts of the Mediterranean world and also because some of the ideas put forward in his most famous book are only now receiving the attention they deserve.

BRAUDEL AS HISTORIAN OF CIVILIZATIONS

One of Fernand Braudel's central concepts was that of "civilisation."[1] In *La Méditerranée*, a chapter was devoted to this topic, taking up about seventy pages in the second edition of the book.[2] Braudel returned to this theme in an article for *l'Encyclopédie française* (1959) and once more in his co-authored *Le monde actuel* (1963). Although the title *Grammaire des civilisations* was only given to this book in its second (posthumous) edition in 1987, the term *civilisation* was used to describe all three parts of the original text, "grammaire des civilisations," "les civilisations non européennes," and "les civilisations européennes."[3]

---

1. Pierre Daix, *Braudel* (Paris: Flammarion, 1995), 363–68, 533–35.
2. Fernand Braudel, *La Méditerranée et le monde Méditerranéen à l'époque de Philippe II*, 1st ed. (Paris: Armand Colin, 1949), 2d ed., 2 vols. (Paris: Armand Colin, 1966).
3. Fernand Braudel, "L'histoire des civilisations" (1959), reprinted in idem, *Ecrits sur l'histoire* (Paris: Flammarion, 1969), 255–314; Fernand Braudel et al., *Le monde actuel* (Paris; Belin, 1963); Fernand Braudel, *Grammaire des civilisations* (Paris: Arthaud, 1987).

Civilisation matérielle was also the title of a book Braudel published in 1967, the first volume of what became the trilogy *Civilisation matérielle, économie et capitalisme.*[4] The concept was also important in *Le modèle italien*, a study first published in Italian in 1974.[5] If Braudel had lived long enough to finish his history of France, that work would have included a section on French *culture.*[6]

What did Braudel mean by "civilisation"? In 1949, he used the term as synonymous with culture, following the anthropologist Marcel Mauss's lecture of 1930 on the elements and forms of "civilisations" (Mauss's use of the term in the plural is worth noting).[7] In Braudel's later work, on the other hand, *culture* "signifies a level lower than that of a civilization" (thus inverting the classic German distinction between *Kultur* and *Zivilisation*).[8]

Braudel's work on cultural history has two distinctive features, features which were particularly remarkable at the time in which his books and articles were written. The first is his interest in cultural frontiers. Early in *La Méditerranée*, for example, the author notes the importance of what he calls the "barrière sociale, culturelle" between mountaineers and plainsmen.[9] Later in the book, he discusses the importance of "frontières culturelles" such as the Rhine and the Danube from ancient Rome to the Reformation. In a late essay, he returned to the argument that it was no accident that the frontiers of Catholicism, the Rhine, and the Danube were also the frontiers of the Roman Empire.[10]

The second is his concern with cultural resistance, or as he calls it, "refusal to borrow" [*refus d'emprunter*], associated with the resilience of civilizations, their power of survival, their "force de résistance." His examples include the Bulgarians under the rule of the Turks and the Moriscos under

4.   Fernand Braudel, *Civilisation matérielle, économie et capitalisme*, 3 vols. (Paris: Armand Colin, 1979).
5.   Fernand Braudel, *Le modèle italien* (Paris: Flammarion, 1989).
6.   Fernand Braudel, *L'identité de la France*, vol. 1 (Paris: Arthaud, 1986), 19.
7.   Marcel Mauss, "Les civilisations: Éléments et formes" (1931), reprinted in idem, *Oeuvres*, ed. Victor Karady, 3 vols (Paris: Minuit, 1968–69), 2, 456–87.
8.   Fernand Braudel, *The Structures of Everyday Life, trans.* Siân Reynolds (London: Collins, 1981), 589 n 78.
9.   Braudel, *La Méditerranée*, 1st ed., 24.
10. Braudel, *La Méditerranée*, 1st ed., 566; Fernand Braudel, "The Rejection of the Reformation in France," in *History and Imagination*, ed. Hugh Lloyd-Jones (London: Duckworth, 1981), 72–80.

the rule of the Spaniards; the Japanese resistance to the chair and the table; and the "rejection" of the Reformation in Spain, Italy, and France.[11]

After noting these positive features, it is necessary to point to a major absence from Braudel's work: "immaterial culture," as Bronislaw Malinowski called it.[12] In contrast to Lucien Febvre, Braudel showed a remarkable lack of interest in beliefs, mentalities, and even in religious practice, apart from the discussions of the Reformation mentioned above (and even there, material factors are treated as determinants).[13] Although he noted that "Islam et Chrétienté voisinent, fraternisent à l'occasion," he did not discuss this inter-action between Christians and Muslims in the religious sphere, despite the fact that it had already been studied at some length in a remarkable (frag-mentary and neglected) posthumous book by a brilliant but short-lived scholar, Frederick W. Hasluck, fellow of King's College Cambridge and assis-tant director of the British School at Athens.[14] Nor did Braudel concern himself with fundamental values such as honor, shared by the Christian and Muslim cultures of the Mediterranean.

In other words, Braudel's use of anthropology was an extremely restricted one. He entered into dialogue with Claude Lévi-Strauss. He showed an inter-est in economic anthropology. An intriguing passage in the 1949 edition of *La Méditerranée* in the section on "civilizations" declared that "Les travaux des ethnographes et des ethnologues—ceux, remarquables, de Marcel Mauss—nous invitaient à suivre des chemins neufs."[15] However, the sentence was deleted in the second edition. It was rare for Braudel to refer to the Mediterra-nean anthropology which came of age or was institutionalized between the

---

11. Braudel, *La Méditerranée,* 1st ed., 558 ff., 569; Braudel, *Structures of Everyday Life,* 288; Braudel, "Rejection of the Reformation."

12. "Culture," by Bronislaw Malinowski, *International Encyclopaedia of the Social Sci-ences,* 2d ed. (1930).

13. Peter Burke, "Material Civilisation in the Work of Braudel," *Itinerario* (1981): 37–43; Stuart Clark, "The Annales Historians," in *The Return of Grand Theory,* ed. Quentin Skin-ner (Cambridge: Cambridge University Press, 1985), 177–98.

14. Braudel, *La Méditerranée,* 1st ed., 554. Frederick W. Hasluck, *Christianity and Islam under the Sultans,* 2 vols. (Oxford: Clarendon, 1929). When I mentioned this book to Braudel in 1977, he said that he had not heard of it. His relative lack of interest in studies in English is noted in Jack H. Hexter, "Fernand Braudel and the Monde Braudellien" (1972; repr. in Hex-ter, *On Historians,* Cambridge, Mass.: Harvard University Press, 1979), 110.

15. Braudel, *La Méditerranée,* 1st ed., 551.

first and second editions of the *La Méditerranée*, with the exception of the work of Julio Caro Baroja and his "beau livre" on the Moriscos.[16]

MEDITERRANEAN ANTHROPOLOGIES AND HISTORIES

The lack of reference to anthropology in Braudel's writings is scarcely surprising. Like the rest of his work, the discussion of the civilizations of the Mediterranean illustrates both the triumphs and the poverties of the macrosocial approach, the Olympian or global view for which he was famous, the very opposite of the microsocial approach associated with anthropology. All the same, the history and the anthropology of the Mediterranean world have illuminated each other and are capable of doing so to an even greater extent than they have done so far. This section will focus on the present and the recent past, while the following section will consider possible futures.

ANTHROPOLOGIES

Immediately after the Second World War, anthropology was still a small and marginal discipline. Since that time it has not only expanded but also become remarkably influential on the humanities (especially history). Some leading anthropologists, such as Pierre Bourdieu and Clifford Geertz (both of whom have worked on the Mediterranean world in their time), have become names to conjure with, constantly cited, whether they are imitated or criticized.[17]

Mediterranean anthropology was once the preserve of a tiny group meeting for the first time in Burg Wartenstein in 1959. The group originally privileged certain themes, including some neglected by Braudel. Honor and shame, for example, a theme which has inspired conferences as well as monographs concerned with southern Italy, North Africa, Spain, Greece, and elsewhere.[18]

---

16. Braudel, *La Méditerranée,* 2d ed., 124.

17. Pierre Bourdieu and Loïc Wacquant, *An Invitation to Reflexive Sociology* (Chicago: University of Chicago Press, 1992); Richard Jenkins, *Pierre Bourdieu* (London: Routledge, 1992); Ronald G. Walters, "Signs of the Times: Clifford Geertz and Historians," *Social Research* 47 (1980): 537–56; Robert Darnton, *The Great Cat Massacre, and Other Episodes in French Cultural History* (New York: Basic Books, 1984), xiii; Jean-Christophe Agnew, "History and Anthropology: Scenes from a Marriage," *Yale Journal of Criticism* 3 (1990): 29–50.

18. John G. Peristiany, ed., *Honor and Shame: The Values of Mediterranean Society* (London: Weidenfeld & Nicolson, 1965); David D. Gilmore, ed., *Honor and Shame and the Unity of the Mediterranean* (Washington: American Anthropological Association, 1987); John G.

Insults, as a way of destroying honor, and feuds, a way of restoring it in a decentralized society, were connected objects of interest.[19] So was the family and its values, once notoriously described (in a study of Potenza) as "amoral familism." "Moral familism" might have been a better term, in the sense that the author meant that the family is viewed as a moral community, its values overriding those of state and church, at least on occasion.[20]

Saints (Muslim as well as Christian) and the pilgrimages and festivals in their honor are another traditional theme in Mediterranean anthropology.[21] From patron saints it is only a short step (as Jeremy Boissevain has shown), to the study of secular patronage or "friendship," another topic which has preoccupied anthropologists of the Mediterranean world, like the people they study. Is this friendship reciprocal or exploitative? they have asked. What is the place of gifts and hospitality in sustaining the links between patrons and clients?[22]

By contrast, a concern with domestic rituals such as weddings and funerals is more recent.[23] Gender is a another relatively new concern in

Peristiany and Julian Pitt-Rivers, eds., *Honor and Grace in Anthropology* (Cambridge: Cambridge University Press, 1992).

19. Jacob Black-Michaud, *Cohesive Force: Feud in the Mediterranean and the Middle East* (Oxford: Blackwell, 1975); Anton Blok, "Rams and Billy-Goats: A Key to the Mediterranean Code of Honor," *Man* 16 (1981): 427–40; Christopher Boehm, *Blood Revenge: The Enactment and Management of Conflict in Montenegro and Other Tribal Societies* (Philadelphia: University of Pennsylvania Press, 1984).

20. Edward Banfield, *The Moral Basis of a Backward Society* (Glencoe: Free Press, 1958); John G. Peristiany, ed., *Mediterranean Family Structures* (Cambridge: Cambridge University Press, 1976).

21. Jeremy Boissevain, *Saints and Fireworks: Religion and Politics in Rural Malta* (London: Athlone Press, 1965); Ernest Gellner, *Saints of the Atlas* (London: Weidenfeld & Nicolson, 1969); Vincent Crapanzano, *The Hamadsha: A Study in Moroccan Ethnopsychiatry* (Berkeley: University of California Press, 1973); Sydel Silverman, *Three Bells of Civilisation: The Life of an Italian Hill Town* (New York: Academic Press, 1975); Jill Dubisch, *In a Different Place: Pilgrimage, Gender and Politics at a Greek Island Shrine* (Princeton: Princeton University Press, 1995).

22. Jeremy Boissevain, *Friends of Friends* (Oxford: Blackwell, 1974); idem, "When the Saints Go Marching Out," in *Patrons and Clients*, ed. Ernest Gellner and John Waterbury (London: Duckworth, 1977), 81–94, and other essays in that volume.

23. William A. Douglass, *Death in Murelaga: Funerary Rituals in a Spanish Basque Village* (Seattle: University of Washington Press, 1969); Loring M. Danforth, *The Death Rituals of Modern Greece* (Princeton: Princeton University Press, 1982); Vassos Argyrou, *Tradition and Modernity in the Mediterranean: The Wedding as Symbolic Struggle* (Cambridge: Cambridge University Press, 1996).

Mediterranean anthropology (as in anthropology more generally). Pierre Bourdieu's remarkable essay on the Berber house may have been influential in this respect as well as for its brilliant structural analysis and its concern with material culture.[24] The old discussions of honor and shame have recently been recast as analyses of gender.[25]

One recurrent theme in Mediterranean gender studies is the apparent or real subordination of women, pursued through studies of public and private space, language and silence, property, and most recently of the veil, which has been viewed as an instrument of liberation as well as of oppression.[26] Another—an especially rich vein in the Mediterranean world—is the construction of masculinity through language, gesture, and ritual.[27] These new themes reflect not only debates about gender in the anthropologists' own societies, but also an increasing interest in the problem of identity.

Despite the suspicion of these "soft" topics, which British anthropologists ("social" as opposed to their "cultural" colleagues in the United States), used to share with Braudel, beliefs and "modes of thought" have always been central to Mediterranean anthropology. Attitudes to time, for example, have been discussed more than once.[28] History, on the other hand, has long been

24. Pierre Bourdieu, "La maison kabyle ou le monde renversé," in *Echanges et Communications: Mélanges offerts à Claude Lévi-Strauss*, 2 vols. (The Hague: Mouton, 1970), 2:739–58.

25. Jill Dubisch, ed., *Gender and Power in Rural Greece* (Princeton: Princeton University Press, 1986); Peter Loizos and Evthimios Papataxiarchis, eds., *Contested Identities: Gender and Kinship in Modern Greece* (Princeton: Princeton University Press, 1991).

26. Lucienne Roubin, "Espace masculin, espace féminin en communauté provençale," *Annales E.S.C.* 25 (1970): 537–60; Vanessa Maher, *Women and Property in Morocco* (Cambridge: Cambridge University Press, 1974); Susan Harding, "Women and Words in a Spanish Village," in *Toward an Anthropology of Women*, ed. Rayna R. Reiter (New York: Monthly Review Press, 1975), 283–308; Rayna R. Reiter, "Men and Women in the South of France: Public and Private Domains," ibid., 252–82; Lidia Sciama, "The Problem of Privacy in Mediterranean Anthropology," in *Women and Space*, ed. Shirley Ardener, rev. ed. (1981; repr. Oxford: Berg, 1993), 89–110; Lila Abu-Lughod, *Veiled Sentiments: Honor and Poetry in a Bedouin Society* (Berkeley: University of California Press, 1987), 159–65; Leila Ahmed, *Women and Gender in Islam* (New Haven: Yale University Press, 1992), 144–68.

27. Stanley Brandes, *Metaphors of Masculinity: Sex and Status in Andalusian Folklore* (Philadelphia: University of Pennsylvania Press, 1980); Henk Driessen, "Male Sociability and Rituals of Masculinity in Rural Andalusia," *Anthropological Quarterly* 56 (1983): 125–32; Michael Herzfeld, *The Poetics of Manhood: Contest and Identity in a Cretan Mountain Village* (Princeton: Princeton University Press, 1985); David D. Gilmore, *Manhood in the Making: Cultural Concepts of Masculinity* (New Haven: Yale University Press, 1990).

28. Pierre Bourdieu, "The Attitude of the Algerian Peasant toward Time," in *Mediterranean Countrymen: Essays in the Social Anthropology of the Mediterranean,* ed. Julian Pitt-Rivers

marginal. The history-mindedness of Julio Caro Baroja and Ernesto de Martino, already explicit in the 1950s, was rare among their anthropological colleagues, who were committed at that time to a timeless functionalism. Today, however, a "historical turn" is clearly visible in anthropology, including Mediterranean anthropology, just as an "anthropological turn" has been visible in history for a generation.

HISTORICAL ANTHROPOLOGY

Historical anthropologists or "anthropological historians" work on a variety of regions and periods. The many contributions to the historical anthropology of ancient Greece—by French, British, German, and American classicists in particular—are well known, and go back to the beginning of the century. Among historians of nineteenth-century Europe, Eric Hobsbawm and Edward Thompson have admitted their debt to anthropology.

The historical anthropology or "anthropological history" of early modern Europe is also far from an exclusively Mediterranean enterprise. Keith Thomas, for example, has been working on the anthropology of early modern England since the 1960s. Alan Macfarlane has led a double life as a historian (focusing on early modern England) and an anthropologist (concentrating on the Gurung of Nepal), allowing the ideas of one discipline to fertilize the other.[29] The Dutch too have found this approach congenial. The anthropologist Anton Blok has produced a major study of Dutch brigands in the eighteenth century, while historians of the early modern period such as Willem Frijhoff have interrogated their documents from an ethnographic standpoint.[30]

Scandinavia is another center of historical anthropology. It was a Swedish anthropologist Börje Hanssen who produced the first serious "microhistory"—long before the term came into use—in his study of the village of

---

(Paris: Mouton, 1963), 55–72; Anna Collard, "Investigating Social Memory in a Greek Context," in *History and Ethnicity*, ed. Elizabeth Tonkin et al. (London: Routledge, 1989), 89–103.

29. Alan Macfarlane, *The Family Life of Ralph Josselin* (Cambridge: Cambridge University Press, 1970); idem, *Resources and Population: A Study of the Gurungs of Nepal* (Cambridge: Cambridge University Press, 1976).

30. Anton Blok, *De Bokkerijders: Roverssbenden en Geheime Genootschappen in de Landen van Overmas, 1730–1774* (Amsterdam: Prometeus, 1991); Willem Frijhoff, "Historische Antropologie," in *Cultuur en maatschappij in Nederland 1500–1850: Een historisch-antropologisch perspectief*, ed. Peter te Boekhorst, Peter Burke, and Willem Frijhoff (Meppel: Boom; Heerlen: Open Universiteit, 1992).

Österlen in Skåne in the eighteenth century, a study first published in 1952.[31] Hanssen's influence is still working in Scandinavia, as a recent study of a Danish estate between 1750 and 1980, written by one of his pupils and dedicated to him, bears eloquent witness. The author, Palle Christiansen, did fieldwork (including agricultural labor) on the estate as well as going to the archives.[32] Modern Swedish social history has been rewritten from an ethnographic standpoint in a study which does not confine itself to the peasants, following ethnographic traditions, but has much to say about the values and lifestyles of the middle classes.[33] Again, a Danish anthropologist trained in England has carried out her fieldwork among the dead and produced a two-volume historical anthropology of Iceland from 1000 to 1800.[34]

There is also a shelf of studies on the historical anthropology of Central Europe, some by local scholars and others by historians from other parts of the world.[35] In the case of Hungary, there was already enough interest for a conference on the subject to be held in 1983. The study of shamanistic elements in Central European witchcraft is one example of the uses of anthropology for historians of Hungary.[36] In Germany and Austria, there is a group which centers on the journal *Historische Anthropologie* (founded in 1993), among whom Hans Medick is probably the best known.[37] Further east, Aron Yakovlevich Gurevich has put the ideas of Malinowski, Mauss, and other anthropologists to good use in his work on medieval gifts, individualism, orality, and other topics.[38]

31. Börje Hanssen, *Österlen: Allmoge, köpstafolk & kultursammanhang vid slutet av 1700–talet i sydöstra Skåne,* 2d ed. (1952; Östervåla: Gidlunds, 1977).

32. Palle O. Christiansen, *A Manorial World: Lord, Peasants and Cultural Distinctions on a Danish Estate, 1750–1980* (Oslo: Scandinavian University Press, 1996).

33. Jonas Frykman and Orvar Löfgren, *Culture Builders: A Historical Anthropology of Middle-Class Life* (New Brunswick: Rutgers University Press, 1987).

34. Kirsten Hastrup, *Culture and Society in Medieval Iceland: An Anthropological Analysis of Structure and Change* (Oxford: Clarendon, 1985); idem, *Nature and Policy in Iceland 1400–1800: An Anthropological Analysis of History and Mentality* (Oxford: Clarendon, 1990).

35. David Sabean, *Power in the Blood: Popular Culture and Village Discourse in Early Modern Germany* (Cambridge: Cambridge University Press, 1984); Robert W. Scribner, *Popular Culture and Popular Movements in Early Modern Germany* (London: Hambledon Press, 1987).

36. Gábor Klaniczay, *The Uses of Supernatural Power* (Cambridge: Polity Press, 1990), esp. 129–50.

37. Hans Medick, *Weben und Überleben in Laichingen, 1650–1900: Lokalgeschichte als Allgemeine Geschichte* (Göttingen: Vandenhoeck & Ruprecht, 1996).

38. Aron Y. Gurevich, *Historical Anthropology of the Middle Ages* (Cambridge: Polity Press, 1992).

In what follows, however, the emphasis will fall on the Mediterranean world in the early modern period and on anthropology, especially Mediterranean anthropology, as an inspiration to some of its historians.

HISTORICAL ANTHROPOLOGY OF THE MEDITERRANEAN

Some anthropologists of the Mediterranean have accused their colleagues of indifference to history, or of using the past as no more than a backdrop, a kind of "historical landscaping."[39] All the same, there is also a tradition of taking history seriously. The first name to mention is surely that of the late Julio Caro Baroja, who wrote both on history and on anthropology.[40] His work has been continued by Carmelo Lisón Tolosana, a Spanish anthropologist trained in England, whose interests run from witches to courts.[41] Spanish historians, on the other hand, have not shown much interest in this approach, though there are signs that their attitudes are changing.[42] A similar point might be made about Portugal, where Francisco Bethencourt stands almost alone.[43]

In France, Emmanuel Le Roy Ladurie might be described as a historical anthropologist of the Mediterranean, not only on account of his famous *Montaillou* (which acknowledged a debt to Laurence Wylie's *Village in the Vaucluse* as well as to Ronald Blythe's *Akenfield*), but also for a cluster of studies on Dauphiné, Provence, and elsewhere.[44] Yves Castan's study of honor in eighteenth-century Languedoc also draws on anthropological theory.[45] A number of French historians have studied the history of their neighbors Spain and Italy along anthropological lines.[46]

39. John Davis, *Peoples of the Mediterranean* (London: Routledge, 1977).

40. Julio Caro Baroja, *Los moriscos del reino de Granada* (Madrid: Instituto de Estudios Políticos, 1957); idem, *El Carnaval* (Madrid: Taurus, 1965); idem, *Etnografía histórica de Navarra*, 3 vols. (Pamplona: Aranzadi, 1971–72).

41. Carmelo Lisón Tolosana, *Belmonte de los Caballeros* (Oxford: Clarendon, 1966); idem, *Brujeria, estructura social y simbolismo en Galicia* (Madrid: Alianza, 1979); idem, *La imagen del rey: Monarquía, realeza y poder ritual en la Casa de los Austrias* (Madrid: Espasa Calpe, 1991).

42. Ricardo García Carcel, *Herejia y sociedad en el siglo xvi: La Inquisición en Valencia, 1530–1609* (Barcelona: Ediciones Península, 1980).

43. Francisco Bethencourt, *O imaginário da magia: Feiticeiras, saludadores e nigromantes no século xvi* (Lisbon: Universidade Aberta, 1987).

44. Laurence Wylie, *Village in the Vaucluse* (Cambridge, Mass.: Harvard University Press, 1957); Emmanuel Le Roy Ladurie, *Montaillou, village occitan* (Paris: Gallimard, 1975); idem, *Le Carnaval de Romans* (Paris: Gallimard, 1979), among others.

45. Yves Castan, *Honnêteté et relations sociales en Languedoc, 1715–1780* (Paris: Plon, 1974).

46. For example, Bartholomé Bennassar, *L'homme espagnol: Attitudes et mentalités du*

In Italy, it was the polymath Ernesto de Martino who was the pioneer of historical anthropology in his studies of popular religion in the South.[47] He has been followed by a network centering on the journal *Quaderni Storici*. Carlo Ginzburg has rightly attracted international attention, but the work of other members of the group should not be forgotten: Giovanni Levi, for instance, Edoardo Grendi, Carlo Poni, and more recently Osvaldo Raggio and Angelo Torre.[48]

In the United States, historical anthropologists of the Mediterranean world include Natalie Davis and some of her many pupils; Robert Darnton, who has collaborated with Clifford Geertz in Princeton; William Christian (who began his working life as an anthropologist but moved from the field to the archive); Peter Sahlins (the son of the anthropologist Marshall Sahlins), and a group of historians working on Renaissance Florence and Venice.[49]

In Britain, despite the example set by Keith Thomas, early modern historians have shown much less interest in anthropology than their colleagues in the United States. In the case of Mediterranean studies, an interdisciplinary group set up at the University of East Anglia in the 1960s has since dissolved, though individual former members and other British historians (myself included) continue to pursue this approach.[50]

It should be noted that the historical anthropology of the Mediterranean has so far concentrated on certain parts of the area, northwestern rather than

XVIe au XIXe siècle (Paris: Hachette, 1975); Christiane Klapisch, *Women, Family and Ritual in Renaissance Italy* (Chicago: University of Chicago Press, 1985).

47. Ernesto de Martino, *Sud e magia* (Milan: Feltrinelli, 1959); idem, *La terra di rimorso* (Milan: Il Saggiatore, 1961).

48. Carlo Ginzburg, *Il formaggio e i vermi: Il cosmo di un mugnaio del '500* (Turin: Einaudi, 1976); Giovanni Levi, *l'Eredità immateriale: Carriera di un esorcista nel Piemonte del '600* (Turin: Einaudi, 1985); Osvaldo Raggio, *Faide e parentele: Lo stato genovese visto dalla Fontanabuona* (Turin: Einaudi, 1990); Angelo Torre, *Il consumo di devozioni: Religione e comunità nelle campagne dell'Ancien Regime* (Milan: Angeli, 1995).

49. Natalie Davis, *Society and Culture in Early Modern France* (Stanford: Stanford University Press, 1975); Darnton, *Great Cat Massacre;* William A. Christian, *Person and God in a Spanish Valley* (New York: Academic Press, 1972); idem, *Local Religion in Sixteenth-Century Spain* (Princeton: Princeton University Press, 1981); Peter Sahlins, *Boundaries: The Making of France and Spain in the Pyrenees* (Berkeley: University of California Press, 1989); idem, *Forest Rites: The War of the Demoiselles in Nineteenth-Century France* (Cambridge, Mass.: Harvard University Press, 1994); Richard Trexler, *Public Life in Renaissance Florence* (New York: Academic Press, 1980); Edward Muir, *Civic Ritual in Renaissance Venice* (Princeton: Princeton University Press, 1981); idem, *Mad Blood Stirring: Vendetta and Faction in Friuli during the Renaissance* (Baltimore: Johns Hopkins University Press, 1993).

southeastern. Little has been written from this point of view on North Africa, for instance, Lebanon, Greece, Turkey, Cyprus, and Malta. Among the rare exceptions is Lucette Valensi's study of Tunisian peasants, which draws on the theories of Michael Polanyi and Pierre Bourdieu and makes comparisons with the fieldwork of Ernest Gellner and Paul Stirling.[51]

CONCEPTS, THEORIES, AND METHODS

It is time to turn from description to analysis. Exactly what has been appropriated from anthropology by historians and in what ways has it been used or transformed? The choice of some historical topics obviously has been inspired by Mediterranean anthropology, and some of these topics are treated (allowing for the differences in sources) in much the same way (with the proviso that the style of anthropology has itself been changing over the years and that ideas which come to the notice of workers in another discipline may already be on their way out). Honor and shame, for example, are topics that have attracted many early modern historians, and this framework now accommodates a growing number of studies of insults, vendettas, and duels.[52] Saints, together with the whole apparatus of "local religion," especially local festivals, have also been studied quite intensively in a quasi-anthropological manner.[53]

50. James Casey, *The History of the Family* (Oxford: Blackwell, 1989); Stephen Wilson, *Feuding, Conflict and Banditry in Nineteenth-Century Corsica* (Cambridge: Cambridge University Press, 1988). Cf. Peter Burke, *Historical Anthropology of Early Modern Italy: Essays on Perception and Communication* (Cambridge: Cambridge University Press, 1987); Paul Sant Cassia and Constantina Bada, *The Making of the Modern Greek Family: Marriage and Exchange in Nineteenth-Century Athens* (Cambridge: Cambridge University Press, 1992).

51. Lucette Valensi, *Fellahs tunisiens* (Paris: Mouton, 1977); cf. Sant Cassia and Bada, *Modern Greek Family*, and Carmel Cassar, *Witchcraft, Sorcery and the Inquisition: A Study of Cultural Values in Early Modern Malta* (Msida: Mireva, 1996).

52. Julio Caro Baroja, "Honor and Shame," in *Honor and Shame*, ed. Peristiany, 79–124; Castan, *Honnêteté et relations*; Bennassar, *L'Homme espagnol*, 167–84; Peter Burke, "Insult and Blasphemy in Early Modern Italy," in *Historical Anthropology*, 95–109; Thomas V. Cohen, "The Lay Liturgy of Affront in Sixteenth-Century Italy," *Journal of Social History* 25 (1992): 857–77; Muir, *Mad Blood Stirring*; cf. Daniel L. Smail, "Factions and Vengeance in Renaissance Italy," *Comparative Studies in Society and History* 38 (1996): 781–89.

53. Christian, *Local Religion*; Muir, *Civic Ritual*; Donald Weinstein and Rudolph Bell, *Saints and Society: The Two Worlds of Western Christendom, 1000–1700* (Chicago: University of Chicago Press, 1982); Peter Burke, "How To Be a Counter-Reformation Saint" (1984; repr. in Burke, *Historical Anthropology*, 1987): 48–62; James Amelang, *Honored Citizens of Barcelona* (Princeton: Princeton University Press, 1986), 195–210; Jean-Michel Sallmann, *Naples et ses saints à l'âge baroque, 1540–1750* (Paris: PUF, 1994); Torre, *Il consumo di devozioni*.

Historians' current concern with kinship in the broad sense (including godparenthood) as opposed to the longer-established study of the household and the nuclear family, has also been inspired by the example of Mediterranean anthropologists, for whom, for example, the *compadre* and its equivalents (the *compère*, the *kombaros*, and so forth) have long been objects of concern.[54] Bourdieu's interest in the spatial structure of the house has inspired at least the occasional historian to follow his example.[55]

Other historical topics have a rather more complicated relation to Mediterranean anthropology. In the case of literacy studies, which began long before historians made contact with anthropologists, it is a particular approach, to the meanings or "uses of literacy," as opposed to its measurement, which has been encouraged by their work.[56] Art historians have become concerned with the relation between art patronage in the traditional sense of the term and wider patronage structures or "Big Man systems," but apart from Michael Baxandall and his concern with the "period eye," few of them have engaged in a historical anthropology of art.[57]

Historians of patrons, clients, and the gifts which pass between them have both learned and diverged from anthropology. Political historians, for example, differ from anthropologists by paying somewhat more attention to contemporary criticisms of patronage as "corruption" as well as to the relation between patronage systems and the formal structures of the state.[58]

54. Le Roy Ladurie, *Montaillou, village occitan;* John Bossy, "Godparenthood," in *Religion and Society in Early Modern Europe,* ed. Kaspar von Greyerz (London: Allen & Unwin, 1984), 194–201; Klapisch, *Women, Family, and Ritual;* Casey, *History of Family;* Raggio, *Faide e parentele.*

55. Le Roy Ladurie, *Montaillou, village occitan;* Peter Burke, *Popular Culture in Early Modern Europe* (London: Temple Smith, 1978), 81, 86–87.

56. Jack Goody, *The Domestication of the Savage Mind* (Cambridge: Cambridge University Press, 1977); Brian Street, *Literacy in Theory and Practice* (Cambridge: Cambridge University Press, 1984); cf. Peter Burke, "The Uses of Literacy," in Burke, ed., *Historical Anthropology,* 110–31.

57. Werner L. Gundersheimer, "Patronage in the Renaissance: An Exploratory Approach," in *Patronage in the Renaissance,* ed. Guy F. Lytle and Stephen Orgel (Princeton; Princeton University Press, 1981), 3–23; Francis W. Kent and Patricia Simons, eds., *Patronage, Art, and Society in Renaissance Italy* (Canberra: Humanities Research Center; Oxford: Oxford University Press, 1987); Michael Baxandall, *Painting and Experience in Fifteenth-Century Italy* (Oxford: Oxford University Press, 1972).

58. Robert Harding, "Corruption and the Moral Boundaries of Patronage in the Renaissance," in *Patronage in the Renaissance,* ed. Lytle and Orgel, 47–64; Jean-Claude Waquet, *De la corruption: Morale et pouvoir à Florence aux 17e et 18e siècles* (Paris: Fayard, 1984); Sharon

Witchcraft has long been a center of interest for historians of early modern Europe. Some historians of witchcraft are familiar with the work of anthropologists, but those anthropologists have generally worked on Africa, and the differences between European and African societies have not always been taken sufficiently into account by those following anthropological models.[59] By contrast, witchcraft has not been an important topic for Mediterranean anthropologists, despite a monograph on Galicia and a few studies of belief in the evil eye.[60] Again, in their studies of ritual, early modern historians have been inspired by Victor Turner's work on Africa and that of Clifford Geertz on the "theater state" in Bali rather than by ethnographies of the Mediterranean world.[61] In similar fashion the increasing concern with the informal settlement of disputes in early modern Europe, outside the courts, has been influenced by the anthropology of law in general, rather than by Mediterranean anthropology in particular, although Mediterranean studies of this kind do exist, including one on the *qadis* of Morocco.[62]

At a more general level, it is necessary to emphasize the convergence of the anthropological concern with "modes of thought" and the revival of the "history of mentalities" in the third generation of the *Annales* group, who in some respects at least returned (as Robert Mandrou put it), to the "Annales première manière" of Marc Bloch and Lucien Febvre. Like the anthropologists, Bloch owed a good deal to the ideas of Emile Durkheim. Microhistory

Kettering, *Patrons, Brokers and Clients in Seventeenth-Century France* (New York: Oxford University Press, 1986); Ronald F. E. Weissman, "Taking Patronage Seriously: Mediterranean Values and Renaissance Society," in *Patronage, Art, and Society,* ed. Kent and Simons, 25–45.

59. Robert Rowland, "European Witch-Beliefs in Comparative Perspective," in *Early Modern European Witchcraft: Centers and Peripheries*, ed. Bengt Ankarloo and Gustav Henningsen (Oxford: Clarendon, 1990), 161–90.

60. De Martino, *Sud e magia;* Lisón-Tolosana, *Brujería, estructura social;* Anthony H. Galt, "The Evil Eye as Synthetic Image and Its Meaning on the Island of Pantelleria," *American Ethnologist* 9 (1982): 664–81.

61. Trexler, *Public Life;* Muir, *Civic Ritual;* cf. Sean Wilentz, ed., *The Rites of Rulers: Symbolism, Ritual and Politics since the Middle Ages* (Philadelphia: University of Pennsylvania Press, 1985); David Cannadine and Simon Price, eds., *Rituals of Royalty* (Cambridge: Cambridge University Press, 1987); Edward Muir, *Ritual in Early Modern Europe* (Cambridge: Cambridge University Press, 1997).

62. John Bossy, ed., *Disputes and Settlements* (Cambridge: Cambridge University Press, 1983); Thomas Kuehn, *Law, Family and Women: Toward a Legal Anthropology of Renaissance Italy* (Chicago: University of Chicago Press, 1991). Cf. Max Gluckman, *Custom and Conflict in Africa* (Oxford: Blackwell, 1955); Simon Roberts, *Order and Dispute* (Harmondsworth: Pelican, 1979); Lawrence Rosen, *The Anthropology of Justice: Law as Culture in Islamic Society* (Cambridge: Cambridge University Press, 1989).

too may be seen as a kind of convergence, or as a product of an encounter with anthropological extended case studies by scholars who were already familiar with the tradition of local history.

Problems naturally remain, in particular, two opposite dangers. In the first place, the problem of insularity not uncommon in community studies, forgetting the need to relate microsocial events and structures to the larger culture and society surrounding them.[63] In the second place, the danger of assuming an undifferentiated Mediterranean. The emphasis on the unity of the Mediterranean in the work of both Braudel and the first generation of Mediterranean anthropologists (John Peristiany, Julian Pitt-Rivers, and others), was extremely valuable at the time, because it broke away from insularity and pointed to common features underlying national frontiers and religious divisions. However, such an emphasis has its own dangers, such as reifying the concept of the Mediterranean and failing to attend to important distinctions between periods, social groups, and what Mauss and Braudel called "aires culturels."[64]

In short, the historical anthropology of the Mediterranean should not follow the older Mediterranean anthropology in every respect. Rather than treat the Mediterranean as a unity or, conversely, as a number of cultural islands, it may be useful to view it as an arena of interaction, of encounters and exchanges.

FRONTIERS AND EXCHANGES

This third section, oriented towards the future, concentrates on the twin themes of cultural exchanges and cultural frontiers, on which historians have written relatively little since Braudel. Political or military frontiers have continued to receive the lion's share of attention.[65] Anthropology has a place in this discussion because the anthropological concern with "symbolic boundaries" might help historians to develop themes which Braudel only

63. Ulf Hannerz, "Theory in Anthropology: Small Is Beautiful?" *Comparative Studies in Society and History* 28 (1986): 362–67.

64. Davis, *Peoples of the Mediterranean;* Michael Herzfeld, "The Horns of the Mediterranean Dilemma," *American Ethnologist* 11 (1984): 439–54; Gilmore, *Honor and Shame.*

65. Among the most important early modern studies are William H. McNeill, *Europe's Steppe Frontier, 1500–1800* (Chicago: University of Chicago Press, 1964); idem, *Venice, the Hinge of Europe, 1081–1797* (Chicago: University of Chicago Press, 1974); Andrew Hess, *The Forgotten Frontier: A History of the Sixteenth-Century Ibero-African Frontier* (Chicago: University of Chicago Press, 1978); Sahlins, *Boundaries.*

sketched, notably the creative "reception" of items of culture, material and immaterial, and the construction of identity by distinguishing the self from the "other."[66] Two Mediterranean case studies may serve to introduce these general issues.

The first example is that of the Ottoman-Habsburg frontier. According to Braudel, "Les deux grands empires de la Méditerranée vivent au même rythme."[67] Was this true for culture as well as for demographic, economic, and political trends? That it was indeed the case was the conclusion of a study made some thirty years before Braudel, a study concerned with religious interaction, or as the author put it, with "transferences," at an unofficial level, such as the pilgrimages by Muslims to the shrines of Christian saints and vice versa.[68] Art historians have come to similar conclusions in their studies of the common material culture of the frontier, noting for example the use of the Turkish scimitar by Polish soldiers and the kaftan by the Polish nobility.[69] Historians of literature have compared the epic heroes on both sides of the border, the Turkish Dede Korkut, for example, and the Greek Digenes Akritas, whose very name means "two-blooded frontiersman."

In short, the frontier zone, whether Muslim or Christian, had a common culture which may be contrasted to the rival centers of Istanbul and Vienna.[70] This does not mean that there were no differences at all. Whether or not Andrew Hess was right to speak of an increasing "divergence" between the Habsburg and Ottoman Mediterraneans in the later sixteenth century, his point about differences is well taken.[71] To reveal those differences more clearly it is now possible to draw on some recent studies of a kind of border crossing, conversion (generally from Christian to Muslim, though the famous case of Leo the African may remind us of the traffic in the opposite direction).[72]

---

66. Fredrik Barth, ed., *Ethnic Groups and Boundaries* (Bergen: Universitets Forlaget; London: Allen & Unwin, 1969); Pierre Bourdieu, *La distinction* (Paris: Minuit, 1979); Anthony Cohen, *The Symbolic Construction of Community* (Chichester: Horwood, 1985).

67. Braudel, *La Méditerranée*, 1st ed., 525.

68. Hasluck, *Christianity and Islam*.

69. Tadeusz Mankowski, *Orient w Polskiej Kulturze Artystycznej* (Wroclaw and Cracow: PWN, 1959).

70. Halil Inalcik, *The Ottoman Empire: The Classical Age, 1300–1600* (London: Weidenfeld & Nicolson, 1973).

71. Hess, *Forgotten Frontier*, 1–3, 297, 209–10.

72. Lucia Rostagno, *Mi faccio turco* (Rome: Istituto per l'Oriente, 1983); Bartolomé and Lucille Bennassar, *Les chrétiens d'Allah: L'histoire extraordinaire des rénégats, 16e–17e siècles* (Paris: Perrin, 1989); Lucetta Scaraffia, *Rinnegati: Per una storia dell'identità occidentale* (Rome: Laterza, 1993).

The second case study is that of Spain, which Braudel once compared to China as an example of the "superimposition of two cultures."[73] From the time of Americo Castro in the 1940s onwards, some historians have emphasized the symbiosis or *convivencia* of Spanish Jews, Christians, and Muslims and the importance of the cultural exchanges between them, mainly in the Middle Ages but to a lesser degree in early modern times as well. For example, Jewish scholars were fluent in Arabic, and Hebrew poetry was inspired by the Arabic lyric. As on the eastern European border, the warriors on both sides used similar equipment and seem to have had similar values. The material culture of the "Mozarabs" (Christians under Muslim rule) and the "Mudejars" (Muslims under Christian rule) combined elements from both traditions. Some Catholic churches (like some synagogues) were built in the Muslim style, with horseshoe arches, tiles, and geometrical decoration on doors and ceilings. It is generally impossible to say whether pottery and other artifacts in the "Hispano-Mauresque" style were made by or indeed for Christians or Muslims, the repertoire of themes being a common one.[74]

Exchanges also took place in the immaterial domains of language and literature. Many people were bilingual. Some wrote Spanish in the Muslim script and others Arabic in the Roman alphabet. Some people used two names, one Spanish and one Arabic, which suggests that they had two identities. Romances of chivalry written in a similar style were popular on both sides of the religious frontier. Some lyrics switch from Spanish to Arabic within a single line. The most spectacular examples of symbiosis, however, come from the practices of popular religion. As was the case on the Ottoman-Habsburg border, there were shrines, such as that of San Ginés, which attracted devotion from Muslims and Christians alike.[75]

These two case studies do not stand alone. Our understanding of the Italian Renaissance, for example, has been enriched and illuminated by studies

---

73. Braudel, *Civilization and Capitalism, 15th to 18th Centuries,* 3 vols., trans. Siân Reynolds (London: Collins, 1981), 1:291.

74. Henri Terrasse, *L'art hispano-mauresque des origines au 13e siècle* (Paris: Institut des hautes études marocains, 1932); idem, *Islam d'Espagne: Une rencontre de l'Orient et de l'Occident* (Paris: Plon, 1958); Fernando Marías, *El largo siglo xvi* (Madrid: Taurus, 1989), 181–202.

75. Amerigo Castro, *España en su historia: Christianos, moros y judíos* (1948); English translation, *The Structure of Spanish History* (Princeton: Princeton University Press, 1954); Angus Mackay, "The Ballad and the Frontier in Late Medieval Spain," *Bulletin of Hispanic Studies* 52 (1976): 15–33; Vivian Mann, Thomas F. Glick, and Jerrilyn D. Dodds, eds., *Convivencia: Jews, Muslims and Christians in Medieval Spain* (New York: Braziller, 1992).

emphasizing both Jewish and Arab contributions to the movement.[76] The point of the examples cited above is simply to put cultural exchanges onto our agenda. To discuss these exchanges, historians and anthropologists have at their disposal a rich (indeed, an embarrassingly rich) array of concepts, among them acculturation, syncretism, creolization, and resistance. These four concepts will be discussed in order.

Braudel himself does not seem to have employed the term "acculturation," though other French historians have done so.[77] An American, Oscar Handlin, appears to have been the first historian to use the term, appropriately enough, since the word had been coined in the United States in the late nineteenth century, principally to describe the effects of Euro-American culture on the Indians. One reason for its appeal (to Melville Herskovits, for example) was that it was more precise than the traditional term "diffusion," and expressed a concern with the differential selection of traits.[78]

The criticisms of this concept (or more exactly of its use) are well known; three in particular. In the first place, neglecting the negative side of the process: conflict, cultural shock, distintegration or "deculturation."[79] In the second place, forgetting reciprocity. For this reason the Cuban sociologist Fernando Ortiz preferred to speak of "transculturation," and Malinowski for one came to agree with him.[80] Others speak of cultural "exchange," while Hasluck discussed what he called "transferences" from Christianity to Islam and vice versa. In the third place, in discussions of Europe, there is the danger

---

76. Fritz Rosenthal, *The Classical Heritage in Islam* (London: Routledge, 1975); Robert Bonfil, "The Historian's Perception of the Jews in the Italian Renaissance," *Revue des Etudes Juives* 143 (1984): 59–82; Nancy Siraisi, *Avicenna in Renaissance Italy* (Princeton: Princeton University Press, 1987).

77. Alphonse Dupront, *Dell'acculturazione* (Turin: Einaudi, 1966); Nathan Wachtel, *La vision des vaincus* (Paris: Gallimard, 1971), English trans. Ben and Siân Reynolds, *The Vision of the Vanquished* (Hassocks: Harvester Press, 1977); Robert Muchembled, *Culture Populaire et Culture des Elites dans la France Moderne* (Paris: Flammarion, 1978).

78. Oscar Handlin, *Boston's Immigrants: A Study in Acculturation* (Cambridge, Mass.: Harvard University Press, 1941); Melville J. Herskovits, *Acculturation: The Study of Culture Contact* (New York: Augustin, 1938); George Foster, *Culture and Conquest: America's Spanish Heritage* (Chicago: University of Chicago Press, 1960).

79. Emmanuel Le Roy Ladurie, *Les paysans de Languedoc* (Paris: S.E.V.P.E.N., 1966).

80. Fernando Ortiz, *Contrapunteo cubano del tabaco y el azucar* (Havana, 1940), Eng. trans., Harriet de Onis, *Cuban Counterpoint* (New York: Random House, 1947), with preface by Bronislaw Malinowski.

of exaggerating the cultural distance between different groups within the same society. It is more accurate to describe them as subcultures than as cultures.[81]

Another term that anthropologists have sometimes used in this context is "syncretism." Herskovits, for example, found that the concept "helped to sharpen" his analyses of culture contact, especially the turn from observing a "mosaic" to analyzing "re-integration." The Brazilian sociologist Gilberto Freyre preferred the term "hybridization" or *mestiçagem*, an idea with which Braudel was acquainted (as he was with Freyre himself), but a term Braudel did not employ, despite its uses in the study of the early modern Mediterranean world.[82] Hasluck described what he called the "complete fusion" of Christian and Muslim cults.[83]

Recent students of culture contact have been less enthusiastic about the idea of syncretism. One has called for a rethinking of the concept, others have criticized Herskovits for forgetting the social actors.[84] As an alternative, some anthropologists have borrowed a term from the linguists and now speak of cultural "creolization."[85]

The term "creolization" is used by linguists in situations in which a simple lingua franca or pidgin develops a more complex structure as people begin to use it as their first language and for general purposes. Linguists argue that what was once perceived simply as error, as "broken" English or "kitchen" Latin, ought to be regarded as a variety of language with its own rules. A similar point might be made about, say, the language of architecture on the frontiers between cultures or between cultural "periods." In the Renaissance, for example, there was a shift from an earlier eclecticism to a later concern with the "grammar" of architecture, in other words with the ancient rules for the combination of different elements.

Cultural resistance should not be forgotten. Since Braudel's day there has been a growth of interest in this idea. Anthropologists too have been

81. Peter Burke, "A Question of Acculturation?" in *Scienze, credenze occulte, livelli di cultura*, ed. Paola Zambelli (Florence: Olschki, 1982), 197–204. Cf. Jean Wirth, "Against the Acculturation Thesis," in Greyerz, *Religion and Society*, 66–78.

82. Gilberto Freyre, *Casa Grande e Senzala* (Rio: Olympio, 1933).

83. Hasluck, *Christianity and Islam*, 1:264.

84. Andrew Apter, "Herskovits' Heritage: Rethinking Syncretism in the African Diaspora," *Diaspora* 1 (1991): 235–60.

85. Lee Drummond, "The Cultural Continuum," *Man* 15 (1980): 352–74; Ulf Hannerz, "The World in Creolization," *Africa* 57 (1987): 546–59; idem, *Cultural Complexity: Studies in the Social Organization of Meaning* (New York: Columbia University Press, 1992); Jonathan Friedman, *Cultural Identity and Global Process* (London: Sage, 1994), 195–32.

interested in the problem of resistance to change. For example, a study of the Pakot, a people from western Kenya, concerned with the 1950s, contrasted their resistance to political, economic, and religious change with the acceptance of change by their Bantu neighbors. It is a pity that the author apparently knew nothing about Braudel's work, or the later Braudel about his.[86]

Syncretism may be a form of resistance, as in the case of African-Americans for whom equations such as Shango/St. Barbara may have served as a cover for their continued practice of their traditional religion. Paradoxically enough, antisyncretism may also be seen as a form of resistance, as in the case of multiculturalism and ethnic revival today, as visible and powerful in the Mediterranean world today as anywhere on the globe, but perhaps to be understood as a rearguard action against the forces of globalization.[87]

There are no problem-free concepts. All the same, I take it as a good sign that the language of historians is changing, that their analytical vocabulary is becoming more rich, not least the vocabulary for discussing the cultural changes and cultural encounters that figure increasingly on their agenda. It is appropriate that this vocabulary should draw on many traditions, disciplinary and regional, as well as on the ideas of many individuals. The result of these appropriations, at least at the moment (when we are still, perhaps, in our pidgin phase), may recall the Tower of Babel. Fortunately, a few voices remain audible, among them the deep bass of Braudel.

86. Harold K. Schneider, "Pakot Resistance to Change," in *Continuity and Change in African Cultures,* ed. William R. Bascom and Melville J. Herskovits (Chicago: University of Chicago Press, 1959), 144–67.

87. Rosalind Shaw and Charles Stewart, *Syncretism Anti-Syncretism* (London: Routledge, 1994) .

PART 4

Crises and Transformations: Politics and People

Chapter 6

DUST AND ASHES

The History of Politics and War[1]

M. J. RODRÍGUEZ-SALGADO

Et cependant, l'histoire ne peut pas être seulement ces grandes pentes déclives du temps, consommatrices de masses humaines et de siècles, ces réalités collectives lentes à nouer ou dénouer leurs rapports. L'histoire est aussi cette poussière d'actes, de vies individuelles attachées les unes aux autres, parfois un instant libérées comme si les grandes chaînes se rompaient.

—Fernand Braudel, *La Méditerranée,* 1st. ed.

Braudel's initial steps in history scarcely hinted at the unconventional course he was to follow. His research into Philip II's Mediterranean policy was timely and much needed; the area had been unjustifiably neglected, and the reign of Philip II was in need of rigorous and balanced analysis. Interest in the king had intensified with the exploration and publication of primary sources from a number of major archives in the second half of the nineteenth century, and Lucien Febvre's extraordinary study of Philip II and the Franche-Comté was to inspire other historians besides the young Braudel, who later declared Febvre the greatest French-language historian "of our, time."[2] Admittedly, Febvre's book was not so much about Philip II as about

---

1. The title of this chapter was inspired by Braudel's use of the term "poussière" to describe human life and events which seemed to call for a similar term to evoke the other part of my title, "war." This article is an expanded version of my comments in the session on "Politics and Diplomacy: War and Revolt." It is not intended as a comprehensive bibliographical sketch and is necessarily eclectic in its use of examples. I would like to thank Professors Hamish Scott, Helli Koenigsberger, and David Stevenson for their useful suggestions.

2. Lucien Febvre, *Philippe II et la Franche-Comté* (Paris: H. Champion, 1911); Braudel wrote it in the introduction to the 1970 Paris edition.

the Franche-Comté; it was a study of "la vie intérieure d'une individualité politique" during the king's reign. Febvre encouraged Braudel to turn the focus away from the king and towards another collective entity, the Mediterranean during this period. Braudel's choice of the area was naturally affected by his personal circumstances in Algiers, but it should also be seen in the context of renewed scholarly interest in North Africa, notably among French and Spanish scholars. Major documentary collections such as the *Colección de Documentos Inéditos para la Historia de España*—available since the 1840s—and *Les sources inédites de l'histoire du Maroc*, which saw its first volume published in Paris in 1905, were a reflection of this.[3]

As his thinking on the subject evolved, Braudel came to see his original research on Philip II's Mediterranean policy as the least important part of his study, and he relegated it to the third and last part of *The Mediterranean* under the tripartite title: "Events, Politics and People" [Les événements, la politique et les hommes]. The fusion of these three elements is revealing, as is the fact that humans are the last of this trinity. Moreover, it is significant that while the title suggests that Philip II is the star of the work, the king is sidelined frequently. Braudel had an eye for a good story, so he ended the book with the king's death, yet he used the occasion to drive home the point that the protagonist of the title scarcely mattered in the wider context of life in the Mediterranean. He emphatically asserted that Philip II's death "was not a great event in Mediterranean history."[4] In fact, Braudel doubted in 1949 whether this section should be included in the book of the thesis, although it was a thorough, well-researched, and detailed exposition of Spain's intervention in the Mediterranean. He came to the conclusion cited at the start of this article: the section must be retained. The lives of people are an integral part of history. He went on to clinch the argument with the words: "L'histoire est l'image de la vie sous toutes ses formes. Elle n'est pas choix. Notre enquête ne serait donc pas complète si nous laissions ce plan événementiel hors de prise."[5]

3. *Colección de Documentos Inéditos para la Historia de España*, 112 vols. (Madrid, 1842–96); Henry Castries et al., *Les sources inédites de l'histoire du Maroc. Première série: Dynastie Sa'dienne* (Paris: E. Leroux, 1905–).

4. Fernand Braudel, *The Mediterranean and the Mediterranean World in the Age of Philip II*, 2 vols., trans. Siân Reynolds (London: Collins, 1973), 2:1237.

5. Fernand Braudel, *La Méditerranée et le monde Méditerranéen à l'époque de Philippe II*, 1st ed. (Paris: Armand Colin, 1949), 721.

By the time of his second, expanded edition, Braudel's historical concerns had moved even farther away from "events, politics, and people." Along with other practitioners of what came to be known as the Annales School, he was fully convinced that long-term "structural" forces, whether geographic, demographic, or economic, were the key to history. Moreover, this third section was, as he candidly admitted in 1966, now very "traditional" methodologically.[6] It had acquired greater volume and was full of fascinating details from archives hitherto little known or unexplored, but it remained conceptually unchanged. Not surprisingly, given his own intellectual evolution and the advances of other types of history, Braudel now asked himself not only if it was worthwhile to include this material, but whether it amounted to "a valid, a particular kind of history." He decided in the end that "it must be included, for there is more to history than the study of persistent structures and the slow progress of evolution," but he was emphatic that these two elements were "the essentials of man's past" even if "they cannot provide the total picture."[7] Yet he no longer believed in political history per se; it had to be fused with—if not indeed subsumed under—economic elements. As he put it: "for us, there will always be two chains—not one."[8] Political and military events were more clearly presented as part of irresistible, long-term economic forces rather than human volition; consequently, the book had a more integrated intellectual vision and went some way towards meeting criticisms that Braudel had not sufficiently integrated the three main parts. But the effect of these changes was to reduce the role of humans and political events even further.[9] Braudel admitted that "to make this connection clearer, I have deliberately excluded explanations advanced by historians who have concentrated on the outstanding personalities and events of the time.... I have also neglected...the long-term political explanation." This, despite the fact that he admits, "politics and institutions can themselves contribute to the understanding of politics and institutions."[10] His eagerness to reduce the role of human beings and politics led him to underestimate not just the role of individuals but also the crucial role that

6. Braudel, *The Mediterranean*, 2:901.
7. Braudel, *The Mediterranean*, 2:901.
8. Braudel, *The Mediterranean*, 2:902.
9. The message was reinforced by stress placed in earlier sections on war and empire, where the reader is told that "circumstances...dictate," and that men act "through force of circumstance," responding to this economic, "compelling factor," which they seldom appreciate or understand; Braudel, *The Mediterranean*, 2:677.
10. Braudel, *The Mediterranean*, 2:678.

the state played in the manipulation of those powerful economic forces which Braudel identified as the main agent of human history.

Braudel's conversion to a belief in the primacy of "structural" forces was not the only reason for his rejection of political historiography. He became contemptuous of the manner in which most historians selected events, criticizing the tendency to write "serial history," that is, a history composed of seemingly important events that are inevitably judged to be those which led to further developments.[11] He emphasized the point in an interview with Peter Burke and Helli Koenigsberger in May 1977: "l'histoire événementielle me paraît surtout dans le domaine de la politique une histoire pas toujours très raisonnable. Les hommes ont des illusions sur ce qui se passe de leur temps. Il y a beaucoup d'événements qui font beaucoup de bruit et qui n'en traînent rigoureusement rien derrière eux. Mais il y a des événements qui ne font pas beaucoup de bruit, et qui entraînent des conséquences qui sont les conséquences considérables."[12] This unease would lead him and other *Annalistes* to a rejection of narrative, which they regarded as inseparable and interchangeable with "serial history" associated with great events and "great men."[13] Yves-Marie Bercé, for example, criticized "mainstream history, by which people mean political history" because of its "linear quality"—although he acknowledged that "events are linked together into an inevitable sequence." He particularly objected to the habit of selecting events "only in terms of the relation it bears to the present" and deliberately studied popular revolts that had not made a significant impact.[14] It is ironic, therefore, to see how popular revolts have became an indispensable ingredient of present-day party political and regional politics—not least because of the way in which Bercé and others stressed the permanent, timeless nature of such popular opposition.

11. Braudel, *The Mediterranean*, 2:901–2, serves as an example.

12. I am very grateful to Helli Koenigsberger for allowing me to see the transcription of this BBC Radio 3 program, recorded in May 1977.

13. The conflation of different types of history as well as of method and approach was emphasized by Philippe Carrard, *Poetics of the New History* (Baltimore: Johns Hopkins University Press, 1992).

14. Yves-Marie Bercé, *Histoire des Croquants: Etude des soulèvements populaires au XVIIe siècle dans le sud-ouest de la France* (Geneva: Droz, 1974), in the abridged English edition as *History of Peasant Revolts: The Social Origins of Rebellion in Early Modern France*, trans. Amanda Whitmore (Cambridge: Polity, 1990), 320 and 2 respectively. He takes a passing swipe also at economic historians whose obsession with numerical data has made them "forget the influence of repetition of events, isolation, and changelessness" (343). Unfortunately, Professor Bercé was unable to attend this conference.

Braudel's public disdain of political history intensified partly because of the criticisms leveled against his work for diminishing the role of events and human volition. Towards the end of the second edition of *The Mediterranean* he argued that "not being a philosopher, I am reluctant to dwell for long on questions concerning the importance of events and of individual freedom."[15] But it was also partly due to his changing vision of what *The Mediterranean* had contributed to the discipline. The essence of his work, he argued, was an analysis of the different levels of time—"qu'il y avait des temporalités différentes, une histoire très rapide, une histoire lente, une histoire immobile"—and how these timescales related to each other. He also maintained later that the shortest timescale—which is represented by the sphere of politics and events—need not have covered political history at all, but that he could have used other subjects such as art history or economics. The reason he had chosen political history, he claimed, was only indirectly related to the fact that this was his original research topic; it was dictated by utility: "j'ai pensé que le langage de la politique était un langage très supérieur et qui portait plus loin."[16]

Once again his pupils and followers echoed similar sentiments. Bercé, for example, accepted that early modern states were primarily shaped by the fiscal pressures prompted by warfare,[17] and his own great work on popular revolts demonstrated that the new power of the state in the seventeenth century was crucial in that century's evolution. But when asked to halve his original work for publication in English, the chief casualties were the first six chapters, which dealt mostly with war and the state, especially military taxation, the destruction of castles, army supplies, enlisting soldiers, billeting, and royal taxes. Whereas other sections that were cut were replaced by summaries, this part was simply obliterated. Ultimately, Bercé, like Braudel, felt that "political" or "mainstream" history could be dropped entirely from their oeuvre without damaging the essence of their work.

Braudel's negative attitude towards military history and the study of war was naturally affected by his general attitude towards political history and traditional historiography. From the first, he announced his decision to play

15. Braudel, *The Mediterranean*, 2:1243.

16. These arguments are evident in the second edition of *The Mediterranean*, but much more sharply expressed in the interview with Peter Burke and Helli Koenigsberger of May 1977, which I cite here.

17. Bercé, *History of Peasant Revolts*, 323: "[T]he modern state of France was built by vigorous fiscal policies which were implemented according to the demands made by European war."

down combat and campaigns—what he calls, "l'histoire-bataille, uniquement événementielle."[18] Military history was a largely discredited area by the time Braudel published, noted for its lack of rigor and its narrow, nationalistic bias. Frequently written by retired military officers without adequate historical training, it was replete with simplistic works revolving around great men and events. Yet to understand Braudel's treatment of war in *The Mediterranean*, we must go beyond the historiography to more personal considerations. He wrote the core of the book—"l'essentiel"—between 1939 and 1945, that is, in the midst of a devastating world war and while enduring the hardships of a prisoner of war camp. These painful circumstances seem to me to go some way towards explaining Braudel's search for the enduring, meaningful aspects of universal existence in *The Mediterranean*. The book is full of references to destiny and to permanent forces which are the equivalent of a *deus ex machina*. It is devoted largely to that which is, if not unchangeable, at least untouched by our brief, often violent and tortured lives. Human existence is dwarfed by the "structural" forces of the universe which gain heroic proportions in Braudel's universe. Moreover, human actions take on a different meaning when seen as unconscious reactions to forces that cannot be seen or resisted, rather than as an expression of their own destructive and petty volition.

Braudel accepted that he must include war in *The Mediterranean* because of its centrality to human existence—"ce formidable remous de la vie des hommes." This prompted him to include a section on bureaucracies because he recognized that war is the business of states.[19] But from the start he was limited by his determination to treat war as a neutral construct, a product of structural forces rather than human action. He argued that war and peace were consequences of economic conjunctures, and he related different levels of economic crisis to different types of war. His two main categories were internal, that is, within one civilization, and external, "between two mutually hostile worlds." While the former occur in "fair weather," the latter were a product of adverse economic circumstances.[20] Such categorizations now seem facile as well as flawed, particularly in the absence of in-depth analyses of ideological and technological factors, but they reflect his obsession with economic forces. Braudel admitted that the analysis had to be taken further,

18. Braudel, *La Méditerranée*, 1st ed., 661. He refused to discuss the role of individuals in war outside of the section on events.

19. Braudel, *La Méditerranée*, 1st ed., 664.

20. Braudel, *The Mediterranean*, 2:842, 897–99.

but he was not prepared to do so until scholars had identified "the long-term patterns, regular rhythms, and relationships underlying the history of events." As late as 1973 he used the lack of progress in this sphere to justify his refusal to provide "philosophical" explanations (his term) about the nature of war.[21]

Behind the intellectual explanation lay a deepening pessimism. Whereas in 1949 he wrote, "la guerre n'est pas, sans plus, la contre-civilisation," noting, however, that wars exhausted states and did not always bring benefits; by the 1960s he appreciated more keenly that war "touched every human activity" and that it was "a waste of money."[22] His pessimism can be traced in one of those poetic passages that still make this book a pleasure to read. Reflecting in the 1940s on the frequency of war during the second half of the sixteenth century, he had written,

> On n'a heureusement pas le droit de tirer, d'une familiarité avec cinquante années de luttes diverses, mais continues en Méditerranée, des conclusions sur la guerre en général. Cinquante années sont peu de chose dans la vaste histoire des hommes. Ainsi s'évitera-t-on une conclusion assez pessimiste, à savoir que la guerre, à travers ses formes diverses, ses relèves, ses changements, maintient sa perpétuité, que ses fils rouges ne cessent jamais de se mêler, quoi qu'il arrive, à la trame du temps. Et que jamais enfin sa vie ne peut s'éteindre.[23]

By the second edition, the tone had darkened: "we are forced to a pessimistic conclusion…war in its metamorphoses, revivals, Protean disguises, and degenerate forms, reasserts its perennial nature."[24] And he goes on in what veers between poetry and prayer: "Bellum omnium pater, the old adage was familiar to the men of the sixteenth century. War, the begetter of all things, the creature of all things, the river with a thousand sources, the sea without a shore: begetter of all things except peace, so ardently longed for, so rarely attained. Every age constructs its own war, its own types of war."[25]

---

21. Braudel, *The Mediterranean*, 2:836.

22. Braudel, *La Méditerranée*, 1st ed., 661; on 665 we find: "On sait qu'elles accablent les états: innombrables sont alors les guerres qui ne paient pas." Compare with Braudel, *The Mediterranean*, 2:840, 842.

23. Braudel, *La Méditerranée*, 1st ed., 715.

24. Braudel, *The Mediterranean*, 2:891.

25. Braudel, *The Mediterranean*, 2:891. Compare this with Braudel, *La Méditerranée*, 1st ed., 716: "C'est banalité alors, de reprendre avec Rabelais le vieil adage, *pecunia nervus belli* ou

❧ ❧ ❧

In view of Braudel's dramatic downgrading of politics, events, and war, it is not entirely surprising that a conference dedicated to *The Mediterranean* should have allocated only a small section to these topics. Yet given the organizer's laudable intention to examine the interrelationship of history and the other social sciences, as well as to look into the future of the discipline, there was every reason to expand this section. Because in spite of (or perhaps because of) the attacks and criticisms of Braudel and the so-called New History, political, diplomatic, and war history survived and evolved so dramatically that it is in these areas that we can find the current "cutting edge" of the discipline.

There is no denying the fact that much political, diplomatic, and war history at the turn of the century was narrow, parochial, patriotic, and obsessed with kings and queens and ministers, as well as with the institutions that were considered to be the foundations of modern bureaucratic government. But it did not remain so. As Geoffrey Elton candidly pointed out, the attacks and criticisms were a vital "stimulus given to political history to improve itself."[26] The obsession with the modern nation-state, which condemned generations of students to turgid studies of constitutions and battles, gave way to sophisticated analyses grounded in extensive archival work, detailed criticism of sources, and the use of nondocumentary material, and gave way to subtle studies of the mentalities and conditions of different periods.

The transformation of diplomatic history throws into sharp relief trends that have helped to bring about similar changes in other sectors of the discipline. When Braudel initiated his research, diplomatic history was only marginally less discredited than military history. It was mainly concerned with narrow narratives of the diplomatic correspondence of monarchs and ministers, frequently culled from a single source and dealing with bilateral relations. It seemed for a time that it would disappear as a distinctive branch, with its practitioners either merging into mainstream history or

---

comme Rabelais encore, l'expression de Plutarque, ce 'bellum onnium pater' [sic] qu'avaient déjà recueilli les *Adages* d'Erasme. Père de toutes choses, fils aussi de toutes choses, fleuve aux mille sources diverses.... Père de toutes choses, mais pas toujours de la paix elle-ême, tant rêvée, si rarement atteinte."

26. Juliet Gardiner, ed., *What Is History Today?* (Atlantic Highlands, N.J.: Humanities Press, 1988); see G. R. Elton's comments on 19–21, quote 20.

defecting to international relations. That this branch of the discipline has survived owes a great deal to the value and power of its original methodology as well as to its ability to adapt and embrace other methodologies. By the 1950s quite a different type of approach was evident amongst some of its practitioners. The use of multiple archives and diverse source material was accompanied by far more rigorous analyses of these sources. The study of participants other than monarchs and ministers further broadened and deepened the subject, but perhaps more significant was the appreciation that to study foreign policy effectively it was vital to analyze the broader trends within internal and international politics. Economic issues loom large, but so do ideological issues.[27] Now, as Gordon Martel, the editor of the New International History series, noted, there is a consensus that "ideology, culture, immigration, communications, myths, stereotypes, trade, and finance... all these are essential for good international history."[28]

Consequently, this type of history has been, in the hands of the best practitioners, one of the most powerful forms of historical study, "seeking to reconstruct the *Weltanschauung*" of monarchs, statesmen, and diplomats, and "to explore the interplay between the imperatives of political decisions within a system of competitive states and the societies and polities... which produced these decisions."[29] This was said recently of one of the "new international history" founders, Ranghild Hatton, whose wide-ranging concerns and meticulous methodology remain crucial underpinnings of the discipline. The results of this new approach were so positive that two years after Braudel published his second, revised edition of *The Mediterranean,* which further dwarfed man, a leading international historian, James Joll, could assert proudly: "It is only by studying the minds of men that we shall understand the causes of anything."[30]

Hatton and Joll were early exponents of the incorporation of history of ideas into diplomatic history, and both also promoted the use of art and

---

27. Robert Oresko, G. C. Gibbs, and H. M. Scott, eds., *Royal and Republican Sovereignty in Early Modern Europe: Essays in memory of Ragnhild Hatton* (Cambridge: Cambridge University Press, 1997); there is an excellent detailed account of these trends in its lengthy introduction, 1–42.

28. Taken from the Introduction to R. J. B. Bosworth, *Explaining Auschwitz and Hiroshima: History Writing and the Second World War, 1945–1990* (London: Routledge, 1993), ix.

29. Oresko, Gibbs, Scott, *Royal and Republican Sovereignty,* 25 and 24 respectively.

30. "1914: The Unspoken Assumptions," inaugural lecture, London School of Economics (1968). It is a typically witty play on the school's motto: "Rerum Cognoscere Causas."

literature, which has immeasurably enriched the historian. It proved a small step to go from this to court studies, which were developing independently under the tutelage and influence of art history, literary criticism, sociology, and anthropology. It looked for a while as if a new trend would be set by the German émigré historical sociologist Norbert Elias.[31] Significantly, while he was and is much read, it did not open a new route for court studies, which remained largely in the domain of art history and folklorism. Few of the works closely tied to nonhistorical methodologies were incorporated into the historical canon, and only gradually has significant progress been made in the incorporation of court studies into political and diplomatic history. Fundamental change did not come about because of the use of sociology or anthropology, but as a result of the extension of more traditional historical methodologies and approaches. Even a notable work such as Peter Burke's *The Fabrication of Louis XIV,* which was strongly influenced by what one reviewer called his unrivaled knowledge of "associated disciplines," is marked by its essentially narrative structure and integration into political history and events.[32] It is no coincidence, however, that international historians have been at the forefront of developing court studies, which seem to me to be currently the most complex and exciting field of historical research. The subject requires the fusion of economics, art, ritual, patronage, and politics; it combines the study of such diverse topics as gift giving and the distribution and use of space. Internal and international aspects are fully integrated, whether in terms of trade or politics. Unsurprisingly, "The Court as an Economic Institution" was chosen as a plenary session in the World Congress of Economic Historians (1998)—yet the international group that participated included virtually no specialists in what is known as economic history, but several with traditional diplomatic and political history backgrounds.[33]

Another historical field that has suddenly expanded and experienced major changes recently is the study of identities. Identity is not only a current political obsession but a potentially fascinating area of historical research for early modern scholars, who are still developing ways of handling the partial and problematic materials that survive. Once the preserve of sociologists,

31. Norbert Elias, *Die höfische Gesellschaft* (1969), trans. Edmund Jephcott, *The Court Society* (New York: Pantheon, 1983).

32. Peter Burke, *The Fabrication of Louis XIV* (New Haven: Yale University Press, 1992); the comment was made by Keith Thomas.

33. Maurice Aymard and Marzio Romani, eds., *La Cour comme institution économique* (Paris: La Maison des Sciences, 1998).

anthropologists, and nonmainstream historians, the study of identities is in the process of being claimed and incorporated by so-called political and diplomatic historians, many of whom have approached it from the vantage point of nationalism. Like the court, the subject of identities brings political history (as well as diplomatic and war history) into contact with a broad spectrum of art, ritual, psychology, culture, and so forth. The subject is still at a stage where it can benefit hugely from direct contact with associated disciplines, as I appreciated at a conference in 1997 which brought historians, sociologists, and anthropologists together to explore the subject. Given the fast learning curve of history, it would not be surprising if historians quickly absorbed the lessons of these related disciplines and formulated new analytical structures to aid research.[34] L. Colley's *Britons* is a precocious and admirable example of how fruitful a predominantly historical perspective (or analysis) can be.[35] The dispersed Spanish monarchy of Philip II has prompted a number of recent studies on the issue which show the different approaches historians are bringing to bear on the subject. Scholars such as Anthony Pagden and Pablo Fernández Albaladejo have produced illuminating accounts that rely more on the history of ideas and on textual analysis, and which concentrate primarily on the elite. Others such as I. A. A. Thompson and Richard Kagan have focused on local, mainly urban levels; my own work has linked the subject more to international relations and war.[36]

Already in the mid-1980s Geoffrey Elton compared political history to a portmanteau or "a vacuum cleaner sucking in the products of other forms of historical study." He referred to social history as a "service industry" for political history.[37] That was exaggerated and unkind—and was probably intended to be—but it embodies an evident truth, that what is sometimes

34. The conference was organized by Peter Marshall and Roy Bridges. A sample of the papers is included in *Transactions of the Royal Historical Society*, 6th ser., vol. 8 (October 1998): 189–355.

35. L. Colley, *Briton: Forging the Nation 1707–1837* (London: Pimlico, 1992).

36. Pablo Fernández Albaladejo, *Fragmentos de Monarquía* (Madrid: Alianza, 1992); Anthony Pagden, *Spanish Imperialism and the Political Imagination* (New Haven: Yale University Press, 1990); I. A. A. Thompson, "Castile, Spain and the Monarchy: The Political Community from *patria natural* to *patria nacional*," and Richard L. Kagan, "Clio and the Crown: Writing History in Habsburg Spain," both in *Spain, Europe and the Atlantic World: Essays in Honour of J. H. Elliott*, ed. Richard L. Kagan and Geoffrey Parker (Cambridge: Cambridge University Press, 1995); M. J. Rodríguez-Salgado, "Christian, Civilised and Spanish: Multiple Identities in Sixteenth-Century Spain," *Transactions of the Royal Historical Society*, 6th ser., vol. 8 (October 1998).

37. Gardiner, ed., *What Is History Today*, 19–20.

referred to as "mainstream" history has absorbed the lessons of social history, and is in the process of absorbing much that economic history, demography, mentalities, and the like have provided, both in terms of questions and methodologies. The closure of separate social and economic history departments in Britain, and the division of such historians into two extremes of econometrics or mainstream history demonstrates the significant transmutation of this type of history. Publication ventures for new histories reflect these trends, abandoning in many instances separate series for political, social, and economic history.

Currently, a sound study of early modern politics entails an analysis of how power was manifested and imposed, involving work on display in art and ritual as well as examining law, religion, political ideas, and the links between monarch, court, elites, and nonelites. It is a true hybrid, integrating traditional archival work and even the most traditional forms of genealogical and family studies alongside sophisticated analyses of patronage and clientèle systems shaped by sociology and anthropology. The importance of economics and finance is widely acknowledged but stripped of the determinism implied in some of the *Annales*-inspired works. While most research-based publications concentrate on one or a few of these aspects, it is generally accepted that a sound understanding will only come with the integration of these varied strands. The study of politics, including work on the monarchy and the state, has embraced the broadest possible subject matter and research base.

It is significant in this respect that a group of scholars working on Philip II's court, led by José Martínez Millán, have recently eschewed some of the popular, nonhistorical methodologies used in the study of patronage, especially those taken from sociology and anthropology. While acknowledging the benefits that had initially come to history from such borrowing, Martínez Millán was concerned at the way historical research was being shaped by methodologies that seek to establish universal and timeless models and typologies which he regards as antithetical to historical concerns. He has appealed for historians to return to full consciousness of changes over a specific timescale. Consequently he and others have deliberately resorted to traditional, document-based, archival work as the primary form of investigation for clientèles.[38] The way forward is not by stepping back, of course, but by reclaiming the fundamental, time-bound element that lies at the heart of history.

---

38. José Martínez Millán, ed., *Instituciones y Elites de poder en la monarquía hispana durante el siglo XVI* (Madrid: Universidad Autónoma Madrid, 1992), 12–13.

Martínez Millán is among those historians currently broadening as well as deepening court and political studies by incorporating issues of religious ideology and confessionalism. Religious history, which was for many years even more discredited than political history, is another area which has been utterly transformed over the last couple of decades. Innovative and exciting studies from historians such as John Bossy, Julio Caro Baroja, Louis Châtellier, Norman Cohn, Carlo Ginzburg, Ronnie Po-chia Hsia, Robert Scribner, Keith Thomas, and others have altered our perception of both popular and elite culture as well as religion. Their very names evoke the geographical and national dispersion of these authors and the widespread impact of this historiographical trend, not least as a result of the beneficial influence of the Annales School. Instead of looking back through the lens of later doctrinal controversies and development, religious history has focused on contemporary beliefs and mentalities. A necessary process of fusion is currently taking place as these findings are incorporated into broader political and diplomatic history. The theme of confessionalization, which Heinz Schilling has done so much to sensitize us to, is particularly crucial. The study of ideological issues in the early modern era is helping us to review a wide range of topics from the nature of legitimization and propaganda to the differences between personal and public faith.

Like religious history, military history was characterized by narrow, partisan work, and its practitioners were seldom university trained. Yet the situation was changing even as Braudel was writing his first edition of *The Mediterranean*, particularly in Germany where before the First World War battle accounts were showing a marked drift away from heroic narratives to a stress on changing technologies. Braudel was largely unreceptive although not blind to such changes. In the first edition of *The Mediterranean* he complained that historians had focused on states and paid little attention to such things as "techniques"—which I take to imply both strategy and technology—but this was omitted from the second edition.[39] He made a significant contribution by his emphasis on the importance of the introduction of artillery to galleys, which entailed both technological advance and tactical changes, but it was left to John Francis Guilmartin to demonstrate that technological and tactical innovations within a narrow, clearly defined time-space, were as crucial for the decline of the early modern

---

39. Braudel, *The Mediterranean*, 1st ed., 663; 2d ed., 2:837.

Mediterranean as the long-term factors Braudel had identified.[40] Guilmartin's book on Mediterranean warfare can also serve as an excellent example of how by then military history was far more than a matter of battles, and—as political and international history—was free to experiment with different chronological and nonlinear forms of narrative to enhance the analytical impact of the historian.

Nevertheless, it is true to say that military history remained more closely bound than most other forms of history to the dictates of ideology and governments, and this hindered innovation and development. For instance, Gioacchino Volpe's research in the 1920s uncovered a picture of industrial unrest and defeatism in Italy during the First World War, which radically altered the received (heroic) view of fellow historians. Mussolini put a stop to Volpe's work, as well as to that of Angelo Gatti, on the grounds that Italy needed myths more than it needed history.[41] Authoritarian regimes, whether fascist or communist, appreciated the need to control history and did so, as democratic regimes are doing now by a mixture of targeting grants and offering political and personal favor.[42] From the dark days of 1939, when Charles Oman felt impelled to write "a plea for military history," the field has evolved into a most innovative and fascinating historiographical area, as Frank Tallet emphasized.[43] The narrowly nationalist orientation and narrative of campaigns ("operational history") gave way, particularly after the 1970s, to a wide-ranging, analytical discipline better defined as "the comprehensive understanding of the relations between armed forces and society."[44] Borrowing heavily from social and economic history as well as work on mentalities, "the historian who studies war," as Michael Howard noted in 1976, does so "not to develop norms for action but to enlarge his understanding of the past." In fact, he claimed, "there is no branch of human activity which is

40. John Francis Guilmartin Jr., *Gunpowder and Galleys: Changing Technology and Mediterranean Warfare at Sea in the Sixteenth Century* (London: Cambridge University Press, 1974).

41. Piero Melograni, "L'Historiographie Italienne de la Première Guerre Mondiale," *Bulletin du Centre de recherche, Historial de la Grande Guerre* 3 (1991): 10.

42. For an example of such manipulation, see Michael Burleigh, *Germany Turns Eastwards: A Study of Ostforschung in the Third Reich* (Cambridge: Cambridge University Press, 1988); one of the most striking recent instances of political manipulation through finance and ideological reinforcement occurred in France over the anniversary of the revolution.

43. Frank Tallett, *War and Society in Early Modern Europe, 1495–1715* (London: Routledge, 1992), 1–20.

44. Geoffrey Best's words; André Corvisier and Arthur Marwick were key figures in this transformation; see Gardiner, ed., *What Is History Today?* 4–17, quote 13.

not to a greater or lesser extent relevant to his subject. He has to study war not only…in the framework of political history, but in the framework of economic, social, and cultural history as well. War has been part of a totality of human experience, the parts of which can be understood only in relation to one another."[45]

The general approach was summed up by Modris Ekstein thus: to explain war the historian has to look not just at the high command, strategy, weapons, organization, tanks, politicians, but the morale and motivation of the common soldiers. Events and material culture have to be investigated, and more importantly how people responded, because "if this point is apposite to the study of modern culture then it is also pertinent to the study of modern warfare."[46] In the last two decades further progress has been made by dint of cross-disciplinary borrowing: sociology, in the case of Tony Ashworth's *Trench Warfare 1914–1918*, which focused on the experience of ordinary men; psychology in the works of Eric Leed, such as *No Man's Land*; literary evidence and literary theory in the case of Paul Fussell's *The Great War and Modern Memory*,[47] and by the broader cultural-cum-philosophical enquiry in Modris Eksteins's *Rites of Spring*. German war history was largely changed by historical sociology. In English-speaking countries, gender studies have led to interesting studies of masculinity and war, as well as the role of women, all of which have helped to create a distinctive "school."[48]

War history has often crossed large time frames, and this may help to account for the rapid adoption of innovations and general approaches.[49]

---

45. Michael Howard, *War in European History* (London: Oxford University Press, 1976), ix–x.

46. Modris Eksteins, *Rites of Spring: The Great War and the Birth of the Modern Age* (Boston: Houghton Mifflin, 1989), 17: The historians of war, he goes on to say, must "unearth manners and morals, customs and values, both articulated and assumed. As difficult as the task may be cultural history must at least try to capture the spirit of an age."

47. Michael Ashworth, *Trench Warfare 1914–1918: The Live and Let Live System* (New York: Holmes & Meier, 1980); Eric Leed, *No Man's Land: Combat and Identity in World War I* (New York: Cambridge University Press, 1979); Paul Fussell, *The Great War and Modern Memory* (London: Oxford University Press, 1975). See also "La Grande Guerre: Pays, histoire, mémoire," *Bulletin du Centre de Recherche, Historial de la Grande Guerre* 2 (August 1990) and 3 (February 1991). I am most grateful to Professor D. Stevenson for bringing this work to my attention.

48. Surveyed in *La Grande Guerre*, 2:3–7.

49. See for example, John Keegan's influential contribution on the experience of ordinary men in battle, *The Face of Battle: A Study of Agincourt, Waterloo and the Somme* (London: Jonathan Cape, 1976).

Early modern specialists were among the earliest to embrace new trends and explore the interaction of armies and society and to bring back into center stage ideological factors and the internal and external impact of war finance: for example, Geoffrey Parker's *The Army of Flanders* juxtaposed records of mutinies and of state finance; Herbert Langer's work on the Thirty Years' War used cartoons and visual material to illustrate how armies lived.[50] Recently, however, early modern war studies have been diverted by an exaggerated preoccupation with the so-called Military Revolution Debate prompted by Michael Roberts's lecture of 1955 and set alight by Parker's reworking of the theory in 1988. As Clifford Rogers noted, the positive side of this debate has been to help bring military history into mainstream history and to make it second nature for early modernists to look at the interaction between war, technology, and state formation. The growth in bureaucracy and the state, fiscal problems, the nature of popular revolts, the impact of technological change and even the expansion of the West are areas which have benefited from the debate.[51] The downside is that it has drawn attention away from other interesting perspectives. It is ironic that the microhistory techniques so skillfully used by early modernists such as Emmanuel Le Roy Ladurie, Natalie Zemon Davis, and Robert Darnton have been successfully employed recently by Michael Geyer to analyze the German massacre of Italian civilians in Civitella on 29 June 1944.[52]

Braudel's dream of turning war into a typological exercise has been largely rejected by historians but more recently taken up and realized by international relations specialists. The results have essentially confirmed the nonhistorical nature of such an approach. Wars have been collected, dissected, and collated; collective causes have been identified and labeled—

50. Geoffrey Parker, *The Army of Flanders and the Spanish Road, 1567–1659* (Cambridge: Cambridge University Press, 1972); Herbert Langer, *The Thirty Years' War,* trans. of *Hortus Bellicus,* C. S. V. Salt, trans. (New York: Hippocrene Books, 1980).

51. Geoffrey Parker, *The Military Revolution: Military Innovation and the Rise of the West, 1500–1800* (Cambridge: Cambridge University Press, 1988); for a collection of the most influential articles in the debate, see *The Military Revolution Debate: Readings in the Military Transformation of Early Modern Europe,* ed. Clifford J. Rogers (Boulder: Westview, 1995), 2–3.

52. Michael Geyer, "'Es muß daher mit schnellen und drakonischen Maßnahmen durchgegriffen werden.' Civitella in Val di Chiana am 29. Juni 1944," in *Vernichtungskrieg: Verbrechen der Wehrmacht, 1941–1944,* ed. Hannes Heer and Klaus Naumann (Hamburg: Hamburger Edition, 1996). I am grateful to Professor M. Knox for bringing this work to my attention.

largely in order to predict or prevent future conflicts. The aims of such studies are laudable; their findings at times verge on the nonsensical, such as the conclusion reached by some analysts that frontiers play no role in war. According to Kalevi Holsti, it is only quite recently that such researchers "reached a consensus that monocausal explanations are theoretically and empirically deficient." The attempt to create an abstract and universal model out of a highly diverse phenomenon in which personalities and other unpredictable factors play a key role, has not significantly advanced historical understanding of war and peace.[53] The path Braudel charted has not proved fruitful for the historian.

The distinctive mix he offered in *The Mediterranean*, which highlighted economic factors and underplayed the role of human and ideological factors, has recently been the subject of controversy once again because it is at the heart of Paul Kennedy's popular survey, *The Rise and Fall of the Great Powers*.[54] Kennedy, like Braudel, rejects simple economic determinism, yet his analysis mostly suggests a direct causal link between great power status and finance. For rather different reasons, Kennedy too has underestimated the role of ideology and of individuals in war, and this has been strongly criticized, as has his aim of trying to fit complex and changing power relationships into a single model.[55] Other similarities lie in the fact that Kennedy sees military conflict as inevitable yet does not deal explicitly with the role of war, but gives greater importance to external than to internal factors when accounting for it. Curiously, however, the roots of their work are rather different. Far from rejecting pre-twentieth-century historiography, Kennedy was inspired by Leopold von Ranke's essay of 1833. This is an obvious reason why Kennedy's approach has been widely dismissed as "old-fashioned." Although one often encounters the argument that broad studies such as those offered by Braudel and Kennedy cannot encompass "everything," it is surely significant that now, as fifty years ago, dramatically reducing the role of humans and ideology while emphasizing the power of economic and other external forces is considered by many as essentially unhistorical.

53. Kalevi J. Holsti, *Peace and War: Armed Conflicts and International Order 1648–1989* (Cambridge: Cambridge University Press, 1991), reviews some of the trends briefly at the start of his book. To create his model he used 177 conflicts from varied timescales and areas.

54. Paul M. Kennedy, *The Rise and Fall of the Great Powers: Economic Change and Military Conflict from 1500 to 2000* (London: Unwin Hyman, 1988). I am not aware that anyone else perceives what are to me evident similarities with Braudel.

55. David Reynolds's review in *Historical Journal* 32 (1989): 475–87, is a good example of the issues raised by the debate.

❧ ❧ ❧

Reflecting on Braudel's *Mediterranean* highlights the fact that books with brilliant insights and radical innovations are seldom an effective or rapid way to bring about change in historical research and writing. The more striking and diverse a work is, the more it crosses boundaries, the more likely it is to remain a unique insight: enduring, certainly, appearing almost as fresh to later generations as to his own, but still something apart from the main-stream. Moderators, in the sense of writers who demonstrate how these innovations can be applied and who successfully fuse innovations with tradi-tional and well-established practice, often play a crucial role in the dissemi-nation and transmission of such works.[56] Language barriers too frequently exacerbate the distance between new and older types of history and retard its adoption. Commenting on new works about the First World War by the "Anglo-Saxon school of cultural history," Annette Becker remarked that until those works were widely available in translation, their impact on France would be small since they dealt with mentalities in a way that was alien to the French historiographical tradition.[57] A similar process of linguistic barri-ers and the shock of the new approach hindered the dissemination of Brau-del's work in the English-speaking world. Peter Burke's efforts to get *The Mediterranean* translated into English foundered for many years, during which he acted as a transmitter and mediator of the Annales School in gen-eral by both practicing new types of history and by publishing translations of key articles.[58]

Yet the difficulties of integrating the most profound insights of *The Med-iterranean* have proved insuperable for reasons other than language and nov-elty. Braudel's exploration of time in *The Mediterranean* was arguably its most startling and enduring contribution, and as noted earlier, he subse-quently judged it to be its most important element. Although in the hands

---

56. For example, I suspect Richard Overy, *Why the Allies Won* (London: Jonathan Cape, 1995), which incorporated new insights into war with more traditional forms of study, will make a greater impact on the historiography than the more novel books cited earlier.

57. Annette Becker, *La Grande Guerre*, no. 2, p. 16, was referring to Mosse, Fussell, and Eksteins: "ils ne sont pas écrits à la manière dont les Français conçoivent l'histoire des menta-lités."

58. For example, Peter Burke, ed., *Economy and Society in Early Modern Europe: Essays from Annales* (London: Routledge & Kegan Paul, 1972). Burke has been notable from the start for his extraordinary range and habitual "borrowing" from other disciplines.

of less skilled emulators it led to some dire historical writing in which fairly traditional research topics were surrounded (that is, burdened) with introductory sections of third-rate geographical material and simplistic narratives of long-term trends, the experimentation of different layers of time combined with the use of different types of narrative and nonnarrative structures in history has been crucial to the improvement of the discipline and its enduring vitality. Significantly, however, Braudel failed to incorporate the different levels of time, particularly the third and most popular historical level, the world of human lives and political events, and his successors have been no more successful. Moreover, by leaning so far towards economic determinism and underplaying the role of Philip II and of people in general, as well as ideology, Braudel cut himself off from a major direction taken by history since. He continued to emphasize the long-term not least because he believed it was the crucial crossroad for the social sciences, its vital meeting point.[59] Consequently, his impact on Philip II studies or the history of the Spanish monarchy has not been profound. One point that has been generally incorporated is his perceptive work on distances and their impact on policy. For the most part, however, *The Mediterranean* is used for details on events and trends in the area, and as a historiographical object in itself. By sidelining human agency Braudel ensured that he would not transform history.

It is not the startlingly innovative Braudel, but John Elliott who has long dominated the field of early modern Hispanic history. Elliott, like Braudel, was much influenced by Lucien Febvre's *Philippe II et la Franche-Comté*, but his work developed along other routes. Elliott too had creative vision that allowed him to grasp at once the advantages of imposing a different vantage point to illuminate the workings of the early modern state, yet he did not shy away from studying central state authority or from tackling the biography of major statesmen. His work is characterized by extraordinary attention to contemporary documentation and a great sensitivity to the mentality of the period that has little to do with historical fashions.[60] Elliott demanded the same scholarly rigor and breadth from his students and facilitated this by

---

59. This came through clearly in Braudel's article on "History and the Social Sciences" from *Annales E.S.C* (1958), published in *Economy and Society*, 11–42.

60. John Huxtable Elliott, *The Revolt of the Catalans: A Study in the Decline of Spain, 1598–1640* (Cambridge: Cambridge University Press, 1963); idem, *The Count-Duke of Olivares: A Statesman in an Age of Decline* (New Haven: Yale University Press, 1986); a taste of some of his other work: idem, *Spain and Its World, 1500–1700: Selected Essays* (New Haven: Yale University Press, 1989). On Febvre's influence, see: *Solemne investidura de Doctor Honoris Causa al Profesor Sir John Elliott* (Barcelona: University of Barcelona, 1994).

encouraging them to approach other scholars with complementary interests and methodologies such as international history, demography, quantification, economic history, and social history.[61] It seems fitting, therefore, that one of his students, Geoffrey Parker, still dominates Philip II studies.[62]

If a young Braudel, with his breadth of vision and enthusiasm, were planning research on Philip II and the Mediterranean now, would a study of the history of events, of politics, diplomacy, and war have looked so dismal as to prompt a wise adviser to suggest that a study of the sea was preferable to a study of man, politics, and war? Of course my conclusion that he would have opted for the world of man rather than that of mountains and water is hardly surprising. It could be argued that once Braudel had traced many of the enduring or long-term patterns in the life of the Mediterranean, there is little left besides ephemeral events and narrower dimensions, but the recent 984-page tome on Philip II and "his time" is reminder enough that big books are not impossible on the subject even now.[63] Moreover, given Braudel's philosophical bent and circumstances, he might well have turned another subject besides history into a contemplation of time. My point is that his original thesis was not a good topic and that he would have changed it now also. Given the current state of historiography, however, he would not have been able to dismiss the realms of politics and war as mere dust and fireflies.[64] My own fascination with Philip II's Mediterranean policy took me along the path Braudel had trodden and it was soon evident that the subject needed a broader context. The two most obvious options, it seemed to me, were either to look at both sides of the ideological and political divide—lessons in classical Arabic and Ottoman Turkish combined with limited employment opportunities put an end to that—or to focus on the monarch and his empire. The king's Mediterranean policy made no sense unless located within a broad study of his political, ideological, and economic

61. See their "Appreciation," esp. 10–11, in *Spain, Europe and the Atlantic World,* ed. Kagan and Parker.

62. The biography by Geoffrey Parker, *Philip II* (Boston: Little Brown, 1978), is still in print and the most widely read. Equally influential have been Parker's works on Spanish foreign policy, e.g., idem., *Spain and the Netherlands 1559–1659: Ten studies* (London: Collins, 1979).

63. M. Fernández Alvarez, *Felipe II y su tiempo* (Madrid: Espasa, 1998). The book is divided into three sections: a general review of the period 1527 to 1598 with topics ranging from bureaucracy to daily life; then events and a final section with a profile of "the man."

64. Braudel, *The Mediterranean,* 2:901: "Events are the ephemera of history; they pass across the stage like fire-flies, hardly glimpsed before they settle back into darkness and as often as not into oblivion."

worlds. I took a contrary path to Braudel, going deep within a very short timescale.[65] Philip II remained an enigma to Braudel; familiar yet shadowy and remote. The alternative option was to make Philip the center of study, and to perfect our understanding of the monarch and his time.

For today's historian, such a choice does not imply a narrowing of boundaries. The geographic and economic projections of Philip II's world are worldwide; the mental worlds that need to be explored are of extraordinary breadth and complexity. My own work continues to lean strongly towards political and international dimensions, while increasingly incorporating ideas, art, and culture. By contrast, Fernando Bouza, who started with politics and ideas, has gone on to explore Philip II in the context of broad cultural trends, fitting him into such diverse contexts as studies on reading and libraries, court jesters, and most recently, within the prevailing culture of praise and opposition.[66] The range and potential of the available options have not made the problems facing the historian in terms of choice of subject matter, events, or methodology any easier, of course. If anything, the diversification of the history of politics, states, and war has made the choices much more difficult. The very thing that made Braudel so uncomfortable with mainstream history, therefore, would haunt him still.

One of Braudel's most significant contributions to history was his ardent advocacy of the integration of the social sciences, and he attempted to demonstrate the way in which history could successfully borrow from related disciplines. It could be argued that Braudel borrowed more successfully from outside the discipline of history than from within. The immense richness of current historiography is in part due to its incorporation of sociology, anthropology, and economics along the way, with the odd foray into fields such as psychology. But is this necessarily the only, or even the best way forward for

65. A revised version of my original research was published as M. J. Rodríguez-Salgado, *The Changing Face of Empire: Charles V, Philip II and Habsburg Authority, 1551–1559* (Cambridge: Cambridge University Press, 1988). The original research was to 1565, but the work was too substantive for one volume.

66. Some examples: Fernando J. Bouza Alvarez, *Portugal no tempo dos Filipes: politica, cultura, representações(1580–1668)* (Lisbon: Edições Cosmos, 2000); idem, "La Biblioteca de El Escorial y el orden de los saberes en el siglo XVI," in *El Escorial: Arte, poder y cultura en la corte de Felipe II* (Madrid: Universidad Compluteade de Madrid, 1989); idem, "La majestad de Felipe II: Construcción del mito real," in *La corte de Felipe II,* ed. J. Martínez Millán (Madrid: Alianza Editorial, 1994); idem, "Servidumbres de la soberana grandeza: Criticar al rey en la corte de Felipe II," in *Imágenes históricas de Felipe II*, ed. Alfredo Alvar Ezquerra (Madrid: Centro de Estudios Cervantinos): 141–79.

history now? After decades of interaction, it is hardly surprising that many of the questions and some of the methods of the sociologist, anthropologist, and economist have been absorbed and become the staple of "mainstream" history. They have become integral parts of the historian's craft. But one should not make the mistake of ascribing improvements in historiography solely to its interaction with the social sciences. Take the topic of popular revolts, for example. In the late 1960s it benefited greatly from incorporating sociological and anthropological elements as well as economics, but to a great extent these advances were the result of the fruitful (if not always cordial) conflict between Marxist and non-Marxist historians, particularly the clash between Roland Mousnier and Boris Porchnev. Similarly, it is worth noting that the earliest accounts of the lives and experiences of the ordinary soldier which lie at the heart of the "regeneration" of war history were the result of ideologically influenced fascist history. Only later was it affected by sociology.[67]

While borrowing and interacting with the social sciences is a good and useful thing for the historian, it has serious limitations. Chronology lies at the heart of history, and its etymology serves as a necessary reminder of our own roots: *chronos* is the Greek for time; *logos* means discourse. Time and the word are our foundations, and these are not boundaries that many of the social sciences will admit. Even Braudel kept coming back to the fundamental point that the historian's time is at the heart of its division from the other social sciences, which can ignore time and duration. More vital is the interaction with other historians. It is significant in this respect that the topic of popular revolt, while continuing to produce informative works, has long been stagnant. It will not really move further until its practitioners resist the lure of more ethnography and rediscover and reintegrate with political and war history.[68] Questions of ideology—religion, patriotism, identity, and the like—the interplay of local elites and court factions, the impact of external factors such as international politics and so on need to be integrated fully. It will advance by coming into line with the historical fields which some of its researchers once thought backward and old-fashioned, but which have, in some ways, overtaken them.

67. André Corvisier, *Armies and Societies in Europe, 1494–1789* (Bloomington: Indiana University Press, 1976), vii.

68. The publishers marketed Yves-Marie Bercé's, *History of Peasant Revolts*, "not only to historians of early modern Europe but also to sociologists and anthropologists as well as general readers." He commented: "A touch of ethnology is an improvement on scholarship pure and simple" (2).

While engaged in writing *The Mediterranean*, Braudel too inclined to the view that the future of history lay in discarding traditional forms such as political, diplomatic, and war history, and integrating instead with the other social sciences. For the majority of historians this did not prove an attractive or fruitful option. Traditional historiography reformed and transformed itself—partly, we should acknowledge, by dint of learning from associated social sciences and partly by broadening its area of competence and refining its analytical tools. It is a consequence of and a tribute to these multiple changes that we should, once again, be at a stage of linguistic chaos with regard to the name of our discipline. "Traditional," "political," "mainstream," "general"—these are the most favored in current usage yet none of these labels fits. Perhaps it is time that we should reclaim the original and best title: history. The appeal has been made before, but the concession is still pending. While Braudel had serious doubts fifty years ago over the need to continue with a history of politics and war, I dare to assert that he would recognize now that the "old" history of politics and war has so renewed itself that it now best achieves that totality he himself aimed at: "L'histoire est l'image de la vie sous toutes ses formes."

Chapter 7

THE *LONGUE DURÉE* AND CYCLES OF REVOLT IN EUROPEAN HISTORY

JACK A. GOLDSTONE

Fernand Braudel's *Mediterranean* pulses with varied rhythms. The yearly turn of the seasons governs the harvest, the sailing of battle fleets, and the range of the olive and the vine. Over decades, harvests rise and fall, while nations and civilizations ebb and flow across the shores of the Mediterranean Sea. Over the century from 1480 to 1580, the population doubles, trade expands, and cities flourish, an expansionary wave which crests at the end of the century, to be followed by financial crises and rebellions across the whole of the Mediterranean basin in the early-to-mid-seventeenth century, from North Africa to Turkey, from Portugal to Naples and Sicily.

Calling attention to these varied beats in historical time was one of the great virtues of Braudel's work. In the fifty years since Braudel wrote, however, even longer cycles have been discerned in European and global history.[1] The most fascinating of such waves have been the waves of social and political revolts that have swept across Europe and the world, at ever shorter intervals, four times since the High Middle Ages: in 1280–1380, in 1580–1680, in 1770–1870, and from 1910 to the present day (using whole centuries to roughly mark out these periods). Over the last nine hundred years, these four centuries were distinguished by unusually frequent and widespread incidences of social and political revolts; the remaining five centuries, though hardly devoid of suffering, military conflicts, and local disorders, nonetheless show a markedly lower incidence of major assaults on the political and social order.

---

1. Immanuel Wallerstein, *The Modern World System* (New York: Academic Press, 1974); idem, "Long Waves as Capitalist Process," *Review* 7 (1984): 559–75; Jack A. Goldstone, "The Causes of Long Waves in Early Modern History," in *The Vital One: Essays in Honor of Jonathan R. T. Hughes,* Joel Mokyr, ed. (Greenwich, Conn.: JAI Press, 1991).

What can account for these waves of revolt and revolution? What hidden drummer is pounding out the beat according to which states rise and fall? This has been a puzzle for social scientists and historians for two generations.[2] On the one hand, most historians have sought the origins of these revolts in the particular elements of national histories, or at the most, in trends that have underpinned a particular century. On the other hand, social scientists have offered theories of revolution designed to span a large number of cases across time and space. I wish to suggest that, in this stark form, both approaches are misguided. However impressive and ambitious theories may be, it is wrong to seek the same single drummer beating her lonely drum, and forcing all kings and emperors to march in line, across the centuries. Yet it is equally wrong to treat each revolution as unique, as having no internal rhythms or processes in common with other episodes of revolution and revolt. Causal uniformity is an almost certain error in explaining cycles of revolt and revolution, but trying to understand the *processes* that lead states to falter and peoples to rise can help make sense of otherwise paradoxical patterns in the last millennium of global history.

I wish to consider four general explanations that have been offered to account for revolts and revolutions: one based on variations in climate, one based on innovations in technology, one based on shifts in political culture, and one based on demographic change (and, despite some interpretations of my work, I do not privilege the last).

CLIMATE

For Braudel, climate was the one great unifying force in the early modern Mediterranean basin. Climate "imposed its uniformity on both landscape and ways of life."[3] But did climate also impose a temporal uniformity, trailing

---

2.   Jack A. Goldstone, *Revolution and Rebellion in the Early Modern World* (Berkeley: University of California Press, 1991); Theda Skocpol, *States and Social Revolutions* (Cambridge: Cambridge University Press, 1979); Barrington Moore Jr., *Social Origins of Dictatorship and Democracy* (Boston: Beacon Press, 1966); Yves-Marie Bercé, *History of Peasant Revolts* (Cambridge: Polity Press, 1990); Geoffrey Parker and Lesley M. Smith, *The General Crisis of the Seventeenth Century* (London: RKP, 1996); Trevor Aston, ed., *Crisis in Europe, 1560–1660* (New York: Doubleday, 1972); R. B. Merriman, *Six Contemporaneous Revolutions* (Hampden, Conn.: Archon Books, 1963); Roland Mousnier, *Peasant Uprisings in France, Russia, and China* (New York: Harper & Row, 1970).

3.   Fernand Braudel, *The Mediterranean and the Mediterranean World in the Age of Philip II*, trans. Siân Reynolds (New York: Harper Colophon Books, 1972), 231.

long waves of favorable and unfavorable conditions all across Europe, and even into Asia?

The likelihood of such long waves of climate has certainly been explored by many scholars of the Annales School,[4] but with somewhat uncertain results. Recently, new evidence on possible sources of long-term global climate change promises to revitalize this debate.

Photographs of clouds of icy comets crashing into the Earth's atmosphere above the poles, as well as the more spectacular crash of comet Shoemaker-Levy into the mists of Jupiter, have dramatized the impact that collision events can have on planets. The British astronomer S. V. M. Clube has published several papers describing how the entry of comet fragments into Earth's atmosphere could disperse substantial volumes of dust and affect the albedo (reflectivity) of the cloud layer, leading to significant cooling. According to Clube's research, icy comets periodically enter sub-Jovian orbits, and then break up, leaving comet fragments strewn across the planetary plane. As Earth encounters such remnants, the effects will depend on the size and density of the fragments, but could include fireballs in the sky (larger fragments), more frequently observed showers of meteorites (smaller fragments), and—most important for the historian of the *longue durée*—a period ranging from decades to centuries of global cooling.[5]

The incidence of such cooling is dependent on how often such comets are captured in near solar orbit and break up. Clube has estimated, from Chinese records of observations of meteoroid showers that he believes represent swarms of comet fragments (and not the rarer rocky meteoroids from asteroid fragments), that particularly significant incursions took place in A.D. 0–100, 400–600, 1040–1100, 1400–1460, 1500–1540, 1640–1680, and 1760–1800.[6] In each of these periods, the heightened flux of cometary debris would produce climate deterioration and sporadic fireballs and cometary apparitions. Clube thus suggests that the long-standing folktales that associated comet sightings with "bad times" was based on actual associations, not just superstition. If we take the Chinese periodic waves of heightened meteoroid sightings and superimpose them on the history of the West, we find that most of them do correspond with periods of demographic and/or political

---

4. Most widely known in Emmanuel Le Roy Ladurie, *Times of Feast, Times of Famine* (Garden City, N.Y.: Doubleday, 1971).

5. S. V. M. Clube, "The Nature of Punctuational Crises and the Spenglerian Model of Civilization, *Vistas in Astronomy* 39 (1995): 673–98.

6. Clube, "Punctuational Crises," 693.

calamities. The first occurred near the overthrow of the Roman republic and the wars of Augustus (as well as the birth and ministry of Christ). The second period spanned both the fall of the western Roman empire and the great plague under Justinian; the third and fourth periods were times of demographic stagnation; and the fifth, sixth, and seventh periods match almost exactly with the great waves of revolution and revolt; for example, the German peasant wars, the "crisis" of the seventeenth century, and the Atlantic revolutions. Clube thus suggests that there may be a physical mechanism linking cosmic influence, earthly climate, and perceptions of historical events behind the folk litany found in this warning: "blazing stars threatening the world with famine, plague and war; to princes death; to kingdoms many curses; to all estates many losses; to herdsmen rot; to ploughmen hapless seasons; to sailors storms; to cities civil treasons."[7]

Was Shakespeare then wrong, so that our fortune is indeed found in the stars, rather than in ourselves? I think it is far too soon to conclude that it is so. For despite the neat correspondence between Clube's imputed heightened cometary flux and some European disasters, the key intervening link—the climate—simply does not show such neat earthly manifestations. Since early in this century, when research on sunspot cycles showed a correspondence between solar cycles and apparent cooling trends, climate historians have sought to fine-tune the periodization of warming and cooling trends in historical times. The most dramatic such fluctuation is the so-called Little Ice Age, a period of markedly cooler temperatures, with longer and harsher winters. Unfortunately, the various sources of data on climate—from tree ring analysis, to combing the records of vine harvests and cherry blossoms, to the analysis of ice cores from Iceland and Greenland, to surveys of the advance and retreat of the frontier of upland cultivation, to estimates of the advance and retreat of the glaciers—simply fail to agree on any particular periodicity for this phenomenon. According to one author, the Little Ice Age extended from 1500 to 1880, with peaks in the 1590s, 1690s, and 1810s; according to another, it merely coincided with the Maunder minimum in sunspot observations, lasting from 1640 to 1710. A third author notes that ice sheets started advancing in Europe shortly after 1300.[8]

If we are seeking to link climate change to the waves of revolution and revolt in early modern and modern Europe and Asia, this simply will not do. The waves of revolt, thankfully, are fairly well defined. But climate fluctuations show as much local spatial variation as they do temporal variation. As

---

7. Clube, "Punctuational Crises," 673.

Ian D. Whyte recently observed, "There is no agreement on when the Little Ice Age started, when it ended, or even what its basic climatic features were."[9]

More importantly, even if climate *did* fluctuate with some uniformity across time, that would not imply that its effects on the ground would be the same everywhere. As Andrew Appleby has noted in his inquiry into the effect of climate on the incidence of famine in England, "human responses to the climate were more important than the climate itself both in causing famine and eliminating it."[10] The impact of climate cooling on harvest and health depends on the quality of land, on the ability to add animal and labor inputs, and on the availability of fuel and good housing to defeat the rigors of climate. Uplands and valleys, grain and meadow, would be differently affected. And of course if we sought extensions to Asia, the tropical and sub-tropical areas of monsoon rice agriculture would be affected quite differently than (and perhaps opposite to) the temperate, seasonal rain-fed agricultural of the Eurasian plains.

This is not to say that climate had no impact on the course of civilizations; only that any such impact must reflect careful tracing of intermediate mechanisms to establish alleged links. I personally think it likely that a period of cooling after 1300 exacerbated the vulnerability of Eurasian populations to the great plague of the Black Death, as the level of housing and heating technology would have encouraged close huddling of people (and rats) to escape severe cold, facilitating the spread of the plague bacillus. But any more specific connections strike me as implausible. Looking at the long term, Scandinavia through most of the early modern period sustained growing populations, dynamic and successful monarchies, and aggressive military machines, despite a cooler climate and shorter growing season than Germany, Britain, or northern France. Italy's political fragmentation and Spain's frequent internal political struggles after 1700 do not seem to have been put off by their generally warmer climates. Global cooling presumably would have made England, the Netherlands, northern France, and Germany more like Scandinavia, and made Spain, Italy, Greece, and southern France a bit

8. Christian Pfister, "The Little Ice Age: Thermal and Wetness Indices for Central Europe," in *Climate and History,* ed. Robert I. Rotberg and Theodore K. Rabb (Princeton: Princeton University Press, 1981), 85–116; Andrew B. Appleby, "Epidemics and Famine in the Little Ice Age," in ibid., 63–83; Ian D. Whyte, *Climatic Change and Human Society* (London: Arnold, 1995), 46.

9. Whyte, *Climatic Change and Human Society,* 47.

10. Andrew Appleby, "Epidemics and Famine in the Little Ice Age" in *Climate and History,* ed. Rotberg and Rabb, 83.

more like the northern "core" regions of the major European monarchies. Thus any assertion that global cooling would necessarily lead to major population declines, widespread disorders, or weakening of social and political bonds strikes me as unreasonable.

In the shorter term, stretches of bad weather in France between 1782 and 1789 and in Europe between 1842 and 1848 may have contributed to the food crises that helped trigger the French Revolution of 1789 and the European revolutions of 1848. But even worse weather caused horrific harvests in the 1590s in England and France, and in Europe in 1810, without giving rise to state breakdown. In short, I can find no conclusive general linkage between climatic trends or events and the waves of revolts and revolutions.

TECHNOLOGY AND COMMUNICATIONS

Let us now consider another of Braudel's favorite themes: technology, particularly the technology of communication. Leonard Dudley has advanced a bold thesis regarding advances in communication technology since the Middle Ages, suggesting that major shifts in the cost of transmitting or storing information have been associated with shifts in population growth rates and with changes in the relationships among rulers and the ruled that lead to revolutions or constitutional change.

Dudley identifies four major innovations in communications technology: the adoption of the standardized Carolingian script for Latin documents at the outset of the High Middle Ages; the invention of the printing press at the outset of the Renaissance; the development of industrialized printing, bookbinding, and distribution (including steam-powered printing presses, new ways to more quickly make moveable type and broadsheets, and their distribution by train) at the outset of the Industrial Revolution; and the complex of telephony/FAX/TV media in the course of the twentieth century. Each of these breakthroughs had two effects. First, by facilitating the spread of information regarding farming, markets, and other elements of production and trade, each led to an increase in population and economic output. Second, by distributing knowledge more broadly—first to elites, and then more widely as literacy spread, and then universally with TV—the new techniques laid the bases for challenges to royal and elite hegemony. Thus standard Latin script facilitated the spread of charters and early constitutions (Dudley gives the example of the Magna Carta), which limited monarchical rights over their subjects; early printing helped spread Protestantism and literacy, which laid the basis for the Dutch challenge to

Spain, the Puritan challenge in England, the Mazarinades in France, and the complex of wars and revolts and religious agreements that constituted the Thirty Years' War. Further improvements in printing and distribution helped fuel the pamphlet wars of the American and French Revolutions, and the middle and working class mobilization in the early nineteenth century up through 1848. And in the twentieth century, FAX and video technology played a key role in empowering the people of Eastern European nations in their challenge to communist autocracies.[11]

Dudley is clearly on to something important here. The number of people who had access to a visual or written message, the speed at which the message traveled, and the number of people to whom it could be simultaneously communicated did undergo episodic and drastic changes in the past millennium. Studies of the impact of printing have been a staple for historians, who have argued that the emerging power of the press played a major role in revolutionary and rebellious actions.[12] Yet as with climate, before bowing to the power of a striking correlation, we must ask: Can we plausibly connect changes in communication technology with what actually happened in specific periods of revolt and revolution, and do changes in communications play a consistent role across the several waves of contestations?

With regard to the first period of upheavals, from 1250 to 1350, we confront a problem that we shall revisit several times. What is distinctive about all these periods of conflict is that they combined revolts on different levels of society—not only elites against the crown, but also urban revolts against municipal elites, as well as peasant uprisings, either against landlords or agents of the crown. The spread of standard Latin for charters and other state documents may have aided the codification of elite rights. But that in no way explains why peasant revolts were so widespread in the late fourteenth century. In the next period, the association is more plausible, as some connection between the printing press and the spread of vernacular Bibles and Protestantism is unassailable. Still, the German peasant war of 1525 occurred before printed Bibles were widespread; in Puritan England, it was

---

11. Leonard Dudley, *The Rationality of Revolution* (Montreal: C.R.D.E., 1995), elaborates this argument with a rational-choice model that determines the type of revolutionary/ constitutional challenge, depending on the shift in communications costs, but I fear historians will find that reasoning wholly implausible. Thus I only give Dudley's main argument here, which I think is suggestive and provocative.

12. Elizabeth Eisenstein, *The Printing Press as an Agent of Change* (Cambridge: Cambridge University Press, 1979).

the public preacher and not the text that was the key to popular mobilization in the 1640s (although once the revolution had begun, various factions churned the printing press with pamphlets to plead their particular case). The newspaper and the café, and the new profession of *journaliste* do seem inseparable from the wave of revolutions from 1776 to 1848, and much excellent scholarship has emerged on the role of media in revolutions, the French Revolution in particular.[13] And in our day, the common jibe regarding "revolution by CNN," referring to the key role played by news media in disseminating information regarding demonstrations and government reactions, seems to substantiate Dudley's suggestion that we have now entered yet another new information age with significant political implications.

But to follow Mark Elvin's lead in his contribution to this volume, a quick glance at China for a comparative check knocks the legs out from under Dudley's argument. For China did not parallel the West's stages in the advance of communications; in this area, China moved to its own rhythm. A standardized script in China was never lost in a dark age, and survived as the basis of the imperial bureaucracy despite the rise and fall of dynasties. From the time of the Southern Song, canonical texts were enshrined in a form that would be standard for nearly a millennium. It is true that the Buddhist perfection of woodblock printing allowed a widespread distribution of "radical" folk literature in the late Ming, but this was an old technology pressed into new service. And there was no new communications technology behind China's great nineteenth-century Taiping rebellion (although as an inspiration for the rebellion's leader, Western Bibles did play a key role). Probably only the Chinese communists, whose printing of standardized propaganda in the hundreds of millions of copies, could claim to be using new communications technology for revolutionary ends. But even there, the main challenges to state hegemony in China in the last thirty years have come not from any great technological breakthrough, but from subversive wall posters—an old but noble technology of protest. The content of what was communicated in China certainly changed dramatically over centuries, but quite unlike the West, it seems impossible to connect any breakthroughs in printing or communications with the periodic eruption of elite and popular rebellion that toppled or disrupted Chinese regimes in the fourteenth, seventeenth, nineteenth, and twentieth centuries.

To an even greater extent than climate, we will want to incorporate the role of changing communication technologies into our understanding of the

---

13. Jeremy Popkin, ed., *Media and Revolution* (Lexington: University of Kentucky Press, 1995).

initiation and spread of revolutions and revolts, especially in western Europe. But given the limited role of literacy in popular mobilization prior to the eighteenth century, and the lack of a clear connection between changing communications technology and major revolts in China, we cannot give communication technology the dominant role Dudley claims for it as the underlying force driving the waves of global political crises.

Mentalités and Political Culture

In recent years, European history in general, and the origins of revolutions and revolts in particular, have come to center on changes in the outlook and values of people, rather than on changes in their material circumstances. Although the social and material world still features in such genres as the history of the environment or the history of particular cities or regions, the role of the social and material world as the foundation for major historical trends and events has been reduced to a minimum, a shift in viewpoint that would greatly distress Braudel.

In large part, this has come about due to the discrediting of two major approaches to history born in the social sciences. The first was modernization theory, rooted in the work of Emile Durkheim, Ferdinand Tonnies, Max Weber, and (to a degree) Karl Marx, and further developed by Talcott Parsons, Gabriel Almond, Alex Inkeles (among many others). In modernization theory, the key theme of history is the transition from a traditional mode of social organization (for example, feudalism, empires) to a modern mode (liberal democracy or mass-party-based states). Although modernization theory gave historians a positive light to shine on events such as the Industrial Revolution, Colonialism and Imperialism, and the English and French Revolutions, such a happy face seemed increasingly out of touch with post-Vietnam and postmodern sensibilities. Horrified and embarrassed by the miseries and slaughters brought on by industrialization, colonialism, imperialism, and revolutionary terrors and civil wars, historians could hardly treat these events as the desirable and inevitable outcome of a positive and liberating historical process. Moreover, modernization clearly denigrated the histories of non-Western and premodern societies.

The second such social theory that failed was of course Marxism. Marxism ordered history by seeing Western history as a transition from feudalism to capitalism, Eastern history as a failure to make that transition, and the main movers and shakers of history as first the bourgeoisie and then the proletariat. It is hard to believe now, but in the 1960s the Marxist approach to history was so dominant—in France, England, the United States, and Japan, as well as in the U.S.S.R. and China—that it was as much a part of common wisdom as "modernization." Indeed, in regard to the French and English Revolutions, the Marxist approach was so much the dominant framework for relating social and material conditions to political conflict that it was simply *the* social interpretation of these events.[14] Nonetheless, despite decades of research inspired by Marx and aimed to support his views, the entire edifice of Marxist history crumbled before an avalanche of contradictory evidence.

Early modern scholars are familiar with the story—for both the English and French Revolutions, it became clear that there was no coherent bourgeoisie behind the revolutions, for the merchant communities in both countries were split between large wholesale merchants and bankers who supported the crown, and smaller merchants, shopkeepers, and artisans who generally supported the opposition. The nobility was also split, with many nobles and aspiring nobles among the ranks of revolutionary leaders in both cases. The groups that were most firmly in the revolutionary camp—lawyers, lesser officials, and ecclesiastics (such as the Abbé Sieyes and various Puritan preachers)—simply should not have been there, or were invisible in Marx's theorizing. Worse yet, the English and French Revolutions did not provide any clear breakthroughs for capitalism or capitalists (aristocratic dominance returned with the fall of the revolutionary regimes in both countries). The proletariat had their *journeés* and their June Days, their Commune and their communist revolutions. But all for naught—the tide of history went out on Marx's heroes, leaving them without victories (unless one counts the eighty years of Soviet dominance as a Pyrrhic triumph).

As belief in modernization and Marxist interpretations dissolved, historians turned away from any social interpretations of history, and sought refuge in the study of events, ideas, and words. Such histories took three major forms: a return to narratives, the study of *mentalités*, and the study of shifts in political culture.

Multifaceted narratives again came to dominate accounts of the English and French Revolutions, stressing the role of turning points, key actors, and key events.[15] Instead of inevitable culminations of social forces,

14. Alfred Cobban, *The Social Interpretation of the French Revolution* (Cambridge: Cambridge University Press, 1965).

15. Lawrence Stone, "The Revival of Narrative: Reflections on a New Old History," *Past and Present* 85 (1979): 3–24.

these revolutions became avoidable accidents, sequences of events that sadly spun out of control.[16] If Charles I had simply had more patience, if Necker hadn't manipulated the French crown's accounts, if Laud had been more reasonable, if the weather in 1788 hadn't been so bad—in short, except for a few bad breaks, counterfactual history could have become real, and we would have been spared decades of scholarly effort and forests of timber spent debating the origins of these unnecessary events. While such narratives inevitably bow in the direction of long-term social and material changes, such changes do no more than set the stage for key actors to make their choices, and it is those choices, plus historical accidents or contingencies, that plunge countries into decades of civil war, social unrest, and institutional change.

The second new direction in history is the ingenious study of values and outlooks, much influenced by anthropology and literary theory. The outstanding examples of this genre take a single deviant individual or community, or an outlandish folktale, and by a brilliant process of inversion and reflection, decipher the values and outlooks of the entire mainstream society in which the focus of their study is embedded.[17] While the virtuosity of these performances is evident, the pattern they set for historical study has worried even leading historians who focus on the study of symbols and ideology. Joyce Appleby, Lynn Hunt, and Margaret Jacob have voiced their fear that "If postmodernist cultural anthropology is any guide, the concern with developing causal explanations and social theories would be replaced in a postmodernist history with a focus on self-reflexivity and on problems of literary construction."[18]

To return to causal explanation without descending into the muddy depths of social theory, historians of the French Revolution have suggested

---

16. Mark Kishlansky, *A Monarchy Transformed: Britain 1603–1714* (London: Allen Lane, 1996); François Furet, *Interpreting the French Revolution*, trans. Robert Forster (Cambridge: Cambridge University Press, 1981). In Furet's description, the French Revolution was a result of the "convergence of several heterogeneous series, surely a fortuitous situation" (25).

17. Natalie Zemon Davis, *The Return of Martin Guerre* (Cambridge, Mass.: Harvard University Press, 1983); Robert Darnton, *The Great Cat Massacre, and Other Episodes in French Cultural History* (New York: Basic Books, 1984); Carlo Ginzburg, *The Cheese and the Worms* (Baltimore: Johns Hopkins University Press, 1980); Emmanuel Le Roy Ladurie, *Montaillou* (New York: Vintage Books, 1979).

18. Joyce Appleby, Lynn Hunt, and Magaret Jacob, *Telling the Truth about History* (New York: W. W. Norton, 1994), 227.

the causal trope of a shift in "political culture."[19] Focusing on analyses of public opinion, as displayed in court decisions and the popular press,[20] these scholars argue that the fall of the French monarchy came about because people's (especially the emerging middle class's) view of the monarchy changed. Instead of viewing the king as "hedged with divinity," the king (and especially the queen) became an object of derision, accused of being irresponsible and undeserving of respect, much less of ultimate power.

The study of political culture has no doubt revealed an important truth—attitudes toward the monarchy had changed. But this puts the question only one step back: Why did this change come about? Where did disillusion with the monarchy come from? At this point, the shift to political culture retreats to narrative. A whole series of events (perhaps avoidable?) discredited the king: Jansenist controversies with the church, unnecessarily harsh confrontations with the parlements, the wanton behavior of Marie Antoinette, rising food prices, arrogant ministers, lack of fiscal rectitude—all sapped the notion that the king was a desirable guide for the nation. Enlightenment attitudes—anticlericalism, skepticism, humanism—combined to raise the opinion of the inquiring, honest citizen above the moldy orthodoxies of church and court.

The story seems complete. And yet, anyone who surveys the entire span of French history from 1600 to 1800 cannot help but feel that this story has been told before. The judicial elites who chased Mazarin and the young Louis XIV out of Paris in 1648 seem to lack the deep respect for the king that is alleged to have prevailed prior to the administration of Louis XV. Anticlericalism, skepticism, and humanism have raised their heads before: Descartes was a man of the seventeenth century, not the eighteenth; as Paul Hazard observed, "virtually all those ideas which were called revolutionary round about 1750, or for the matter of that, 1789, were already current as early as 1680."[21] Indeed, many of the ideas that dominated the early stages of the revolution had been around as early as 200 B.C., for initially the revolutionaries

19. Keith Baker et al., eds., *The French Revolution and the Creation of Modern Political Culture* (Oxford: Pergamon Press, 1987–).

20. Arlette Farge, *Subversive Words and Public Opinion in Eighteenth Century France*, trans. Rosemary Morris (Cambridge: Polity Press, 1994); Mona Ouzouf, "War and Terror in French Revolutionary Discourse," *Journal of Modern History* 56 (1984): 579–97; Sarah Maza, "Le tribunal de la nation: Les mémoires judiciares et l'opinion publique à la fin de l'ancien régime," *Annales, E.S.C.* 42 (1987): 73–90.

21. Paul Hazard, *The European Mind (1680–1715)*, trans. J. L. May (London: Hollis & Carter, 1963), xviii.

revived the ideal of the Roman republic as their guiding light.[22] One is reminded of the "virtualités subversives" that underlay seventeenth-century urban revolts, noted by Yves-Marie Bercé. It was not simply new ideas, the birth of a "modern political culture," that overturned the French monarchy. It was a new salience, a widely felt cogency, of some old and some very old ideals.

DEMOGRAPHIC CHANGE

If we return to the phenomenon of global waves of revolt and revolution, it does appear that one variable marches neatly in step with these disorders, and that is the oscillation of population growth. In each wave, in the century and a half or so leading up to the climax of revolts, circa 1350, 1640, 1848, and the present day, populations grew by 30 to 100 percent or more in the countries or regions most affected. And yet, a close inspection shows that population growth will not serve as a drum major any better than our other choices.

M. M. Postan first proposed a Malthusian disaster as the reason for the decline and disarray of medieval society after 1250.[23] Population pressure may well have created problems from 1250 to 1350, as there is strong evidence for a vastly increased population in England in that period.[24] Yet the major peasant revolt in England, as well as Jacqueries in France, occurred well after 1350, by which time population pressures had been unpleasantly eliminated by the Black Death. It was arguably the sudden and drastic fall in population, making labor scarce and leading to contestation over serfdom, that led to the widespread revolts.

One can find population increases in the years leading up to the French peasant revolts and the Frondes, the English Revolution, the French Revolution, and the revolutions of 1848. Yet the magnitudes of this growth are so varied as to raise questions about consistent causes. In the seventeenth century, one finds populations that have increased by 50 percent or more in the century preceding the revolutions and major revolts; but in the nineteenth

22. Harold T. Parker, *The Cult of Antiquity and the French Revolutionaries* (New York: Octagon Books, 1965); Claude Mossé, *L'Antiquité dans la Révolution française* (Paris: Albin Michel, 1989).

23. M. M. Postan, *The Medieval Economy and Society* (Hammondsworth: Penguin, 1972).

24. John Hatcher, *Plague, Population, and the English Economy, 1348–1530* (London: Macmillan, 1977).

century, population growth in England, France, and Prussia does not seem at all germane to the pattern of crises. From 1800 to 1850, the population of England grew by 92 percent; the population of France grew by only 31 percent, and that of two of the German states most affected in 1848 (Württemberg and Bavaria) grew only 24 percent and 33 percent, respectively.[25] Yet England was least affected by political crises in the 1840s.

And as I have pointed out, in the century and a half prior to the Meiji Restoration in Japan in 1868, a truly revolutionary episode of civil war and social restructuring, population was basically unchanging from 1721 to 1846, rising only for a couple of decades before the fall of the Shogunate.[26] To turn to the most recent wave of revolutions, while one does find population rapidly increasing in the developing nations that experienced twentieth-century revolutions, from Mexico in 1910 to Iran and Nicaragua in 1979, such increases are not markedly greater than that in countries that have not had revolutions, from South America to Thailand. And in the most dramatic revolutions of 1989, in Eastern Europe and the U.S.S.R., population increases were only rapid in the Central Asian (and least revolutionary) Soviet Republics, while growth was slow or absent in Russia, the Baltics, and most East European states. Clearly, neither in Europe nor in the rest of the world can we find a consistent relationship between population increase and major revolts and revolutions.

SOCIAL REPRODUCTION AND SOCIAL SCIENCE

What then can social science offer to historians, to help understand the major waves of revolutions and revolts? After the bankruptcy of modernization and Marxism, and the indecisiveness of climate and population change, what remains?

As one of the greatest comparative/historical sociologists, Charles Tilly, has frequently remarked, historians should beware of social scientists bearing universal causes.[27] Causes are generally particular to specific times and places;

---

25. The German data is actually for the period 1816–64, the dates of the most complete nineteenth-century German censuses; the actual increase to 1848, just prior to the potato blight and major waves of emigration, may have been considerably greater. Population trends for all these areas and timespans is summarized in Goldstone, *Revolution and Rebellion*, 290.

26. Goldstone, *Revolution and Rebellion*, 404.

27. Charles Tilly, "Les Bourgeois Gentilhommes," in *Debating Revolutions*, ed. Nikki Keddi (New York: New York University Press, 1996).

as such, they are in the special provenance of history. Nonetheless, sociologists can tell us some things about relationships and social processes that do seem to be general, and that can help us find our way among the complex and twisting narratives of particular incidents.

When historians think of social stability, or the reproduction of a society over time, they generally think of durable institutions—a monarchy, a particular elite, a set of rules that define the relationships of peasants to the land, to landlords, to the church, and to the state. Yet such institutions do not simply reproduce themselves, automatically persisting across generations.[28] If we think of social reproduction as the task of assigning real human beings to particular positions in a society, and then continually reassigning people to institutional places as new generations take the place of old, we gain a better sense of what is required for social institutions to persist.

For example, let us imagine an agrarian bureaucratic society (like the French monarchy between 1500 and 1850) in which peasants till the land, pay rents to landlords, and pay taxes to the state, and the state dispenses patronage to, and relies on the services of, noble and nonnoble bureaucrats and elites. What is required to stably reproduce this society across generations?

If the number of peasants should double, then to maintain the same relationships, the amount of land under cultivation should double too. Otherwise, either the technology of farming must improve, or labor intensity increase, or some peasants must leave the land (either for rural industry or cities), or the output of peasant families will decrease. Assuming that even technology and greater effort cannot quite double yields, then either peasant incomes will fall, or migration to cities will increase, or both. Already, the rural structure of society is undergoing change. For if peasants migrate to the city or rural industry, how will they be fed? As cities grow, the penetration of markets or state provisioning forces must reach further into the country to feed the urban population; as more people buy their food, the roles for merchants (and their profits) are increased.

How will these urban merchants be fit into the existing structure of the elites? If elites have enough children to survive to double their numbers, where will those children go to reproduce the existing class and status system? Will the state double the number of elite positions to which it offers patronage and authority? If so, where will the state get the resources to do so?

---

28. Anthony Giddens, *New Rules of Sociological Method*, 2d ed. (Stanford: Stanford University Press, 1993), has best expressed the simultaneously constructed and persistent character of social institutions through his theory of "structuration."

If the doubled number of peasants can pay double the rent and double the taxes, all is well—society successfully reproduces its key relationships. But if peasants cannot double their incomes or their payments, how will state and society adjust? Will peasants be more heavily taxed than before? Will the number of elite positions fail to keep up with the number of claimants seeking elite positions? Will the state have to borrow to meet its needs?

In short, population increase poses challenges to the reproduction of society in an agrarian bureaucratic society. But such challenges can be met, or can emanate from other causes. For example, if the state develops an overseas empire to employ aspiring elites, or expands its urban industrial base to absorb most of the peasant children leaving the land for cities, the aspirations of elites and popular groups can be met. Society may well change some of its key institutions (this is the story of nineteenth-century England), but it will not be caught trying to maintain institutions whose reproduction is breaking down under the impossibility of reconciling their reproduction with increased numbers.

Alternatively, technological change may so increase the opportunities for elites and peasants and workers that population increase is not a worry; that is, as long as access to jobs and the rewards of work are fairly distributed. Should the state be so corrupt or inept as to intervene to block social mobility and grossly maldistribute output, the reproduction of social institutions will again be under threat. Thus despite their stable populations, the East European communist countries found that vastly expanding higher education while at the same time blocking access to professional advancement for most of the college-educated population, created a situation in which most of that population lost any desire to reproduce communist institutions.[29]

As mentioned above, after 1350 in England, and prior to 1868 in Japan, a declining or stable population could threaten social reproduction. Labor shortages can lead to pressures to change the rules for the relationships among workers, the land, and their landlords. Or (as in Japan), a constant population that captures all the returns of gains in agriculture, leaving a smaller and smaller share of social output to go to the state, will not desire or need to obey the dictates of that state indefinitely.

In short, in almost any society, early modern or modern, reproducing the relationships among the state, elites, and the working and farming population

29. Jack A. Goldstone, "Theories of Revolution and the Revolutions of 1989 in the U.S.S.R. and Eastern Europe," in *Revolution and Political Change*, Alexander Groth, ed. (Aldershot, U.K.: Dartmouth, 1996), 491–508.

can never be assumed; it requires the maintenance of particular balances in the production and distribution of resources and positions. Any shift that undermines those balances—an increase in population without accompanying increases in productive technology or land to farm; a technological change that allows some group to get more resources at the expense of other groups, or lets a new group of claimants to income and status emerge, even a change in climate that reduces yields without also reducing population—will undermine social reproduction.

What happens when social reproduction is disrupted? This takes us back to *mentalités*. All societies seek to inculcate in their members values that support, and expectations that correspond to, what is likely to be delivered within existing social institutions. A set of symbols that encapsule the relationships among superiors and inferiors, state and society, church and society, and so forth are common currency. Yet that currency can be debased by the persistent departure of social conditions from what is expected under the prevailing value system. Disruption of social reproduction thus leads to the denigration of the symbols and values associated with existing social institutions, and to a search for, and increasing salience of, alternative symbols and values. Whether taken from an idealized past or formulated from readily available contemporary ideas, the challenge to existing symbols and values creates a shift toward a "new" political culture.

On the other hand, the steady reproduction of social institutions reinforces the legitimacy and stability of those institutions. During the reign of Louis XIV, the population of France did not increase. Harvests rose and fell, but there was no overall tendency for cities to grow or prices to rise. Instead of excess aspirants for elite positions overwhelming the crown, noble lands and titles tended to pass from father to sole surviving sons (or for those without sons at all, to nephews or sons-in-law). Social reproduction, in other words, was almost effortless. Is it any wonder that the Sun King's reign seemed to be one of extraordinary grace?

Nor is this link between social reproduction and *mentalités* limited to the political realm. Braudel notes in his *Mediterranean* that witchcraft was a widespread social problem in sixteenth-century Europe. This too may have been linked to social relationships and social reproduction. The sixteenth century was a period of high population growth and falling real wages. Population growth meant that families had more surviving younger children, and either had to subdivide their landholding among progeny, or send landless younger offspring out into the world. Falling wages made it harder for workers to support a family and accumulate savings. The result was that more younger sons were around who could not marry, or only married late. More daughters were around as well, but given the situation of the men, the incidence of marriage for women declined, and the number of unmarried single women in the population greatly increased.[30] As they aged, these women became spinsters. By the late sixteenth and early seventeenth century, Europe harbored an unprecedented number of elder, unmarried women—exactly the people who were most often the target of witchcraft scares. By the later seventeenth century, when populations in northern Europe stopped their growth, the incidence of marriage returned to earlier high levels, and the excess of spinsters faded away.

To repeat, the location and identification of specific causes of social change is the provenance of history. But how to locate, among thousands of possible events, trends, and changes, the causes of a particular social change? The sociologist can offer historians this clue: look to the processes that guide social reproduction; look to see how individuals and families find their way into economic, social, and political roles. If you can find factors that interfere with the reproduction of relationships across time and across generations, you will have found the causes of changes in both social and political relationships and values and *mentalités*.

MATERIAL CHANGE AND *MENTALITÉS*

What then should we do with the relationship between material change and *mentalités*? It will not do to assert that material change always guides changes in *mentalités*. This is simply not true. At times when social reproduction is breaking down, from whatever cause, the search for new institutions, relationships, and practices will be guided by values, outlooks, and the meanings attached to particular practices. Those values, outlooks, and meanings can be transformed by revolts and revolutionary struggles, but they can also take the lead in setting the direction of change.[31]

Let me offer a metaphor. Material conditions and *mentalités* are like two horses harnessed together, pulling the chariot of history. At the moment, some historians have put such huge blinders on themselves and on their chosen horse of *mentalités* that they feel safe in assuming the material conditions are not there. Others have attacked and hobbled the horse of material history, in the belief that this will free their mount on *mentalités* to run faster

30. E. A. Wrigley and R. S. Schofield, *The Population History of England 1541–1871* (London: Edward Arnold, 1981).

31. I develop this argument at length in Goldstone, *Revolution and Rebellion*, chap. 5.

and run free. But this leaves historians with only half a story to tell; only half a team to pull their wagon.

Braudel realized, and left a magnificent argument, that material conditions and *mentalités* are harnessed together. Over the course of history, sometimes one, and sometimes the other, will take the lead, set the pace, and determine the direction of change. What historians and social scientists together can do is pay close attention to how material conditions and *mentalités* are connected, and—at a given moment—which is setting the lead. By all means, historians are right to discard modernization and Marxism, to reject universal causal theories, and to pay great attention to the nature and evolution of values, ideas, and their role in social change. But none of this requires rejecting social science, nor does it provide a deep understanding of social relationships and social reproduction. Braudel instinctively knew all of this; on the fiftieth anniversary of the first edition of *The Mediterranean*, his great work reminds us not to forget.

PART 5

Constructing Identities
from *Mentalité*

Chapter 8

EARLY MODERN LAW AND THE ANTHROPOLOGICAL IMAGINATION OF OLD EUROPEAN CULTURE

ANTÓNIO MANUEL HESPANHA

SUBJECTS AND OBJECTS

In a chapter of his treatise *On Justice and Law*, the famous Spanish theologian and jurist Domingo de Soto expressed a strange opinion on the legal capacity of beasts and animals:

> It can actually be affirmed that, in their own way, beasts have a
> right to ownership of the grass.... It also seems that the queen
> of the bees has also a dominion over the swarm...and, among
> the brutes, it seems that the fiercest lion reigns over the remain-
> ing animals, just as the hawk seems to exercise dominion over
> the miserable birds. As much again can be said of the inani-
> mate heaven, which has dominion over this sublunar world, by
> spreading the warmth and strength from which the world lives
> and develops itself.[1]

This surprising idea that animals, beasts, and even inanimate things, like the heavens or a rock, were tied together by links of ownership or political power was not a poetic metaphor of an imaginative scholar. Practical writers of prosaic texts on matters of everyday life shared the same conviction that brutes or things could possess the same rights or legal faculties claimed by humans.

---

1. Domingo de Soto, *De iustitia et iure* (Cuenca, 1556), ed. Venancio Diego Carro (Madrid: Instituto de Estudios Políticos, 1968), iv, 1, 2, 284 col. 1.

Ulpian, a well-known Roman jurist, had written about natural law as a rule that "nature teaches to every animal … that springs up on the earth or in the seas, even to the birds."[2] And an early modern German jurist, Hermann Wissman, writing on the symbolism and dignity of colors, conceived the primacy of some of them (such as purple or gold) with legal rights of their own that could be claimed in court.[3]

An infinite number of practical illustrations of this kind of panjuridification of the world can be cited from early modern popular beliefs; for example, animals were liable for injuries or exposed to criminal punishment. As late as the mid-nineteenth century, the Portuguese lawyer Dias Ferreira discussed a lawsuit against an ox that had broken an arm of a neighbor in the small village of Alfândega da Fé in northern Portugal.[4] And a century earlier in 1751, houses were destroyed and lands were salted and made sterile as a "real" punishment for having been owned by the Portuguese dukes of Aveiro, who had been convicted of royal treason. In opposition to such liabilities, landed estates also enjoyed rights of human services (serfdom) or of other estates' privileges, like rights-of-way. And as everyone knows, some men or women (slaves) were legally treated as things, although with a somewhat different rationale.

Current distinctions between persons and things simply did not exist, at least in such a structured way as ours. Creation was a more homogeneous universe, an interrelated universe, where every creature—animated or not, intelligent or brute—was entitled to claims or subject to duties toward others. Creation was a great, although polyphonic, choir where each individual sang in his own way a prayer to God. These distinct songs and different ways of pursuing harmony nevertheless shared the same hierarchy concerning their final purpose. A biblical anecdote expresses quite well this interchangeability of the different chains of being. In his last arrival in Jerusalem, Christ had been blamed by the Pharisees for allowing his disciples to acclaim him. His answer evokes the same unity and intermutability of Creation: "I tell you, even if they are silent, the stones will themselves cry out" (Luke 19:37–40).

A more modern legal sensibility has introduced, on the contrary, an intimate relationship between law, reason, and will. Therefore, a legally active universe had to be restricted to being able to trigger willingly reasoned actions. A decisive distinction has then been introduced between

2. Ulpian, *Justinian's Digest*, 1.1.1.3
3. Hermann Wissman, *De iure circa colores* (Leipzig, 1683).
4. José Dias Ferreira, *Código civil anotado* (Lisbon, 1870), 1:6.

human and nonhuman beings. Humans became clearly the center of Creation and the only subjects of legal order, because they alone could reason and thus be held responsible for their actions. "Only men can be the subjects of rights and obligations," declares emphatically the first article of the 1867 Portuguese Civil Code. The original unity of Creation has been blurred. Since then, legal personhood became the monopoly, and also the specificity, of human beings.

SUBSTANCE AND ROLES:
PERSONS AND STATUS; THINGS AND USES

Discussing the legal relationship between the crown and the house of the dukes of Bragança, the Portuguese royal house from the seventeenth century, a Lusitanian lawyer has written that several symbolic persons could be seen in the physical body of the king, "each one retaining and conserving his nature and qualities and having to be considered distinct from the others."[5] This is another expression of an effect of the superimposition of symbolic entities on the same physical body as it was described by Ernst Kantorowicz in his classic work, *The King's Two Bodies*.[6]

What should be stressed is that such a symbolic reverberation of human physical entities was not exclusive to royal persons. Society, according to legal imagination, included an infinite number of persons, each of whom corresponded to a particular insertion of any individual in the social hierarchy, that is to say, each corresponded to a status. As Manuel Álvares Pegas, a Portuguese lawyer of the late seventeenth century, wrote, "It is neither new nor contrary to the terms of reason that one and the same man uses different rights under different aspects."[7] Besides, there was the theological example of the Holy Trinity for this unfolding of distinct personalities.

Although the relationship between a status and the individual was ambivalent, status could either explode or implode individuals. Disintegration of an individual occurred when status represented attributes, conditions, or positions of the same individual (as father, as son, as professional, as native of a kingdom). Implosion occurred whenever a status gave an identity to a plural

---

5. Manuel Álvares Pegas, *Commentaria ad Ordinationes Regni Portugalliae*, 12 vols. (Ulysipone, 1669–1703).

6. Ernst H. Kantorowicz, *The King's Two Bodies: A Study in Mediaeval Political Theology* (Princeton: Princeton University Press, 1957).

7. Pegas, *Commentaria*, II: ad 2, 35, cap. 265, n 21.

set of individuals ("Father and son are one and the same person in what regards the law," wrote Álvaro Valasco).[8] But status could also change the very physical nature of bodily substance. A daughter who inherited instead of her father (by the so-called right of representation) "had to become" a male in order to inherit goods (for example, fiefs) that could only be bequeathed to men.

From a legal point of view, individuals were as mutable as status was decisive. Law was some kind of impressionist painting where the rigid materiality of things (or physical persons) was substituted by the countless reflexes provoked on them by the different lights of social interaction. Therefore, physical substances became a mere chromatic reverberation. Humans were actors who assumed different social roles. While our contemporary social and legal imagination is actor-centered, the early modern one was personage-centered. The Great Chain of Being, in which people were integrated and played their own roles, was the really important matter. Thus, the definition of things and individuals was related to their functions or roles and not to their isolated essence.

The same "relationism" dominated the imagination of things. In what concerns the imagination of external nonhuman creatures, the legal thought of the great jurists of medieval common law (*ius commune*) was framed by the idea that an order ruled the universe, embracing men and things, and giving them functional or relational definitions. In the case of things, the meaning of function implies the notion of "use." Therefore, more than objects that were physically distinct, things were utilities, that is, devices or procedures through which desires (*affectiones*) could be satisfied. "Thing," according to a common legal definition, "is a general name, that comprehends rights, contracts, and every obligation."[9] And, considering the evanescence and mobility of the defined object, that was "a dangerous definition, although the fact that the definition was a demonstration of the substance of a defined thing, therein could happen many variations, according to the circumstances of the affairs."[10]

Actually, things appeared fully dematerialized. They could exist without any material support (like rights). They could consist in a discontinuous and moveable materiality (like a legacy or a contract). Or they could share the

---

8. Álvaro Valasco, *Consultationum ac rerum judicatarum in regno Lusitaniae* (Ulysipone, 1588; Conimbricae, 1730), cons. 126 n 12.

9. António Cardoso do Amaral, *Liber utilissimus judicum*, 2 vols. *Summa seu praxis judicum* (Ulysipone, 1610; Conimbricae, 1740), "res," n 1.

10. Cardoso do Amaral, *Liber utilissimus judicum*, "res," ad 2, 363.2.

same material object, like the different rights that could fall upon the same thing (ownership, possession, usufruct, communitarian claims, fiscal rights, and so forth). This last feature explains why medieval lawyers were not troubled with the fact that several *dominia* (or property rights)—in principle without limits and exclusivity—could exist, at one time, on the same estate. In fact, their infinite claims could subsist because they applied to different utilities of the underlying common physical object.

All this means that things did not preexist the order of human relationships. On the contrary, things were created by the fact that this order existed and had given them precise utilities.

RITES AND EMOTIONS

The ceremonial was known. If the king of Spain wanted to raise a courtier to the rank of grandee, he would invite the nobleman solemnly, in the presence of the court, to cover his head. This change of protocol expressed the royal feelings of equality and intimacy towards a particular subject. Thereafter, the external manifestation of their social relationship, that is to say, the fact that a nobleman wore a hat before the king, expressed in itself the emotive foundation of their relationship. This is one example of the common idea that there was a relation of necessity between external attitudes and emotions.

Emotional life was supposed to have a rigid architecture. Feelings and emotions were not to be dependent on individual mood. On the contrary, they should be inner dispositions, a kind of psychological commonplace, as they had been identified and evaluated by moral theologians. A good example of such a mapping of the "anatomy of the soul"[11] is Aquinas's set of questions about love and friendship, where different kinds of affections are typified as well as their hierarchy, related feelings, and external manifestations.

The existence of this natural order of emotions turned affections into objective entities with external and prescribed dimensions. Just as faith had to be actualized in works, each kind of emotion was supposed to be expressed in fixed attitudes, rites, and practical dispositions. Thus, political affections (*affectus*) had an objective or nondisposable logic that limited the will or passions of each person and expressed itself in typified acts (*effectus*). Therefore, due affections were to be paid with external behaviors, prescribed by objective patterns which were inscribed in the nature of things.

11. Mario Bergamo, *L'anatomia dell'anima: De François de Sales à Fénélon* (Bologna: Il Mulino, 1991).

To bow or to stand, to kiss the hands or the face, to take off the hat or to put it on were corporal dispositions from which one could infer corresponding internal dispositions. Even the closest relationships had strict prescribed rules of meaning. The dramaturgy of intimate love, for example, was not dependent on one's creativity and emotional ecstasy, but on the natural order of different positions and sexual practices. Honest love, for example, could only be expressed in "[man with woman], in the right position, in the right vessel" ([*vir cum foemina*], *recta position, recto vaso*). In fact, the link between *effectus* and *affectus* was so strong that the former could stand for the latter. Changing of external attitude stood for a mutation of inner feelings.

This idea of a natural order of emotions and of the contiguity between emotions and behavior had a strong influence on the scope of law. As feelings were naturally due and necessarily linked to external attitudes, rites, and ceremonies were not just a matter of style or personal civility, but a matter of respect toward the natural order of things; that is to say, a question of "honor" or "honesty" (*honestas*).

Law, the guardian of order, was then deeply concerned with this subject. Etiquette and manners were a matter of law, and their fulfillment became a proper object for a legal suit. Precedence, corporal disposition—like kissing, bowing, kneeling, or even sexual intercourse—or address were legally due and often claimed in court.

While ruling external behavior, law was also ruling the corresponding inner dispositions. This means that though treating it through a permanent hermeneutics of its external manifestations, medieval and early modern law considered that the inner world had a domain of its own. In this sense, medieval law was not blinder to interiority than ours. Legal formalism or ritualism did not mean that the relevance of the soul was denied, but on the contrary, such legalism meant law's disposition to identify the soul with its external surrogates or its confidence in the possibility of ruling the soul by ruling its corporal dimensions.

Another manifestation of this interchangeability between feelings and external behavior was the blurring of the boundaries between law and other normative orders arising from emotional duties, like love or gratitude. This intimate relation between legal order and the exigencies of affections explains the contiguity modern jurists conceive to exist between the disciplinary mechanisms of law, religion, love, friendship, gratitude, and so forth. Being was Order, in its origin, an act of love, and all beings (including humans) were naturally linked by affections. Law is nothing but a way (although rough and external) of correcting some occasional deficit of that universal sympathy. In this sense, religious duties—as well as duties arising from friendship, debts of gratitude, compensation of favors, debts of honor—are almost legal duties (*quasi legales, antidorales*). Such duties include the worship towards God and the saints, the compensation of favors, the remuneration of benevolent services (like vassal services), the payment of interest on loans, the exercise of charity, the protection of friends. Under European early modern sociopolitical ideals, it is evident that within this circle are comprised almost every social duty that guarantees a well-ordered society.[12]

The wide range of duties of relatives within the family were also drawn from this source of the emotional order. Taking a less direct example, we can quote the Portuguese jurist Baptista Fragoso from 1641 when he distinguishes between mercenary labor, earning by strict law a salary, and the work done by children within the parental household: "the son who works for his father, being under his *patria potestas*, has no right to a salary. Otherwise, he could not be distinguished from an outsider, who does not work without salary.... The reason is that one cannot consider that the son serves his father for wages, but by love, owing compliance to the father."[13]

FREE WILL AND SOCIAL ORDER

Since the late seventeenth century, social philosophy and constitutional theory have been dominated by the hypothesis of a voluntary basis of sociability and political institutions, that is to say, by the hypothesis of a social contract.[14] Even those who searched for a transcendental source to society have found mostly God's will for justifying political rule and political institutions.

Medieval and early modern social theory, on the other hand, made little of the role of free will (even if it was God's will) in the shaping of human interaction. "The law of God is not in his will, but in his understanding,"

12. Bartolomé Clavero, *Antidora: Antropolgia católica de la economia moderna* (Milano: Giuffrè, 1991), and António Manuel Hespanha, "Les autres raisons de la politique: L'économie de la grâce," in António Manuel Hespanha, *La gracia del derecho* (Madrid: Centro de Estudios Constitucionales, 1993).

13. Baptista Fragoso, *Regimem reipúblicae christianae*, 3 vols. (Collonia allobrogum, 1641–1652), 3:648 nn. 117 and 118.

14. António Manuel Hespanha, "Pré-compréhension et savoir historique: La crise du modèle étatiste et les nouveaux contours de l'histoire du pouvoir," in *Juristische Theoriebildung und rechtliche Einheit: Beiträge zu einem rechtshistorischen Seminar in Stockholm im September 1992* in *Rättshistoriska Studier* 19 (1993): 49–67.

wrote Domingo de Soto.[15] Also, human law did not depend upon human free will. That explained why "legal doctrine does not have as its source either praetor's edict, nor the Law of the Twelve Tables, but the very inwardness of philosophy";[16] or why "to discuss the reasons of statutes [as positive laws] reveals more ignorance on law than knowledge."[17] In short, law and will were bound together by prudence. "The light does not exist in the will, which is blind, but in the understanding…from where Plato wisely affirms that one must not pretend or try to say that everything obeys the will, but on the contrary, that our will obeys either prudence or practical reason."[18]

This devaluation of the role of free will in the constitution of political order was pervasive in both the early modern legal and political imagination. On the level of political theory, it provoked a permanent awareness of the natural (that is, not artificial) character of rule, and of its limitation through principles that escaped the royal *arbitrium*.

> Although some claim that it is sacrilegious to discuss royal powers, as the ruler's will is the rule of law, a sure and certain answer can be given to this statement. Actually, what is criminal and sacrilegious is to affirm that it is not allowed to dispute royal powers. This is the very sign of politics without God, sweetened with the suggestion that there is no God. Thus, it is an impious thing—similar to a precept of the Turk—to claim that royal will, unfair, absolute and irregular [that is, arbitrary] has the force of law.[19]

Therefore, royal statutory law had to be enlightened by legal reason (*ratio iuris*)—that is to say, by that knowledge of human and divine things that was discussed by philosophy—in order to become legally fruitful. On the plane of legal theory, this limitation of free will by reason was at the origin of a sensible suspicion vis-à-vis statutory law, in particular when it either contradicted the established principles of doctrinal law (*contra tenorem iuris rationis*) or introduced exceptions to them.[20]

15. Domingo de Soto, *De iustitia et de iure*, I, q. 1, 1a. 1. 1. I, q. 1, art. 1.

16. Soto, *De iustitia et de iure*, Proemio, 5.

17. Soto, *De iustitia et de iure*, Proemio, 5.

18. Francisco Suarez, *De legibus ac Deo legislatore* (Coimbra, 1613), L. I, q. 1, art. 1.

19. João Salgado de Araújo, *Carta que un cavallero biscaino escrivio en discursos politicos y militares, la otra del Reyno de Navarra* (Lisbon, 1643), 15.

20. Cf. *Justinian's Digest*, 1, 3, 14–16.

Specific institutions were also cast in a similar antivoluntaristic mode. Property, for example, was not that unbounded power over things that has characterized our individualistic conceptions of ownership since the early nineteenth century. "To fulfill the concept of property," says Luis de Molina (1535–1600), "it is enough to use things according to one's own will, but only in the way required by nature and allowed by divine and human laws. Thus, a person is master of his slave, although he cannot kill him, or he is proprietor of his own things, although he cannot destroy them."[21]

Contracts were also not the realm of choice and free will, as nineteenth-century liberal law would have it. Here, the protagonism of voluntaristic elements is circumvented by a theoretical construction on the cause of contracts (*causa contractus*), which is frequently disregarded. For legal theoreticians, cause was the element that gave rationality to the will, the underlying motive without which either contractual performances would be senseless or a casual advantage for the opposite part. The French jurist Domat still affirmed in the early eighteenth century, "tout engagement doit avoir une cause honnête" [that is, according to the order of things]. Other authors preferred another dogmatic construction, centered on the idea of the nature of contracts: "Every contract has an inherent nature" (*natura ergo inest omnibus contractibus*).[22] *Natura contractus* would have an objective logic, required by the very nature of each kind of social relationship and embedded in tradition.

In whatever dogmatic construction we examine, the weight of voluntaristic elements in the imagination of contract was very light. The Portuguese lawyer António Cardoso do Amaral summed up quite expressively this unexpected balance between will and socially objective rationality: "Obligation is contracted by things themselves, by words or by writings... and sometimes, also, by the mere assent" (*aliquando tamen obligatur quis solo consensu*).[23] As a leading Italian legal historian has put it, for this naturalistic vision "man disappeared, absorbed by a *rerum natura* [nature of things] full of vital energy."[24]

---

21. Domingo de Soto, *De iustitia et de iure* (Conchae, 1593), I, 18.

22. Mantica, *Vaticanae locubrationes...*, quoted by Paolo Grossi, "Sulla 'natura' del contratto (qualche note sul 'mestiere' di storico del diritto, la proposito di un recente 'corso' di lezioni)," *Quaderni fiorentini per la storia del pensiero giuridico* 15 (1986): 593–619.

23. António Cardoso do Amaral, *Liber utilissimus judicum*, "Obligatio," n 6.

24. Grossi, "Sulla 'natura' del contratto," 161.

This nonconsensual conception of contracts suffered some limitations through the canon law's condemnation of lying ("That which is gone out of thy lips thou shalt keep and perform," Deut. 23:23). But until the (mitigated) triumph of individualism in social philosophy in the mid-eighteenth century, the irrelevance of free will in the imagination of social interaction would be maintained.

One of the best-known consequences of the idea of the unwilling character of social obligations is the strict regime of marriage, where will was almost helpless in the shaping of matrimonial relationship. Even more striking was the stress made by Amaral, for example, of the fact that the natural bounds of friendship and gratitude could, on their own, generate obligations. Therefore, there would be obligations "that do not arise but from the instinct of nature, because of services or benefits, in such a way that we are naturally bound to benefit those who had benefited us."[25] The wide scope of Amaral's (quite commonplace) *scholium* is understandable if we consider the extent that "service," "grace," "mercy," and "charity" had in the structure of human interaction in early modern European society.

The principle that (human) nature mechanically generated obligations comprehended, also, that duties were triggered by moral virtues, like "liberality," "friendship," "charity," or "magnanimity." Friends owed each other "graces" and "favors"; mighty people owed "protection" towards humble people (friendship, liberality). The rich owed alms to the poor (charity). And magnates (like the king), because of the higher rung on which they were located, owed all these in a superlative degree (magnanimity).

The case of usury was remarkable, for example, in the sense of these legally obligated duties generated by nature, even if usury was against Revelation. In fact, several texts of the Bible condemn usury. So does strict canon law. However, nature produced claims in another direction. Whoever borrowed money from another had the obligation of becoming grateful to the lender who had rendered him the service of lending it. Gratitude gave rise to an obligation, and interest was nothing else than the due fulfillment of an obligation generated by nature.[26] This nature-induced obligation prevailed even upon the strict interdiction of usury commanded by the revealed will of God.[27]

25. Amaral, *Liber utilissimus judicum*, "Obligatio," n 4.
26. Cf. Thomas Aquinas, *Summa theologica*, Ia.Iae, q. 78, 2 ad 2.
27. Clavero, *Antidora: Antropolgia católica de la economia moderna.*

LEGAL DOCTRINE AS A SOURCE TO THE HISTORICAL ANTHROPOLOGY OF THE OLD REGIME

The few examples given above lead to some fundamental conclusions about the relationships between law and culture, as well as on the roles legal history can play within historical and legal disciplines. Let us stress three main points.

The first conclusion is that legal institutions can be the object of a cultural hermeneutics that leads to the unveiling of a few categories that organize the perception of society and guide the evaluation of fairness and justice. These categories are not inorganic. They are combined in a global and harmonic interpretation of reality. Leading pieces of this model (or paradigm) are concepts (images or representations) or conceptual oppositions, like order (versus confusion or homogeneity), nature (versus artifact), reason (versus free will), whole (versus parts), persons (versus things), essence or interiority (versus appearance). This paradigm actualizes itself in myriad concrete manifestations of legal or institutional performances, in such a way that it summarizes the institutional whole of medieval and early modern political culture, rendering it familiar and predictable in every detail.

The second conclusion is that such a paradigm is so deeply rooted that it extends over a wide set of normative discourses, like moral theology, ethics, economy (in the ancient sense of *oikonomia*, as management of the household), and politics. At the same time, all these disciplines plunge deeply in common sense and everyday behavior. This explains the anachronism of applying the contemporary organization of knowledge (*arbor scientiarum*) to this whole normative discourse, where law is inextricably connected to theology and ethics. Thereafter, it also clarifies the permanent and pervasive migration of concepts and models of reasoning and justifying from one literary field to another. And finally, it illuminates the reasons for the continuity between this learned literature and daily practices.

The third conclusion deals with the jurists' and lawyers' commonly implicit assumptions about the nature of paradigms underlying law. At least since the German Historical School of the nineteenth century, jurists have been aware of the existence of a coherent system of values behind each singular legal proposition and rule. But, except for the first generation, they still tend to think that those paradigms are the result of an everlasting legal reasoning and not a culturally embedded universe of beliefs. Namely, in what concerned Roman law or the great tradition of continental *ius commune*, it was assumed that modern "rational" legal categories were already there, although still in an embryonic form. Western legal tradition would be an unshaken continuum, where reason developed progressively and without ruptures in its consistent conceptual system.

Therefore, stressing discontinuity and rupture is not a trivial theoretical attitude among jurists, and even legal historians. In fact, the timelessness of legal constructs has been a basic postulate of western legal thought since the Enlightenment, when culturally pervasive rationalism created the utopia of a legal system based on rational axioms developed at a mathematical pace.

Gottfried Wilhelm von Leibniz (1646–1716) and Jeremy Bentham (1748–1832) are two leading representatives of this stream of jurists who conceived legal reasoning and the finding of legal solutions (*Rechtsfindung*) as a form of calculus, albeit specific. Neo-Kantian formalism stressed the tendency to assimilate legal doctrine to a formal science, cut off from any cultural or social context. The last step in this trend was taken by the Pure Theory of Law (Hans Kelsen, 1897–1955), when it measured the scientificity of legal discourse in its capacity to alienate (purify) any other considerations but formal rigor.

Even historicism and sociology have often fallen in such an aculturalist essentialism. In fact, even when social roots of legal institutions or of legal doctrines were problematized, the adopted model considered that social groups, in the present as in the past, shared the same basic models of representing reality or interests. Social conflict or social emulation in history was often represented as if actors were contemporary urban Europeans. For them, wealth would be more important than honor; individual affirmation more decisive than the fulfillment of a natural preestablished role; progress more desirable than stability; rights more imposing than duties; individuals more visible than community; formal legal obligations more stringent than necessary (*praeter*-intentional) natural bonds. This contemporary context of behavior forms a kind of natural practical reason that can be exported to any human situation or taken as a basis for the research of political justice (as in John Rawls's procedural theory of justice).

Current anthropological awareness has given historiography, especially legal historiography, a new sensibility to cultural rupture and historical difference, liberating the autonomous grammar of each of the different institutional cultures of the European past. This liberation of difference has two major effects; one on the legal plane, another on the historical.

On the plane of the theory of law, to recover the sense of historical difference has been a major factor in the recovery of the sense of the localness of Western legal values. Today, European legal consciousness is confronted with the failures of exporting Western legal technologies or with their reticent import by alien cultures. In a world that vertiginously tends to integration, the clash of legal universalism and the corresponding awareness of the localism of law poses the vital problem of rebuilding a general theory of law that can work, liberated from chronocentrism and ethnocentrism, on behalf of pluralism.

In what concerns the historical dimension, the sensitiveness to difference is a condition of a successful re-creation of extinct cultural environments. Medieval and early modern legal culture is one of them. It forms a coherent universe of images, beliefs, and values that gave sense to millions of concrete decisions of everyday life. These now silent and traceless acts can no longer be witnessed. Alternatively, we still have the imposing corpus of the learned tradition of law that worked on the same cultural frame and which had implemented several discursive devices allowing a continuous shuttling between common sense and learned culture. One of them was the permanent openness of legal doctrine to everyday life or established social values, by means of concepts or topics like *equitas* (equity), *bonum* or *rectum* (for example, *bonus paterfamilias*, ordinary person; *recta ratio*, common reason), *natura rerum* (nature of things), *id quod plerumque accidit* (statistical normality), rootedness (for example, *iura radicata*, rooted [in time or tradition] social expectations) and so on. Another device was the role of "topica" as the art of reaching consent on the finding of legal doctrinal solutions. A last word on this point would suggest how it can be the answer to a common question about the potentialities of legal doctrinal literature in becoming a source of cultural and intellectual history.

Notwithstanding the latest developments in the sense of rebuilding a theory of law in everyday life,[28] current legal doctrine (*maxime* in European continental doctrine) is rather impermeable to common sense and desires for social justice. In certain domains where adhesion to common-sense fairness values is crucial, there are some discursive devices that guarantee an open legal conceptual system to everyday life. This is the case of general clauses or open concepts like "good faith" (in contractual matters), "prudent discretion or arbitration" (in judicial adjudication), "wise man" (namely in patrimonial management). But in general, legal concepts are quite stiff and self-referential.

On the contrary, this reference to the world of values and evaluations rooted in common sense was permanent in *ius commune* legal doctrine. Legal learned solutions were continuously justified by the fact that they were accepted by ordinary people for a variety of reasons: because they were long

---

28. Austin Sarat, *Law in Everyday Life* (Ann Arbor: University of Michigan Press, 1996).

used (*usus receptae*), because they were rooted in social practices (*radicatae, praescriptae*), because they respond to the order of things or to the moral order as they were commonly perceived (*honestae, bonnae et aequae*). Even the frame of legal sources of law, as it was acknowledged by the doctrine, expressed this weight of spontaneous sense of fairness. At the top were custom (*consuetudo*), received doctrine (*opinio communis*), and judicial practice (*stylus curiae, praxis*).

Furthermore, this permanent scrutiny of common sense was completed by the decision-making techniques. Rather than infer a solution from a doctrinal rigid standard, jurists reached it in two steps: first (*inventio iuris, ars inveniendi*), by finding and collecting relevant common points of view (*loca communia, topoi*); second, by confronting them according to their casuistic impact on common sense (*iudicium, ars iudicandi*). Common sense was then at the beginning and at the end of the decision-making process. It suggested the set of criteria for decision (*topoi*) as well as the metacriteria of hierarchizing them in each case.

But the intercourse between learned doctrine and common sense did not complete the decision-making process. Once reached, decision—this product of a learned reason—becomes a *bone more* in this moral skeleton of everyday life formed by "received or practiced law" (*ius receptum vel praticatum*). Actually, decided cases would integrate the horizon of moral standards and social expectations of the community. But the process of doctrinal reelaboration of the social sense of fairness was ongoing. Working on this decisional practical *acquis*, jurists distill *regula, brocarda*, short phrases or epigrams where practical legal wisdom was concentrated and could be easily disseminated and assimilated by laypeople. Now, learned constructs structured by common sense return to everyday life, becoming themselves structuring principles. Discourse comes back into life, from its ephemeral refuge in books.

The editor gratefully acknowledges assistance from Julius Kirshner in clarifying the translation and explaining the law and arguments outlined in this chapter.

Chapter 9

STRATEGIES OF SURVIVAL

Minority Cultures in the Western Mediterranean

HENRY KAMEN

Fernand Braudel's approach to Lepanto, a battle that constitutes the focal event of his *Mediterranean*, offers us some evidence of his handling of historical categories. Though the battle occupies a seemingly innocuous place at the very end of his work, as though it were an *événement* of minor consequence in a narrative where the major participants are the eternal invariables of mountain and sea, in reality it predetermines much of what precedes it. When applied to the Iberian peninsula, Braudel's vision of Lepanto calls for the creation of a military scenario. Jews, Muslims, and Christians in Spain are presented as civilizations in conflict, offering a suitably dramatic rehearsal for the stage on which the famous naval battle will eventually be fought. This brilliant panorama is highly convincing. But the evidence that we now have of the centuries-long *convivencia* in Spain offers a different perspective that accords more with what we know of Western society at that time. Martyred Jews, oppressed Muslims, and fanatical Christians all existed in reality; though they come perilously close to being stereotypes of traditional historiography rather than images supported by the documentation. The dramatic sweep of *The Mediterranean* allows little room for us to stop and examine what was really going on among the cultures of the peninsula; we have to hurry on, to join Don Juan at Lepanto.

Braudel, in short, paid proportionately little attention in his work to problems of cultural evolution, what used to be called *mentalités*. This can be seen even in his *Identity of France*. The deficiency has no profound implications, but it inevitably colored the picture he offers us of the past. Brilliant as his few pages on the subject of religion may be, they are too few: Giordano Bruno being burnt on the Campo dei Fiori in 1600, the Valladolid Protestants being burnt in 1559, these are the extent of dissent in the Mediterranean. The

Jews make an appearance, but are considered more in their presumed role as conveyors of capitalism. And in the specific case of Spain, Braudel possibly misjudges the issue by viewing the expulsion of Jews as something inevitable, brought about by Spain's drive for political unity and by the Jews' own unwillingness to compromise. With dissenters and Jews rapidly cleared out of the way, the stage is clear for the struggle between militant Catholicism and militant Islam.

It is the clash between strident and militant faiths that interests Braudel, because his is the total view, taken from an Olympian perspective. One must confess that the problem of *mentalité* seems, by contrast, literally trivial. The greater part of recent original work by early modern historians on the framework of everyday culture, explores the much smaller world of communally shared attitudes, nearly always within the enclosed universe of a village, town, or city.[1] In these cases, the researcher normally does not claim validity for his findings beyond the little universe he has studied.

The restricted framework of this type of cultural research seems to make a traditional *Annales* approach inapplicable; it also makes *mentalités* research fragmented, localized, always open to debate, and in the end somewhat frustrating. However, a sharp contrast must be drawn between this approach and the other, deliberately anecdotal, to be found in some recent Italy-oriented research, where scholars rely on minute case histories or on revealing personal documentation, narrowing the focus down to individuals and their mental horizons. It is doubtful if the cultural history of early modern Spain (or even, perhaps, Italy) can be studied in this way. The social situation of Christians, Muslims, and Jews seems to demand that attention concentrate on the community context of individuals rather than on their private visions. In part, this is dictated by the available documentation, which is mostly administrative and refers to corporate matters (taxes, property, crimes); in part also it follows from the refusal of literate Spaniards in early modern times—of whatever religion—to entrust their thoughts to paper. In the process, mentalities in early modern Spain have more often to be viewed by the historian through the medium of social context than through the (less accessible) medium of religious attitudes.

It is possible to be more specific about this problem of access to private belief, at least for Christians. In a recent very interesting study Carlos Eire

---

1. As in the suggestive study by David Sabean, *Power in the Blood: Popular Culture and Village Discourse in Early Modern Germany* (Cambridge: Cambridge University Press, 1984).

studied some 450 wills from the Madrid area for the period 1520–99;[2] but he assumed that the testators were normally responsible for the statements of religious affirmation in the wills.[3] Had he probed more into the background to wills, he would have found that the religious formulations in them were fairly rigidly laid down by diocesan authority;[4] they were set formulae, instead of expressions of personal belief. There is ample evidence of the Catholicity of Spanish testators, but their wills do not give us reliable access to their beliefs. It is, in short, difficult to find out what Spaniards believed, and more convincing to see how they behaved.

The work done in recent years on the culture of the three historic faiths of Spain seems now to emphasize the local at the expense of the universal. Where Braudel saw self-assured "civilizations" and a secure faith, the evidence offers a perspective of fragmented communities, not pitted against each other but surviving in conditions of relative tolerance. One should emphasize at the outset that this does not mean we can accept the optimistic scenario, still popular among some literary scholars in the United States as a result of the influence of Américo Castro, of a happy *convivencia* between the three faiths. In reality, the long coexistence between three cultures produced both confrontation and survival, leading to a complexity of social responses not found in other Western nations.

The present essay will look very briefly at three aspects of the religious culture of the Christian western Mediterranean: the community-centered evolution of cultural identities, the dogmatic uncertainty of the major faiths, and aspects of interchange and mutual tolerance.[5]

In medieval times Spain was a society of uneasy coexistence [*convivencia*], increasingly threatened by the advancing Christian reconquest of lands that had been Muslim since the Moorish invasions of the eighth century. For long periods, close contact between communities had led to a mutual tolerance among the three faiths of the peninsula: Christians, Muslims and Jews. Even when Christians went to war against the Moors, it was (a thirteenth-century writer argued) "neither because of the law [of Mohammed] nor

---

2. Carlos Eire, *From Madrid to Purgatory: The Art and Craft of Dying in Sixteenth-Century Spain* (Cambridge: Cambridge University Press, 1995).

3. Cf. Eire, *From Madrid to Purgatory,* chap.2.

4. As they were in Catalonia; see Henry Kamen, *The Phoenix and the Flame: Catalonia and the Counter Reformation* (New Haven: Yale University Press, 1993), 10.

5. Some sections of the following text were published in Henry Kamen, *The Spanish Inquisition: A Historical Revision* (New Haven: Yale University Press, 1998).

because of the sect that they hold to,"[6] but because of conflict over land. The different communities, occupying separate territories and therefore able to maintain distinct cultures, accepted the need to live together. Military alliances were made regardless of religion.

There had always been serious conflicts in a society as divided as medieval Spain, at both the social and the personal levels, between Mudéjar and Christian villages, between Christian and Jewish neighbors. But the existence of a multicultural framework produced an extraordinary degree of mutual respect. This degree of coexistence was a unique feature of peninsular society, repeated perhaps only in the Hungarian territories of the Ottoman empire. Communities lived side by side and shared many aspects of language, culture, food, and dress, consciously borrowing each other's outlook and ideas. Where cultural groups were a minority they accepted fully that there was a persistent dark side to the picture. Their capacity to endure centuries of sporadic repression and to survive well into early modern times under conditions of gross inequality was based on a long apprenticeship.

Muslims were possibly the least affected by religious tension in Christian Spain prior to 1492. They were numerically insignificant in Castile, and in the crown of Aragon they lived separately in their own communities, so that friction was minimal. Tension increased from the mid-sixteenth century, precisely the period studied by Braudel, for two main reasons: the forced conversions that made Muslims, now known as Moriscos, subject to growing pressure from the Inquisition; and the military threat from north Africa in the first instance and, more menacingly, from Istanbul itself. Jews, ultimately to be expelled in 1492, lived mostly in urban centers and were more vulnerable to outbreaks of violence. After the accession of Ferdinand and Isabella to the throne in 1474, both minorities began to suffer the consequences of living under the hegemony of a triumphal crusading religion. It is significant that the new rulers of Spain were willing to pursue an intolerant policy regardless of its economic consequences. In regard to both the Jews and the Muslims, Isabella was warned that pressure would produce economic disruption, but she was steeled in her resolve by Cisneros and the rigorists. Ferdinand, responding to protests by Barcelona, maintained that spiritual ideals were more important than material considerations about the economy. Though affirmation of religious motives cannot be accepted at face value, it

---

6. Cited in Américo Castro, *The Structure of Spanish History* (Princeton: Princeton University Press, 1954), 221.

appears that a crusading spirit had replaced the possibility of *convivencia*, and exclusivism was beginning to triumph.

A FOCUS: THE COMMUNITY

Religion, however, was not the only social context within which early modern Spaniards lived; nor did it absolutely divide them from each other. Under Christian rule both Jews and Muslims were from the beginning subjected to an autonomous community structure, negotiated with the seigneur, who in most of Spain was the ruling monarch. As in the case of medieval settlement charters in Christian lands, this structure gave the minorities internal autonomy but facilitated direct agreements over taxation and law, and it also enabled the communities to claim the protection of their lord. Christian society, likewise, functioned for the most part along lines of community organization, but with the evident difference that Christians were the majority society, and were seldom restricted to one sole jurisdiction. In the case of all three faiths, the nature of their legal jurisdiction played a fundamental role in the quality of everyday religion, affording them opportunities for autonomous development that can cause surprise if we think only in terms of persistent conflict.

The "community" had real sociological meaning: it was a localized unit sharing a localized culture. Recent studies emphasize (what may appear obvious to most of us now, but had never previously been studied in the case of Spain) that Spanish Christianity was profoundly localized.[7] This tended to distance Spanish communities from the beliefs and practices of the universal church; in consequence, the evidence suggests that Christian culture, well into the late sixteenth century, was basically traditional rather than orthodox. Religious culture was conditioned by geography (that is, isolation), jurisdiction (the type of seigneur), and language (Catalan, Basque, and so forth); it was in all cases heavily localized rather than universal. But the localization did not express itself in an individualistic faith. Despite Emmanuel Le Roy Ladurie's perception of a Christocentric Cathar belief in the foothills of the medieval Pyrenees,[8] there is no clear evidence of a personalized religion in the western Mediterranean. On the contrary, all early modern religion was communal, as in reality the documentation used in

7. William A. Christian Jr., *Local Religion in Sixteenth-Century Spain* (Princeton: Princeton University Press, 1981); Kamen, *Phoenix,* chap. 1.

8. Emmanuel Le Roy Ladurie, *Montaillou* (London: Scolar Press, 1978), 299.

Ladurie's brilliant study demonstrates. Menocchios may have existed, but behind them was always a conforming community.

The emphasis on local religious practice has helped to shed considerable light on the evolution of Jewish and Islamic communities of Spain. It is well known that from the thirteenth century onwards anti-Jewish legislation became common in Europe. The decrees were never enforced in the Spanish kingdoms, though successive Cortes continued to call for action—in 1371 at Toro and 1405 at Madrid. In most towns Jews began to be restricted to their own community (called an *aljama* when it was organized as a corporate body). Each *aljama* was a separate society within the towns, with its own officials and its own taxes. It was exempt from most municipal obligations except the duty to defend the town. It paid taxes only to the crown, under whose direct control it came. In practice, the crown had few resources with which to protect the *aljamas* against hostile municipalities. In size and numbers the *aljamas* shrank dramatically after widespread massacres in 1391, and indeed in some cities *aljamas* no longer existed. In Barcelona, the medieval Jewish *call* [street] was abolished in 1424 because it was deemed unnecessary. In Toledo, the ancient *aljama* consisted by 1492 of possibly only forty houses. Though Braudel continued in *The Mediterranean* to present the Jews as largely middle class,[9] it is certain that they were no longer significant in this social sector.[10] The massacres of 1391 had driven many to settle in the countryside. By the late fifteenth century, contrary to a widely held view that Jews were mainly town dwellers, Jewish farmers and peasants could be found throughout Spain, but above all in the provinces of Castile. In Toledo, a considerable proportion of Jews seem to have worked their own lands. In Máqueda (Toledo) there were 281 Jewish families to only fifty Christian.[11] Even when they had lands and cattle, however, for practical reasons of religious observance and security the Jews tended to live together, usually in a town or village environment. In Buitrago (Guadalajara), members of the prosperous Jewish community (which in 1492 boasted six rabbis and even a town councilor) owned 165 fields of flax, 102 meadows, 18 market gardens,

---

9. Fernand Braudel, *The Mediterranean and the Mediterranean World in the Age of Philip II*, 2 vols., trans. Siân Reynolds (London: Collins, 1972), 2:814–15.

10. This is the argument followed by Yitzhak Baer, *A History of the Jews in Christian Spain*, 2 vols. (Philadelphia: Jewish Publication Society, 1966).

11. Pilar León Tello, *Judíos de Toledo*, 2 vols. (Madrid: Consejo Superior de Investigaciones Científicas, Instituto "B. Arias Montano," 1979): 2:549–607.

a large amount of pasture, and a few water rights.[12] In Hita, in the same region, they had two synagogues and nine rabbis; the major investment was in wine, with Jews owning 396 vineyards totaling no less than 66,400 vines.[13] Even in the Andalusian countryside, there were Jewish farmers owning lands, vineyards, and herds of cattle.[14] The reduced number of Jews after 1391 did not necessarily imply a cultural decline. The communities preserved their identity, legislated for their people (a comprehensive law for Jews was drawn up by them in 1432 in Valladolid), enjoyed the protection of leading nobles as well as of the crown, and coexisted pacifically with Christians.[15] In Aragon the crown itself favored the recovery of the *aljamas*, which paid taxes directly to the royal treasury. In 1479 Ferdinand expressly confirmed the autonomy of the Jewish community in Saragossa.[16]

In the case of Muslims, who were theoretically Christianized "Moriscos" after the 1520s, their situation varied across the peninsula according to density of population. The highest concentration was in the kingdom of Granada, where Moriscos in the 1560s were some 54 percent of the population; in areas such as the Alpujarra mountains they constituted the totality. In Valencia they formed a third of the population in the late sixteenth century, in Aragon about a fifth. In Catalonia, Moriscos were a tiny group, and in Castile they were proportionately even less, perhaps a total of some twenty thousand in 1502,[17] scattered throughout the country in small urban *morerías* and living at peace with their Christian neighbors.

There were major differences between the Morisco communities. The Granadans, recently subjugated, included a flourishing upper class, preserved their religion and culture intact, and usually spoke Arabic (*algarabía*, the Christians called it). They were an integral Islamic civilization. The

---

12. F. Cantera Burgos and Carlos Carrete Parrondo, "La judería de Buitrago," *Sefarad* 32 (1972).

13. F. Cantera Burgos and Carlos Carrete Parrondo, "La judería de Hita," *Sefarad* 32 (1972).

14. A. A. Bel Bravo, *Los Reyes Católicos y los Judíos Andaluces (1474–1492)* (Granada: Universidad de Granada, 1989), 128.

15. For arguments against a decline, see E. Gutwirth, "Towards Expulsion, 1391–1492," in *Spain and the Jews*, ed. Elie Kedourie (London: Thames & Hudson, 1992), 54–68.

16. M. A. Motis Dolader, "La expulsión de los judíos aragoneses," in *Destierros aragoneses: Judíos y moriscos* (Saragossa: Institución Fernando el Católico, 1988), 84.

17. M. A. Ladero Quesada, *Los Mudéjares del reino de Castilla en tiempo de Isabel I* (Valladolid: Istituto Isabella Católica, 1969).

Valencians were largely a rural proletariat, but because they lived quite separately from the Christian population and were so numerous, they managed
to preserve most of their customs, religion, and language. Elsewhere in
Spain, Arabic was almost unknown among the Moriscos. All spoke a form
of Castilian. In Aragon, where Muslims had lived longest among Christians, the decline of Arabic produced the beginnings, in the sixteenth century, of a Morisco literature written in Spanish. Residual knowledge of
Arabic, however, was sufficient to warrant the import of sacred texts from
abroad.[18] Aragonese Moriscos, for the most part, lived and dressed like their
Christian neighbors; they differed only in religion.[19]

Though deprived of access to Christian society by discrimination, the
Moriscos were not uniformly poor. As a separate community, they had an
economic life parallel to that of Christians. The majority worked the land.
But in Aragon they also herded flocks of sheep and cattle for the market; in
Saragossa they were carpenters, metalworkers, and clothworkers. They were
active in the building industry, and produced swords and arms for sale. Some
were traders, investing their profits in the land.[20] In towns wholly populated
by Moriscos, such as Almonacid de la Sierra (in Aragon), the inhabitants logically produced their own liberal professions: a surgeon, a scrivener, a lawyer,
a noble, in addition to lesser callings.[21]

To maintain their internal integrity, the Muslim leaders also strengthened the social role of their community, the *aljama*. It was an institution that
allowed them to preserve their autonomy and culture, but at the same time
made it possible to cooperate on good terms with the authorities.[22] They
spoke among themselves the version of Spanish known as *aljamía*.[23]

Until the early years of the reign of Philip II the efforts of the Inquisition
to keep Moriscos to their nominal Christianity were little more than a gesture. The largest numbers to be prosecuted were in the crown of Aragon, but
they were only the tip of the iceberg of unbelief in Morisco Spain. There

18. Jacqueline Fournel, "Le livre et la civilisation écrite dans la communauté morisque
aragonaise (1540–1620)," *Mélanges de la Casa de Velázquez* 15 (1979).

19. William Monter, *Frontiers of Heresy: The Spanish Inquisition from the Basque Lands to
Sicily* (Cambridge: Cambridge University Press, 1990), 212.

20. G. Colás Latorre, "Los moriscos aragoneses y su expulsión," in *Destierros aragoneses*,
203–5.

21. M. C. Anson Calvo, in *Destierros aragoneses*, p. 309.

22. Cf. Mikel de Epalza, "Les Morisques," in *Les Morisques et leur temps* (Paris: CNRS,
1983), 38–39.

23. Cf. Mikel de Epalza, in *Destierros aragoneses*, 225.

were two main reasons for the relative absence of prosecutions: the conviction of both church and state that a proper program of conversion should be undertaken, and the strong opposition of Christian seigneurs to any interference with their rights over their Morisco vassals. In Aragon, for instance, nearly 70 percent of the Moriscos were under noble jurisdiction.[24] In January 1526 the leaders of the Valencian Moriscos succeeded in obtaining from the crown and the inquisitor general a secret *concordia* or agreement that if they all submitted to baptism they would be free for forty years from any prosecution by the Holy Office, since it would be impossible for them to shed all their customs at once. In 1528 the *concordia* was made public, and in that same year the Cortes of Aragon, meeting at Monzón, asked Charles to prevent the Inquisition from prosecuting Moriscos until they had been instructed in the faith. Their request was timely, for the guarantee was no more lasting than the one granted to the Mudéjars of Granada. The Holy Office interpreted the *concordia* to mean that it could bring to trial those converts who had slipped back into Islamic practices.

Although it is customary to emphasize the conflictive nature of Morisco life in Philip II's Spain, as documented in Louis Cardaillac's excellent study,[25] it may be worthwhile to pursue the distinction (already touched on) between ideological tension and social coexistence. Cardaillac demonstrates the uncompromising nature of Muslim resistance to Christian indoctrination; but it was not the only face of peninsular mentalities, and we would be making a serious mistake to think it was. At the level of everyday coexistence the community dimension defused much potential for conflict. It made it possible, on one hand, for Muslims and Christians to continue their social existence together on acceptable terms; on the other, it enabled many Christians, both clergy and laity, to defend the coexistence even while the pressure was growing on all sides for the expulsion of the Moriscos.

Of several examples that demonstrate the way in which a Morisco community could survive within a hostile environment, we may choose that of the town of Arcos de Medinaceli, on the estates of the duke of Medinaceli near the frontier of Castile with Aragon. In the 1550s the town was nine-tenths Morisco in population; though formally Catholic, the Moriscos practiced cultural rites—in their fasts, burials, and ablutions—that set them clearly apart from orthodox Christians. Yet both Moriscos and Christians

---

24. G. Colás Latorre, in *Destierros aragoneses*, 199.

25. Louis Cardaillac, *Morisques et Chrétiens: Un affrontement polémique (1492–1640)* (Paris: Klinksieck, 1977).

coexisted peacefully despite the religious differentiation: they shared municipal posts equally, and when Moriscos were buried the Old Christians attended the funeral.[26] There were abundant conflicts in Spain's multicultural society; but there was also a striking absence of confrontation in many parts of the country throughout the sixteenth century.[27] A historian whose perspective is dominated by Lepanto, or even more crucially by the expulsions of 1609, may tend to look backward and see only the clouds of a gathering storm. Those living under that storm, for their part, knew that for centuries the skies had always menaced but that the storms also tended to dissipate.

TRUE BELIEVERS?

The *mentalité* of the western Mediterranean, in other words, was not defined exclusively by religious conflict but also by strategies of survival. Autonomy of religious communities in Spain produced a remarkable variety of religious attitudes. Spain was not, as often imagined, a society dominated exclusively by zealots. In the Mediterranean the confrontation of cultures was more constant than in northern Europe, but the certainty of faith was no stronger. Jews had the advantage of community solidarity, but under pressure from other cultures they also suffered the disadvantage of internal dissent over belief.[28] The three faiths had coexisted long enough for many people to accept the validity of all three. "Who knows which is the better religion," a Christian of Castile asked in 1501, "ours or those of the Muslims and the Jews?"[29]

Though there were confusions of belief in the peninsula, there seems in late medieval times to have been no formal heresy, not even among Christians. But this did not imply that Spain was a society of convinced believers. In the mid-sixteenth century a friar lamented the ignorance and unbelief he had found throughout Castile, "not only in small hamlets and villages but even in cities and populous towns." "Out of three hundred residents," he affirmed, "you will find barely thirty who know what any ordinary Christian

---

26. Raphael Carrasco, "Morisques anciens et nouveaux Morisques dans le district inquisitorial de Cuenca," *Mélanges de la Casa de Vélazquez* 22 (1986).

27. G. Colás Latorre, "Cristianos y Moriscos en Aragón," *Mélanges de la Casa de Vélazquez* 29, no. 2 (1993).

28. Baer, *History of the Jews in Christian Spain,* vol. 1, chaps 5–6.

29. Carlos Carrete Parrondo, "Nostalgia for the Past among Christian Judeoconversos," *Mediterranean Historical Review,* vol.6, no.2 (1991): 33.

is obliged to know."[30] Religious practice among Christians was a free mixture of community traditions, superstitious folklore, and imprecise dogmatic beliefs.[31] Some writers went so far as to categorize popular religious practices as diabolic magic. It was a situation that church leaders did very little to remedy.[32] Everyday religion among Christians continued to embrace an immense range of cultural and devotional options. There are many parallels to the cases of the Catalan peasant who asserted in 1539 that "there is no heaven, purgatory, or hell; at the end we all have to end up in the same place; the bad will go to the same place as the good and the good will go to the same place as the bad"; or of the other who stated in 1593 that "he does not believe in heaven or hell, and God feeds the Muslims and heretics just the same as he feeds the Christians."[33] When Christian warriors battled against Muslims, they shouted their convictions passionately. At home, or in the inn, or working in the fields, their opinions were often different. The bulk of surviving documentation gives us some key to this dual outlook; only, however, among Christians. In Soria in 1487, at a time when the final conquest of Granada was well under way, a resident commented that "the king is off to drive the Muslims out, when they haven't done him any harm."[34] "The Muslim can be saved in his faith just as the Christian can in his,"[35] another is reported to have said. The inquisitors in 1490 in Cuenca were informed of a Christian who claimed that "the good Jew and the good Muslim can, if they act correctly, go to heaven just like the good Christian."[36] There is little or nothing to tell us how Jews and Muslims thought, but every probability that they also accepted the need to make compromises with the other faiths of the peninsula. Towards the end of the reign of Philip II, for example, a small group of Morisco intellectuals attempted to spring onto unwary Christians

30. Felipe de Meneses, *Luz del alma cristiana* (1554), ed. Ismael Velo Pensado (Madrid: Universidad Pontificia de Salamanca, 1978), 317, 321.

31. This is the argument in Kamen, *Phoenix*, chap. 3.

32. The practice in the diocese of Toledo may be gauged by the prohibitions issued by the provincial council of Aranda in 1473: Juan Tejada y Ramiro, *Colección de cánones y de todos los concilios*, 6 vols. (Madrid: Montero, 1859), 5:24.

33. Institut Municipal d'Historia, Barcelona, section Consellers CXVIII, vol. 8, fol. 95; Archivo Histórico Nacional, Madrid, section Inquisición, lib. 731, fol. 172.

34. *Fontes Iudaeorum regni Castellae*, ed. Carlos Carrete Parrondo, vol. 2: *El Tribunal de la Inquisición en el Obispado de Soria (1486–1502)* (Salamanca: Universidad Pontificia de Salamanca, 1985), 120.

35. *Fontes*, 2:122.

36. Carlos Carrete Parrondo, "'Duelos os dé Dios, e avrá Christiandad': Nueva página sobre el criptojudaísmo castellano," *Sefarad* (1992): ii, 369.

the ingenious fraud of the leaden tablets of Sacromonte (Granada), discovered in a cave and which were engraved in apparently ancient Arabic that claimed to add an Arabic dimension to the Christian revelation.[37] It was, scholars are agreed, an attempt to find a niche for Muslim culture within the framework of Iberian Christianity.

Christians who wished to turn their backs on their own society often did so quite simply by embracing Islam. From the later Middle Ages to the eighteenth century, there were random cases of Spanish Christians who changed their faith in this way. The Moorish kingdom of Granada had a small community of renegade Christians. In Christian Spain it was not uncommon to find many of pro-Muslim sentiment. In 1486 the Inquisition of Saragossa tried a Christian "for saying that he was a Muslim, and for praying in the mosque like a Muslim."[38] Long after the epoch of *convivencia* had passed, many Spaniards retained at the back of their minds a feeling that their differences were not divisive. In the Granada countryside in the 1620s, a woman of Muslim origin felt that "the Muslim can be saved in his faith as the Jew can in his," a Christian peasant felt that "everyone can find salvation in his own faith," and another affirmed that "Jews who observe their law can be saved."[39] The attitude was frequent enough to be commonplace, and could be found in every corner of Spain.

A SHARED SOCIETY

Though coexistence among the faiths has occasionally been idealized by historians, it is timely to emphasize that the communities of Christians, Jews, and Muslims never lived together on equal terms; so-called *convivencia* was always a relationship between unequals. Within that inequality, the minorities played their roles while attempting to avoid conflicts. In fifteenth-century Murcia,[40] the Muslims were an indispensable fund of labor in both town and country, and as such were protected by municipal laws. The Jews, for their part, made an essential contribution as artisans and small producers,

37. Cf. *The Legacy of Muslim Spain,* ed. Salma Khadra Jayyusi (Leiden: Brill, 1992), 228–29.

38. Monter, *Frontiers,* 24.

39. María de los Angeles Fernández García, *Inquisición, comportamiento y mentalidad en el reino de Granada (1600–1700)* (Granada: M. Fernández García, 1989), 110, 246.

40. Denis Menjot, "Les minorités juives et musulmanes dans l'économie murcienne au bas Moyen-Age," *Minorités et marginaux en Espagne et dans le Midi de la France (VIIe–XVIIIe siècles)* (Paris: CNRS, 1986).

in leather, jewelry, and textiles. They were also important in tax administration and in medicine. In theory, both minorities were restricted to specified areas of the towns they lived in. In practice, they preferred to live together and the laws on separation were seldom enforced. In Valladolid at the same period, the Muslims increased in number and importance, chose their residence freely, owned houses, lands, and vineyards.[41] Though unequal in rights, the Valladolid Muslims were not marginalized. The tolerability of coexistence paved the way to mass conversion in 1502.

In community celebrations, all three faiths participated. In Murcia, Muslim musicians and jugglers were an integral part of Christian religious celebrations. In times of crisis the faiths necessarily collaborated. In 1470 in the town of Uclés, "a year of great drought, there were many processions of Christians as well as of Muslims and Jews, to pray for water."[42] In such a community, there were some who saw no harm in participating with other faiths. "Hernán Sánchez Castro," who was denounced for it twenty years later in Uclés, "set out from the church together with other Christians in the procession, and when they reached the square where the Jews were with the Torah he joined the procession of the Jews with their Torah and left the procession of the Christians." Coacceptance of the communities extended to acts of charity. Diego González remembered that in Huete in the 1470s, when he was a poor orphan, as a Christian he received alms from "both Jews and Muslims, for we used to beg for alms from all of them, and received help from them as we did from the Christians." The kindness he received from Jews, indeed, encouraged him to pick up a smattering of Hebrew from them. It also led him to assert that "the Jew can find salvation in his own faith just as the Christian can in his."[43] There was, of course, always another side to the coexistence. It was in Uclés in 1491 that a number of Jewish citizens voluntarily gave testimony against Christians of Jewish origin. And Diego González, twenty years later when he had become a priest, was arrested for his pro-Jewish tendencies and burnt as a heretic.

41. Adeline Rucquoi, "Juifs et musulmanes dans une ville de la Castille septentrionale," in *Minorités et marginaux en Espagne et dans le Midi de la France.*
42. Carlos Carrete Parrondo, "Los judaizantes castellanos," in *Inquisición y conversos.* III Curso de cultura hispano-judia y sefardi (Toledo: Asociación de Amigos del Museo Sefardí, 1994), 201.
43. Cited Carlos Carrete Parrondo, *El judaismo español y la Inquisición* (Madrid: MAPFRE, 1992), 103.

These examples are, of course, from the period when coexistence still existed, but was breaking down. Very soon, after the Jewish expulsions of 1492, there would be no further Jewish presence. And very soon the abolition of Islam in Spain—in Castile in 1500, in Aragon in 1526—would put Catholics and Muslims on a collision course. The war in Africa and the Mediterranean acted as a reference point for ideologies within the peninsula: Moriscos celebrated in the streets in 1578 when news arrived of the annihilation of the army of Portugal at Alcazarquivir. Yet, despite everything, there remained a *mentalité* that bound Muslims (as, of course, Jews would always feel bound) to Spain. In Cervantes's *Quixote* the refugee Morisco is quoted as saying that "wherever we are, we weep for Spain, for we were born there and it is our native land." It was not mere literary rhetoric. No evidence can be more illustrative of the Morisco dilemma than that of an agent of the English government in Morocco in 1625 who reported that the Moriscos there "complain bitterly of their cruel exile, and *desire deeply to return under Christian rule*."[44]

Suffering, it seems, was an integral part of a plural civilization in the western Mediterranean; and conflict with rival faiths may have served to produce the remarkable phenomenon of an absence of formal "heresy" in late mediaeval Spain. The three faiths, even while respecting each other, attempted to maintain in some measure the purity of their own ideology. In times of crisis, as with the rabbis in 1492 or the Muslim *alfaquis* in 1609, they clung desperately to the uniqueness of their own truth. Christianity, for its part, remained so untarnished by formal heresy that the papal Inquisition, active in France, Germany, and Italy, was never deemed necessary in medieval Castile and made only a token appearance in Aragon. In the penumbra of the three great faiths there were, it is true, a number of those who, whether through the indifferentism born of tolerance or the cynicism born of persecution, had no active belief in organized religion. But the virtual absence of organized heresy meant that though defections to other faiths were severely punished in Christian law, no systematic machinery was ever brought into existence to deal with nonbelievers or with those forced converts who had shaky belief. For decades, society continued to tolerate them, and the policy of burning practiced elsewhere in Europe was little known in Spain.

44. My italics; cited in Guillermo Gozalbes Busto, *Los Moriscos en Marruecos* (Granada: T. G. Arte, 1992), 115.

The appearance and activity of the Inquisition consequently plays a smaller role in this essay than some might expect. Braudel states explicitly that "during the long sixteenth century the peninsula turned itself into the Church Militant."[45] It is a valid viewpoint if one has one's eye on Lepanto, and the statistics show clearly that more Moriscos suffered at the hands of the Inquisition under Philip II than at any other period. But viewed from within the peninsula even the Inquisition takes on diminished and localized proportions that help us comprehend its role in the formation of religion. On one hand, it has now become possible to revise very radically the figures given for Inquisitorial persecution. A recent carefully considered view is that in the years of the high tide of persecution (from 1480 to about 1530), executions for heresy were a fragment of the figures frequently given by scholars.[46] Taking into account all the tribunals of Spain up to about 1530, it is unlikely that more than two thousand people were executed for heresy in the half-century of the most intense activity of the Inquisition.[47] The famous period of persecution of Protestants, resulting in the autos de fe of 1559 and 1562, is also a good example of how the standard image of Spanish religious ferocity needs to be defused; the city courts of Antwerp between 1557 and 1562 alone executed 103 heretics,[48] more than died in the whole of Spain in that period. Prosecutions of Moriscos in the later sixteenth century were numerous, but severity of punishment was rare.[49] And the day-to-day contact of the Holy Office with the Spanish Christian population was minimal. In Catalonia, "in over 90 per cent of the towns, during more than three centuries of existence, the Holy Office never once intruded."[50] For the rest of the peninsula, especially outside the heartland of Castile, the situation seems to have been comparable.

45. Braudel, *The Mediterranean,* 2:824.
46. Monter, *Frontiers,* 15, 21. The diagram of cases in Aragon in Motis Dolader, "Los judíos zaragozanos en la época de Fernando II de Aragón," *Minorités et marginaux en Espagne,* 402, suggests even fewer executions, but his data are evidently incomplete. The figures given in Ricardo García-Cárcel, *Orígenes de la Inquisición española: El tribunal de Valencia, 1478–1530* (Barcelona: Ediciones Península, 1976), 174, according to which some 700 people were executed, are unproven. Monter, *Frontiers,* 21 n 36, concludes that García-Carcel's figures are "inaccurate."
47. Monter, *Frontiers,* 53, makes a lower estimate of 1,500 executions.
48. F. E. Beemon, "The Myth of the Spanish Inquisition and the Preconditions for the Dutch Revolt," *Archiv für Reformationsgeschichte* 85 (1994): 255.
49. Kamen, *Spanish Inquisition,* 225.
50. Kamen, *Phoenix,* 436.

If we set out with an exaggerated image of a militantly Catholic Mediterranean, the exceptional heretics such as Giordano Bruno or Menocchio will surprise and startle. Established historiography in Spain has always, for reasons that cannot be explored here, accepted the militant image. The limited evidence at our disposal does not support the alternative, and quite implausible, image of a largely pagan society. But there is little doubt that the Iberian peninsula harbored extensive communities of "unbelief" that make it far easier for us to understand the de-Christianization of the Mediterranean in the nineteenth century. "I really don't know," a Spanish noble commented to the superior of the Jesuits in Andalusia in 1615, "why the fathers of the company go to Japan and the Philippines to look for lost souls, when we have here so many in the same condition who do not know whether or not they believe in God."[51] If we choose any date in the subsequent period, we find similar evidence. Bishops' parish visitations of the eighteenth century give no reason to be optimistic about the nature of belief among Christians in Spain. The fallacy in such cases, of course, is to assume that the *mentalité* of the people is predicated on "belief." In reality, the moral and spiritual discourse of the people was based on the norms of the community, and not on ideological orthodoxy.

We may conclude by touching extremely briefly on the mentality of a minority about whom much has been written: the *conversos*. The *conversos* started their historical existence as Jews, then subsequently were forced into the Christian fold, where they became notorious for their doubtful Christianity. Since literary scholars at one time used to explain virtually the whole of peninsular culture down to the eighteenth century in terms of the *converso* mentality, the subject has a certain relevance.

Emphasis recently has been given to the suggestion that Spain contributed, through a community tradition that extended down to Spinoza, a wholly new Judeo-converso consciousness in western Europe. The consciousness, once again, was based not on religious belief but on philosophic and community links. Within the peninsula most *conversos* remained cut off from the development of international Jewry. It is remarkable, for instance, that the millenarian movement of Sabbatai Zvi, which shook the entire Jewish world and found its ablest controversialist in the north African rabbi Jacob Sasportas,[52] seems to have caused no tremor in Spain, even though the

51. Cited in Kamen, *Phoenix*, 378.
52. For Sabbatai, see the masterly work of Gerschom Scholem, *Sabbatai Zevi: The mystical Messiah 1626–1676* (Princeton: Princeton University Press, 1973).

Inquisition was aware of the phenomenon and warned its tribunals to keep a watch at the ports for any unusual emigration of *conversos*.

But a feeling for Spain (*Sefarad*) permeated the thought of west European Jews and helped to stimulate developments in thought and literature. Ironically, the *conversos* who lived abroad felt that they were different from others, and different even from other Jews, precisely because they were from Sefarad. The cultivation of Iberian cultural habits became a distinguishing feature of the exile communities.[53] Amsterdam afforded liberty of printing to those who wished to publish. But Sefarad was still home, and many were deeply conscious of their roots there. Among them was the young Spinoza, of Spanish origin even though he lived all his life outside the peninsula. The peninsula itself did not provide congenial ground for Jewish speculative thought.

Iberia, despite the echoes of the Inquisition, gave to Jewish and *converso* exiles a common bond that made them all "men of the nation." Even those who were no longer practicing Jews felt a profound kinship, based less on religion than on origins, with the *converso* world from which they had emerged.[54] A few of those who contributed to the new brand of *converso* consciousness in Europe broke firmly with orthodox Judaism. They included Uriel da Costa, Isaac Orobio de Castro, and at one remove, Spinoza. Orobio, born 1617 in Portugal, moved with his parents around midcentury to Málaga.[55] He studied medicine at the University of Osuna. In 1654 he and his family were arrested by the Inquisition of Seville on a charge of judaizing. They appeared in an auto de fe but were lightly punished and eventually, in 1658, released. A couple of years later they left Spain. Orobio arrived in 1662 in Amsterdam, where he participated in the rich intellectual world of the Jews. In the background of the thinking of the Sephardic diaspora, there always remained the memory of Spain. Through men such as Orobio, "the social thinking of Spain found its way into the writings of the Jews of Amsterdam."[56]

This very brief survey has touched selectively on aspects of religious consciousness in Mediterranean Spain, and attempted to show some features of the almost unique multicultural life of the Iberian peninsula. It is the other

---

53. Miriam Bodian, "'Men of the Nation': The Shaping of Converso Identity in Early Modern Europe," *Past and Present* 143 (1994): 66.

54. Bodian, "'Men of the Nation,'" 70–72.

55. Details from the superb study by Yosef Kaplan, *From Christianity to Judaism: The Story of Isaac Orobio de Castro* (Oxford: Oxford University Press, 1989).

56. Kaplan, *From Christianity to Judaism*, 323.

face to the conflictive picture presented by Braudel. At the same time, I have hinted at the priority of local community-based mentalities over universal concepts of ideology. Even within areas sharing a common faith, there were significant variations among Christians, Muslims, and Jews.

PART 6

Worlds beyond the Mediterranean

Chapter 10

BRAUDEL AND CHINA

MARK ELVIN

For a historian of the Chinese economy and environment, as I am, Fernand Braudel's *La Méditerranée* and *Civilisation matérielle, économie et capitalisme*[1] are an endlessly fascinating evocation of unfamiliar landscapes and seascapes, and the human societies in interaction with them. The wealth of detail is intoxicating. The reader from another mental world sees pass before him mountains, piedmonts, wetlands, islands, plains, and seas, and their part in human production and destruction—economics and warfare—and becomes conscious of the roots of those themes that have been so fruitfully later developed by other scholars of the Mediterranean, such as John Pryor.[2] He shares in the author's delight in specificity: the changes in sailing seasons, transhumance routes and their social institutions, malaria and its influence on human settlement, the transit times needed for letters and journeys across the width of Europe, the glittering spoils of long-distance argosies, the intricate finesses of letters of exchange, and the casino capitalism of yesteryear as elaborated in turn by the Venetians, Flemish, Genoese, Dutch, and English,[3] to choose but a scattering of examples.

---

1. I have used the following editions: Fernand Braudel, *La Méditerranée et le monde Méditerranéen à l'époque de Philippe II,* 1st ed. (Paris: Armand Colin, 1949); 2d ed., 2 vols. (Paris: Armand Colin, 1966), and idem, *Civilisation matérielle, économie et capitalisme, XVe–XVIIIe siècle,* 3 vols. (Paris: Armand Colin, 1979) The translations of citations are my own; I prefer the historic present, the use of which is much commoner in French than in English. The French original is also given in the notes as Braudel's "voice"—his artistry—which is often an element in the discussion.
2. John H. Pryor, *Geography, Technology, and War: Studies in the Maritime History of the Mediterranean 649–1571* (Cambridge: Cambridge University Press, 1988).
3. For the phrase "casino capitalism," see Susan Strange, *Casino Capitalism* (Oxford: Blackwell, 1986).

But, above all, images. The image is the historical truth. "These images are not merely the picturesque aspect of a history rich in color but its principal verity."[4] Its preponderant truth.

The impression establishes itself in the reader's mind that Braudel's driving passion is to bring a vanished world to life again. Thus he writes of the Maremma, the great marsh outside Siena, where the great families had their country castles: "Could there be any better spot to put to death, in the style of Italy and of that century, in the isolation created by malaria and the oppressive heat, a wife who has been unfaithful, or is suspected of having been so? Such a climatic explanation would have delighted Barrès."[5] The reference to the novelist suggests the extent to which Braudel felt himself to be not just a historian but also an artist. Self-consciously.

Evocation is a valid mode of history, at least to my way of thinking.[6] A problem for the reader nonetheless arises in the discontinuity between aperçu and analysis. A few examples will make this point clearer:

4. Braudel, *La Méditerranée*, 2d ed., 1:98. "Ces images ne sont pas seulement la note pittoresque d'une histoire haute en couleur, mais sa vérité majoritaire."

5. Braudel, *La Méditerranée*, 2d ed., 1:68. "Y a-t-il meilleur endroit pour exécuter, à la mode d'Italie et du siècle, dans l'isolement créé par la fièvre et la lourde chaleur, l'épouse infidèle ou soupçonnée de l'être? L'explication climatique eût enchanté Barrès." Maurice Barrès (1862–1923) was the author of such novels as *Du sang, de la volupté et de la mort.*

6. Simon Schama, *Landscape and Memory* (London: HarperCollins, 1995), is a recent example. In general, I have kept away from metahistory such as that to be found in Philippe Carrard, *Poetics of the New History: French National Historical Discourse from Braudel to Chartier* (Baltimore: Johns Hopkins University Press, 1992). I think it would be fair to say that the majority of Western and Western-trained historians of China at the present time implicitly take a quasi-scientific view of their work; the texts and other materials with which they work are analogous to microscopes: dirty, distorting, and of poor resolution, but nonetheless looking at something in some sense "real." Hence, by exercising critical care and aiming at conceptual economy and coherence in interpretation over as wide a range as possible, it is felt possible to develop reconstructions—whether of sequences of events, social structures, or mentalities—that can eventually be ranked in a rough order of plausibility. No doubt some current historiographical fashion regards this as naive; per contra, I would, probably in this like most of my sinological colleagues, feel that a working epistemological position of something of this nature is a prerequisite for having a meaningful dialogue with other scholars—even, in the extreme case, with oneself. Carrard, has some interesting comments—such as the way he links Braudel to Lucien Febvre in terms of Stuart Hughes's perception that the latter was torn between two contradictory impulses, to seize "the pulse of living" and to follow "science and scientific method" (218). On the whole, though, he avoids examining any issues of historical substance in the works of the historians whom he discusses, and it is these that are of primary interest to me.

On the Dalmatian coast Braudel writes:

> A tenuous festoon of Mediterranean life makes its way down between the mountains and the coast, insinuating itself into the interior where gaps open in the mountains' defences.... It is a threadlike space, on a different scale from the huge Zagora, that high country of Karst limestone that...serves as a barrier along the side of the Balkans.

> Could one imagine any contrast more striking? Toward the east, immense mountain landscapes afflicted by the harshness of the winter and the devastating droughts of summer, regions of stock-herding and a precarious livelihood, veritable "hives" from which...people and flocks swarm into the lands beyond, making for Moravian Serbia with its ever-boggy rivulets, toward Shumadia whose woods once made it impenetrable, toward Croatia-Slovenia to the north.... One can hardly conceive of a rougher area, one more patriarchal in character, or, whatever the charms of its culture, one more backward....

> Facing the Turks...the Zagorci are natural warriors, bandits, or outlaws..."fleet of foot as the stags" and of a courage that is legendary.... But [along the coast]...an effective war is waged against the flocks of the Zagorci....

> Here the invader confronts a world that is pre-eminently stable and prudent...a tightly knit rural world that has been patiently put into place, blows from the pick-ax shaping its gardens behind their miniature stone walls, its orchards and its vineyards, even fields where the gradient is not too abrupt.... The people here work hard, and have well-adjusted characters... having to contend with nature, with the huge and menacing Zagora, with the Turks, and, what is more, with the sea. A concentrated effort is required for all of this, not a folk at liberty to act as it best may please them. The peasant in Ragusa...is half a serf.... Around the Venetian villas of the *altra sponda* [the far side] a timid agriculture shelters beneath the protection of soldiery. Peasants sally forth to their obligatory labors each morning and return each dusk safeguarded by armed squads. Here is a situation not conducive

to individualism, nor to the peasant movements for which we nonetheless have evidence.[7]

As a sketch of the interlinking of environment and of society and human psychology this has an extraordinary and characteristic vitality. Its power and its poetry come from the way in which it conveys the sense of the immensity and immutability of the external forces shaping human behavior. Then one stops and wonders. The dependency of the peasants was in fact linked with the quite recent creation of seignorial domains by the Venetians; and, for all the "logic" of the environment, they do seem to have tried to revolt. How, then, do long-term and short-term in fact interact? How immutable is immutability?

Here the hesitations are fleeting. It is fair enough that such a picture should be suggestive, not definitive. But another example throws the problem into sharper relief. Each of the three stages of the development of Lombardy, says Braudel, "corresponded to the putting in place of new layers of people," "different human groups."

---

7. Braudel, *La Méditerranée*, 2d ed., 11:50–51. "Un étroit feston de vie méditerranéenne borde la montagne jusqu'au contact de la côte, s'insinuant dans les brèches vers l'intérieur des terres…un espace filiforme, sans commune mesure avec l'énorme Zagora, ce haut pays de *Karst* qui…fait barrage du côté du continent balkanique.

Peut-on rêver contraste plus saisissant? Vers l'Est, de vastes pays montagnards, désolés par les rigueurs de l'hiver et les sécheresses catastrophiques de l'été, pays d'élevage et de vie instable, vrais «pays-ruches» qui…déversent leurs hommes et leurs troupeaux sur les avant-pays, vers la Serbie moravienne aux sillons fluviaux mal asséchés, vers la Choumadia impénétrable jadis avec ses boisements, vers la Croatie-Slavonie, au Nord.… On ne peut guère imaginer région plus rude, plus patriarcale et quels que soient les charmes de sa civilisation, en fait plus arriérée.… [F]ace aux Turcs…[l]es *Zagorci* sont des soldats nés, bandits ou bannis…«légers comme le cerf» et d'un courage d'épopée.… Mais…[u]ne guerre efficace est faite [sur la côte] aux troupeaux des *Zagorci*.…

[L]'envahissseur se heurte cette fois à un monde éminemment stable et sage…un monde rural serré, patiemment mis en place, qui a façonné à coups de pioche les jardins en murettes, les vergers, les vignobles, les champs là où la pente n'est pas trop forte.… Les gens y sont laborieux, équilibrés.… Il faut lutter contre la nature, contre l'énorme *Zagora* menaçante, et contre le Turc; par surcroît, il faut batailler avec la mer: tout cela réclame un travail coordonné, et non point des gens libres d'agir à leur guise. Le paysan de Raguse…a la situation…d'un paysan à demi serf.… [A]utour des villes vénitiennes de l'*altra sponda*, une agriculture craintive s'abrite sous la protection des soldats. Des corvées de paysans partent chaque matin et rentrent chaque soir, sous la protection de la troupe. Voilà qui n'est pas favorable à l'individualisme, ni aux remuements des paysans dont on a cependant des preuves et des indices."

The upland Lombardy of mountain folk and shepherds…is a domain of smallholders, poor but free, who strive to produce everything from their own plots, even the wretched wine from their vines. Lower down, the estates of the nobles and the church make their first appearance, on an irrigated elevated plain, a region of springs and widespread perennial pastures. This lower level, which is still not the lowest, is the zone of castles, of share-croppers, and of charterhouses set among lofty trees. At the lowest level of all spread out the ricefields of the capitalists whose revolutionary enterprise solved the problem of how to farm these flooded areas. Lombardy rice was to imply…the slavery of the labor force.[8]

Shortly afterwards, he once again asserts that irrigation enslaves: "In Spain, whenever one moves from the *secanos* to the *regadios*—from dryland farming to irrigated—one shifts from peasants who are relatively free to those who are enslaved."[9] The historian of China can accept the accuracy of the specific descriptions; he is obliged to reject the implied causal connection. In China, irrigation as such did not imply slavery.[10] (Nor, in the Chinese context, does reclaiming vast areas of lowlying land for rice have to be particularly "revolutionary" in the sense of requiring protocapitalism.) He also recalls that in Holland, massive hydraulic works, though mainly for drainage and defense against the sea, implied social discipline but no other loss of personal liberty. Little by little the sense of unease with the environmental

---

8. Braudel, *La Méditerranée*, 2d ed., 1:66. "La haute Lombardie, montagnarde, pastorale…est un pays de petits propriétaires, pauvres mais libres, acharnés à tout produire sur leurs terres, y compris le mauvais vin de leurs vignes. Au-dessous, avec le plateau irrigué de la haute plaine, zone des fontaines…et de grands herbages, commence la propriété nobiliaire et ecclésiastique. Ce bas étage, pas encore tout à fait le rez-de-chaussée, est la zone des châteaux, des terroirs à métayers, des chartreuses au milieu des grands arbres. Tout en bas, s'étendent les rizières des capitalistes. Leur entreprise révolutionnaire a résolu le problème de la culture de ces terres inondées…. Le riz de Lombardie aura signifié…l'esclavage de travailleurs."

9. Braudel, *La Méditerranée*, 2d ed., 1:67. "En Espagne, chaque fois que l'on passe des *secanos* aux *regadios*—des terres «sèches» aux terres irriguées—on passe d'un paysan relativement libre à un paysan esclave."

10. See Mark Elvin, "Introduction," in *Japanese Studies on the History of Water Control in China: A Selected Bibliography,* ed. Mark Elvin, Hiroaki Nishioka, Keiko Tamura, and Joan Kwek (Canberra: Institute of Advanced Studies, Australian National University; Tokyo: Centre for East Asian Cultural Studies for UNESCO, Toyo Bunko, 1994).

near-determinism constantly implied by Braudel, which is not of course to say that the reader that we have imagined disputes the relevance of these factors, casts a shadow on the mind.

Sometimes the rhetoric, so effective as rhetoric, leads to an epistemological black hole. Discussing piracy in the sixteenth-century Mediterranean directed against ships carrying grain from Sicily, Braudel says: "Piracy, here as elsewhere, often tends to re-establish a natural balance falsified [that is, disrupted] by history."[11] One can only ask what is to be defined in such a context as "natural," what as "falsified," and how "history" is to be separated from the "natural."

Finally the reader notices how much certain aphorisms sometimes promise but do not deliver. Speaking of the "double imperialism" of Spain and the Ottoman empire at the opposite ends of the Mediterranean, Braudel writes that "politics is only a transfer of an underlying reality."[12] But how and where does this underlying reality get transferred? He follows with a brief discussion of the difference in climatic regimes, and notes that the Turkish navy got moving earlier in the year than the Western navies. The punch line? "In an age when the rhythm of the seasons dictated that of warfare, this was important."[13] True, but this does not even begin to make the case for justifying the challenging metaphor of the environmental-political decalcomania. And not only the paragraph but the section ends at this point.

The same is true of the tidal metaphor that underlies the most famous concept of all, that of the *longue durée*, which is in a sense the fundamental rhythm hypothesized to underlie the swifter rhythms of event history:

> Ordinarily, history only takes an interest in crises, in the paroxysms that occur in the course of these slow changes. We must remember, though, that immense preparations precede these crises, and endless consequences follow them. It happens, too, that, in their slow way, these movements little by little reverse direction.... Furthermore, in these almost static circumstances, it is not only these slow tides that are at work; these oscillations in the general relationships between humankind and the environment within

11. Braudel, *La Méditerranée*, 2d ed., 1:107. "La course, ici comme ailleurs, tend souvent à rétablir un équilibre naturel faussé par l'histoire."

12. Braudel, *La Méditerranée*, 2d ed., 1:125. "La politique ne fait que décalquer une réalité sous-jacente."

13. Braudel, *La Méditerranée*, 2d ed., 1:126. "A une époque où le rhythme des saisons commandait celui de la guerre, la chose est importante."

which humankind exists, are joined by other fluctuations in the economy, slow at times but usually of shorter duration. All these movements are superposed. Together they rule the never-simple lives of human beings. Our observation of the *longue durée* leads us to the slowest oscillations known to history.[14]

It seems churlish, faced with this vision, to ask if the wave metaphor can be justified, if history really may usefully be conceived of as a Fourier synthesis of superposed waves, and, if so, how one is to do the Fourier analysis?[15] In historian's terms, it goes without saying. Yet can we in the end, if we are serious, avoid asking? And, so far as I am aware, we are not shown how it is to be done. Since Braudel's time it has also become apparent that waves may be the wrong metaphor. Modern complexity theory suggests that in systems like human history and the evolution of species there are no qualitative discontinuities between short-, medium-, and long-term events. A better metaphor is a pile of sand at a critically steep slope: dropping further single grains onto it will from time to time unleash avalanches over a wide range of magnitudes. And the pattern will not be periodic.[16]

It seems to me that these strictures are justified, yet also unjust. Braudel appears in *La Méditerranée* as, above all, the founder of the environmental history of the Mediterranean, and perhaps not only the Mediterranean. As the heir of Paul Vidal de la Blache, of course;[17] but above all as the pioneer who opened the way for John McNeill and others.[18] In other words, he

14. Braudel, *La Méditerranée*, 2d ed., 1:92–93. "D'ordinaire, l'histoire ne s'intéresse qu'aux crises, aux paroxysmes de ces mouvements lents. Or d'immenses préparations les précèdent, d'interminables suites leur font cortège. Et il arrive que ces mouvements, dans leur lenteur, changent peu à peu de signe.... Or, dans ces cadres à peu près immobiles, ces marées lentes ne jouent pas seules, ces oscillations des rapports généraux entre l'homme et le milieu où il vit, s'ajoutent à des autres fluctuations, celles parfois lentes mais d'ordinaire plus courtes de l'économie. Tous ces mouvements se superposent. Les uns et les autres règlent la vie jamais simple des hommes.... L'observation de la longue durée nous conduit vers les plus lentes oscillations que connaisse l'histoire."

15. For an introduction to the real thing, see J. F. James, *A Student's Guide to Fourier Transforms* (Cambridge: Cambridge University Press, 1995).

16. Per Bak, *How Nature Works: The Science of Self-Organized Criticality* (Oxford: Oxford University Press, 1997).

17. A point stressed by Jean Baechler, letter, 21 January 1998, who adds that "the great French tradition" of human geography inaugurated by Vidal de la Blache is "today close to dying or having died" [aujourd'hui à peu près moribonde ou morte].

18. John McNeill, *The Mountains of the Mediterranean World: An Environmental History* (New York: Cambridge University Press, 1992).

showed these contemporaries of ours—and also I would guess to some extent, if only by some sort of intellectual osmosis, those of us concerned with the other end of Eurasia—that there are phenomena to examine, where human action interfaces with the rest of the natural world, which are important and have been to a great extent neglected. Maybe, after all, it was the vision, not the analysis, that was crucial.

However, as the reader from the Chinese world turns to Braudel's other great work, *Civilisation matérielle*, published a generation later, he or she is, I think, ineluctably impelled to invert this tribute, and to express regret that Braudel was not, in his turn, more influenced by the modern historians of China's economy and society. This not in any spirit of arrogance but of sadness at the loss of the insights that a genuine dialogue might have elicited. Braudel had some guides of quality in Chinese history, such as Henri Maspero and Étienne Balasz.[19] He drew much less, however, on their successors, such as Jacques Gernet, for all that he commissioned Gernet's magisterial *Le monde chinois* for Armand Colin, and even less on Michel Cartier (though he refers to the work of both).[20] This was an omission of some consequence. By the middle 1970s the economic history of China had been so transformed that it challenged nearly every familiar generalization made about probable causal patterns in European economic history, and had discredited nearly every older received idea about China's historical economy. Whether because of age, or because his conceptions had crystallized, or because he was incurably Eurocentric,[21] or for some other reason, Braudel missed this. To his and to our misfortune.

19. A point to some extent confirmed by Jacques Gernet, letter of 15 January 1998: "I think that he must have talked matters over with Balasz and, as you do, I seem to detect traces of the influence of Balasz (who was obsessed with a hatred of the Chinese bureaucratic system which he likened to Nazism" [Je pense qu'il a dû discuter avec Balasz et il me semble voir comme vous des traces de l'influence de Balasz (dont l'idée fixe était la haine du système bureaucratique chinois qu'il assimilait au nazisme)].

20. Gernet, letter of 15 January 1998, observes that "to tell the truth, Braudel only rarely questioned me about China" [à vrai dire, Braudel m'a rarement interrogé sur la Chine]. He adds that "after he left the EHESS Braudel became more solitary. It [also] seems to me that Cartier entered the EHESS too late for him to have had discussions with Braudel" [après son départ de l'EHESS Braudel est devenu plus solitaire. Cartier me semble être entré trop tard à l'EHESS pour qu'il ait discuté avec Braudel].

21. Gernet, letter of 15 January 1998, recalls of Braudel's *Civilisation matérielle*, that "the book dropped from my hands so full did I find it of ethnocentric prejudices" [le livre m'était tombé des mains tellement je l'avais trouvé plein de préjugés ethnocentriques].

❧ ❧ ❧

The pages of Braudel's major books are scattered with references to China, but, with some important exceptions, discussed later, they are mostly decorative. In terms of current scholarship, some are true, some problematic, some more or less certainly false. No useful end would be served by evaluating them one by one more than twenty years after publication. What is critical is that none of them is placed in the context of an understanding of the *longue durée* pattern of the evolution of the Chinese economy and environment over the last thousand years or so that has been reconstructed by sinologists during the last third of the century just past.

Essentially, though in somewhat oversimplified terms, what Braudel missed was that China in the central period of the Middle Ages—let us say in the period 1100 to 1300, that is, mostly under the Southern Song in the south, and the Jin (Jurchen) and then the Mongols in the north—was well "ahead" of the Europe of this time when measured by most of the key indicators. These may be summarized as agricultural productivity (demonstrably by unit area, and probably also by hour of labor and seed-yield ratio), cheapness and scale of transportation networks, the commercialization and almost ubiquitous monetization of the economy, the use of fiduciary money and credit instruments, urbanization, literacy (through woodblock printing), formalized bureaucratic administration, the technology of everyday life and warfare, and protoscience. Technology included water-powered mechanized spinning and silk-twisting, and mass production of certain armaments (such as metal arrowheads); scientific instrumentation, for its part, hydraulic celestial clockwork that rotated to match the apparent rotation of the skies. All of this was in the public—though mostly anglophone—domain before *Civilisation matérielle* was published. Had he been aware of it, I find it hard not to believe that his sense of the patterns of causation would have been transformed. In terms of the most apparently compelling general economic historical analysis up to and through the 1960s, it now appeared that Song China had already solved virtually all the strategically difficult problems along the way to economic modernity, and yet had—patently—failed to arrive at what might be called "modern economic growth," to borrow Kuznets's term.[22] Awareness of the awkwardness of the Chinese case, had it been at his disposal, ought to have

---

22. Simon Kuznets, *Modern Economic Growth: Rate, Structure, and Spread* (New Haven: Yale University Press, 1966). Gernet, letter of 15 January 1998, makes the comment that "the

reoriented, by juxtaposition, by comparison and contrast, his intuitions about what was genuinely and significantly different about western Europe—features, both the relatively culturally stable and the conjuncturally labile, that are nothing like as obvious as he or virtually all his contemporaries thought they were, and that still present a serious challenge to historical analysis.

I will look at this question in the fourth section of this survey, foreshadowing here only the curious issue of technology. On the one hand, Braudel is fascinated by technology. "Power, supremacy, spheres of influence—when what is at issue is the life of a maritime sector, does it amount to anything other than the technical details: sails, oars, rudders, the contours of hulls, or the tonnage of shipping?"[23] Likewise, at the beginning of the two chapters devoted to technology in *Les structures du quotidien*, he states bluntly: "Everything is technology."[24]

On the other hand he appears at times—especially in the second and third volumes of *Civilisation matérielle*—to have an extraordinary, even willful, indifference to the causes of technological change. He speaks of "the general rise of technology"[25] without ever, it seems, asking where this upsurge may have come from. "Processes often develop in the world of work as if automatically."[26] Dismissing with unsubstantiated disdain the Schumpeterian innovator, he declares that "the innovator is carried along as if by the upsurge of the rising tide."[27]

If there is any lesson that the Chinese countercase has for the economic historian of Europe, it is that it is possible to have a rising tide of furious

technological genius of China seems to me to have always been remarkable and does not date just from the Song dynasty, although all sorts of factors seem to have come into play at this time in favor of a veritable technological, scientific, and intellectual explosion" [le génie technique de la Chine me semble avoir toujours été remarquable et ne date pas que des Song, bien que toutes sortes de facteurs semblent avoir joué à ce moment en faveur d'une véritable explosion technique, scientifique, intellectuelle, etc.], a view with which I would concur.

23. Braudel, *La Méditerranée*, 2d ed., 1:113. "[P]uissance, suprématie, zones d'influence, quand il s'agit de la vie d'un secteur maritime, est-ce souvent autre chose que les détails techniques: voiles, rames, gouvernails, profils de coques, tonnages des navires?"

24. Braudel, *Civilisation matérielle*, 1.291. "Tout est technique."

25. Braudel, *Civilisation matérielle*, 2.280. "L'essor général de la technologie."

26. Braudel, *Civilisation matérielle*, 2.280. "[L]es procédés s'élaborent comme souvent d'eux-mêmes dans le monde de travail."

27. Braudel, *Civilisation matérielle*, 2.337. "Le novateur est porté par le flot de la marée montante."

economic activity without necessarily having major technical progress. This much is implicit in the title of the third section of my book *The Pattern of the Chinese Past*,[28] namely "Economic Development without Technological Change," which deals with the late-imperial period, approximately that with which Braudel is most concerned in Europe. Further documentation, with some marginal qualifications, was available by 1975.[29] No echo reached the Place Marcelin-Berthelot.

Detailed inquiry into technological change is swept aside with rhetoric: "In and of itself, the event-history of inventions is but...a game of distorting mirrors."[30] Possibly so, but that does not justify not examining important specific advances in a broad, multicausal context. The stunning, and to be frank, the embarrassing truth is that Braudel had not read the early volumes of *Science and Civilisation in China* by Joseph Needham and his collaborators.[31] The first of these appeared in 1954; at the time of my writing these words the seventeenth book, on the sugar industry and forestry, by Christian Daniels and Nicholas Menzies, has just been published.[32] The embarrassment arises from the fact that the vast majority of technological skills described by Braudel in his chapters as being important in Europe also existed in China, where many of them had either originated (such as the stern-post—or better, "axial"—rudder, the nautical compass, military gunpowder, printing and paper, and so on), or at the least existed from early medieval times (such as the efficient forms of horse harness). There were a few sectors where China was significantly inferior, most notably in the drainage and ventilation of mines; and the Chinese type of windmill, which was essentially a horizontally set merry-go-round with ship's sails around the perimeter of the rotating disk,

---

28. Mark Elvin, *The Pattern of the Chinese Past: A Social and Economic Interpretation* (Stanford: Stanford University Press, 1973).

29. Mark Elvin, "Skills and Resources in Late Traditional China," in *China's Modern Economy in Historical Perspective,* ed. Dwight Perkins (Stanford: Stanford University Press, 1975). Reprinted in idem, *Another History: Essays on China from a European Perspective* (Sydney: Wild Peony Press / Honolulu: University of Hawaii Press, 1996).

30. Braudel, *Civilisation matérielle,* 1.293. "Réduite à elle seule, l'histoire événementielle des inventions n'est...qu'un jeu de faux miroirs."

31. Joseph Needham, with Wang Ling, *Introductory Orientations,* vol. 1 of *Science and Civilisation in China* (Cambridge: Cambridge University Press, 1954–).

32. Christian Daniels and Nicholas K. Menzies, *Biology and Biological Technology,* pt. 3: *Agro-Industries: Sugarcane Technology,* vol. 6, pt. 3 of *Science and Civilisation in China* (Cambridge: Cambridge University Press, 1996).

required nothing so sophisticated as the gearing of an advanced Dutch wind-mill.[33] Some techniques, however, that Braudel thinks were not known in China, were in fact very well known; an example is the vertical overshot waterwheel, used to power all sorts of machinery.[34] The errors that he makes in these two chapters with regard to China are so numerous that it would be tedious, and pointless, to list them all.

The analytical issue is, on the contrary, central. If China, up to about the seventeenth century, could be in broad terms on a level with Europe at the same date, it is crucial to ask why China did not proceed much further there-after, but came close to a technological standstill. Equally crucial is to try to determine why Europe, on the contrary, accelerated. Braudel's one-sentence solution of the problem of the causes of invention is ingenious: "There is no doubt but that the condition of progress is a reasonable balance between a ubiquitous use of human labor and other, alternative, sources of energy."[35] This contains a certain truth, and it would be wrong to dismiss his conclu-sion that "in China…the use of machinery was ultimately blocked by the cheapness of human labor,"[36] as wholly mistaken. It is not, but neither is it adequate. To begin with, medieval China had a lot of machines; some of these later disappeared, such as the water-powered spinning of hemp roving (in north China in the thirteenth and early fourteenth centuries), but *not* during a period of notably denser population (early Ming in all probability). Second, the cost of labor only appears to be critical in the eyes of a potential employer: artisans and peasants welcome any affordable machine that aug-ments returns to their own hours of work. Third, some devices could save labor profitably even in a Chinese context (such as *norias* driven by water power in places where streams flowed strongly enough to turn them). Fourth, some technical changes could economize on resources (rather than

33. Elvin, "Skills and Resources," gives an outline account of the technology of both these sectors.

34. There are illustrations of both vertical overshot and horizontal waterwheels in Sung Ying-hsing, *T'ien-kung k'ai–wu: Chinese Technology in the Seventeenth Century,* trans. E-tu Zen Sun and Shiou-chuan Sun (University Park: Pennsylvania State University Press, 1966), for example 93 (vertical overshot wheel driving multiple trip-hammers off a camshaft) and 103 (a rolling mill for grain driven by a horizontal waterwheel).

35. Braudel, *Civilisation matérielle,* 1.297. "La condition du progrès, sans doute est-ce un équilibre raisonnable entre le travail omniprésent de l'homme et les autres sources énergé-tiques de remplacement."

36. Braudel, *Civilisation matérielle,* 1.297. "En Chine…le machinisme a été finalement bloqué par le travail à bon marché de l'homme."

labor), improve quality (mechanized silk-reeling), or make possible what had previously been problematic or difficult (such as sailing year-round in the dangerous waters off the northern Chinese coast). Fifth, when the Chinese population fell for a time in the seventeenth century, there was no surge of labor-saving inventions. Hence the cost of labor, though very important, was not the only dimension.[37] It is also worth noting that the pressures placed on the environment by economic growth, notably the rising cost of fuel and timber for construction caused by deforestation, were broadly similar at the two extremities of the Old World.[38]

It seems reasonable to hypothesize that Braudel's ideas about the Chinese economy in historical times crystallized just before the work of scholars like Robert Hartwell, Shiba Yoshinobu, Bill Skinner and his collaborators,[39] and—if I may be permitted to say so—myself, reset the paradigms of Chinese economic history, to a great extent by thinking through the implications of the detailed studies made of China's historical economy by Japanese scholars, following Katô Shigeshi's pioneering efforts before the Second World War, in the generation following the war's ending.

There were, nonetheless, earlier hints in the francophone literature. Thus Jacques Gernet wrote in 1959 in his *La vie quotidienne en Chine à la veille de l'invasion mongole:*[40]

> The commercial development of China from the eleventh to the thirteenth century took place at the same time as a similar process in Europe. Moreover, the powerful upsurge that occurred at this time was on a different scale from its western counterpart. The importance of the growth of trade in China was commensurate with her population, wealth, size, and high level of technological development. The exaggerations of Marco Polo at the end of the thirteenth century only bear witness to the stupefaction of a western traveller at the sight of commercial

37. Elvin, "Skills and Resources," discusses materials relevant to all these points.

38. Mark Elvin and Ts'ui-jung Liu, eds., *Sediments of Time: Environment and Society in Chinese History* (New York: Cambridge University Press, 1997), chapters by John McNeill, Eduard Vermeer, and Anne Osborne.

39. Braudel was of course aware of Skinner's early work on Chinese marketing structure, but interpreted it as being essentially "traditional," whereas "late-imperial" would perhaps have been more appropriate; see Braudel, *Civilisation matérielle*, 2.95–98.

40. Jacques Gernet, *La vie quotidienne en Chine à la veille de l'invasion mongole* (Paris: Hachette, 1959.)

activity far more intense than that of Genoa or Venice at this date. Be that as it may, the sudden rising of the sap in the economies both of Europe and the Far East did not have the same effects in the two regions.[41]

Gernet then goes on to explain the difference in terms derived from Étienne Balasz, namely, that the imperial state was too powerful in China, and does not pause—but it was still early days—to ask why this same state should have been so conducive to such a commercial and technical explosion and then, and under what conditions, should have become—if indeed it was—such an obstacle to it. Even at this point reflection should have indicated that the use of static analysis based on all-but-unchanging ideal types, in other words, the attribution of more or less fixed characteristics to "China" and "Europe," was not going to work.[42]

Braudel does at one or two points briefly play with the thought-experiment of a counterfactual: "Shall we for a moment suppose that Chinese junks had rounded the Cape of Good Hope in 1419...and that the mastery of the world had worked to the advantage of this vast and distant country at

41. Gernet, *Vie quotidienne*, 65–66. "Le développement commercial de la Chine du XIe au XIIIe siècle est contemporain d'un développement analogue en Europe. Cependant, la vigoureuse poussée qui se produit alors est sans commune mesure avec son correspondant occidental. L'importance du mouvement commercial en Chine est en rapport avec la population, la richesse, l'immensité et le haut degré de développement technique de ce pays. Les exaggérations de Marco Polo à la fin du XIIIe siècle témoignent seulement de l'étonnement du voyageur occidental au spectacle d'une activité commerciale beaucoup plus intense que celle de Gênes ou de Venise à la même époque. Pourtant, cette brusque montée de sève dans l'économie de l Europe et de l'Extrême-Orient n'eut pas ici et là les mêmes effets."

42. Gernet, letter of 15 January 1998, comments with characteristic perception:

"Might I risk making certain remarks to you while asking you to forgive what may appear to be the 'fixed characteristics' that you rightly condemn...?

It seems to me that the technological genius of China was always remarkable.... On the Western side there has been, since the days of the Greeks and Romans, a traditional contempt for work, fine for slaves and serfs, that was not so much in evidence in China.

As to machines, one might ponder which were more useful: the simple and economic (exemplified by the extraordinary use made in China of bamboo, or the low cost of woodblock printing...) or the complex and expensive (machines made of metal, the printing press...) but more durable and requiring investments.

What of the spirit of competition which was Greek and continued, under other conditions, throughout the entire history of the West (competition being thought of in China as being simply ill-bred)...etc.?

[Puis-je vous hasarder certaines remarques en vous demandant d'excuser ce qui peut paraître comme des 'fixed characteristics' que vous condamnez à juste titre...?

the other extremity of the densely inhabited universe?"[43] Not a particularly far-fetched possibility, as these junks did in fact at one point reach Malindi just north of Zanzibar.[44] He does not follow this idea up, but the phrasing suggests his implicit sense of the crucial pattern of causation: the "mastery of the world" was to be decisive. Yet Gernet's accurate perception of the Lilliputian nature of Europe compared to China in some respects held even up until the beginning of the Industrial Revolution. In 1833, China, already with a vast domestic production of cotton, was importing more raw cotton from India than ten times the total yearly consumption of Britain at the time of the invention of the spinning frame.[45]

Gernet, who was later to be for many years the holder of the chair of Chinese social and intellectual history at the Collège de France, moved away from the economic history in which his great reputation was initially and deservedly made, and into cultural history. Thus a full-scale francophone debate that might have transformed Braudel's vision seems never to have been joined. Gernet's *Le monde chinois*,[46] to which Braudel refers at several

---

[La génie technique de la Chine me semble avoir toujours été remarquable.... Il y a du côté occidental de l'Eurasie, depuis l'antiquité gréco-romaine, un mépris traditionnel pour le travail, bon pour les esclaves et les serfs, qui n'était pas aussi prononcé en Chine.

[Pour ce qui est des machines, on peut poser la question de savoir ce qui vaut le mieux: le simple et l'économique (avec l'extraordinaire usage qui a été fait en Chine du bambou, le faible coût de la xylographie...), ou le complexe et le coûteux (les machines métalliques, l'imprimerie...), mais plus durable et qui demande des investissments.

[Quid de l'esprit de *compétition* qui était grec et s'est maintenu, dans d'autres conditions, tout au long de l'histoire en Occident (la compétition était considérée en Chine comme de la simple goujaterie)... etc.?]

I have no difficulty with regarding some cultural characteristics being extremely long-lived, this being after all a matter of empirical observation in each case, only with the assumption that this is necessarily always so, and I think that we would both agree on this.

43. Braudel, *Civilisation matérielle,* 2:518. "Supposons, un instant, que les jonques chinoises aient doublé le cap de Bonne Espérance en 1419...et que la domination du monde ait joué en faveur de l'énorme pays lointain, de cet autre pôle de l'univers des peuplements denses?"

44. For a map of the Ming voyages and the maritime links of late-imperial China, see Caroline Blunden and Mark Elvin, *A Cultural Atlas of China* (Oxford: Phaidon, 1983), 38–39.

45. Mark Elvin, "The High-Level Equilibrium Trap: The Causes of the Decline of Invention in the Traditional Chinese Textile Industries," in *Economic Organization in Chinese Society,* ed. W. Willmott (Stanford: Stanford University Press, 1972); reprinted in idem, *Another History,* 36.

46. Jacques Gernet, *Le monde chinois* (Paris: Armand Colin, 1972.)

points, and arguably the best single-volume general history of China to date, does indicate something of the Chinese medieval economic revolution. Gernet speaks of how the improvement and spread of rice agriculture "favored the development of exchanges between regions, the commercialization of agricultural products, the rise of the artisan class, and the growth of large cities."[47] He mentions how the quantity of cast iron in 1078 was more than one and a half times greater than that of England in 1788, how "the appearance of large concentrations of mercantile activity...led to a general reorganization of the commercial circuits operating through the large cities," and the completion of "the gigantic navigable network formed by the Yangzi River and its tributaries, which was unique in the world." China's principal riches in this period were not agricultural but "of artisanal origin"; there was "a diffusion of the money economy," extensive international trade, and China "was the largest maritime power in history during the four and a half centuries that spanned the consolidation of the Song empire to the great period of the expansion of that of the Ming."[48] In spite of these well-made basic points, Gernet's treatment is sketchy, perhaps as befits an introduction, and he does not tackle in any systematic way the economy of the later empire or underlying patterns of causality.

Braudel would have needed extraordinary intuition at this time, extraordinary even by his standards, to have foreseen the full extent of the shifting of the intellectual tectonic plates in Chinese economic history that was being prepared. In the middle 1960s, Hartwell began to write of a "revolution" in iron and coal in Song China.[49] It was here that Braudel came nearest to seeing the problem: "The use of coal for heating [in China] very early allowed...the

47. Gernet, *Le monde chinois*, 281. "A favorisé le développement des échanges entre régions, la commercialisation des produits agricoles, l'essor de l'artisanat, la croissance des grandes villes."

48. Gernet, *Le monde chinois*, 282–87. (1) "L'apparition de grandes agglomérations marchandes...a entraîné une réorganisation générale des circuits commerciaux en fonction des grandes villes." (2) "Cet immense réseau navigable, unique au monde, que forment le Yangzi et ses affluents." (3) China "fut la plus grande puissance maritime de l'histoire pendant les quatre siècles et demi qui vont de la consolidation de l empire des Song à la grande période d'expansion de celui des Ming."

49. R. Hartwell, "Markets, Technology, and the Structure of Enterprise in the Development of the Eleventh-Century Iron and Steel Industry," *Journal of Economic History* 26 (1966), and idem, "A Cycle of Economic Change in Imperial China: Coal and Iron in Northeast China, 750–1350," *Journal of the Economic and Social History of the Orient* 10 (1967).

production and use of cast iron. This great precocity did not lead to the systematic use of coke at the time of the extraordinary Chinese upsurge in the thirteenth century, although it is likely that coke was known of.... This failure is a remarkable argument in favor of our thesis: China, in its thirteenth-century vigor, may be regarded as having had the means to open the most important of all doors to the Industrial Revolution, and did not do so!"[50] In fact, Needham had already suggested in 1958 that the Chinese crucible method made it unnecessary to use a refined fuel in iron smelting,[51] and coke continued to be used for smelting silver and copper during the Qing period.[52]

By 1970, Elvin had shown that land tenure and servile and quasi-servile status in China had evolved over the last millennium in a way that presented many parallels with much of western Europe—towards fragmentation and freedom for the most part.[53] Shiba's definitive *Commerce and Society in Sung China* was translated into English from the Japanese in 1972,[54] revealing a society permeated through and through by trading. Elvin's *The Pattern of the Chinese Past* outlined the new paradigm in 1973,[55] stressing the contrast between medieval Chinese technological creativity and late-imperial technical near-stagnation. Finally, in 1977 the collective volume inspired and edited by G. W. Skinner, *The City in Late Imperial China*, drastically reshaped the urban history of China, showing *multa inter alia* that un-Braudelian phenomenon, on a subcontinental scale, of a massive but nearly acephalous urban hierarchy.[56] By now, as we have seen, it was too late. The last two volumes of

50. Braudel, *Civilisation matérielle*, 1:325. "[En Chine] la chauffe au charbon de terre permit très tôt...la production et l'utilisation de la fonte de fer. Cette énorme précocité ne conduisit pas à l'utilisation systématique du coke lors de l'extraordinaire poussée chinoise du XIIIe siècle, bien qu'il soit probable que celle-ci ait été alors connue.... Sans quoi, quel argument pour notre thèse: la Chine vigoureuse du XIIIe siècle aurait eu le moyens d'ouvrir la porte majeure de la Révolution industrielle et elle ne l'aurait pas fait!"

51. Joseph Needham, *The Development of Iron and Steel Technology in China* (London: Newcomen Society for the Study of Engineering and Technology, 1958), 14.

52. Elvin, "Skills and Resources," in *Another History*, 73.

53. Mark Elvin, "The Last Thousand Years of Chinese History: Changing Patterns in Land Tenure," *Modern Asian Studies*, 2 (April 1970) 4.2; reprinted in idem, *Another Country*.

54. Shiba Yoshinobu, *Commerce and Society in Sung China* (Ann Arbor: Center for Chinese Studies, University of Michigan, 1972.)

55. Mark Elvin, *The Pattern of the Chinese Past* (Stanford: Stanford University Press, 1973.)

56. G. William Skinner, ed., *The City in Late Imperial China* (Stanford: Stanford University Press, 1977); see the graph on p. 248, showing that even huge Beijing [Peking] was in a sense "too small" for a country the size of China.

Civilisation matérielle, économie et capitalisme, XVe–XVIIIe siècle were presumably completed and in or close to being in press.[57] Eric Jones, in *The European Miracle* (1981), was the first Western historian to grasp the new comparative intellectual challenge posed by the restructured Chinese economic history, one radically different from that perceived more than a generation earlier by Max Weber.[58] By the time of Baechler, Hall, and Mann's *Europe and the Rise of Capitalism* the debate had already changed out of recognition.[59]

I shall return to the question of the nature of the new debate in the conclusion to the present essay. The essential point is that it accepts, as one of its premises, that up to the seventeenth or eighteenth century or thereabouts the economic and technological differences between China and western Europe were relatively slight. This presents a choice of strategy in the argument: either one has to demonstrate that one or more of these slight differences were strategically critical, or one has to turn to factors that lie outside the economic and technological domains, or else identify underlying conjunctural changes that were decisive. In *La dynamique du capitalisme* Braudel proposed what was in effect a version of the first of these: "If one compares the European economy with those of the rest of the world, it seems to have owed its more advanced development to the superiority of its [financial] instruments and institutions: stock exchanges and the various forms of credit."[60] More specifically, "exchange in China was, to sum it up, flattened and lacking a topmost level," and "this had a great importance with regard to the failure of a Chinese capitalism to develop."[61] This relative ranking of Chinese financial institutions is not entirely baseless, but could mislead the uninformed, because one has to go to the very top before it becomes tenable.[62] Beyond, that is, the Shanxi banks that routinely transmitted large

57. Fernand Braudel, *Les jeux de l'échange* and *Le temps du monde* (Paris: Armand Colin, 1979). The first volume appeared in 1967.

58. Eric Jones, *The European Miracle* (Cambridge: Cambridge University Press, 1981). Mark Elvin, "Why China Failed to Create an Endogenous Capitalism: A Critique of Max Weber," *Theory and Society* 13.3 (May 1984).

59. Jean Baechler, J. Hall, and M. Mann, eds., *Europe and the Rise of Capitalism* (Blackwell: Oxford, 1988).

60. Fernand Braudel, *La dynamique du capitalisme* (Paris: Flammarion, 1985). This little book was based on lectures given in 1976, prior to the publication of Braudel, *Civilisation matérielle*. Idem, 38: "Si on la compare aux économies du reste du monde, l'économie européenne semble avoir dû son développement plus avancé à la supériorité de ses instruments et de ses institutions: les bourses et les diverses formes du crédit."

61. Braudel, *La dynamique*, 37. "L'échange en Chine est en somme écrêté, arasé," and "cela a eu sa grande importance pour le non-développement du capitalisme chinois."

sums of money from one end of China to the other, beyond the [copper] cash bills and silver bills issued by the money shops in quantities well in excess of their metallic reserves, and beyond the reliable clearing systems used by the bank guilds, such as those in Shanghai.[63] It is essentially correct to say that "in the East and the Far East one does not meet with institutionalized stock exchanges such as those of Amsterdam, London [and so forth]."[64] But no further explanation of the mechanism in Europe linking summit financial institutions with the advent of modern economic growth is provided. In *Civilisation matérielle,* he was later to ask, in a spirit of rhetorical skepticism: "But do economic progress, the entrepreneurial spirit, and technical innovation always come from above?"[65] He also of course offers a number of other explanations, both geo-economic and sociopolitical, for China's failure in this regard, which we will look at in detail later.

We can cite as an illustration of the use of the second approach, namely, the invocation of a crucial element outside the economic sphere, Jean Baechler's *Le capitalisme.*[66] Baechler writes that his central thesis is that in its origins, "capitalism is an expression of democratic modernity,"[67] though, once invented, borrowable "by other régimes, under certain conditions." Democracy, or a democratizing tendency, is thus identified as the crucial missing extraeconomic component.[68] There was, in fact, a very faint, but

---

62. See, for example, W. Rowe, *Hankow: Commerce and Society in a Chinese City* (Stanford: Stanford University Press, 1984), esp. chap. 5. There were "large, intercity banking networks" in late-imperial times, and a plethora of paper instruments, but seemingly no institutionalized markets in stocks or bonds, or commodity entitlements. Insecurity was a serious problem at times.

63. On the first two, see Elvin, *Pattern*, 293–94; on the last, see the details in London, Public Record Office, FO 228/2506–8 (on the 1910 financial crisis), which show the superiority in many respects of the late-imperial Shanghai Banking Guild to modern Western banks early in the present century.

64. Braudel, *Civilisation matérielle,* 2:104. "En Orient et en Extrême-Orient, ne se reconcontrent pas de Bourses institutionalisées comme celles d'Amsterdam, de Londres [etc.]."

65. Braudel, *Civilisation matérielle,* 2:372. "Mais le progrès économique, l'esprit d'entreprise et l'innovation technique viennent-ils toujours d'en haut?

66. Jean Baechler, *Le capitalisme* (Paris: Gallimard, 1995), 2 vols.

67. Baechler, *Le capitalisme,* 1:136. "Le capitalisme est une expression de la modernité démocratique."

68. Gernet, letter of 15 January 1998, suggests a top-down version that has much in common with this line of thought: "The Manchus imposed, in the name of Confucianism, a doctrine of absolute submission that was not in general of a nature to make people open-minded." [Les Mandchous ont imposé, sous le nom de confucianisme, une doctrine de la soumission absolue qui n'était pas faite en général pour ouvrir les esprits.]

real, democratizing tendency in late-imperial China, which formed the subject of my own doctoral thesis.[69] I would not, however, take issue with Baechler on these grounds. *Le capitalisme*, we may also observe in passing, constitutes an almost total contrast to *Civilisation matérielle*: rigorously argued from the first page to the last, virtually without images, lacking that sense of the texture of life—like that of Chardin—which makes almost every sentence of Braudel a conjured reincarnation of the past, but redeemed—and how!—by the power of its un-Braudelian abstract clarity.[70]

The third approach, the conjunctural, may be exemplified, for the decline in economic vitality in the fourteenth century, by Janet Abu-Lughod's suggestion: "Could the economic difficulties experienced by China have been caused, at least in part, by the fact that the [thirteenth-century] world system had collapsed around it...the final fragmentation of the larger circuit of thirteenth-century world trade in which China had played such an important role[?]"[71] For the late-imperial technological stagnation it may be illustrated by the Sinha-Elvin "high-level equilibrium trap": easily exploitable China had largely "filled up" demographically by the later eighteenth century (and in several regions before this), and a pre-modern technological quasi-ceiling had been reached in intensive agriculture, hydraulics, and inland water transport that required what amounted to a discontinuous scientific and technical leap to break through. It should

69. Mark Elvin, "The Gentry Democracy in Shanghai, 1905–1914" (Ph.D. dissertation, Cambridge University, 1968). For an outline summary see chapter 5 of Elvin, *Another History*.

70. Jean Baechler, letter 21 January 1998, writes of Braudel's work: "Having recognized these merits [of his works as masterpieces of historical human geography], I have always regarded Braudel's writings as being a compilation of filing-cards and items of information waiting for a theory that might provide them with meaning." [Ces mérites reconnus, j'ai toujours considéré que les écrits de Braudel étaient une compilation de fiches et de renseignements en attente d'une théorie susceptible de leur donner un sens.] He notes "the total absence of a comparativist perspective [l'absence complète d'un point de vue comparativiste], adding that "this methodological vice is a direct consequence of the theoretical void" [ce vice méthodologique est une conséquence directe du vide théorique]. "...In short, I do not think one can be a historian if one is not a sociologist, and vice versa, and I would add, without also being a philosopher." [Bref, je ne pense pas que l'on puisse être historien sans être sociologue, et réciproquement, et ajouterai–je, sans être aussi philosophe]. Thus, "with respect to what you write about my own contribution, you are right to see in me a radical anti-Braudel" [quant à ce que vous écrivez sur ma contribution personnelle, vous avez raison d'y voir un anti-Braudel radical].

71. Janet L. Abu-Lughod, *Before European Hegemony: The World System A.D. 1250–1359* (New York: Oxford University Press, 1989), 345.

be noted that this theory was presented in the context of social characteristics of late-imperial Chinese economic behavior, some of them rewarding in the short term but probably inhibiting in the longer run, such as preferring to use commercial means for tasks that in the West have tended to be assigned to management internal to a business.[72]

At moments Braudel seems to have had a certain presentiment of the way in which his relative neglect of the world outside Europe had handicapped his work. He is concerned that he may have "too conveniently Europocentric a vision."[73] He reflects: "If the cogwheels of exchange that we have just described, for Europe alone, exist outside Europe—and they exist in China, India, across the Islamic world, and in Japan—can one use them as the basis of an attempt at comparative analysis?"[74] He wishes to see if the gap between Europe and non-Europe, so evident later, was "already apparent before the Industrial Revolution, if Europe was, or was not, ahead relative to the rest of the world."[75] Yet he ends by ranking China, "used to living off her own resources," just above the "primitive" economies and in the bottom place among "nonprimitive" economies.[76] It is interesting, in this context, to recall what Adam Smith said in *An Inquiry into the Nature and Causes of the Wealth of Nations*: "[T]he great extent of the empire of China, the vast multitude of its inhabitants, the variety of climate, and consequently of productions in its different provinces, and the easy communication by means of water carriage between the greater part of them, render the home market of so great extent as to be alone sufficient to support very great manufactures, and to admit of very considerable subdivisions of labour. The home market of China is...not much inferior to the market of all the different countries of Europe put together." If an expanded foreign trade were to be added to this, Smith thought, "the Chinese would naturally learn the art of using and constructing themselves all the different machines made use of in other countries."[77] He shares something of Braudel's faith in the magic of overseas

72. See Elvin, *Pattern*, chap. 17.

73. Braudel, *La dynamique*, 33. "Une vision eurocentriste trop commode."

74. Braudel, *La dynamique*, 33. "Si les rouages de l'échange que nous venons de décrire, pour l'Europe seule, existent hors d'Europe—et ils existent en Chine, dans l'Inde, à travers l'Islam, au Japon—peut-on les utiliser pour un essai d'analyse comparative?"

75. Braudel, *La dynamique*, 33. "Déjà visible avant la Révolution industrielle, si l'Europe était, ou non, en avance par rapport au reste du monde."

76. Braudel, *La dynamique*, 39. "Habituée à vivre sur elle-même."

77. Adam Smith, *An Inquiry into the Nature and Causes of the Wealth of Nations*, 2 vols. (1776; repr. London: Dent & Sons, 1910), 2:174.

trade; he would have been startled, I think, at the idea that China in the eighteenth century was economically barely above the level of the primitive.

❧ ❧ ❧

One of the leitmotifs of Braudel's work is his insistence on the extraordinary contribution of long-distance trade to generating new concentrations of wealth and new economic practices. "Just as in Europe, long-distance commerce is at the heart of the highest-level capitalism in the Far East."[78] It is therefore disconcerting to find him saying, when discussing why China did not make an endogenous breakthrough to modern economic growth, "compared to this immensity [that of China's coastline] the zones of life seem to have been that much smaller [than in Europe], along the lines followed by the circulation of ships, goods, and human beings."[79] Now it is fair to say, for late-imperial times, that there was something of an economic dualism in China, distinguishing areas that had easy access to cheap transport by water, and those that had to rely primarily on land transport,[80] but to treat the distances as negative influences in this context does not seem logically consistent with the rest of the book. It is also at variance with what the facts we have suggest. For example, after 1684, a fleet of about thirty-five hundred ships, each carrying between 65,000 and 400,000 pounds of cargo, regularly made several trips a year between Shanghai and Manchuria, exchanging southern cotton cloth and tea for northern beans, bean-cakes, and wheat.[81] This is about half the total length of the eastern Chinese littoral. In the background of this trade, which was even so only a part of the market they supplied, stood wholesalers, some at least of whom sold on the order of a million bolts of cotton cloth each a year.[82] For Braudel, though, within China, only the south seems to have fostered protocapitalism a little: "Does the same not hold true all along the southern shores of China, hemmed with

78. Braudel, *Civilisation matérielle*, 2: 104. "Tout comme en Europe, le commerce au loin est au coeur du plus haut capitalisme de l'Extrême-Orient."

79. Braudel, *Civilisation matérielle*, 2:519. "Relativement à cette immensité, les zones vivantes semblent d'autant plus étroites, au long des lignes où circulent les navires, les marchandises et les hommes."

80. Elvin, *Pattern*, 304, discusses this.

81. Elvin, "High-Level Equilibrium Trap" (1972), reprinted in Elvin, *Another History*, 36–37. Cp. Elvin, "Skills and Resources," in *Another History*, 81–83.

82. Elvin, *Pattern*, 278–79, 286–87.

sunken coastlines where the sea makes deep inroads into the land, from Fuzhou and Amoy as far as Canton? Here travel and seagoing ventures were associated with a certain Chinese capitalism that could only assume its true importance when it broke free of a China that was under surveillance and constrained it."[83] But Shanghai, built on recent alluvial mudflats at the mouth of the Yangzi, was well north of the last traces of sunken coastline, and its trade, south to Fujian, up the Yangzi, to Manchuria, even, it seems, Japan,[84] was *tous azimuts*. Case dismissed.

Toward the end of *Les jeux de l'échange* Braudel puts forward the theory that the existence of deeply rooted, long-lived lineages, both noble and mercantile, threatened neither by "a power-concentrating tyranny, nor the despotism of an arbitrary ruler,"[85] was essential for "the patient accumulation of riches and the development of multiple forces and hierarchies in a diversified society."[86] To explain the absence of (a modern) capitalism in China he summons up the bureaucratic polity as in some sort a *Diabolus ex machina*. In his view, this was the primary reason why "China...is the perfect demonstration that a capitalist superstructure does not arise from the mere fact of the existence of a vigorously pulsing economy."[87] We have here to confront the delicate task of evaluating a sequence of assertions, both factual and analytical, that are almost never wholly wrong or wholly right. A lengthy quotation imposes itself at this point to indicate precisely what is at issue:

> The obstacle in China is the state, the coherence of its bureaucracy.... Public works, the construction of river levees, highways, canals, security, and urban administration...all depend on the state. The same is true of the struggle against

83. Braudel, *Civilisation matérielle,* 2:519–20. "N'en est-il pas de même tout au long de la côte méridionale de la Chine, ourlée de rias, où la mer enjambe le littoral et s'y enfonce, depuis Fou-tcheou et Amoy jusqu'à Canton. Ici le voyage, les aventures de la mer sont complices d'un certain capitalisme chinois qui ne peut prendre sa vraie dimension que lorsqu'il s'échappe d'une Chine surveillée et contraignante."

84. On the trade to Japan from the lower Yangzi region, on which we still know relatively little, see Elvin, "Skills and Resources," in *Another History,* 82.

85. Braudel, *Civilisation matérielle,* 2:234. "Ni la tyrannie totalisante, ni la tyrannie du prince arbitraire."

86. Braudel, *Civilisation matérielle,* 2:234. "L'accumulation patiente de richesses et, dans une société diversifiée, le développement de forces et hiérarchies multiples."

87. Braudel, *Civilisation matérielle,* 2:535. "La Chine...est la démonstration parfaite qu'une superstructure capitaliste ne se met en place, *ipso facto*, à partir d'une économie d'un rhythme vif."

famines...; sanctioning from time to time cash advances to peasants, to producers of silks, to entrepreneurs; filling the public granaries to serve as emergency reserves;...allowing only the state the right to tax its subjects.... Individual landed property goes back to the Han dynasty...but in principle the government remains the owner of the soil.... In like fashion the government, in its capacity as an entrepreneur on an enormous scale, keeps for itself all the obligatory labor due from the peasants.

...Likewise the businessmen and the manufacturers whom the Argus-eyed administration can always call back to order, manipulate as if holding them on a leash, or limit in their activities.... All the cities are in similar fashion under surveillance, set with snares, divided into quarters and into separate streets that close their barriers every evening. Under such conditions neither merchants nor moneylenders, nor again money changers nor manufacturers...have good chances.

...In a system such as this, accumulation is only possible for the state and the state apparatus.... The example of China supports our determination to draw a sharp distinction between "economy" and "capitalism." This is because...China has a solid market economy, with its networks of local markets...the pullulation of its shops and urban meeting-points..., but above there is the omnipresent tutelage of the state—and its unambiguous hostility toward any individual who may be seen as having grown rich in an abnormal fashion.... Hence no capitalism, except within defined groups sanctioned by the state...such as the thirteenth-century salt merchants [read "eighteenth-century" M.E.]....

In China, bureaucratic society covers over Chinese society with a unique upper layer that is impossible in any practical fashion to rip open.... Not a few mandarins...put money on deposit with merchants, who are happy to purchase the former's goodwill.... The prestige of the mandarins often induces well-to-do merchant families to push their sons in the direction of these enviable positions...such is their way of "betraying" [their class]. But...neither the fortunes nor the power of the mandarins is perpetuated smoothly down the lines of descent of the dominant families.[88]

This is a confusing conflation here of often widely separated periods and of different organizational levels. Thus, northern rural China was indeed tightly controlled by the state in the earlier part of the Tang dynasty (in the seventh century), but by Qing times, a millennium later, with counties that had on the order of two hundred thousand inhabitants each, a form of indirect rule through imperially recognized local elites, and depending on cooperation with powerful local forces such as merchant guilds, was the norm. Emergencies apart, the last time the Chinese state envisaged advancing money to peasants was probably in the eleventh century. Major hydraulic works were indeed organized by the state; but the operation of smaller systems was, to an increasing degree, essentially only supervised by the state,

---

88. Braudel, *Civilisation matérielle*, 2.524–31.

"En Chine, l'obstacle c'est l'État, la cohérence de sa bureaucratie.... Travaux publics, endiguement des fleuves, routes, canaux, sécurité et administration des villes... tout cela relève de l'État. De même la lutte contre les famines...; consentir à l'occasion des avances d'argent aux paysans, aux producteurs de soie, aux entrepreneurs; remplir les greniers publics pour constituer des réserves de sécurité; ... ne reconnaître qu'à l'État le droit de taxer les sujets.... La propriété individuelle de la terre remonte aux Han... mais le gouvernement reste, en principe, le possesseur du sol.... De même, le gouvernement se réserve, énorme entrepreneur, toures les corvées paysannes.

"...De même les négociants ou les manufacturiers que l'administration aux cent yeux peut toujours rappeler à l'ordre, tenir en laisse et limiter dans leurs activités.... Toutes les villes sont pareillement surveillées, piégées, divisées en quartiers, en rues différentes qui, chaque soir, ferment leurs barrières. Dans ces conditions, ni les marchands, ni les usuriers, ni les changeurs, ni les manufacturiers... n'y ont partie belle.

"...Dans un pareil système, l'accumulation n'est possible qu'à l'État et à l'appareil de l'État.... [L]'exemple de la Chine vient appuyer notre obstination à distinguer fortement *économie* et *capitalisme*. Car... la Chine a une solide économie de marché, avec ses guirlandes de marchés locaux... le pullulement de ses boutiques et rendez-vous urbains... mais *au-dessus*, la tutelle omniprésente de l'État—et son hostilité nette vis-à-vis tout individu qui s'enricherait «anormalement».... Alors pas de capitalisme, sinon à l'intérieur de groupes précis, cautionnés par l'État, ... tels marchands de sel du XIIIe siècle [entendre, du XVIIIe M.E.]....

"En Chine, la société bureaucratique recouvre la société chinoise d'une unique couche supérieure, pratiquement indéchirable.... Bien des mandarins... placent de l'argent auprès des marchands, qui achètent volontiers leur bienveillance.... Le prestige de mandarins entraîne souvent les familles marchandes aisées à pousser leurs fils vers ces positions enviables... c'est leur façon de «trahir». Mais... [n]i la fortune, ni la puissance des mandarins ne se perpétuent sans accroc dans les lignages de familles dominantes."

which arbitrated disputes, or rarely, reorganized systems that were in disarray, but mostly left day-to-day running in the hands of locals selected in a wide variety of ways. The state's theoretical claim to the ultimate ownership of land was of virtually no significance in what was an almost totally commercialized market in land from at least the Ming on (and had also been earlier under the Song). Urban cellularization for the purposes of security was often found in archaic, early-imperial, and even midimperial times.[89] It was much less marked after the Song, though urban policing could be strict at times, as in Beijing in the middle of the Qing dynasty,[90] but whether the resulting security was hurtful to commerce seems at least doubtful.

One crucial problem with Braudel's approach has already been flagged: if the Chinese regime, envisaged for the moment (as he does) as changing little over time, was so detrimental to high-level economic activities, how did China ever achieve her medieval economic eminence? A second problem, with which we shall concern ourselves here, is, at what point did these alleged negative effects, if they existed, impinge on the social structure of the economy? There were large accumulations of both mercantile and entrepreneurial capital in late-imperial China. In the later part of the sixteenth century, Shen Sixiao wrote of the great merchants of Zelu that "if they do not possess 100,000 ounces of silver they are not regarded as rich."[91] Since a Chinese ounce was about the same as the European one, these were serious sums of money. Somewhat later, Yan Ruyu wrote of the ironworkers of the border area between Hubei, Shaanxi, and Sichuan as follows:

> Their iron furnaces are seventeen or eighteen feet in height.... Charcoal is put in at the bottom and ore in the middle.... At each side more than ten persons will take it in turn to work the bellows. The fire is not put out either by day or by night...the liquid metal turning into iron which is cast as slabs.... More than ten artisans are hired to serve each furnace. The largest numbers of men are needed for transporting timber and building the [charcoal] kilns...and for opening up the seams and extracting ore.... The distances that the ore and charcoal have

89. See Yang Kuan, *Zhongguo gudai ducheng zhidu shi yanjiu* [Studies on the history of capital cities in China during antiquity] (Shanghai: Shanghai guji chubanshe, 1993).

90. See Mark Elvin, "Introduction," in *The Chinese City between Two Worlds,* ed. M. Elvin and G. W. Skinner (Stanford: Stanford University Press, 1974), 1–2.

91. Elvin, *Pattern,* 296.

to be taken vary, but over a hundred men are required for each furnace. Thus six or seven furnaces will give employment to not less than a thousand men. Once the iron has been cast into slabs it is sometimes manufactured locally into pots and farm tools. A thousand and several hundreds of men are also required for this work, and for the transport [of the goods]. Thus the larger iron-works in Sichuan and the other provinces regularly have two thousand or three thousand persons, and the smaller ones with but three or four furnaces well over a thousand.[92]

The details of the organizational structure are not available, and may well have involved some subcontracting; but the scale is not trivial, and the question has to be put to the Braudelian theory, how far does the accumulation of capital shown here, and in like cases, clearly coexisting with the allegedly oppressive state, fall short of "capitalism"?—not that all allegations of economic constraint are necessarily entirely false. E-tu Zen Sun has shown that the Chinese government was at times apprehensive that large groups of miners could cause disturbances, especially when ores ran out, and might move to stop their formation, though equally often valuing mining as a source of employment and a provider of strategic raw materials like iron, copper (for coinage), and sulfur. Sometimes it even promoted mining, by the practice technically known as "recruiting merchants," and this was a slightly paradoxical combination of promotion on the one hand and some measure of constraint on the other.[93]

It is also possible to find at least a limited number of mercantile enterprises that lasted more than two hundred years in late-imperial China.[94] In like fashion, we therefore have to ask, how long is long enough? And, what number is needed at least to cast serious doubt on the theory?

As it happens, I tend to feel, more intuitively than analytically, that the character of China's polity did in fact create problems for a homegrown breakthrough to economic modernity; but identifying them in a plausibly formulated and potentially provable fashion is not easy.

        ॐ ॐ ॐ

92. Elvin, *Pattern*, 285–286.
93. E-tu Zen Sun (Ren Yidu), *Selected Essays in Chinese Economic History* (Taipei: Taiwan xuesheng shuju, 1981), chaps. 6 and 7.
94. Elvin, *Pattern*, 297.

The lethal silence in *Civilisation matérielle* is that concerning the nonmaterial, that is to say, science. In recent years there have been fashionable ways of eliding any concern with modern science in the context of discussions of the origins of economic modernity. One of these ways has been to posit the possibility of a multiplicity of equally valid sciences. "Valid" in some radical epistemological or anthropological sense, since all systems of thought require at least a handful of culturally given terms, not further definable without circularity or infinite regress. The practical historian, in his turn, can elide this elision by concentrating not on "validity" in some such ultimate sense but on close "comparability" to modern Western science, in the spirit simply of the descriptive taxonomist.

Another, more widespread, evasion has been to posit a complete dichotomy between early modern science and early modern technology, and to argue that the first steps of early modern technology owed little or nothing to "science" in this sense, science only assuming its role as the underlying motor of the apparent (even if in the last analysis illusory) *moto perpetuo* of modern economic growth some time in the nineteenth century. This is to fail to understand that both early modern science and early modern technology were developed through the refinement and, sometimes, the creation of certain styles of thinking that, in the last analysis, underlay both. When De Bélidor, the great French hydraulic engineer, used geometrical analysis to determine the optimal slope of, and optimal dimensions for, pallet chain-pumps early in the eighteenth century, was he engaged in science or in technology? The only reasonable answer is "both."[95]

Modern science, as the late Alistair Crombie showed, is best grasped as an ensemble, ever more tightly intertwined, of styles of thinking.[96] China around 1600 had some understanding of all but one of the required styles (the absentee being the probabilistic mode), but mostly in a fairly attenuated form, and was soon to fall ever further behind.[97] The modern western European ensemble of styles of scientific thinking had roots that in some cases reached back to classical antiquity, had a significant European medieval input, and, although they drew at one critical period to a substantial degree

95. F. B. de Bélidor, *Architecture hydraulique: Ou l'art de conduire, d'élever et de ménager les eaux pour les différens besoins de la vie* (Paris, 1737–53), 1:362.
96. Alistair C. Crombie, *Styles of Scientific Thinking in the European Tradition* (London: Duckworth, 1994).
97. Mark Elvin, "The Man Who Saw Dragons: Science and Styles of Thinking in Xie Zhaozhe's *Fivefold Miscellany*," *Journal of the Oriental Society of Australia* 24–25 (1994–95).

on the science preserved and advanced in the Islamic world, could not have been easily paralleled in China. (China was of course also in a position to borrow from Islamic science, a point that can be illustrated by its familiarity with the Islamic tradition of astrology, but on the whole did not.) When one is playing with possible counterfactuals, either in the spirit of Braudel (Chinese junks rounding the Cape of Good Hope) or, indeed, of Abu-Lughod (no collapse of the thirteenth-century world system), I suspect that it is a falsification of the problem to omit any consideration of early modern science.

That question, however, must await another occasion.

I am particularly grateful to Jacques Gernet, Professeur Honoraire au Collège de France, and to Jean Baechler, of the Groupe d'étude des méthodes de l'analyse sociologique, Université de Paris–Sorbonne, at the Maison des Sciences de l'Homme in Paris, for their letters answering various points that I raised with them about their relations with and attitudes towards Braudel and for permission to cite portions of what they have written.

Chapter 11

PLUS ULTRA

America and the Changing European Notions of Time and Space

ANTHONY PAGDEN

To discuss the place of the "discovery" of (or "encounter" with) America, of human perceptions of time and space in Fernand Braudel's work is, perhaps, to ask what his friend Lucien Febvre famously described as a "question mal posée." It is to ask what place human agency has in a history whose prime objective was to deny that human agency played any significant role at all. *La Méditerranée et le monde Méditerranéen a l'époque de Philippe II* was, as its author says in the preface, the history of a sea, or more precisely of the regions that border that sea.[1] In some respects this is an oxymoron. The book is not an account of a body of water or a landmass, significant though they are in the narrative—for such things do not have histories in any meaningful sense. It is the history of those peoples who lived by, on, and off the Mediterranean in the "long" sixteenth century. Throughout his own long career Braudel insisted time and again that people were the irreducible products of the places in which they lived. Cultures, civilizations, polities, and communities were for him all, in the first instance, the creatures of environments. The "human science" with which he always had most affinity was geography. It is why he found Oswald Spengler and Arnold Toynbee slightly absurd— although he professed to enjoy reading them, and his comments on these old, and now largely forgotten, New Historicists make for interesting reading and are highly revealing about his own work. Braudel's history was one of the determination of human agency by a specific, and ultimately bounded non-human location. It is a history that has little space for individual human

---

1. Fernand Braudel, *La Méditerranée et le monde Méditerranéen à l'époque de Philippe II,* 2d ed., 2 vols. (Paris: Armand Colin, 1966).

actions, described—or rather dismissed—as "une agitation de surface"[2] of the *longue* or *moyenne durée*, very little for the arts and sciences, and still less for human reflection. It might, therefore, seem merely a category error to demand some account of how the humans who were shaped by these places understood their position within them.

But *La Méditerranée* does, famously, employ a concept—or rather concepts—of time, which are, somewhat uncertainly, played off against an equally varied, if also conventional, notion of space. As we all know, Braudel divided time into three: the *longue durée*,[3] the time of man's interaction with his environment, the time of "une histoire quasi immobile";[4] the *moyenne durée* (although he does not employ that term) of "une histoire sociale; celle des groupes de groupements," and finally the traditional history, the history, significantly, "non de l'homme, mais de l'individu," what he also called, borrowing a term from François Simiand and Paul Lacombe, the "histoire événementielle."[5] The first two belong to the time of what Braudel calls (following Claude Lévi-Strauss) "structures," the third to that of *conjuncture*, that is, the time of individual human actions. To make any sense of the third, he claimed that they had to be understood in the context of the first two. Most *structures* were, it seemed, inescapably composed of human actions—the development of economies, trade routes, technologies, and the like, but they were all far more than simple aggregations of those actions; indeed they possess something of the timelessness of rock formations. And it is significant in this context that perhaps one of the most profound influences on Braudel's thinking, as indeed on Lévi-Strauss, was the French geographer Paul Vidal de la Blache.

In its day, Braudel's tripartite division of historical time was a compelling model, partly because it did away with the merely contingent explanation for historical change, and because it, in effect, demolished the older, entirely voluntarist, historical narrative which lurched uncertainly from one seemingly causally unintelligible event to the next. However, all theories of history have their limits and Braudel's limit is, in effect, any complex under-

2. Braudel, *La Méditerranée*, 2d ed., 1:16.
3. The phrase seems to have been first used in an essay: Fernand Braudel, "Histoire et science sociales: La Longue durée," *Annales E.S.C.* 4 (1959): 725–53, now reprinted in Fernand Braudel, *Écrits sur l'histoire* (Paris: Flamarion, 1969), 41–83, and trans., Fernand Braudel, "History and the Social Sciences: The *Longue Durée*," in *On History*, trans. Sarah Matthews (Chicago: University of Chicago Press, 1980), 25–54.
4. Braudel, *La Méditerranée*, 2d ed., 1:16.
5. Braudel, *Écrits sur l'histoire*, 45.

standing of agency. People are, for Braudel, precisely and only what they did. In general, his work is silent about how historical agents looked upon, or attempted to represent, their own worlds. Since the *longue durée* is accumulative and indeterminate, it cannot plausibly accommodate the history of mental actions. His praise of Pierre Francastel's *Peinture et société*, and Ernst Curtius's *Europäische Literatur und lateinischer Mittelalter* as serial histories misses the point, at least of Curtius's work, and runs the risk of reducing his own theoretical model to little more than the claim that the historian should not limit his or her interests to short periods of time.

Braudel also assumed that history has a determined recoverable shape. Of Georges Gurvitch's attempt to pluralize time, Braudel's comment was, "How could a historian believe in all this? Given such a range of colors, he could never reconstitute a single, white light—and that is something he cannot do without."[6] Texts—as technologies—belong in such a conception of time, and so do their consumers (the *histoire du livre* is a characteristically Braudelian venture); but the contents of texts, or the mind-sets of their authors clearly do not. The *longue durée* has, therefore, had the unfortunate consequence of reducing most intellectual activity to something called *mentalités*. But these are at best only suggestive, at worst merely indeterminate, and their history, which by definition is one of unreflective "structures," cannot accommodate the products of what is misleadingly called the "high culture," nor—and this applies to other aspects of the *longue durée*—explain how these mentalities come into being in the first place, or how they changed over time. (The general assumption of most historians of mentalities is that these, too, belong to the *longue durée*, thus shelving, if not exactly solving, the problem.)

The same limitations apply to Braudel's notion of a civilization, which in its reordering of the traditional neo-Kantian distinction between *Zivilisation* and *Kultur*, derives largely from Spengler.[7] Cultures are "primitive"

6. Braudel, *Écrits sur l'histoire*, 78.
7. Oswald Spengler, *The Decline of the West: Form and Actuality*, trans. Charles Francis Atkinson, 2 vols. (London: George Allen & Unwin, 1934), 1:31–32: "For every culture has *its own* civilization. In this work for the first time the two words, hitherto used to express an indefinite, more or less ethical distinction, are used in a *periodic* sense, to express a strict and necessary *organic succession*.... Civilizations are the most external and artificial states of which a species of developed humanity is capable. They are conclusions, the thing-become succeeding the thing-becoming, death following life, rigidity following expansion, intellectual age and the stone-built petrifying world-city following mother-earth and the spiritual childhood of Doric and Gothic. They are an end, irrevocable, yet by inward necessity reached again and again."

nontechnological, static. "The societies which correspond to culture," Braudel wrote in *Grammaire des civilisations*, "have a tendency to maintain themselves indefinitely in their initial state, which explains, furthermore, why they appear to us as societies without history and without progress...whereas civilizations are founded on hierarchical societies with...changing tensions, social conflicts, political struggle, and perpetual evolution."[8] Yet even these "civilizations" evolve as slowly as the shape of the landscape itself, and are as resistant to the "impact" of a passing human act, or the reflections of persons upon those acts, as the landscape is to a hurricane, a landslide, or an earthquake. *La Méditerranée* is, in large part, a book about communications, at a period when those were themselves undergoing rapid and spectacular transformations. If climate and terrain was determinant of the *longue durée*, so too the links between peoples across terrains. But if the Roman and Latin-Christian world was to be counted as a "civilization," then its identity was to be found precisely in its "refusals to borrow, by its resistance to certain alignments, by its resolute selection among the foreign influences offered to it." Precisely, that is, by its closure to the benefits that the new systems of communication might bring. All these are, of course, very general claims and, as with many of Braudel's more theoretical utterances, they are ultimately left unresolved. But one thing does seem obvious: Braudel's "civilizations" have no obvious origins, and no mechanism which might explain how they resist those "certain alignments."

Braudel's history is also, explicitly, and in many respects curiously, Eurocentric—the limiting effects of which, as Mark Elvin points out, he seems to have felt intuitively.[9] The world is what he called a "global Mediterranean," which reached all the way to India and Africa and America. But at its "radiant center whose light grows less as one moves away from it, without one's being able to define the exact boundary between light and shade is the Mediterranean itself."[10] It is, perhaps unsurprisingly, a very Hegelian perception of the conjuncture between time and space. For Hegel, although he was writing very much from the viewpoint of an intellectually and culturally emergent north, the Mediterranean was still the "uniting element" of the

8. Fernand Braudel, *Grammaire des civilisations* (Paris: Flammarion, 1987), 48. For a more extensive critique of Braudel's conception of "civilization," see Steven Feierman, "Africa in History: The End of Universal Narratives" in *After Colonialism: Imperial Histories and Postcolonial Displacements*, ed. Gyan Prakash (Princeton: Princeton University Press, 1995), 40–65.

9. See Mark Elvin, "Braudel and China," chap. 10 above.

10. Braudel, *La Méditerranée*, 2d ed., 1:168.

"three quarters of the globe" and "the center of world history." (America belonged firmly in the domain of the future, "where in the ages that lie before us, the burden of the world's history shall reveal itself.")[11] Little wonder then perhaps that the "discovery" of America (and in this context it was that and not an "encounter") has relatively little place in the Braudelian calculus, despite the importance of American silver, American foodstuffs, as well as the role played by America in finally shifting the equilibrium of Philip II's political power from the Mediterranean itself toward the Atlantic.

It is that "discovery," and how it was understood, that I want to consider as a limiting case of the *longue durée*. It is a narrative—only, of course, one of many—whose origins are to be found in the Ancient geographical vision of the world. The frontier of Braudel's Mediterranean was crucially an ocean, indeed the Ocean—*Okeanos*. In Antiquity this was conceived as an encircling river that constituted the final *periodos* and *peirata*, the boundaries and the limits that enclosed humanity (which makes nonsense of Braudel's description of the Greek and Phoenician expansion between the tenth and the sixth centuries B.C.E. as "la découverte d'une Amérique," charming hyperbole though it may be).[12] This, of course, is the geography of the *Odyssey*. But just as the *Odyssey* is itself a poem about the limits of space (and, though it is another matter, time) so there were always those who sought some wider, more densely populated universe. Herodotus, for instance, recast these geographical images in terms of human populations scattered throughout numerous, unconnected spaces, populations which, though they might know nothing of each other's existence, nevertheless shared a common humanity. To this hypothetical collectivity, which included both Greek and barbarian, the recorded and the still-to-be-encountered, he gave the name *oikoumene* (and was one of the earliest to do so). Herodotus's vision marked the terms of an enduring Indo-European conflict: a conflict between settlement and migration, between the *cives* and the denizen of a bounded, known space, on the one hand, and the *homo viator* (in Saint Francis's term), the wanderer, the pilgrim, the navigator on the other. It marks, too, a concern (which is present in all Braudel's work) for the possibilities for communication which existed between the various members of the species. In Cicero's

11. Georg Wilhelm Friedrich Hegel, *The Philosophy of History*, trans. J. Sibree (New York: Dover, 1956), 86.

12. Fernand Braudel, *Les mémoires de la Méditerranée: Préhistoire et antiquité*, ed. Roselyne de Ayala and Paule Braudel (Paris: Éditions de Fallois, 1998), 207. The original manuscript of this book was written in 1969, and then abandoned.

Somnium Scipionis, one of the most popular of the Latin texts which sought to capture some of this anxiety about the limits of human space, the Roman general Scipio Aemilianus is granted a vision of four inhabited but separate landmasses.[13] No communication was possible with the peoples who inhabited these other regions, which lay beyond the limits of the "orbis terrarum" except in dream travel, or what for the Romans came to much the same thing, oceanic navigation. For Cicero the lesson to be learned from Scipio's dream had been the relative futility of earthly fame. When, however, Macrobius in the fifth century wrote his Neoplatonic commentary on Scipio's dream voyage, his concern, which would be repeated again and again as the European understanding of the world expanded, was that the human groups which inhabited the world lacked the ability for reciprocal communication, something which Macrobius at least seems to have regarded as a violation of the human condition.[14] Communication between such widely separated peoples could only be achieved by oceanic travel and the Ancients had, of course, always looked upon oceanic voyages as not merely perilous, but somehow unnatural, the main reason, in Abraham Ortelius's opinion, for their failure to discover America.[15]

The European explorations of the late fifteenth century, however, first of Africa then of Asia, loosened the hold which the image of an encircling Ocean and of scattered oceanic landmasses had upon the European geographical and anthropological imagination. "Hence we can see," wrote the Portuguese cosmographer Duarte Pacheco Pereira in 1508, "that the Ocean does not surround the earth as the philosophers have declared, but rather the earth surrounds the sea that lies in its hollow and center."[16] The final discovery of a new continent confirmed this image of a near continuous global landmass, and the altered image of the space which humankind occupied led inexorably to a changed conception of humankind in space. To insist, as

13. Cicero, *De re publica*, 6.19–20.

14. On Macrobius's vision, see John M. Headley, "The Sixteenth-Century Venetian Celebration of the Earth's Total Habitability: The Issue of the Fully Habitable World for Renaissance Europe," *Journal of World History* 8 (1997): 1–27, at 6.

15. James Romm, "New World and '*novos orbes*': Seneca in the Renaissance Debate over Ancient Knowledge of the Americas," in *European Images of the Americas and the Classical Tradition,* ed. Wolfgang Haase and Meyer Rheinhold, vol. 1, pt. 1 of *The Classical Tradition and the Americas* (Berlin: Walter de Gruyter, 1994), 105.

16. Duarte Pacheco Pereira, *Esmeraldo de situ orbis*, quoted in W. G. L. Randles, "Classical Models of World Geography and Their Transformation following the Discovery of America," in *The Classical Tradition and the Americas*, 1:5–76, at 63.

Horace had done, that the seas had been created by the gods precisely to keep men apart was to deny mankind a crucial part of their true nature. It was in implicit response to Horace and Claudian that Pietro Bembo makes his Columbus declare "the globe of the earth is of such a nature that to man has been given the capacity for going through all its parts."[17] It was this which, for Richard Hakluyt, made the new astronomers, geographers, and navigators the heroes of the modern age, as the great philosophical synthesizers had been of the Ancient. "Was not divine Plato," asked Hakluyt, "(who lived so many years ago and plainly described their West Indies under the name of Atlantis) was not he (I say) instead of a Cosmographer unto them? Were not those Carthaginians mentioned by Aristotle *lib. de admirabil. auscult.* their forerunners?"[18] Samuel Purchas, who inherited the project Richard Hakluyt had begun in the *Principal Navigations* of 1589, displayed a similar recognition that the modern world to which he belonged had transcended the limits which the Ancients had placed upon the possibilities of human communication. His "Pilgrimes,"—as he called his collection of travel narratives—"not being, a Booke of Travels in the World, but the World historified in a World of Voyages and Travels."[19]

For these new historians of oceanic navigation, for Hakluyt and Purchas, for the earliest natural historian of America, Gonzalo Fernández de Oviedo, and for the Spanish chronicler royal Antonio de Herrera, for Pierre-François Charlevoix, the Ocean was no longer a boundary, a frontier, but a highway, another kind of *via* that would eventually link together all the peoples of the world both known and still unknown.

In the Ancient conception of the relationship of humankind to its geographical environment, humans were ultimately sedentary beings, whose mastery over themselves depended upon the creation of confined spaces the *politeai* and *urbes* of the ancient world beyond which, as Aristotle had said, there lived only beasts and heroes. But these communities, these "civilizations," had all in the first instance been the creations of wanderers. Furthermore, like the expansion into Africa or the creation of new trade routes into Asia, the discovery of America came to be seen as a special instance of the exercise of European technology. Ever since Aristotle (at least) the capacity to

17. Headley, "Sixteenth-Century Venetian Celebration of the Earth's Total Habitability," 16.
18. "Preface to the Principal Navigations, 1598," in *The Original Writings and Correspondence of the Two Richard Hakluyts*, ed. E. G. R. Taylor, 2 vols. (London: Hakluyt Society, 1935), 2:435.
19. Samuel Purchas, *Purchas His Pilgrimes*, 5 vols. (London, 1625), vol. 4, dedicatory letter.

transform the world according to human needs was held to be a defining feature of the species. The natural world had been created, in Copernicus's celebrated phrase, for human use "propter nos." But it had been created in a
state of potentiality, whose actuality could only be realized through purpose-
ful action. It required art, *techne*, to realize in a tree its capacity for transformation into a chair. For the Greeks, this *techne* had been a form of
knowledge (*logos*). It is the abstract form of *tikto* to "generate" or "engender";
humans are thus the *teknotes*, the genitors, and the *tekna* are their offspring.
Techne was precisely the power to set in motion, a power that none besides
humankind and the gods themselves possessed. And although civility, polity,
could only be acquired in settled communities, it remained the case that the
true *teknotes* were always those who moved out by their own will, beyond the
periodos, the boundaries which the inactivity of nature had imposed.

The classical conception of the origins of human technology was further
complicated by the Christian concept of the Fall, for this entailed not merely
a loss of God's grace, but also a loss of cognitive understanding. In the Garden of Eden, Adam had been empowered to name all the works of creation
because their properties had been fixed, and because he—Adam—knew
what they were. In the altered world beyond Paradise, that knowledge had to
be reacquired within an environment in which ultimate causes—as Newton
insisted time and again—had been hidden and would, in all probability,
remain forever so. The Basle reformer Simon Grynaeus, in the preface to one
of the earliest attempts to adjust the older spatial understanding of the world
to accommodate the existence of America, the *Novus orbis regionum ac insularum veteribus incognitarum* of 1532, praised the new travelers for having
recovered by their action the *dominium* over the natural world once enjoyed
by Adam.[20] Traveling into uncharted space had become, in the modern age
in which Grynaeus was conscious of living, a manner of overcoming the cognitive damage inflicted by the Fall. The traveler, together with the geographer, the mathematician, and the astronomer, were God's self-fashioning
instruments for the subjugation of nature to man's needs. For Grynaeus these
are men[21] whose mission is comparable, both in its nobility and the distrust

20. Simon Grynaeus, *Novus orbis regionum ac insularum veteribus incognitarum* (Basle,
1532), "Epistola nuncupatoria," fols. 92r–93r.
21. And they always are *men*—Eve's role is prompting Adam to make a bid for the
knowledge reserved for God; the knowledge as the scholastics would say of first causes pre-
cluded her from any role in *scientia*—the human quest for the attainable understanding of
secondary causes.

it aroused in the ignorant, to those (the Saints) who had similarly abandoned the settled known world in order to seek a knowledge of God. The new navigators, the desert fathers, even Christ and his disciples themselves, now share something of the same identity. Nearly a century later, the tirelessly punning Samuel Purchas also appropriated the legend of the expulsion from Eden as the source for the transformation of man's condition from the stationary to the migratory. For mankind, "preferring the Creature to the Creator, and therefore is justly turned out of Paradise to wander, a Pilgrime over the world." This act of divine retribution transformed for Purchas all human history—including the story of Christ's passion, "the greatest of all peregrinations," from God to man and back again—into a narrative of human movement, a narrative which, at least as far as the modern world was concerned, had been initiated by Christ himself and the Evangelists, who since they also "planted the Church and settled on her foundations," were not only the first Christian travelers; they were also—and the association was crucial—the first colonists.[22]

All these narratives of modernity are, in broad outline and in the moments of creation and transmission which they employ, familiar enough. The triumph of human *techne* over the natural world had been given many beginnings, but by the late sixteenth century most writers would point to three moments in which a new technology, a new *scientia*, could be said to have resulted in the transformation of the understanding of the world: they were the discovery of America and the new sea route to India, the invention of gunpowder, and of the printing press. Each of these (except initially gunpowder—but I shall come back to that) had two properties. They made Europeans more mobile, and they made them better able to communicate with one another and increasingly with those whom they encountered in the worlds beyond their own. And, if there is anything which separates the modern from the premodern world, it is mobility and communication. This was clear enough to Braudel himself, clearer still perhaps to his mentor Lucien Febvre, the founder of *Annales* whose emblem was the figure of Hermes, the messenger of the gods.

Since these achievements had been limited to, and broadly shared by, those whom Samuel Purchas described as "we in the West," they became a collective means of self-presentation, not merely Portuguese or Spanish or later English and French, but in some broader sense, European. In 1559, the French savant Louis Le Roy makes "the voice of our common mother

22. *Purchas His Pilgrimes*, 1:49–50.

Europe" declare "I who in the past hundred years have made so many discoveries, even things unknown to the ancients—new seas, new lands, new species of men: with Spanish help I have found and conquered what amounts to a New World."[23] In Johannes Stradanus's engraving of 1589 it is European science, here embodied by Amerigo Vespucci, which is shown literally drawing aside the curtains upon a new world of which neither Africa nor Asia, nor even Europe's own, now sometimes dubious, ancient ancestors had any knowledge. In Stradanus's fanciful representation of the first moment of encounter between Old World and New, Vespucci is shown with an astrolabe, the emblem of his empowering knowledge, in his hand. The figure of America, in recumbent allusion to Vespucci's own image of the continent as an ever-available female, is raising herself naked from the long sleep of her ignorance.

But this image, if only in what it implies from what we, and Stradanus, know about what will follow in the narrative of the discovery, is not an innocent celebration of scientific knowledge. The presence of gunpowder in the list of significant modern achievements ties, as does Grynaeus's association of navigation with the recovery of *dominium*, travel and the knowledge it provided—indeed all human technology—to possession. (The various uses to which the world *dominium* itself was put, especially within the Roman juridical tradition, makes this clear. For one may have equally *dominium* over a thing, as *dominium* over one's own being, and *dominium* in some field of knowledge.) The histories of technology implied not merely power over a nature created solely for "us," as a species, but also power over others by "us," understood as a single social group, a single, in Braudel's term, "civilization," for although all true humans were *teknotes*, not all were equally skilled. Some, the *barbaroi* for instance, might have no direct access to *techne* at all, or to its moral equivalent, practical wisdom (*phronesis*), save via some other more gifted being. *Techne* could thus be conceived as that power which is exercised not by humankind over nature, but by one human group over another. As Michel Foucault once pointed out, what in the Greek Church was called *techne technon* and in the Latin *ars artium* was not only the creation of things in the world, but also the direction of the conscience, and thus ultimately the government of men.[24] The narratives of the progress of

23. Louis Le Roy, *De la vicissitude ou variété des choses en l'univers* (Paris, 1579), fols. 98 v–99 v.

24. Michel Foucault, "Qu'est-ce que la critique (Critique et Aufklärung)," *Bulletin de la Société française de la Philosophie* 84 (1990): 5–63.

the European peoples could thus link the instruments of *communio* and *communicatio,* the compass and the book, with that of political and territorial dominium, with gunpowder and steel. The immensely popular stories of the conquest of Mexico and Peru where vast numbers of men had been vanquished by a handful of adversaries armed with canon, horses, and steel swords, or of the subjugation by Portuguese shipboard canons of the peoples of the West African coast and southern India, became as much stories of the triumph of a particular way of looking at the world as tales of individual heroism and divine preference. Cesare Ripa's *Iconologia* of 1603, a work that provided artists with an easy set of iconographic rules, instructs its readers to depict Europe wearing a crown, "to show that Europe has always been the leader and queen of the world." And this is how Europe appears in Sebastian Münster's *Cosmographia* in the Basel edition of 1588.

To know a space, therefore, was to acquire dominium over it, first in the form of a map or a description (for ekphrasis, too, confers ownership), a list of attributes, something that, in Bruno Latour's brilliant metaphor, can be "made mobile" and carried back to Europe.[25] Later, reversing the direction of travel, would follow the colonies, commerce, and conversion. There was nothing modern in this. The thirteenth-century natural scientist Roger Bacon had linked in this way Seneca's *Quaestiones naturales* with his "patron" Nero's aspirations to universal dominium, just as, in Bacon's view and also Purchas's, Aristotle had written *De Caelo* for Alexander the Great.[26] Anything resembling disinterested scientific knowledge was unimaginable before the great scientific explorations of the eighteenth century such as those of Bougainville, Cook, and Charles de la Condamine, and even these had barely concealed political agendas. But the discoveries of the fifteenth and sixteenth centuries were believed, rightly, to have enhanced the real potential to be derived from harnessing science to power, exploration to expropriation to an unprecedented degree. Giovanni Battista Ramusio, in *Discorso sopra il commercio delle spezie* (1547), referring to the vast but yet unknown resources of the "Southern Continent" (still in the mid-sixteenth century a geographical fiction), claimed that the most admirable act that a great prince could perform would be "to get the men of our hemisphere to come to know those of the opposite hemisphere." This, he explained, could easily be carried out in the traditional manner, first by voyages of exploration, then by "dispatching into diverse

25. Bruno Latour, *Science in Action: How to Follow Scientists and Engineers through Society* (Milton Keynes: Open University Press, 1987), 227.
26. *Purchas His Pilgrimes,* 1:91.

places of that hemisphere colonies and settlers. In the manner which the Romans did."[27] Ultimately all such communication involved political *dominium*.

The discovery of America, however, was not an event which could merely be added to the chronologies of human—or more precisely European—inventiveness. For, like the invention of printing and gunpowder, it marked a moment of transition. This moment, the action not of one (despite the prominence of Columbus in most of these accounts), but of several, is precisely, of course, the beginning of the modern world. For this discovery, unlike the explorations of Africa and Asia that preceded it (but like the discoveries in the Pacific that followed), had, or so it seemed, resulted in the recognition of a "new" world. It should be stressed, however, that the term "new" implied only prior ignorance. When the great Dominican theologian Domingo de Soto argued in 1556, "we speak of a New World or a New Earth of islands and a continent which encompasses vast spaces," we use the term in the same ways as did the poet Lucan when he wrote the line, "Arabs you have come to a world unknown to you."[28] No one supposed that these places were literally "new." They were simply new to Europeans. Despite the accusations leveled at them by twentieth-century historians, Europeans had always been conscious in this way of the antiquity of the autochthonous identity of the New World. Fernández de Oviedo, for instance, in his account of Nuño de Guzmán's expedition to the region he named "New Galicia" objected forcibly to this apparently indiscriminate use of the adjective, for "the Spaniards called this New Galicia, not because it is more or less ancient than Old Galicia, but simply because the Christians have recently encountered [*hallaron*] it."[29] Indeed it was precisely America's identity, so very striking in being so unlike Europe, its existence prior to its "discovery," which made the "discovery" at all remarkable.

America's entry into European time, however, implied for most an entry into history. For both Bartolomé de las Casas (for whom Columbus's voyages had constituted an expression of God's favor to the moderns) and Ramusio

27. *Navigazioni e viaggi*, ed. Marica Milanesi, 6 vols. (Turin: Einaudi, 1978–88), 2:980. See Marica Milanesi, *Tolomeo sostituito: Studi di storia delle conoscenze geografiche nel XVI secolo* (Milan: Edizioni Unicopli, 1984), 219; and Headley, "Sixteenth-Century Venetian Celebration of the Earth's Total Habitability," 13–14.

28. Domingo de Soto, *De iustitia et iure* (Salamanca, 1556), 306.

29. Gonzalo Fernández de Oviedo, *Historia general y natural de las Indias*, 14 vols., ed. Perez de Tudela Bueso, Biblioteca de Autores Españoles, nos. 117–21 (Madrid: Ediciones Atlas, 1959), 4:269, 278.

(who believed that God had hidden America from human, that is, European, eyes until the time was ready) the ignorance of past generations, and crucially, of course, the ignorance of the Ancients with regard to America, constituted part of God's manipulation of human time. Only in the modern age, as it was coming to be understood, had Christendom been prepared for the burdens, and the opportunities, which America represented. The discovery thus became a device for measuring the distance that now separated the "new" world of modern Europe from that of what Henry IV's cosmographer royal André Thevet called "those toadstools of philosophers."[30] The textual authority of those Ancients who had defined most scientific understanding had been shattered, at least in the areas of geography, navigation, and by implication as more and more became known about its structure and its inhabitants, meteorology, botany, biology, and anthropology. For America was, in the telling phrase of the Basle humanist Glareanus in 1527, "regiones extra Ptolemaeum,"[31] about which everything was as yet too uncertain to be the subject of proper scientific inquiry. Ptolemy, as the Neapolitan man-of-letters Giambattista Manso observed to Galileo in 1610, "had been judged to be a new Hercules, beyond whose limits it was impossible to go."[32] The text of Ptolemy's geography had acted as a *periodos* for the European scientific imagination as surely as Scylla and Charybdis had for the Ancients marked the frontier between the inhabited world and *Okeanos*. Because of this, the historiographer royal Antonio de Herrera in 1601 at the start of his great celebration of his nation's conquest of these new, extra Ptolemaic spaces wrote: "These Western Indies were regions so far removed from the imagination of mankind that it was held to be a madness to think of [the possibility] of them."[33]

The discovery had thus freed at least one part of the modern imagination from its dependence upon a canon. It offered, too, a vision of a radically altered future. Ever since Seneca's *Quaestiones naturales* had raised the apparently prophetic possibility of future discoveries, the recognition of the existence of a *novus orbis* had carried with it the possibility of a *novus ordo*

30. André Thevet, *Le grand insulaire et pilotage d'André Thevet angoumoisin, cosmographe du roi* (1588) in *André Thevet's North America: A Sixteenth-Century View*, ed. and trans. Roger Schlesinger and Arthur Stabler (Montreal: McGill-Queens University Press, 1986), 222.

31. Henricus Glareanus, *D. Henrici Glarsani poetae laureati De Geographia liber unus* (Basle, 1527), fol. 35 r.

32. See Anthony Pagden, *European Encounters with the New World, from Renaissance to Romanticism* (New Haven: Yale University Press, 1993), 98.

33. Quoted in Headley, "The Sixteenth-Century Venetian Celebration of the Earth's Total Habitability."

saeclorum. Because America was the prime location of the exercise of all that modernity was now thought to imply—description, exploitation, and possession, the supreme exercise of the *ars artium*—it, unlike either Asia or Africa which shared some but not all of these attributes, offered the possibility of a final *translatio.* In America, "new" Europe had not merely demonstrated its capacity for outstripping the old; America itself might actually become the fixed site of the new. This perception, familiar enough from nineteenth-century immigrants' tales, in fact reaches all the way back to Braudel's sixteenth century. For many of the Spanish missionaries, the fact that Hernán Cortés had entered Mexico at roughly the same date that Luther nailed his celebrated thesis to the church door at Wittenberg was evidence that God had offered this new world to the Catholic church as a compensation for the substantial losses it had sustained in the old. The Franciscans in New Spain labored hard in the first years of the occupation to bring about a new apostolic church to redeem the vices and corruptions of the old. Richard Hakluyt envisaged a kind of commercial version of the same transference. America, he assured the reader of the *Discourse on Western Planting,* contained within it all the climatic features of the old world. "Being answerable in climate to Barbary, Egypt, Syria, Persia, Turkey, Greece, all the islands of the Levant sea, Italy, Spain, Portugal, France, Flanders, high Almayne, Denmark, Estland, Poland, and Muscovy may presently or within a short space afford unto us for little or nothing and with much more safety either all or a great part of the commodities which the aforesaid countries do yield us at a very dear hand, and with manifold dangers."[34] Finally, he believed the new world would come to replace not merely the agricultural lands of northern and southern Europe but even, "I may well and truly conclude with reason and authority that the commodities of poor old decayed and dangerous trades in all Europe, Africa and Asia haunted by us, may in short space for little or nothing and many for the very workmanship in manner be had in that part of America." If that is, he added, "by our slackness we suffer not the French and others to prevent us."[35] Hakluyt, of course, was attempting to persuade, and his text, with its account of the balmy climate of Newfoundland, is willfully misleading. But the image of America as a place that offered to Europe the possibility not merely of an extension, or a place of refuge, but of a renewal had already by 1584 become an established

34. Hakluyt, *Original Writings,* 2:222.
35. Hakluyt, *Original Writings,* 2:233.

part of the discourse of discovery and occupation. Later, of course, there would be other translations, culminating in the late eighteenth century in a series of attempts in both the north and the south of the continent to effect the most radical political translation in European history since the collapse of the Roman republic, attempts which would, of course, occasion the final irrevocable severance of the two continents.

If America was "new" precisely, and only, because it had been unknown to the Ancients, then for those who had first been driven to reflect upon its significance, the discovery suggested the possibility for an entire reordering of historical time. For the discovery of America had this other property, as contemporaries soon realized: if one continent of which the Ancients had had no knowledge might exist where before there was assumed to be only ocean and a few scattered islands, then there might exist others still to be discovered. As the celestial guide in Juan de Maldonado's modernized version of the *Somnium Scipionis* (1581) caustically observes, having "occupied a few of its beaches," the Spaniards, "think they have found a New World." What lay beyond those beaches, and beyond America itself, lay as yet in the future. Thus, when Purchas divided the world, as had now become traditional, into the Old and the New, he took "new" to mean not only all that was not available to the Ancients, but also those other shadowy regions still awaiting discovery. "Now for the *New World*," he wrote, "we begin it at China, which the Ancients knew not, and take all the East and North parts of *Asia* from the *Caspian Sea*, the Arctoan [sic] regions, all *America* and *Terra Australis*, comprehending all in that *New Title*."[36]

This had indeed always been an implicit possibility in the languages employed by the European powers to establish their rights over not merely known worlds, but also over all possible future worlds. The pillars of Hercules stood at the entrance to the Atlantic and thus the exit from the Mediterranean. They were, however, as the supposedly classical tag *non plus ultra* indicated, not merely a self-imposed limit, but the measure of the possible. When in 1516 Charles V added Hercules's pillars (now transformed into neat Doric columns) to his coat of arms but transformed the line by rendering it as "plus ultra," he was not only celebrating the fact that his "imperium" had passed beyond the limits of that of Augustus, whose name he frequently assumed: He was also making a statement about the further possibilities that now remained. The pillars now stood not on the boundaries of the known,

36. *Purchas His Pilgrimes*, 1, "To the Reader."

but at the entrance to the still-to-be-known.[37] Indeed from the moment of Columbus's return from his first voyage, the political claims to sovereignty over the world were always couched in the future tense. The famous Bulls of Donation of 1493, by which the pope had granted to Ferdinand and Isabella territorial rights over the Americas, defined these lands as all those "as you have discovered or are about to discover"[38] and which were not already occupied by another Christian prince. One year later Spain and Portugal divided the entire *orbis terrarum*, of which they possessed only the most primitive geographical knowledge (even the 370 leagues west of the Cape Verde Islands, approximately 46°30′ W, along which the Tordesillas Line was drawn could not be established with accuracy), into two discrete spheres of jurisdiction. As Alexander von Humboldt remarked from the vantage point of the late eighteenth century, by thus "extending the circle of what is known," the existence of America had not only created for the Europeans a new world, it had also "opened further the prospect of what still remains to be overcome."[39]

What "remained to be overcome" had a definite, if still wholly imaginary, shape as the Southern Continent, the *Terra australis incognita*—an oxymoron, as contemporaries pointed out, but one which carried with it an implicit future condition. This first appeared in Mercator's world map of 1569 and on all subsequent world maps. As with America before it, the Southern Continent provided future possibilities, of mineral abundance, and of course, European domination. Persuaded by Vittorio Ricci's very unusual projection of 1676, the Vatican in 1681 even created a prefecture for it.[40]

The recognition that the presence of America marked not merely the end of the fixed, limited, and known world, but the beginning of a possibly limitless one, threw into uncertainty not only all future geographical knowledge. It also had a deeper, and as yet still little understood, impact on

37. See Earl Rosenthal, "*Plus ultra, non plus ultra*, and the Columnar Device of Emperor Charles V," *Journal of the Warburg and Courtauld Institutes* (1971): 34, 204–28. The device, which was not necessarily related to America—although it did clearly imply territorial expansion—was of Italian and Burgundian, rather than Castilian, inspiration.

38. In Manuel Giménez Fernández, "Nuevas consideraciones sobre la historia y el sentido de las letras alejandrinas de 1493 referentes a las Indias," *Anuario de estudios americanos* 1 (1944): 173–429, at 181. This is taken from the Bull *Inter cetera* of 3 May 1493.

39. Quoted in Anthony Pagden, *European Encounters with the New World*, 115.

40. W. A. R. Richardson, "Mercator's Southern Continent: Its origins, influence and gradual decline," *Terrae Incognitae* 25 (1993): 67–98, at 95.

other orderings of human time. As Domingo de Soto argued in 1556, the Latin term *terra* had traditionally been used to describe the territorial limits of the jurisdiction of the Roman people. Since, however, it was now obvious that this "world" was no longer fixed, but was continually expanding, and despite the limits imposed by God on all space, might do so for some considerable time to come, it should now be understood in the terms employed by Soto's contemporary, the jurist Vázquez de Menchaca, in the indefinite (or subjunctive) mode, as limited in its application to a condition that was still only potential.

If the discovery of America had demonstrated that the world existed, for its European inhabitants at least, in a state of potentiality, then no claim to possession of it could be made in future time. For Soto, and even more forcibly for Vázquez, the Bulls of Donation had thus been rendered void by the very facts they were intended to bring under control, for clearly no man, not even a pope, can have dominium over what is potential, since he would have no means of knowing just what it was he was claiming power over.[41] So long as the full extent of the inhabited world was as yet unknown, any claim to universal sovereignty could only be based upon a tacit assumption that each new society, as it came to light, would have to conform to a rule—the juridical concepts of western Europe—which had been devised with no prior knowledge of its existence. Furthermore, if such a rule were to be at all legitimate it would also have to be one that had been created for the "exclusive use" of peoples whose particular needs were as yet unknown to those who had drafted it. And that, concluded Vázquez, would be "worthy of laughter and mockery."[42] The point both Soto and Vázquez were making assumed, of course, that societies could only be legitimate if they acted in the interests of those whom Vázquez referred to as their *cives et subditi*, something which neither the drafters nor the beneficiaries of the Bulls of Donation had assumed. But it was also a rejection of the whole notion of a universal sovereignty on the grounds that such sovereignty could never be realized in a world which, for its European explorers, had been so clearly demonstrated to be in a state of perpetual becoming. America had forced upon these men a very modern conception of the limitlessness of time. For Vázquez the expanding regions of the new worlds, known and still to be known, meant

---

41. Fernando Vázquez Menchaca, *Controversiarum illustrium aliarumque usu frequentium, libri tres* [1563], ed. Fidel Rodriguez Alcalde, 3 vols. (Valladolid, 1931), 2:30.

42. Vázquez Menchaca, *Controversiarum illustrium*, 2:29.

that everything about human history could only be contingent. The law, hitherto considered to be timeless, was "for this moment only. On the next it dies." Futurity, which the jurists had sought to appropriate for themselves, now belonged only to God.

The discovery of America became, then, not an end but a beginning. When Alexander von Humboldt came to write what was in effect a history of the geographical-temporal imagination of Europe, he began his narrative with the Crusades, the first attempts by Europeans to break free from their spatial prison, to reclaim their human heritage as travelers; he passed through genealogies of the arts and sciences before coming to rest on the much mythologized figure of Columbus himself. For it is Columbus's venture which is the beginning, not, as it was to be for Michelet, of the discovery *of* "mankind," so much as the discovery of a way of being in the world *for* mankind. Before that discovery, Europeans had conceived time, and their progress through it, in terms of a set of responses to what Humboldt called "external circumstances." With the addition of America to humankind's "objects of contemplation," the European intellect "henceforth produces… grand results by its own peculiar and internal power in every direction at the same time." "We may record," he continued, "how since the grand era, a new and active state of the intellect and feelings, bold wishes, and hopes scarcely to be restrained, have gradually penetrated into the whole of civil society." For Humboldt, the discovery of America marked the beginning of modernity. This, too, is its own *longue durée*, but one conceived in terms of moments of transition, not virtually unshifting continuities. What is crucial is precisely that this "event" has not merely added to a range of possible objects of knowledge. It has altered the ways in which humans (European humans at least) have understood the intersection between space and time.

And where does this leave the *longue durée*? First, as a conception it constitutes a rejection, not only of the older *res gestae* style of historiography, but also of the entire structure of the Indo-European narrative tradition. This has always been primarily foundational (its role is to explain origins not developments). It has always, however unambitious its individual subject matter, conceived humanity under the aspect of time, and in a time that is measured in terms of moments of creation and transmission. A number of the critics in this volume have already commentated on the limitations imposed by Braudel's "Olympian" viewpoint. But it is not so much the distance from its subject which makes the Braudelian model suspect; it is, I think, the fact that its subject is not, as the term has been understood since Thuycidides, a historical one. True, Braudel is writing about the past and about certain processes over time. And it might seem merely frivolous to claim that he was not writing *historia*. But his is a narrative that ultimately begins and ends nowhere, not even, as Henry Kamen has indicated, with the Battle of Lepanto.[43] We are offered an account of *conjunctures*, but it is impossible from this to extract any account of how this process operates. Furthermore, it is clear from his description of the history of human agency as "une histoire à oscillations brèves, rapides, nerveuses," that the structure is itself wholly unmodified by the events of which it is, in part at least, composed. It is clear that Braudel's model cannot provide answers to the kind of questions that have generally troubled historians in the past and will continue to trouble them in the present. In asking it to do so, we may simply be asking the wrong kind of questions. It is perhaps also worth reflecting that if the *longue durée* cannot accommodate how humans perceive their own place within it, nor ultimately how we, and our world, are linked to that of the sixteenth century, then this may in part be due to an overdependence upon now discredited natural scientific models. For Braudel was not only indebted to Spengler, he was also indebted—and more than to any other single theorist—to Lévi-Strauss. The objections I, and others in this collection, voice about Braudel are much the same as those that were raised, many years ago now, against structuralism. Both perhaps owe their startling originality—and their ultimate demise—to their imaginative debt to the natural sciences—and in this case, in particular to geology, which brings us aptly full circle to Braudel's original foundation on Vidal de la Blache.

43. Henry Kamen, "Strategies of Survival," chap. 9 above.

Contributors

Peter Burke, Emmanuel College, University of Cambridge

Jan de Vries, University of California, Berkeley

Mark Elvin, Australian National University, Canberra

Jack A. Goldstone, University of California, Davis

Antonio Manuel Hespanha, Universidade Nova de Lisboa

Henry Kamen, Consejo Superior de Investigaciones Científicas, Institució Milà i Fontanals, Barcelona

John A. Marino, University of California, San Diego

Ottavia Niccoli, Università degli Studi di Trento

Anthony Pagden, University of California, Los Angeles

M. J. Rodríguez-Salgado, London School of Economics

Bartolomé Yun Casalilla, Universidad Pablo de Olavide de Sevilla

A SHORT
BRAUDEL BIBLIOGRAPHY

Aguirre Rojas, Carlos A., et al. *Primeras Jornadas Braudelianas*. San Juan Mixcoac, Mexico: Instituto Mora/UNAM/IFAL, 1993.

———. *Segundas Jornadas Braudelianas: Historia y Ciencias Sociales*. San Juan Mixcoac, Mexico: Instituto Mora/UNAM/IFAL, 1995.

Arcangeli, Bianca, and Giovanni Muto, eds. *Fernand Braudel: Il mestiere di uno storico*. Naples: Edizioni Scientifiche Italiane, 1988.

Aymard, Maurice, et al. *Lire Braudel*. Paris: La Découverte, 1988.

Braudel, Fernand. *Civilization and Capitalism 15th–18th Century*, trans. Siân Reynolds. 3 vols. New York: Harper & Row, 1981. Trans of *Civilisation materielle, economie et capitalisme, XVe–XVIIIe siècle*. Paris: Armand Colin, 1979.

———. *The Mediterranean and the Mediterranean World of Philip II*, trans. Siân Reynolds. 2 vols. New York: Harper & Row, 1972–73. Trans. of *La Méditerranée et le monde Méditerranéen à l'époque de Philippe II*, 2d rev. ed. Paris: A. Colin, 1966; orig., Paris: A. Colin, 1949.

———. *On History*, trans. Sarah Matthews. Chicago: University of Chicago Press, 1980. Trans. of *Écrits sur l'histoire*. Paris: Flammarion, 1969.

———. "Personal Testimony," *Journal of Modern History* 44 (1972): 448–67.

Burke, Peter. *The French Historical Revolution: The Annales School, 1929–89*. Cambridge: Polity Press, 1990.

———. *History and Social Theory*. Ithaca: Cornell University Press, 1992.

Daix, Pierre. *Braudel*. Paris: Flammarion, 1996.

"Dossier: Fernand Braudel, le patron de la nouvelle histoire," *Magazine Littéraire* 212 (November 1984): 16–39.

Gemelli, Giuliana. *Fernand Braudel e l'Europa universale*. Venice: Marsilio Editore, 1990; Fr. ed. 1995.

Hexter, J. H. "Fernand Braudel and the *Monde Braudellien*," *Journal of Modern History* 44 (1972): 480–539.

Horden, Peregrine, and Nicholas Purcell. *The Corrupting Sea: A Study of Mediterranean History*. Oxford and Malden (Mass.): Blackwell, 2000.

Huppert, George. "Storia e scienze sociali: Bloch, Febvre e le prime *Annales*," in: *Gli strumenti della ricera*, pt. 2, *Questioni di metodo: Il Mondo contemporaneo*, vol. 10. Florence: La Nuova Italia, 1983. 734–50.

Kinser, Samuel. "Annaliste Paradigm? The Geohistorical Structure of Fernand Braudel," *American Historical Review* 86:1 (1981): 63–105.

McNeill, William H. "Fernand Braudel, Historian," *Journal of Modern History* 73 (March 2001): 133–46.

Marino, John A. Review of Giuliana Gemelli, *Fernand Braudel e l'Europa universale* (Venice: Marsilio Editore, 1990) in *Journal of Modern History* 65:2 (1993): 375–77.

Mulroney, Kelly A. "Discovering Fernand Braudel's Historical Context," *History and Theory* 37:2 (1998): 259–69.

Revel, Jacques. "Histoire et sciences sociales: Les paradigmes des *Annales*," *Annales: E.S.C.* 34:6 (1979): 1360–76.

Review 1, nos. 3/4 (1978). "The Impact of the Annales School on the Social Sciences." Inaugural Conference of the Fernand Braudel Center for the Study of Economies, Historical Systems, and Civilizations. State University of New York, Binghamton, 13–15 May 1977.

Stoianovich, Trian. *French Historical Method: The "Annales" Paradigm*. Ithaca: Cornell University Press, 1976.

Trevor-Roper, H. R. "Fernand Braudel, the *Annales*, and the Mediterranean," *Journal of Modern History* 44 (1972): 468–79.

INDEX